The Early Nizārī Ismailis and their Neighbouring Powers

The Institute of Ismaili Studies
Ismaili Heritage Series, 16

General Editor: Farhad Daftary.
Series Editor: Daryoush Mohammad Poor

Previously published titles:

1. Paul E. Walker, *Abū Yaʿqūb al-Sijistānī: Intellectual Missionary* (1996)
2. Heinz Halm, *The Fatimids and their Traditions of Learning* (1997)
3. Paul E. Walker, *Ḥamīd al-Dīn al-Kirmānī: Ismaili Thought in the Age of al-Ḥākim* (1999)
4. Alice C. Hunsberger, *Nasir Khusraw, The Ruby of Badakhshan: A Portrait of the Persian Poet, Traveller and Philosopher* (2000)
5. Farouk Mitha, *Al-Ghazālī and the Ismailis: A Debate in Medieval Islam* (2001)
6. Ali S. Asani, *Ecstasy and Enlightenment: The Ismaili Devotional Literature of South Asia* (2002)
7. Paul E. Walker, *Exploring an Islamic Empire: Fatimid History and its Sources* (2002)
8. Nadia Eboo Jamal, *Surviving the Mongols: Nizārī Quhistānī and the Continuity of Ismaili Tradition in Persia* (2002)
9. Verena Klemm, *Memoirs of a Mission: The Ismaili Scholar, Statesman and Poet al-Mu'ayyad fi'l-Dīn al-Shīrāzī* (2003)
10. Peter Willey, *Eagle's Nest: Ismaili Castles in Iran and Syria* (2005)
11. Sumaiya A. Hamdani, *Between Revolution and State: The Path to Fatimid Statehood* (2006)
12. Farhad Daftary, *Ismailis in Medieval Muslim Societies* (2005)
13. Farhad Daftary, ed., *A Modern History of the Ismailis* (2011)
14. Farhad Daftary and Shainool Jiwa, ed., *The Fatimid Caliphate: Diversity of Traditions* (2018)
15. Dagikhudo Dagiev, *Central Asian Ismailis: An Annotated Bibliography of Russian, Tajik and Other Sources* (2022)

The Early Nizārī Ismailis and their Neighbouring Powers

Politics in the Caspian Provinces

Miklós Sárközy

I.B.TAURIS
in association with
The Institute of Ismaili Studies
LONDON, 2024

I.B. TAURIS
Bloomsbury Publishing Plc
50 Bedford Square, London, WC1B 3DP, UK
1385 Broadway, New York, NY 10018, USA
29 Earlsfort Terrace, Dublin 2, Ireland

In association with The Institute of Ismaili Studies
Aga Khan Centre, 10 Handyside Street, London N1C 4DN
www.iis.ac.uk

First published in Great Britain 2024

Cover design: Adriana Brioso
Cover image © dpa picture alliance / Alamy Stock Photo

A catalogue record for this book is available from the British Library.

A catalog record for this book is available from the Library of Congress.

ISBN: HB: 978-0-7556-5668-4
PB: 978-0-7556-5667-7
ePDF: 978-0-7556-5670-7
eBook: 978-0-7556-5669-1

Series: Ismaili Heritage Series

Typeset by RefineCatch Limited, Bungay, Suffolk
Printed and bound in Great Britain

The Institute of Ismaili Studies

The Institute of Ismaili Studies (IIS), established in 1977, has an extensive programme of multilingual and interdisciplinary research and publications. Informed by rigorous scholarly research, we endeavour to make available texts relating to Islam and Muslim communities in their historical and contemporary contexts. Our focus is on Ismaili and related Shiʿi studies, Qur'anic studies, and Islam's diverse devotional, literary, intellectual, artistic, and esoteric traditions. Many of these publications highlight the relationship of faith and practice to broader dimensions of society, culture, and modern life.

IIS publications take the form of monographs; critical editions and translations of significant primary or secondary texts; edited volumes and conference proceedings; reference works such as bibliographies, manuscript catalogues, and encyclopaedias; occasional papers and essays; and trade non-fiction works aimed at lay audiences.

Authors of the Institute's publications hail from various parts of the world and express a range of views and ideas, which are not necessarily those of the Institute itself.

A full list of the publications of the Institute of Ismaili Studies can be found on our website at www.iis.ac.uk.

Ismaili Heritage Series

A major Shiʿi Muslim community, the Ismailis have had a long and eventful history. Scattered in many regions of the world, in Asia, Africa, and now also in Europe and North America, the Ismailis have elaborated diverse intellectual and literary traditions in different languages. On two occasions they had states of their own, the Fatimid caliphate and the Nizari state of Iran and Syria during the Alamut period. While pursuing particular religio-political aims, the leaders of these Ismaili states also variously encouraged intellectual, scientific, artistic and commercial activities.

Until recently, the Ismailis were studied and judged almost exclusively on the basis of the evidence collected or fabricated by their detractors, including the bulk of the medieval heresiographers and polemicists who were hostile towards the Shiʿis in general and the Ismailis among them in particular. These authors in fact treated the Shiʿi interpretations of Islam as expressions of heterodoxy or even heresy. As a result, a 'black legend' was gradually developed and put into circulation in the Muslim world to discredit the Ismailis and their interpretation of Islam. The Crusaders and their occidental chroniclers, who remained almost completely ignorant of Islam and its internal divisions, disseminated their own myths of the Ismailis, which came to be accepted in Europe as true descriptions of Ismaili teachings and practices. Modern orientalists, too, studied the Ismailis on the basis of these hostile sources and fanciful accounts of medieval times. Thus, legends and misconceptions have continued to surround the Ismailis through the 20th century.

In more recent decades, however, the field of Ismaili studies has been revolutionized due to the recovery and study of genuine Ismaili sources on a large scale – manuscript materials which in different ways survived the destruction of the Fatimid and Nizari Ismaili libraries. These sources, representing diverse literary traditions produced in

Arabic, Persian and Indic languages, had hitherto been secretly preserved in private collections in India, Central Asia, Iran, Afghanistan, Syria and the Yemen.

Modern progress in Ismaili studies has already necessitated a complete re-writing of the history of the Ismailis and their contributions to Islamic civilization. It has now become clear that the Ismailis founded important libraries and institutions of learning such as al-Azhar and the Dar al-ʿIlm in Cairo, while some of their learned *daʿis* or missionaries developed unique intellectual traditions amalgamating their theological doctrine with a diversity of philosophical traditions in complex metaphysical systems. The Ismaili patronage of learning and extension of hospitality to non-Ismaili scholars was maintained even in such difficult times as the Alamut period, when the community was preoccupied with its survival in an extremely hostile milieu.

The Ismaili Heritage Series, published under the auspices of the Department of Academic Research and Publications of the Institute of Ismaili Studies, aims to make available to wide audiences the results of modern scholarship on the Ismailis and their rich intellectual and cultural heritage, as well as certain aspects of their more recent history and achievements.

To Krisztina and Rusztem

Contents

Preface and Acknowledgements xiii
List of Abbreviations xv

Chapter 1: Introduction: Sources and Studies 1

Chapter 2: The Political Relations of the Nizārī Ismaili State in the Caspian Provinces under Ḥasan-i Ṣabbāḥ 21

Chapter 3: The Development of Local Powers in the Caspian Region during Saljūq Decline 48

Chapter 4: Nizārī Bāwandid Competition for Hegemony, 534–565/1140–1170 54

Chapter 5: Nizārī Bāwandid Confrontation in the Late 6th/12th Century 80

Chapter 6: The Last Decades of the Nizārī Ismaili State 115

Chapter 7: ʿAlāʾ al-Dīn Muḥammad III and the End of the Nizārī Ismaili State in the Caspian Provinces 131

Chapter 8: The Economy and Social Structure of the Nizārī Ismaili State 166

Conclusion 177

Appendix I Maps of the Caspian Provinces 184

Appendix II The Dīwān-i Qāʾimiyyat, Extracts in Translation 189

Appendix III Dynastic Tables 193

Notes 196
Select Bibliography 220
Index 231

Preface and Acknowledgements

This book was conceived as a way of bringing the local history of the Nizārī Ismailis in the Caspian region between 483/1090 and 655/1257 to a wider audience. It is intended to provide what it is hoped will be an examination of the local history and local policies of the Nizārī Ismailis using material both from medieval histories and from other texts. Apart from the major chronicles written in the post-Alamūt era, mainly by Sunni historians working for the Īl Khāns, the local history of the Nizārīs can be extracted from various sources, such as Zaydī texts, artefacts and the results of archaeological investigations.

The introductory chapter discusses the sources and provides a general outline of the Caspian region before the founding of the Nizārī Ismaili state in 483/1090. Subsequent chapters endeavour to characterise the local history and contacts of the Nizārī Ismailis with their neighbours, their territorial gains and losses, and their attitudes towards the Twelver Shiʿi, Zaydī and Sunni polities in the surrounding areas, culminating in the Mongol invasion and the campaign led by Hülegü Khan in 654/1256. The final chapter presents a provisional reconstruction of the socio-economic conditions under which the Nizārī Ismaili state in the Caspian region existed for 166 years. Additional information is given in a series of appendices, including genealogical tables of local ruling families and three maps, which represent an initial step in displaying graphically the changing boundaries of the Nizārī-controlled areas in the Caspian region.

Although a large number of primary sources have been utilised, this book by no means claims to provide a comprehensive survey of the entire local history of the Caspian Nizārīs. Many important archaeological aspects have had to be left out due to the fact that investigation of Nizārī-related sites in northern Iran is still very much in its infancy. This means that it is not yet possible to examine the material culture of the Nizārī fortresses in northern Iran.

The publication of this book would not have been possible without the support of The Institute of Ismaili Studies (IIS), London, the Károli Gáspár University of the Hungarian Reformed Church and the Oriental Collection of the Hungarian Academy of Sciences. The author is especially grateful for the generous help and immense support offered by these esteemed institutions.

The author is also particularly appreciative of the contributions by Farhad Daftary, the late Wilferd Madelung, Jalal Badakhchani, Gurdofarid Miskinzoda, Shafique Virani, Delia Cortese, Christopher Atwood, István Vásáry, István Hajnal, the late Mohsen Jaʿfarī-Madhab, Toby Mayer, Arzina Lalani, Orkhan Mir-Kasimov, Mushegh Asatryan, Alessandro Cancian, Ferenc Csirkés, Benedek Péri, Hajnalka Kovács, Agnes Nemeth, Kinga Devenyi, Tamas Ivanyi, Istvan Kristo-Nagy and the late Jinghiz Bayburdi, all of whom kindly helped with their important comments and suggestions.

At the Institute of Ismaili Studies the author would like to thank Russell Harris, for creating the maps for this volume as well as for his careful editorial work on an earlier draft, and Isabel Miller for preparing the final typescript, and Tara Woolnough, Omar Alí-de Unzaga, head of the Qurʾanic Studies Unit in the Department of Academic Research and Publications, Wafi Momin, head of the Ismaili Special Collections Unit (ISCU) and Nourmamadcho Nourmamadchoev, Research Associate and Projects Coordinator at the ISCU for all their help and for granting the author access to manuscripts and coins held by the ISCU. Thanks are also due to the staff of the Aga Khan Library.

Several other colleagues at the Institute gave me their time and expertise at various stages in the production of this book, and I would like to acknowledge in particular Julia Kolb, Nadia Holmes, Marjan Afsharian, Wendy Robinson, Najam Abbas, Rahim Gholami and Yahia Baiza.

Abbreviations

BSOAS	*Bulletin of the School of Oriental and African Studies*
EI	*Encyclopaedia of Islam*, first edition, ed. M. Th. Houtsma et al., Leiden–London, 1913–1938, reprinted, London, 1987
EI2	*Encyclopaedia of Islam*, New edition, ed. H.A.R. Gibb et al., Leiden–London, 1960–2004
EI3	*Encyclopaedia of Islam Three Online*, ed. Kate Fleet et al., 2010—
EIs	*Encyclopaedia Islamica*, ed. W. Madelung and F. Daftary, London, 2008—
EIR	*Encyclopaedia Iranica*, ed. E. Yarshater, London–New York, 1982—
IJMES	*International Journal of Middle East Studies*
JRAS	*Journal of the Royal Asiatic Society*
SI	*Studia Islamica*
ZDMG	*Zeitschrift der Deutschen Morgenländischen Gesellschaft*
Tārīkh-i Ṭabaristān I	*Tārīkh-i Ṭabaristān* of Ibn Isfandiyār, vol. 1, ed. A. Iqbāl. Tehran, 1320/1941
Tārīkh-i Ṭabaristān II	*Tārīkh-i Ṭabaristān* of Ibn Isfandiyār, vol. 2, ed. A. Iqbāl. Tehran, 1320/1941

Chapter 1

Introduction: Sources and Studies

Primary Sources

This work addresses the subject of the regional relationships of the Nizārīs between 483/1090 when the Ismaili *dāʿī* Ḥasan-i Ṣabbāḥ established a centre at the castle of Alamūt and 654/1256 when the Mongols captured Alamūt and other castles nearby, forcing the surrender of the Ismaili Imam. This study relies on seven groups of primary sources.

The Nizārī Ismaili sources for the Alamūt period

As far as Nizārī Ismaili sources are concerned primary material, including chronicles, relating to the 166 years of the Ismaili state is extremely limited. Due to the complete lack of administrative records, correspondence, epigraphic material and the existence of only a very limited amount of numismatic data, research must rely on two main types of source material relating to the Alamūt period: historical chronicles and doctrinal works, of which only a limited number have survived.

As regards historical works, one needs to stress the fact that none of these chronicles have survived in their entirety. It is possible that a lack of interest in historiography may have played a role in the very limited number of historical works that seemingly were produced in the Nizārī period. A hostile political atmosphere meant that the Nizārīs frequently had to live clandestinely and they regularly practised *taqiyya*, or precautionary dissimulation, in order to conceal their identity, ideas and actions. Had the Nizārīs of the era written openly about their manners, customs and the lives of their rulers, the very existence of the community could have been endangered. The result is that only a very limited number of genuine historical works, chronicles or annals, were produced during the Alamūt era.[1]

However, at the fall of the Nizārī Ismaili state after 654/1256, a few of Nizārī historical chronicles were saved and parts of them are quoted in later works by writers who were mostly Sunnis, bureaucrats serving the Ilkhanid state (654–735/1256–1335). Though most of these later sources display a marked enmity towards the Ismailis, they nevertheless preserved a significant amount of valuable material from these earlier Nizārī sources providing a vital, albeit partial and incomplete, impression of these lost works. This state of affairs particularly concerns material for the early Nizārī Ismaili period before the reign of the third lord of Alamūt, Muḥammad b. Buzurg-Umīd (r. 532–557/1138–1162), which is well represented in these Nizārī fragments whereas later Nizārī history suffers from a scarcity of autochthonous historical works.

The most important historical work from the early Nizārī period is the biography of Ḥasan-i Ṣabbāḥ, entitled *Sargudhasht-i Sayyidnā*, which is a partly historical and partly doctrinal biography of the first Nizārī Ismaili lord of Alamūt. The actual author of this work remains unknown, but it is seen as a very popular work since the second part survived the destruction of Alamūt both as an independent manuscript and in paraphrase as part of the chronicles by Juwaynī, Rashīd al-Dīn and Kāshānī, the main Ilkhanid historians to write about the Nizārī Ismaili state.

The availability to academics of two manuscripts of the *Sargudhasht-i Sayyidnā* held by the Ismaili Special Collections Unit (ISCU) of The Institute of Ismaili Studies at the Aga Khan Centre constitutes a major advance in the history of Nizārī sources, providing ample evidence for the survival of hitherto unknown parts of texts dating to the Alamūt period. It also implies that such a text could have been more widely circulated in the community in the post-Alamūt period than previously thought, and the existence of surviving manuscripts may somewhat question the 'discovery story' of the work in Alamūt by Juwaynī as related in his *tārīkh-i jahān-gushā*. Furthermore, there is another manuscript of *Sargudhasht-i Sayyidnā*, held in the Majlis Library in Tehran.[2]

The enormous influence of the *Sargudhasht-i Sayyidnā* on the study of early Nizārī Ismaili history is unquestionable. Traces of the original work can be found in hitherto unpublished later variants of the *Sargudhasht-i Sayyidnā* preserved by the ISCU.[3] Since, to the best of our knowledge, many primary sources were destroyed in the Mongol assault on the Nizārī fortresses, the possible rediscovery of new historical material containing new information relating to Nizārī Ismaili history is more than welcome. In the light of these newly-emerged pieces of evidence (i.e. the two ISCU manuscripts), there is an urgent need to reassess the importance of the *Sargudhasht-i Sayyidnā.* The importance of the work as doctrinal text and work of history in Ismaili communities from the 6th/12th century onwards is also apparent from the reception and use of a version of it in Sunni historiography.[4]

In many ways, the two manuscripts of the *Sargudhasht-i Sayyidnā* display strong similarities with the variants of the *Sargudhasht-i Sayyidnā* as preserved and reworked by Juwaynī, Rashīd al-Dīn and by other Persian historians, proving that all of these traditions go back to a certain 'Urtext', a fact which makes the discovery of these versions all the more important.

Nonetheless, significant differences between the ISCU *Sargudhasht-i Sayyidnā* manuscripts and the accounts of Rashīd al-Dīn and Juwaynī are apparent. Apart from a few differences in names and places, as well as alternative sequences of events, there are other more important differences. One of the most striking discrepancies is that in the ISCU manuscripts Ḥasan-i Ṣabbāḥ's lineage is traced back to the fifth Imam, Muḥammad al-Bāqir (d. ca. 114/732). Among further differences, one notices the following: according to the ISCU manuscripts Ḥasan-i Ṣabbāḥ's youth was spent not the city of Rayy itself but in a place called Muḥammad-ābād, albeit not far from Rayy.

In the ISCU manuscripts the geographical emphasis is put rather more on regions of northern Iran: for instance, the place where Ḥasan-i Ṣabbāḥ met ʿAbd al-Malik b. ʿAṭṭāsh is given as Rūdbār (a place not far from Alamūt), again rather than Rayy as in the versions by Juwaynī and Rashīd al-Dīn; Ḥasan-i Ṣabbāḥ's relationship with him is described as one of *khidmat* (service), rather than *nayābat* (deputyship), although the position of *khidmat* incidentally never features in descriptions of the Ismaili *daʿwa* hierarchy in its various forms.[5] The most striking discrepancy (and a mystery still to be solved) is that only one date in these two new manuscripts, Rajab 484/

September 1091, is given for Ḥasan-i Ṣabbāḥ's takeover of the castle of Alamūt. The near total lack of dates in the ISCU manuscripts confirms the supposition that the anonymous editors of these writings sought to transform the material they had to hand from a historical biography to a more religio-doctrinal text. Finally, the ISCU manuscripts end with a legendary account of Ḥasan-i Ṣabbāḥ's reception of the news of al-Mustaʿlī's usurpation of the Fatimid throne in Egypt in Dhu'l-Ḥijja 487/December 1094 and the capture of Nizār in 488/1095, here presented as Ḥasan-i Ṣabbāḥ's elder brother.[6]

Besides the *Sargudhasht-i Sayyidnā*, there are other chronicles composed in the early Nizārī period in Northern Iran; yet all these works perished in the post-Alamūt period with only a few excerpts surviving in the chronicles of Juwaynī, Rashīd al-Dīn and Kāshānī. One of these lost works was the so-called *Kitāb-i Buzurg-Umīd*, itself a biography of the second lord of Alamūt, Kiyā Buzurg-Umīd (r. 518–532/1124–1138), part of which was incorporated in later Ilkhanid accounts of the Nizārīs. Another possible Nizārī chronicle could have been composed under his son and successor, Muḥammad b. Buzurg-Umīd (532–557/1138–1162), the third lord of Alamūt, written by Dihkhudā b. ʿAbd al-Malik Fashandī, fragments of which have also survived in later Ilkhanid accounts. However, there is no evidence of chronicles written by Nizārī authors after the era of Muḥammad b. Buzurg-Umīd, though it is conceivable that there were later continuations of these early Nizārī annals which unfortunately do not seem to have survived.[7]

As for the second group of sources, the so-called non-historical Nizārī works, mention must be made of the *Dīwān-i Qā'imiyyāt*, another recently discovered and published genuine work,[8] a collection of *qaṣīdas* dedicated to the *qiyāma* declaration of 559/1164.[9] Albeit a predominantly religious and literary work, the *Dīwān-i Qāʿimiyyāt* nevertheless contains important material on perceptions of Mongol-Nizārī encounters prior to the Mongol conquest of Alamūt in 654/1256. Besides this work, there is a group of other doctrinal sources possibly dating back to the Nizārī period (487–654/1094–1256). Among these is Ḥasan-i Maḥmūd-i Kātib's *Haft bāb-i Bābā Sayyidnā*, which contains important information on the historical circumstances of the *qiyāma* declaration of Ḥasan *ʿalā dhikrihi'l-salām*, an event of huge religious and political importance.[10] In addition, some aspects of the *Rawḍat al-taslīm* by the great 7th/13th-century polymath, Naṣīr al-Dīn al-Ṭūsī (d. 672/1274) are also useful when examining the forms of theology and philosophy current among the Nizārī elite in the final decades of the state. Al-Ṭūsī himself played an active role in Nizārī politics, and it is likely that his role as an adviser to the last Imams of Alamūt as well as a transmitter of Nizārī traditions in the early Ilkhanid period was more significant than previously understood.

Apart from these works, there are two texts in Persian attributed to Ḥasan *ʿalā dhikrihiʾl-salām* (r. 557–561/1162–1166) and addressed to high-ranking Nizārī officials in northern Iran. The texts consist of a dialogue between Ḥasan *ʿalā dhikrihiʾl-salām* and Dihkhudā ʿAlī Abū Shujāʿ and a letter in the name of Nūr al-Dīn Muḥammad and are thought to have been composed not long after the declaration of the *qiyāma* in 559/1164. They are probably authentic, though more careful philological study is required.[11]

Sources chronicling the history of the major powers of the age

The main historical sources for the era were composed in Persian in the Ilkhanid empire and contain essential material on Nizārī history. The most important of these are those by Rashīd al-Dīn, Juwaynī and Kāshānī mentioned above, which all contain common elements that are either excerpts from Nizārī texts or represent information derived originally from anonymous Nizārī authors. The importance of the few surviving Nizārī chronicles, or those parts of them which have survived, such as the so-called *Kitāb-i Buzurg-Umīd*, cannot be overestimated. These historical fragments from the pre-654/1256 period contain valuable information about the contacts and interactions of Nizārī communities with their neighbours.

Juwaynī, Rashīd al-Dīn and Kāshānī all used these early Nizārī sources extensively, and the tenor of their writing changes noticeably when these authors have exhausted such sources. The early Nizārī period, up until the era of Muḥammad b. Buzurg-Umīd (r. 532–557/1138–1162) contains more elaborate accounts of events than do the years after it.

Juwaynī, arguably the most famous member of a family of Sunni intellectuals and bureaucrats from Khurāsān, accompanied Hülegü, the first Īl Khān of Persia (r. 654–663/1256–1265), on his military expedition to the Islamic lands of the Middle East and thus came with his armies to Rūdbār in the Caspian region in 653/1256. He played a crucial role in the negotiations between the Nizārīs and the Mongols bringing the *yarlīgh* (decree) of Hülegü to the Imam Rukn al-Dīn Khurshāh, the last lord of Alamūt, then staying in the castle of Maymūndiz, granting him safe conduct upon his complete surrender. Juwaynī was also allowed to examine the library of Alamūt before its destruction by the Mongols. Among the documents he said he collected were a few 'choice books', including the *Sargudhasht-i Sayyidnā* of which, as pointed out above, in fact a number of manuscripts have survived. Juwaynī's account of the Ismailis (completed in about 658/1260) is still an important source for the Alamūt period, despite its anti-Ismaili sentiments.

Rashīd al-Dīn, the author of our second source, showed more understanding of the Nizārīs in his *Jāmiʿ al-tawārīkh*, or 'Compendium of Histories'. His work was completed fifty years after Juwaynī's, around 709/1310, when memories of the Persian Nizārīs and their alleged threat had perhaps become a less sensitive matter than previously at the Ilkhanid court; this might be the reason for a more objective account. Rashīd al-Dīn appears to have had access to several Nizārī sources, and his account is more elaborate than that of Juwaynī. It should also be borne in mind that his relatives, notably his grandfather, Muwaffaq al-Dawla ʿAlī, were guests of the Nizārī Imam when Alamūt surrendered to the Mongols.[12]

The third major source is a work by Kāshānī, who was of Twelver Shiʿi origin. His *Zubdat al-tawārīkh* was discovered in 1964 and it contains the most detailed account of the Persian Nizārīs written in the Ilkhanid period. Kāshānī claimed in this work that he also wrote much of Rashīd al-Dīn's 'Compendium'.[13]

Sources relating to the Saljūq sultans and the Khwārazmshāhs also include large parts of Nizārī history, especially the episodes recounting their diplomatic relations and missions. The parts of the *Taʾrīkh* of Ibn al-Athīr (d. 630/1233) that deal with the Iranian and Syrian Nizārīs is of great importance, offering a rare insight into some otherwise unknown issues. As for its importance more generally on this subject, one can note it provides the most detailed biography of Ḥasan-i Ṣabbāḥ to be found in Classical Arabic historiography.[14]

Al-Maqrīzī's short but important biographical notes on the life of Ḥasan-i Ṣabbāḥ preserve a partly different tradition, including mystical and supranatural elements. The biography survives in two versions. In 1837, his fragmentary *Kitāb al-Muqaffā' al-kabīr* was referred to for the first time in the western Orientalist tradition by the French scholar, Etienne Quatremère. This work contains the biographies of rulers and famous individuals who had visited Egypt. In it al-Maqrīzī provides a brief but interesting summary of the life and deeds of the founder of the Nizārī Ismaili state. Although its contents do not greatly differ from other legends regarding Ḥasan-i Ṣabbāḥ that have been preserved, nevertheless it can be said that, setting the legends aside, the *Kitāb al-Muqaffā' al-kabīr* offers a balanced portrayal of Ḥasan-i Ṣabbāḥ's life and actions. It has a distinct connection to astrological texts as well, as pointed out recently by Carole Hillenbrand.[15] Another similar biography can be found in al-Maqrīzī's more famous history of the Ismaili Imams, the *Ittiʿāz al-hunafā'*.[16]

Al-Nasawī was secretary to the last Khwārazmshāh, Jalāl al-Dīn Mingburnī (r. 616–628/1220–1231), and also wrote his biography, *Sīrāt-i Jalāl al-Dīn Mingburnī*, which has a unique place among sources relating to the Nizārīs since it contains a first-hand account of his diplomatic mission to Alamūt and his negotiations with ʿAlā' al-Dīn Muḥammad on behalf of Jalāl al-Dīn.[17]

The *Nuṣrat al-fatra*, written by ʿImād al-Dīn Muḥammad al-Iṣfahānī in 579/1183, is perhaps the earliest contemporary Saljūq account of the Nizārīs, though it has only survived in a much abbreviated form dating from 623/1226. Ẓahīr al-Dīn Nīshāpūrī's *Saljūqnāma* is a dynastic history which stops in 590/1194, at the end of Saljūq rule in the Persian lands. It was very popular, and later authors, such al-Rāwandī, relied heavily on it for their accounts of the Nizārīs.[18]

The local chronicles of Ṭabaristān

Ṭabaristān, in the eastern part of the Caspian region, has a rich tradition of historical literature beginning in the early 7th/13th century and represents a hitherto largely ignored and very important group of sources for Nizārī Ismaili history. These chronicles were written at the courts of the local rulers of Ṭabaristān, who were sometimes allies and sometimes enemies of their neighbours the Nizārīs.

The first local work was written in the 7th/13th century, and up until the 13th/19th century one finds a series of other compilations dealing with the history of the Caspian region. However, works written after the 9th/15th century mainly repeat material found in previous works, hence their analysis is beyond the scope of this monograph.

The first and probably the most important work on Ṭabaristān is Ibn Isfandiyār's *Tārīkh-i Ṭabaristān*, written at the beginning of the 7th/13th century. A Twelver Shiʿi diplomat and courtier for the Bāwandid rulers of Ṭabaristān, Ibn Isfandiyār started writing his work around 606/1205 at the bequest of Bāwandid *iṣfahbad*,[19] Ḥusām al-Dawla Ardashīr I (r. 568–602/1173–1205), and was still writing it at the time of the murder of his successor, the *iṣfahbad* Naṣīr al-Dawla Rustam, in 606/1210. Subsequently he travelled to Khwārazm, where he continued to work on his history. He assembled many, now lost, sources for this work which is the earliest Persian account of the history of Ṭabaristān.[20]

We know that Ibn Isfandiyār was still alive in 613/1216,[21] however he did not finish his book, possibly because he was killed by the Mongols during their invasion of the Khwārazmian empire in 616–617/1219–1220. One may therefore argue that the *Tārīkh-i Ṭabaristān* was continued by an unknown author or authors up to the fall of the last Bāwandid ruler in the 8th/14th century. One of the possible authors of the continuation is Awliyāʾ Allāh Āmulī, the author of the *Tārīkh-i Rūyān*. According to Melville, the structure of the *Tārīkh-i Ṭabaristān* is rather vague, with coherence often being sacrificed for the sake of personal anecdotes or legendary stories.[22] Indeed, both the *Tārīkh-i Rūyān* of Āmulī and the later works of Marʿashī (see below for more details about this author), offer more for the historian, being better constructed than Ibn Isfandiyār's history. The dissolution of the Bāwandid court, the elimination of royal patronage in 606/1210, the personal and intellectual goals of Ibn Isfandiyār, along with his possible death in the first Mongol invasion of the Islamic lands all contributed, it can be argued, to the somewhat incoherent structure of the *Tārīkh-i Ṭabaristān*.[23] Yet, despite these issues, this work contains invaluable material for any study of the Nizārīs in the Caspian region and the complex relations they had with the Bāwandids and the Bādūspānids.

The second major work on Ṭabaristān is the *Tārīkh-i Rūyān* of Āmulī, who was a court historian of the Bādūspānids, another Caspian dynasty, in the mid-7th/13th century when they reached the zenith of their power. The *Tārīkh-i Rūyān* was apparently designed to be a record of this. In his work, Āmulī largely followed the outlines of Ibn Isfandiyār's history, concentrating for the most part on the local affairs of Rūyān, in the western part of Ṭabaristān near Nizārī-controlled Rūdbār.[24] Āmulī's history is much less detailed than Ibn Isfandiyār's, but nonetheless contains valuable material on local events in the 6th and 7th/12th and 13th centuries.

The third local history is a work by Ẓahīr al-Dīn Marʿashī (ca. 815–after 894/1412–1489), entitled *Tārīkh-i Ṭabaristān va Ruyān va Māzandarān.* Marʿashī was a well-known figure of his time, one of the renowned Marʿashī *sayyids* and, through his mother, a descendant of the Bāwandids.[25] His father, Sayyid Naṣīr al-Dīn Marʿashī, was expelled from Māzandarān in the reign of the Timurid Shāhrukh Mīrzā (r. 801–850/1398–1447), and the family moved to the province of Gīlān. After many unsuccessful struggles to regain his paternal inheritance, Marʿashī was appointed governor of Gulijān and Gurjīyān by the ruler of Lāhījān, Karkiyā Naṣīr Kiyā. He died in 894/1488 at the age of eighty.[26]

Marʿashī wrote two very important chronicles of the Caspian provinces. His main work is undoubtedly the *Tārīkh-i Ṭabaristān va Rūyān va Māzandarān,*[27] which was intended as a more elaborate continuation and revision of Ibn Isfandiyār's *Tārīkh-i Ṭabaristān.*[28] Towards the end of his life he also wrote the *Tārīkh-i Gīlān va Daylamistān*, which is considered one of the main sources for any study of the Caspian provinces in the 8th–9th/14th–15th centuries.

Marʿashī's works are of considerable historical value and one can often observe efforts being made to 'adjust' what was written by earlier authors.[29] Marʿashī was a reliable informant but an even better editor of his works. His genealogical lists are essential for a study of the local history of many Caspian dynasties prior to the mid-9th/15th century. Marʿashī wrote extensively about the local history of the preceding centuries, and in many cases his accounts seem more reliable than those provided by Ibn Isfandiyār.

Zaydī works

The Caspian provinces served as a refuge for the Zaydīs and their ʿAlid rulers from the 3th/8th until the early 10th/16th century. Local families played important political and religious roles, especially in Gīlān and Daylamān, but the Zaydīs occasionally extended their political influence to Ṭabaristān and as far as Gurgān. Although all the Zaydī communities in the Caspian provinces disappeared after the early Ṣafavid period (mid-10th/16th century), their literary traditions and biographical works have been preserved in Yemen. With the help of Zaydī sources discovered in Yemen one can reconstruct some details of Zaydī history in the Caspian provinces too. One of the most important Zaydī works is, undoubtedly, *al-Ḥadā'iq al-wardiyya* of al-Muḥallī,[30] an important biographical work of the 7th/13th century, which relates many Zaydī-Nizārī clashes in the 5th–6th/11th–12th centuries in Daylamān.[31]

Other, non-historical, works

Certain sources of a clearly non-historical nature can be useful in providing some tangential historical detail. As far as the Caspian provinces are concerned, there are a number of poems, letters and theological-doctrinal treatises which contain material about the region before the establishment of the Nizārī Ismaili state there.

The *Kitāb al-naqḍ* of ʿAbd al-Jalīl Qazwīnī Rāzī, a Twelver Shiʿi author of the mid-6th/12th century, also contains a significant amount of material about the politico-religious propaganda of the Bāwandids in his time. The title (*The Book of Refutation*) indicates that this is a polemical work refuting the ideas of an anonymous Twelver Shiʿi apostate, excerpts from whose pro-Sunni work (entitled *Baʿḍ faḍā'iḥ al-Rawāfiḍ*) are extensively cited in Rāzī's own book. The date of composition (556/1161) coincides with the heaviest Bāwandid attacks against the Nizārīs. Despite refuting the anti-Shiʿi remarks of his opponent, Rāzī also makes repeated attempts to reconcile the Uṣūlī Twelver Shiʿis and Ḥanafī Sunnis.

In spite of its being predominantly doctrinal, Qazwīnī Rāzī's voluminous work does not lack elements of actual policy. He seems to be one of the main proponents of a Saljūq-Bāwandid alliance against the Nizārīs. The main reason for this unusual alliance is no doubt his own relentlessly anti-Nizārī stance. Although as his name indicates he hailed from Qazwīn, he spent most of his life in Rayy at a time in the 6th/12th century when both of these urban centres were at the forefront of both Nizārī and anti-Nizārī military operations. As a Twelver Shiʿi scholar, Qazwīnī Rāzī witnessed the decline of the once powerful Twelver Shiʿi educational centre in Rayy, which he attributed to the threat represented by the Nizārīs. The virulence of his rhetoric reflects his thorough hatred of the Nizārīs.[32]

Sources such as the *Kitāb al-Naqḍ* or the *Dīwān* of Muḥammad b. ʿAbd al-Malik Muʿizzī[33] of the early 6th/12th century, although mainly literary and religious, contain valuable material for the study of events in northern Iran.

Armenian and Chinese sources for Nizārī history in northern Iran

The last decades of the Nizārī Ismaili state in northern Iran are dominated by Mongol imperial policy. Mongol armies overran northern Iran, Anatolia and the Caucasus several times between 616/1220 and 655/1257. Contemporary Armenian sources, especially those by Smbat Sparapet and Kirakos of Gandzak, throw light on interesting and hitherto relatively neglected incidents relating to Armenian-Nizārī and Mongol-Nizārī relations prior to Hülegü's campaign.[34]

All assessments of Mongol-Nizārī relations have been given a new impetus with the publication of Chinese sources, which several times refer to the presence of '*mulayid*' envoys[35] in the Mongol capital Karakorum and also negotiations between Nizārīs and Mongols. These sources, principally the *Yuanshi* and the *Shengwu qinzheng lu*, major Chinese sources written after the Yüan period (677–768/1279–1368), are important for the western campaigns of the Mongols; and in them encounters with the Nizārīs are mentioned.[36]

Numismatic sources and recent archaeological discoveries

Alongside written primary sources, the importance of archaeological findings must be emphasised. Nizārī archaeology in Iran is still in an incipient state. Despite the efforts of Wladimir Ivanow (1886–1970) and Manūchihr Sutūda (1913–2016) in the 20th century there have been only a few actual excavations in formerly Nizārī-populated areas. The decade-long excavations in Alamūt by Ḥamīda Chubak and some of her articles on the newly-unearthed Alamūt-related objects are, however, more than promising, and the findings shed some light on the economy, notably trade and contacts established by the Nizārī Ismaili state, with Central Asia and the Far East.[37] Mention should also be made of the topographical work by Peter Willey on establishing the sites of Nizārī castles in Iran. However, the material published to date highlights the need for further systematic excavations of the former Nizārī Ismaili strongholds in northern Iran in order to enable a more substantive analysis of Nizārī society and economy. Finally, mention must be made of the coinage of the northern Iranian dynasties of this period, including that of the Nizārīs and their neighbours. The number of published numismatic findings is relatively limited. The studies by Miles and Casanova are of particular importance in elucidating these lesser-known sources for Nizārī history.[38] There is also the brief study by Hamdan and Vardanyan at the end of Willey's work on the Ismaili castles.[39]

Studies

The secondary sources about the local contacts of the Nizārīs with their neighbours have so far not been studied or examined as a whole and their number appears to be rather limited.

The most elaborate and critically praised work about the local contacts of the Nizārīs was written by Marshal Hodgson (1922–1968), who, in his *Order of Assassins*, took major steps in elucidating this subject.[40] He collected a vast corpus of material for his study of the early Nizārī Ismaili state, and is to date the only scholar who has shown an interest in attempting to understand the regional importance of the Nizārīs. His study aimed to present a survey of these contacts, using new sources and endeavouring to shed light on other aspects of the issue of local contacts made by the Nizārīs.

Mention must also be made of Hyacinth Louis Rabino di Borgomale, a prolific author and specialist on northern Iran, who produced numerous detailed prosopographical studies in the early 20th century about the local history of Gīlān and Māzandarān, which constitute pioneering advances in the study of medieval and early modern Caspian history. Although his works do not focus especially on the Nizārīs, he provides a thorough overview of other Gilite, and Daylamī dynasties who played a prominent, but sometimes less than eminent, role in the region. The vast amount of material collected by Rabino di Borgomale, using his expertise in local sources, is still a valuable starting place for academic research.[41] The articles of Charles Melville have also had an impact on the study of medieval northern Iran and aspects of its historiography. Yukako Goto has also delved into Caspian studies, and her very detailed essay, based on local sources, on the late medieval and early modern history of northern Iran is very important and useful in many respects.[42]

In his numerous, meticulous works, Farhad Daftary has underlined the importance of local sources for any study of Nizārī history.[43] His oeuvre is particularly important in the area of early Nizārī history. Besides the important contributions of Farhad Daftary, one should mention also Wilferd Madelung's several pioneering works on early Shiʿi groups in the Caspian provinces which offer a significant perspective on religious and historical trends in the region and contribute to the understanding of religious motives behind many historical events involving the Nizārīs and their neighbours.[44] Various articles by Carole Hillenbrand on Saljūq policy and ideology have also provided fertile ground for further research into the regional role of the Nizārīs in the Caspian provinces.[45]

A brief history of the Caspian region before the establishment of the Nizārī Ismaili state

These remote provinces were not conquered by the Arabs until 149/766 and the conquest was not as complete as that of other Iranian provinces so that pre-Islamic Sasanian and local traditions were still reflected in the beliefs of the various local dynasties in the 5th/11th and 6th/12th centuries.

Due to their remoteness, many Shiʿi groups chose the Caspian provinces as a place of refuge, so that from as early the second half of the 2nd/8th century the local population was composed of converts to various branches of Shiʿi Islam, such the Zaydī, Ismaili and Twelver Shiʿi, although local variants of Zoroastrianism also remained influential in the region.[46]

In general, however, western Gīlān remained a staunch stronghold of Sunni Islam, especially that of the Ḥanbalī *madhhab*, throughout the medieval period; and it was from this area that several Ḥanbalī scholars originated with the *nisba* Gīlānī in the Middle Ages. But the eastern areas of Gīlān followed the early Zaydī *daʿwa* from the second half of the 2nd/8th century, and by the early 4th/10th century had almost entirely embraced Zaydī Shiʿi Islam thereby marking the start of an enduring political and religious division in the province.[47]

The provinces of Gīlān and Daylamān remained politically semi-independent. Different branches of the Zīyārids, the Būyids (who themselves came from the Caspian provinces), and later the Saljūqs, attempted to assert their authority here, and these greater dynasties were occasionally able to exact tribute from the provinces but their authority remained largely nominal. The Zaydī chieftains in eastern Gīlān gave active support to local ʿAlids in Hawsam, which was a very important political and religious centre[48] in the centuries preceding the establishment of the Nizārī Ismaili state. Most of the region apparently continued to be controlled by local clan chieftains, though the written sources do not give an entirely clear picture of the political and social conditions of the time.[49]

The history of the mountainous region of Daylamān is even more obscure than that of Gīlān. This region seems to have been a highly disputed area where two local families, the pro-Zaydī Justānids and their opponents the Musāfirids (who could have been possibly the earliest partisans of the Ismaili Shiʿis), emerged in the 3rd–4th/8th–9th centuries.[50] In the 4th/10th century, the Zīyārids and the Būyids attempted to extend their influence over Daylamān.[51]

The Musāfirids (also known as the Sallārids or Kangarids) largely replaced the Justānids in the first half of the 4th/10th century. The first Musāfirid ruler, Muḥammad b. Musāfir married the daughter of Justān III, who was one of the last rulers of the Justānid dynasty. The Ismaili *dāʿī*, Nāṣir-i Khusraw, when passing through Daylam in 438/1046 and visiting the city of Shamīrān, spoke highly of the Musāfirid kingdom, its social institutions and stability.[52] However, the material available for the last decades of the Musāfirid dynasty is very limited, and it is not exactly known when and how their line became extinguished. Alamūt itself might have been a Musāfirid castle sometime before the takeover by the Ismailis.[53]

Besides the local dynasties of Daylam and Gīlān, the Ziyārids, the Būyids and the Kākūyids, all of Caspian origin, played significant roles in the history of the Iranian lands. They quickly emerged as a major force in Iranian history, in the so-called 'Daylamite interlude', and dominated the political scene of western Iran and the declining Abbasid caliphate and also the deeply divided Zaydī ʿAlid movement in northern Iran after 308/920.

The Ismaili *daʿwa* in Gīlān and Daylam was already significant at a very early date. The importance of Ismaili missionary activity prior to the arrival of Ḥasan-i Ṣabbāḥ in 483/1090 and the founding of the Nizārī Ismaili state in northern Iran should not be underestimated. The earliest possible date for the presence of the first Ismaili *dāʿīs* may be around 308/920 and it appears that the early Ismaili *dāʿīs* successfully exploited the internecine clashes of the various Zaydī chieftains. The fact that early Zaydī Islam did not favour strict adherence to any particular branch of the ʿAlids contributed notably to the success of the Ismaili *daʿwa* and the disintegration of Zaydī political cohesion was also of benefit to the Ismailis. To the best of our knowledge the first active Ismaili *dāʿī* in Gīlān and Daylamān was Abū Ḥātim al-Rāzī (d. 322/934), who attracted many new followers to the Ismaili *daʿwa*, among others some leading Daylamī leaders and warlords such as Asfār, Mardāwīj and the Justānid Mahdī b. Khusraw Fīrūz (also known as Siyāh-Chashm), who had been followers of Zaydī Shiʿism.[54] The sons of the Musāfirid ruler Muḥammad b. Musāfir, Wakhsūdān and Marzbān, as well as his vizier, Jaʿfar b. ʿAlī, are known as the first high-ranking Ismaili converts in the first half of the 4th/10th century. In connection with these events one should mention that Ibn Ḥawqal hints at the successes of Ismailis in the province of Ādharbāyjān in 344/955.[55]

Some of these early Ismailis might have belonged to the Qaramiṭa, who awaited the return of Muḥammad b. Ismāʿīl as the Mahdī and did not acknowledge the imamate of ʿAbd Allāh al-Mahdī (r. 297–322/909–934) who established the Fatimid state in Ifrīqiya. After the split of 286/899 following the proclamation of ʿAbd Allāh al-Mahdī's imamate, many Iranian and Central Asian Ismailis followed the Qarmaṭī teachings.

At the end of the 4th/10th century, however, the Fatimid *daʿwa* under Imam-caliph al-Muʿizz li-Dīn Allāh (r. 341–365/959–975) began supporting the *daʿwa* in Daylam. When the Būyid ruler of Fārs, Abū Kālījār, converted to Ismailism just before 438/1046, this act greatly facilitated the spread of the Fatimid Ismaili *daʿwa* in all

Būyid-controlled areas. Indeed many Ismailis had turned to the Fatimid *daʿwa* after the decline of the Qarmaṭīs in the last decade of the 4th/10th century.[56] In the second half of the 4th/10th century, there was heightened Fatimid missionary activity at the Sāmānid court in Bukhārā.[57] Thus, notable progress for Fatimid Ismaili missionary activity could have been seen in Daylamān and Gīlān as well as among the former Qarmaṭī groups and newly converted people of various religious backgrounds. The Ismaili *daʿwa* in the decades preceding the career of Ḥasan-i Ṣabbāḥ appears to have met with success in the highlands of Daylamān whereas the Caspian littoral area of Gīlān tended to remain in the hands of Zaydī clans.[58] This may be due to the fact that many of the local clans in the Caspian provinces were already in contact with the Ismailis in Daylam, and especially in Rūdbār before the emergence of the Nizārī Ismaili state, as Stern noted, that the Ismaili *daʿwa* under Ḥasan-i Ṣabbāḥ was so successful and popular in the region.

In Gīlān and Daylam, the Zaydīs established the centre of their religious authority in the town of Hawsam (modern Rūdsar). It was here that Nāṣir Uṭrūsh was active converting local Gilites in the 3rd/9th century.[59] Hawsam became a centre of learning of the Nāṣiriyya branch of the Zaydīs while at the same time it was the capital of a local ʿAlid clan, established around 320/932 by Abu'l-Faḍl Jaʿfar b. Muḥammad, himself a grandson of Nāṣir Uṭrūsh's brother Ḥusayn Shāʿir and, through his mother, a descendant of Nāṣir himself. This family later embraced the regnal title 'al-Ṭā'ir fi'llāh', though none of these Zaydīs laid claim to the Zaydī imamate.

In the 6th/12th century, Lāhījān replaced Hawsam as the seat of Zaydī ʿAlid rulers and this town, where the Būyid dynasty first appeared on the political scene remained in the hands of different Zaydī clans for several centuries.

Ṭabaristān and Māzandarān

Regarding the internal geographical and administrative divisions of Māzandarān (Ṭabaristān), as with Gīlān one can detect both continuity and gradual change.

The mountainous areas of Ṭabaristān in the early Islamic period, according to al-Iṣṭakhrī, had three main divisions: those of Rūbāndj

(Rūyān) or Rustamdār,[60] Fādūspān (Bādūspān) and Jibāl Qārin. Rūyān was the western-most borderland of Ṭabaristān, lying between Ṭabaristān and Rayy; its political centre was Kajā or later Kujūr.[61] In the 5th–10th/11th–16th centuries, Rūyān was ruled by a local Zaydī dynasty, the Bādūspānids.[62] The small but important district of Ṭāliqān, on the border of Gīlān and Rūyān, was closely attached to Rūyān and was at the forefront of Nizārī Ismaili activities.[63] From the Ilkhanid period, the coastal area of Ṭabaristān was known as Māzandarān, and it was only the mountainous areas which were still designated as Ṭabaristān. In Ilkhanid Ṭabaristān there were three main areas, all of which had ancient names that had been used beforehand: Sawādkūh (areas south-east of Āmul in the upper valley of the Tālār river), Fīrūzkūh (south-eastern border areas of Sawādkūh) and Hazārjarīb.[64]

Political subdivisions in Ṭabaristān and Gīlān often overlapped. Both shared the same amount of very narrow coastal plain and a more extensive but barely populated mountainous region. Both had their major urban centres in the coastal regions. In Ṭabaristān, the main cities were Sārī (formerly Sāriyya), the capital of several indigenous local dynasties from the mid-7th century CE,[65] and also Āmul, by far the richest place in the early Islamic period and the seat of the Abbasid governors in the 2nd–4th/8th–10th centuries (later serving as a twin-capital of the Bāwandids, alongside Sārī).[66] Besides Sārī and Āmul there were several other important urban centres in the *sāḥil* region of Ṭabaristān: Nātil, Chālūs, Kalā (Kalār) Māmṭīr, and Tamīsha.

The area of Jibāl Qārin occupies central Ṭabaristān, where the major dynastic fortresses of the Qārinwands and the Bāwandids, alternating allies and opponents of the Ismailis, were built. The most important fortress was Firīm[67] belonging to the Bāwandids, on the banks of the river Tijan in the medieval Hazārjarīb district, not far from Astarābād.[68] Another ancient dynastic castle was Lafūr, a place once ruled by the Qārinwand amīrs. The third main area was Jibāl Bādūspān, which could have been located around the modern towns of ʿAlīābād and Bārfurūsh.[69]

The political structures of the Caspian region, titles and religious trends, were deeply rooted in the Sasanian past and its culture was strongly influenced by its pre-Islamic past.

As far as the local families of the central and the eastern parts of the Caspian provinces are concerned, one can see similarities with the political situation in the north-western Iranian areas in the time preceding the foundation of the Nizārī Ismaili state. Here different Muslim religious and local Iranian traditionalist families were present and divided up the areas of Ṭabaristān and Māzandarān, yet the traditionalist elements, whose legitimacy was established on pre-Islamic traditions, were more important than those groups who claimed Islamic religious legitimacy.

In the decades before the founding of the Nizārī Ismaili state in 488/1095, we can observe the presence of three local traditionalist dynasties in Ṭabaristān: the principalities of the Qārinwands, the Bāwandids and the Bādūspānids.[70]

The Bāwandid dynasty ruled the most powerful and formidable local principality in Ṭabaristān and the Caspian provinces. claiming to be descendants of Prince Kāwūs, a son of the Sasanian king, Kawād I (r. 488–531 CE).

Various branches of the Bāwandid *iṣfahbad*s ruled vast areas of Ṭabaristān and Māzandarān from the second half of the 2nd/8th century until 750/1349. Their three main lines, the Kā'ūsiyya (144–early 5th/761–early 11th century), the Iṣfahbadiyya (mid-5th century–606/11th century–1210) and the Kinkhwāriyya (635–750/1238–1349), represent an almost unbroken line of continuity in Ṭabaristān.[71]

The Bāwandids, as protagonists of actual political events, first appear in the written sources in 144/761. The Bāwandid ruler, the *iṣfahbad* Qārin b. Shahriyār, converted to Islam in 227/842.

However, Zaydī forces started penetrating Ṭabaristān in the second half of the 3rd/9th century. This led to several wars between the Bāwandids and the early Zaydī rulers, Ḥasan b. Zayd and Muḥammad Zayd.[72] The reasons for these conflicts display parallels with those behind the later Nizārī Ismaili-Bāwandid wars, as the Bāwandids and Zaydīs fought for dominance over the northern Iranian provinces of the Caspian. During Zaydī rule in Ṭabaristān, the Bāwandids Rustam b. Surkhāb (r. 253–282/867–895) and Sharwīn b. Rustam (r. 282–318/895–930) were generally hostile towards the 'newcomer' Zaydīs, although they also occasionally allied with Zaydī rulers, and sometimes marriage alliances took place as well. But the Bāwandids were an indigenous dynasty acknowledging the nominal authority of the Abbasid caliphate, and noticeably autonomous.

After the fall of the Zaydī amirate in Ṭabaristān in 318/930 the Bāwandids found themselves in another conflict. This time, the

Ziyārids had formed a coalition with the Sāmānids, the amīrs ruling Central Asia and eastern Iran, and the Būyids, which aimed to subjugate Ṭabaristān. The result of this was that, from the reign of Rustam b. Sharwīn (r. 351–369/962–980) onwards, the Bāwandids fragmented and split. Rustam's sons, Marzbān, Sharwīn and Dārā caused long-lasting chaos in Ṭabaristān as a result of their own ambitions and the interference of major regional powers. Some descendants of Rustam b. Sharwīn, being loyal to the Ziyārid-Sāmānid coalition, remained Sunni, but Bāwandid vassals of the Būyids embraced Twelver Shiʿi Islam. Eventually, the pro-Būyid Twelver Shiʿi branch of the Bāwandids acquired all the Bāwandid lands.

A new line, the Iṣfahbadiyya, whose first ruler Qārin b. Surkhāb (d. ca. 465–466/1073–1074) was plausibly said to have been the grandson of Shahriyār, was established.[73] Qārin's son and successor, Ḥusām al-Dawla Shahriyār (465–ca. 506/1073–ca. 1113), was the first important ruler of the old-new Bāwandid kingdom; and he was a contemporary of Ḥasan-i Ṣabbāḥ.

The Bāwandids of the new Iṣfahbadiyya branch acknowledged the authority of the new power, the Saljūqs, a few decades before the establishment of the Nizārī Ismaili state. Ḥusām al-Dawla Shahriyār, as the new head of the dynasty, revived and strengthened its influence in the 460s/1070s, and his efforts to rebuild his state occurred in tandem with early Nizārī successes. The main stronghold of the Bāwandids remained their mountain fortresses. Thus, their organisational and military background, to a certain extent, seems similar to that of the Nizārīs. By the beginning of the 5th/11th century they had become Twelver Shiʿis but they nevertheless preserved elements of their apparently pre-Islamic traditions.

Pre-Islamic traditions, a marker of indigenous origin, undoubtedly played a major role in the culture and ideology of some northern Iranian families in their conflicts against new, 'foreign', states in the Caspian provinces. They all invoked legends tracing their origins back to the Sasanians, and indeed they could have at the least belonged to one of the high-ranking aristocratic clans of the Sasanian empire.

Besides these apparently pre-Islamic elements, Twelver Shiʿi doctrine also played a major role in the court ideology of the Bāwandids. A still underestimated fact is how much of a major role the Bāwandids played in the history of the Twelver Shiʿis in pre-Safavid

Persia. From the 4th/10th century, when the Bāwandids first adhered to the Twelver Shiʿi branch of Islam, they gradually also became patrons of the Twelver Shiʿi communities, pledging active and open support to both local as well as more remote Twelver groups in the Islamic world. Their adherence to Twelver Shiʿi beliefs and, at the same time, their strong Iranian traditionalism can be clearly seen in some of the 6th/12th-century sources.[74]

Regarding the wider regional Shiʿi contacts of the Bāwandids, Marʿashī says that they regularly hosted and fed thousands of *sayyid*s. This author mentions the warm Bāwandid welcome and lavish ceremonies and banquets held in honour of large groups of Twelver Shiʿi *sayyid*s of Ḥilla (a major centre of Twelver Shiʿi learning in the medieval era) in Āmul, the Bāwandid capital.[75]

The third local dynasty was that of the Bādūspānids, whose lands were in the western parts of Māzandarān, in Nizārī-controlled Daylamān. Although they were proud traditionalists, claiming to have pre-Islamic roots and that they were a cadet branch of the Dābūyids and therefore descendants of Sasanian king Jāmāsp (496–498 CE), their alleged Sasanian origins are obscure as is their emergence as an important local clan. The Bādūspānid *ustāndār*s were Zaydīs, suggesting that they had strong contacts with Daylamān and Gīlān.[76] Although their official title, *ustāndār*, has a pre-Islamic connotation, according to Madelung the genealogy of the early Bādūspānids is entirely fabricated and the dynasty did not appear historically until the end of the 5th/11th century, when coins depicting the first Bādūspānid *ustāndār*, Nāṣir al-Dawla Sharaf al-Dīn Naṣr b. Shahrīwash, a vassal of the Saljūq sultan Muḥammad I, were minted in Rūyān and Kujūr in 501–502/1108–1109 and 504/1110–1111. It is worth noting that the emergence of the Bādūspānids coincided with the outbreak of the Saljūq-Bāwandid and Saljūq-Ismaili wars in the time of Ḥasan-i Ṣabbāḥ. So, it is likely that the first Bādūspānids, as a newly founded local family that was loyal to the Saljūqs, served Saljūq political interests.[77] The Bādūspānids were the longest lasting native Persian dynasty of the Caspian provinces, coming to an end at the turn of the 11th/17th century.

Chapter 2

The Political Relations of the Nizārī Ismaili State in the Caspian Provinces under Ḥasan-i Ṣabbāḥ

It was in the complex and fragmented conditions described in the previous chapter that the Ismaili *dāʿī* Ḥasan-i Ṣabbāḥ was able to establish the origins of what became the Nizārī Ismaili state. Originally, it is clear, his objectives were far greater than a state in the Caspian region, but the network of castles there became and remained the core and centre of the state until their capture by the Mongols in the middle of the 7th/13th century.

Ḥasan-i Ṣabbāḥ was born into a Twelver Shiʿi family in the city of Qumm, on the borders of the Caspian region. He converted to Ismaili Islam as a young man of seventeen and a few years later was sent to the centre of the Ismaili *daʿwa* in Cairo by the Iranian *dāʿī*, Ibn ʿAṭṭāsh. This was the capital of the empire of the Fatimid Imam-caliphs who sought to establish their authority over the Islamic world as a whole. At that time the reigning Imam-caliph was al-Mustanṣir, who had been on the throne for some forty or more years. After three years in Egypt, Ḥasan-i Ṣabbāḥ returned to Iran in 473/1018. At this point he was simply working for the Ismaili *daʿwa* in Iran and in fact travelled through Iran for the *daʿwa* for some nine years. Iran at the time was ruled by the Saljūqs who had entered the Iranian plateau in 431/1040 at the head of a great movement of Central Asian nomads of Turkic origin, which then spread further into Anatolia and Syria. At some point prior to this, the Saljūqs had converted to Islam in its Sunni form and once in Iran presented themselves as the protectors of the Abbasid caliphs in Baghdad, whose spiritual authority they acknowledged. As far as can be discerned, during his travels the purpose of Ḥasan-i Ṣabbāḥ's mission developed and his objective became to counter directly the Saljūqs who saw themselves as the champions of Sunni Islam. To this end he began to work in the Caspian provinces to install a secure base for the *daʿwa* there from which to launch a counter-offensive against the Saljūq regime.

But it was not until the crisis at the centre of the Ismaili *daʿwa* in Egypt that Ḥasan's activities became explicitly independent. Upon the death of al-Mustanṣir in 487/1094 the powerful Fatimid vizier al-Afḍal disputed the right of al-Mustanṣir's eldest son Nizār to succeed, seeking to place his much younger brother on the throne instead. In the ensuing conflict Nizār, who was declared Imam in Alexandria, was captured and killed and al-Afḍal placed the young al-Mustaʿlī on the Fatimid throne. Ḥasan-i Ṣabbāḥ supported the right of Nizār and his progeny to the imamate, and as a result the *daʿwa* in Iran split from the *daʿwa* of the Fatimid caliphate in Egypt. This split was to be permanent, and the nucleus of Ismaili castles in the Caspian then became the centre of the Nizārī Ismaili state that was openly and avowedly opposed to the Saljūq empire and the dominance of the Central Asian Turks in the Middle East.

But, however expansive the aims of the Nizārī Ismaili *daʿwa* were, it also had to contend with rivals for power at the centre of the state in the Caspian mountains, and the process by which Ḥasan-i Ṣabbāḥ acquired the castles that came to form the axis of this new state was a complex one.

Following the death in 485/1092 of Niẓām al-Mulk and Sultan Malikshāh, the two key figures of central Saljūq government, the relative unity of the Saljūq empire immediately collapsed. The sons of Malikshāh, Maḥmūd, Barkiyāruq, Muḥammad and Sanjar, all attempted to seize the sultanate, with other forces, including leading characters of the central administration, becoming deeply involved in the conflicts that followed. The internecine strife of the Saljūqs clearly reflected the Central Asian nomadic aspects of Malikshāh's legacy. This was because in their Turkic nomadic tradition there was no designated heir to the leadership.[1]

In the wake of this there emerged two local powers in the Caspian provinces: the Nizārī Ismaili state, directed from Alamūt in Rūdbār, and the reinstated Bāwandid kingdom around Shahriyārkūh and Firīm in south-eastern Ṭabaristān. These two can be characterised as old-new formations as both the Ismailis and the Bāwandids can hardly be termed newcomers to northern Iran at the end of the 5th/11th century. In the case of the Nizārī Ismaili controlled area of Girdkūh the Ismaili *daʿwa* appeared there as early as the 4th/10th century.[2]

As for other local states in the Caspian provinces, as has been discussed, the Bādūspānid polity in Rūyān lay in the vicinity of the Bāwandids and Nizārīs, and there were various Zaydī rulers in Daylamān and Gīlān, who were well established in the Caspian provinces before the end of the 5th/11th century.

The Zaydīs of Daylamān in the time of Ḥasan-i Ṣabbāḥ

It is important to note that the Zaydī rulers and, likewise, the Zaydī Bādūspānids did not represent a significant military force and were in a deeply fragmented state by the time of the founding of the Nizārī Ismaili state in the late 5th/11th century. Hitherto powerful in Daylamān and Gīlān the Zaydīs were now profoundly divided between the Qāsimīs and Nāṣirīs, and this fact contributed notably to the success of the Ismailis.[3]

Among the political centres of the Zaydīs in Daylamān with Ismaili connections we must mention first Hawsam and its environs. During the first years Ḥasan-i Ṣabbāḥ's rule in Daylamān, the town of Hawsam (modern Rūdsar) was disputed by two groups of Zaydīs, the descendants of Nāṣir and the descendants of Ṭāhir, who had theological and political disputes with each other.

However, although greatly divided, the Zaydīs still represented a considerable political force in Daylamān in the early years of the Nizārī Ismaili state. Wilferd Madelung examined the sources for the Zaydīs in Daylamān, and on their basis pointed out that the Zaydīs of the Caspian province had evolved into two main branches: the Qāsimī Zaydīs and the Nāṣirī Zaydīs. The Nāṣirīs, in eastern Gīlān and Daylamān, elected their Imams from the descendants of al-Nāṣir li'l-Ḥaqq and his brother Ḥusayn al-Shāʿir al-Muḥaddith, founders of Zaydī rule in Gīlān in the 3rd/9th century. Madelung notes that in terms of law, ritual traditions and practices they were much closer to other Shiʿi groups, such as the Ismailis and Twelver Shiʿis, than were the Qāsimī Zaydīs who were strongly opposed any contact with the Ismailis. This division explains the different attitudes of different local Zaydī rulers towards the Nizārī Ismailis in Daylamān.[4]

Around 432/1040-41 the Nāṣirī Zaydī scholars of Hawsam chose a Nāṣirī Zaydī prince, a certain Ḥusayn b. Jaʿfar Nāṣir, as their Imam.[5] His kingdom eventually extended from Khānakjā on the Safīdrūd river to the borders of Ṭabaristān, and Ḥusayn b. Jaʿfar Nāṣir was able to control the area of Rūyān and presumably the fortress of Alamūt too. Ḥusayn was married to a daughter of a Bāwandid *iṣfahbad*, perhaps Ḥusām al-Dawla Shahriyār, founder of the new Iṣfahbadiyya branch of the Bāwandids in Ṭabaristān. The fact that the Zaydīs tried to build up dynastic contacts with the Bāwandids had more serious ramifications in the decades of Ismaili dominance in Daylamān. Twelver Shiʿi-Zaydī dynastic marriages became very frequent in the 6th/12th century, and various Zaydīs became vassals of the Bāwandids, who acted as their protectors. Although Ḥusayn b. Jaʿfar Nāṣir later came into conflict with his Bāwandid father-in-law, relations usually remained amicable, and on various occasions a very close cooperation between the *iṣfahbads* of Ṭabaristān and various Zaydī clans in Daylamān is evident.[6]

The years directly preceding the Nizārī Ismaili takeover of Alamūt saw a chaotic political situation in Daylamān. The Nāṣirī Zaydī Imam, Ḥusayn b. Jaʿfar Nāṣir, died in 472/1079-80. After his death, a Qāsimī Zaydī ruler, Yaḥyā Hādī Ḥuqaynī, a son of Mahdī Ḥuqaynī, from the other main branch of the Zaydīs in the Caspian provinces, claimed the Zaydī imamate in western Ṭabaristān with the active backing of a group of Qāsimī Zaydī theologians. The city of Langā rejected his claim, and in the eastern parts of Gīlān a scion from the family of the Nāṣir Uṭrūsh, whose name was Abu'l-Riḍā Kīsumī, was elected by local Zaydīs as their Imam, though in fact this ʿAlid never actually claimed the imamate for himself. Owing to endless quarrels between their respective supporters, the two Zaydī Imams eventually divided their lands between them.[7]

The Ismailis led by Ḥasan-i Ṣabbāḥ skilfully exploited the fragmented political landscape of Daylamān after 481/1088. At the time of Ḥasan-i Ṣabbāḥ's return from Egypt, in around 473/1081, the fortress of Alamūt was in the hands of an ʿAlid, Ḥusayn Mahdī, who had it as an *iqṭāʿ* (land grant) from the Great Saljūq, Sultan Malikshāh. A Zaydī, Ḥusayn Mahdī was a descendant of Ḥasan b. ʿAlī al-Uṭrūsh (d. 304/916), the 4th/9th-century ʿAlid ruler of Ṭabaristān also known as al-Nāṣir li'l-Ḥaqq. Ḥusayn Mahdī belonged to the Nāṣirī Zaydī line; and this fact perhaps helps to explain why Ḥusayn Mahdī and his retinue were sympathetic to the Ismaili guests in his fortress. An Ismaili *dāʿī*, Ḥusayn Qāʾinī, working under Ḥasan-i Ṣabbāḥ, became a boon companion of Ḥusayn Mahdī, and this friendship proved to be decisive since it resulted in the arrival of other Ismailis.

Ḥasan-i Ṣabbāḥ directed these movements from the castle of Firīm in Ṭabaristān, which belonged to the Bāwandid dynasty. He arrived at Alamūt on 6 Rajab 483/4 September 1090, and entered the fortress in disguise calling himself Dihkhudā; he did not reveal his identity to Ḥusayn Mahdī, and as time passed he became more and more confident as a large number of the soldiers there began to be increasingly responsive to Ismaili teachings. Subsequently, the Ismailis took over the fortress of Alamūt in a peaceful fashion. Using the resources of the area of Girdkūh and with the help of Ra'īs Muẓaffar, the newly converted commander of the castle at Girdkūh, Ḥasan-i Ṣabbāḥ succeeded in persuading Ḥusayn Mahdī, to leave.[8]

After Ḥasan-i Ṣabbāḥ acquired Alamūt, some Zaydī resistance to the Ismailis continued, albeit on a limited scale, but they apparently failed to halt the Ismaili advance in Daylamān. Hādī Ḥuqaynī, was one of the most vehement Zaydī opponents of the Ismailis in Daylamān.[9] As a minor ruler and religious leader, he issued a legal declaration prohibiting the Zaydīs from coming into contact with the Nizārīs, declaring them to be heretics. He was later said to have been killed by Ismailis in 490/1097. The family of Hādī Ḥuqaynī remained in Daylamān, however, and continued to resist the Ismailis. A possible son of Hādī Ḥuqaynī, Kiyā Buzurg al-Dā'ī ilā'l-Ḥaqq Riḍā b. Hādī,[10] maintained his influence around Hawsam and later joined the Bāwandids in their resistance to the Saljūqs in 521/1127.[11] However, there seems to have been a continual quarrel between different factions of the Qāsimī Zaydīs and certain Nāṣirī Zaydīs, since after the death of Hādī Ḥuqaynī a Nāṣirī called Abu'l-Riḍā Kīsumī rose to power in Hawsam; however the extent of his authority in Gīlān and in Daylamān is not clear.

The local Caspian sources remain largely silent or simply relate anecdotes about the Zaydī rulers after the death of Abu'l-Riḍā Kīsumī. More useful are the Zaydī sources, which provide some biographical details about the Zaydī Imams, their doctrinal background and occasionally some historical facts pertaining to their rule. Thus, we know from these Zaydī sources of the 6th–9th/12th–15th centuries that in 502/1108-09 a great-grandson of a Qāsimī theologian, Mu'ayyad, a certain Abū Ṭālib Akhīr Yaḥyā, claimed the imamate in the city of Khānakjā. The complexity of Zaydī history from the beginning of 6th/12th century is clearly seen in the fact that this Qāsimī Zaydī Imam enjoyed the support of a respected descendant of Uṭrūsh, a Nāṣirid called Nāṣir Riḍā. Besides some attempts at reconciliation between the two groups of Zaydīs in Daylamān, the possible alliance of Nāṣirī and Qāsimī Zaydī forces in Daylamān might perhaps be seen as a sign of their weakening positions vis-à-vis the Ismailis.

Abū Ṭālib Akhīr Yaḥyā quickly gained recognition in eastern Gīlān as far as Hawsam and also in the area of Daylamān, which had not yet been lost to the Ismailis. According to Zaydī sources, he led military campaigns against the Ismailis to reconquer former Zaydī areas in Daylamān. An important Zaydī biographical work of the 7th/13th century, *al-Ḥadā'iq al-wardiyya* by al-Muḥallī, refers to his campaigns against the Ismailis in Daylamān and attempts to glorify Abū Ṭālib Akhīr Yaḥyā for attacking the Ismaili areas. It states that Abū Ṭālib Akhīr Yaḥyā fought numerous wars with the Ismailis, retaking thirty-eight fortresses and even besieging Alamūt, taking over the valley of Alamūt, building camps around the fortress. Abū Ṭālib Akhīr Yaḥyā ordered the execution of captured Ismailis but then greatly fearing that the Ismailis would avenge this act did not leave his house for fourteen years except to pray.[12]

It is not known exactly when, where or how fortresses were captured or how the Qāsimī Abū Ṭālib Akhīr besieged Alamūt; and there is no hint in other sources of an independent Zaydī raid against Alamūt. However, the beginning of his rule might have coincided with Saljūq attacks on Alamūt. According to Rashīd al-Dīn, this first attack was organised by a coalition of local princes, including the Bāwandids, and there were armies from 'Gīl and Daylam' as well as 'other servants' at the siege.[13] Zaydī sources do not mention other forces participating in the attack against Alamūt which, they say, took place around 502/1109. The other possible date for Abū Ṭālib Akhīr Yaḥyā's attack against Ismaili areas is during the series of expeditions against Alamūt led by the Saljūq military leader Anūshtigīn Shīrgīr, which lasted nearly seven years ending in 512/1118.[14] It is clear from our sources that for years Shīrgīr had systematically laid waste to extended areas inhabited or cultivated by the Ismailis and that he was on the verge of capturing Alamūt when his master, the Saljūq sultan Muḥammad II

(r. 498–512/1105–1118), suddenly died, causing the immediate withdrawal of Saljūq forces.[15] Non-Zaydī sources make no mention of any Zaydī participation in these operations. However, given the high number claimed of 'thirty-eight fortresses retaken' by Abū Ṭālib Akhīr Yaḥyā, this may mean that his anti-Nizārī campaigns were very much linked to the intensive military activity of Anūshtigīn Shīrgīr, and that he recruited and despatched Zaydī Daylamī military forces in support of the Saljūq offensives during these years. Shīrgīr was indeed successful to some degree and recaptured some fortresses in Rūyān from the Ismailis, but there is no mention of any specific strongholds taken by the Zaydīs from the Ismailis.

In 512/1118 Abū Ṭālib Akhīr Yaḥyā and his anti-Ismaili actions came to an end after fresh dissent broke out in the Zaydī community of Gīlān and Daylamān in 511/1117. An ʿAlid, Ḥasan Jurjānī, appeared from Gurgān in the last years of Abū Ṭālib Akhīr Yaḥyā's rule, challenged his power and easily captured both Hawsam and Lāhījān from him. With some Gilite military aid and using resources from the confiscated property of the local Zaydī population, Abū Ṭālib Akhīr Yaḥyā was able, temporarily, to drive out his rival but his quarrels with Ḥasan Jurjānī seriously weakened his ability to resist the Ismailis. No doubt the renewed conflicts within the fragmented Zaydī community greatly facilitated Ismaili expansion in Daylamān. The shift of the Zaydī political centre from Hawsam to Lāhījān is clearly linked to the weakening Zaydī position in Daylamān, though Hawsam may have remained under Zaydī influence until 511/1117, the start of the war between Ḥasan Jurjānī and Abū Ṭālib Akhīr Yaḥyā.[16]

Despite the troubled and often chaotic political events engendered by the quarrels between different Zaydī clans, the area populated by the Zaydīs in Gīlān served as a base for the more powerful Twelver Shiʿi Bāwandid rulers. We learn from Marʿashī that when his sons, Najm al-Dawla Qārin and ʿAlāʾ al-Dawla ʿAlī, started fighting each other, Ḥusām al-Dawla retreated first to Āmul and then to Hawsam, the old Zaydī centre in Daylamān, where he built a *khānqah* for himself and engaged in pious devotion and agriculture.[17] The local Gilite and Daylamī aristocracy obeyed the ageing Bāwandid *iṣfahbad* and acknowledged his suzerainty over Hawsam, according to Ibn Isfandiyār.[18] Due to the Ismaili conquest of Hawsam in 503/1110, as well as the close dynastic and religious-political contacts between the

Zaydī family of Mahdī Ḥuqaynī and the Twelver Shiʿi Bāwandids,[19] it is no surprised that Ḥusām al-Dawla Shahriyār received a warm welcome from the Zaydīs of Gīlān.

Thus, in addition to Alamūt, the Zaydīs gradually had to give up much of their lands in neighbouring areas in Daylamān which had belonged to them before 481/1088. The Ismailis succeeded in taking over the fortress of Lamasar in 494/1101 or maybe slightly later, as well as a fortress down river from Alamūt which according to one of our principal sources, Rashīd al-Dīn, the Ismailis swiftly attacked and apparently took over with relative ease, defeating the Zaydīs, Rasāmūj, Lāmsālār and his relatives who held it.[20]

As regards early Ismaili policy in Daylamān, there are indications in the sources of a more conciliatory approach coming from both the Ismailis and the Zaydīs, though more rarely from the latter. The general assumption must be that although the Ismailis' main aim was to extend the regions under their control, due to the Saljūq threat they often allied themselves with the Zaydīs. In order to strengthen their position against the Saljūqs, the Ismailis not only conquered local fortresses or ousted their former owners from such places but sometimes also supported those local kingdoms that were inclined to resist Saljūq attempts at domination.

Signs of this approach can be seen in the case of Lamasar before the Ismailis took control of it. According to Rashīd al-Dīn, in 486/1093,[21] Rasāmūj and Lāmsālār visited Ḥasan-i Ṣabbāḥ in Alamūt and forged an alliance with the Ismailis. However, this alliance proved tenuous as only a year later the same Rasāmūj broke the treaty. The nature and details of this agreement between the Zaydīs in Lamasar and the Ismailis in Alamūt is not known, but if there was some mutual consensus to build friendlier relations this could only have been a sign of a local alliance being formed against the Saljūqs. We are not informed about the religious background of Rasāmūj and Lāmsālār or if they were Nāṣirī or Qāsimī Zaydīs. Regarding the possible date of the conquest of Lamasar, based on Rashīd al-Dīn's claims Hodgson suggests it took place as early as 489/1096. On the other hand, Juwaynī records the conquest as having occurred rather later in 495/1102.[22]

Another sign of a more peaceful approach by the Zaydīs is a gesture made by the *qāḍī* of Langā, called Marwān, who was apparently a Nāṣirī Zaydī[23] and who was in correspondence with the Ismailis. Yet the milder attitude of this Zaydī *qāḍī* greatly enraged Hādī Ḥuqaynī, who ordered his execution. Soon after this, in 490/1097, it is said that Hādī Ḥuqaynī fell victim to a Nizārī Ismaili warrior.[24]

In general, it is evident that the Zaydīs were in a very fragmented state when the Ismailis arrived in Rūdbār and other parts of Daylamān. The fractious nature of the Zaydi polity greatly facilitated the emergence of the Nizārī Ismaili state at the end of the 5th/11th century. However, they were not the only new power to exploit the state of affairs following the deaths of Niẓām al-Mulk and Malikshāh since around the same time the Bāwandid dynasty also came to power.

The emergence of the Bāwandids, the eastern neighbours of the Nizārīs

Let us first examine the striking similarities between the early Nizārī and Bāwandid kingdoms at the end of the 5th/11th century. Over forty-five years, from 487 to 532/1094 to 1138, both the Ismaili Nizārī Ismaili state and that of the Bāwandids benefitted from dynamic and effective rulers: for the Nizārīs Ḥasan-i Ṣabbāḥ and Kiyā Buzurg-Umīd, and in the Bāwandid kingdom, Ḥusām al-Dawla Shahriyār and ʿAlāʾ al-Dawla ʿAlī.

In this period, one can note three main groups around the Ismaili areas in the vicinity of Alamūt and Girdkūh: the Zaydīs in Daylamān and western Gīlān (eastern Gīlān had been in the hands of Sunnis since the early Islamic period); the Bāwandids in Ṭabaristān; and the Bādūspānids in Rūyān, to the west of Alamūt. Both these latter groups were Shiʿi, albeit representing different branches of Shiʿi Islam. The Bāwandids were Twelver Shiʿis, while the Bādūspānids followed Zaydī Shiʿism; yet both families claimed to be descendants of old local families. In addition, the Nizārīs had local contacts with certain Sunni-dominated areas, notably the area of Qazwīn, which at least at that period had a mainly Sunni population.

As far as the chronology of events in these forty-five years are concerned, there are three main sub-periods which can be discerned. Again parallels in the history of the Nizārīs and that of the Bāwandids can be discerned and the chronological boundaries are much the same.

The main characteristic of the three sub-periods can be described as follows:

1. The first sub-period is that of the emergence of the two states and their initial successes against the Saljūqs (487–498/1094–1105).
2. The second covers the time of Saljūq counter-attacks, when the sources relate major military expeditions under Sultan Muḥammad I against both the Nizārīs and Bāwandids (498–514/1105–1120).
3. The third sub-period, after 514/1120, might be termed one of consolidation, when the Nizārīs and Bāwandids respectively started restoring and extending their influence.

As regards the first sub-period, although both these states had been established before 485/1092, in subsequent years they managed to extend their borders, defeating the Saljūqs as well as other local powers. The Bāwandids, though still nominally Saljūq vassals after the death of Malikshāh in 485/1092, expelled the Saljūq governors from Āmul and Sārī, thereby extending their influence from the mountains to the littoral of the Caspian sea.

Meanwhile, the Ismailis extended their power at the expense of the Zaydīs in Daylamān and in the conquered region of Girdkūh as well as in more remote areas, such as Arrajān in the southern Zagros and Shāhdiz near Iṣfahān in an endeavour to establish a larger state. This expansionist policy lasted until nearly 498/1105, when, after the death of Sultan Barkiyāruq, the two surviving sons of Malikshāh, Muḥammad and Sanjar, decided to attack the Nizārīs. This rapid expansion coincided with the founding of the independent Nizārī *daʿwa* after 487/1094, when Ḥasan-i Ṣabbāḥ supported the claim of Nizār,[25] the eldest son of the Imam-caliph al-Mustanṣir in Fatimid Egypt to the Ismaili imamate, as has been mentioned. Nizār was eventually defeated and murdered in 490/1097 by the powerful vizier, al-Afdal, who had elevated his younger brother al-Mustaʿlī to the imamate. This was a definitive breach between the Fatimids and the *daʿwa* at Alamūt and can be said to mark the beginning of an independent Nizārī Ismaili *daʿwa* and state.

In the second sub-period, the Nizārīs and Bāwandids had to withstand determined Saljūq military assaults, both having rejected Saljūq overlordship even before 498/1105. In fact, the first anti-Nizārī expedition of the Saljūqs took place in 494/1101, when, according to Ibn al-Athīr, Sanjar in Khurāsān and Barkiyāruq launched a concerted attack against the Nizārīs of Persia. This first attack, however, proved to be a failure and the Nizārīs managed to keep their strongholds.[26] After 498/1105, the Saljūqs under Muḥammad b. Malikshāh, the sultan in western Iran, were much more successful, capturing the fortress of Shāhdiz in 501/1107, thereby eliminating the Nizārī Ismailis from the vicinity of Iṣfahān.[27] The Ismaili governor of the castle, Aḥmad ʿAṭṭāsh, and most of his followers either perished in the siege or were later tortured and killed.[28] After this successful siege, Muḥammad b. Malikshāh commenced attacking the Nizārī heartlands in Rūdbār and Daylamān.

The loss of Nizārī strongholds near Iṣfahān and the end of Nizārī rule in the region around Arrajān, curtailing the idea of a broader Nizārī Ismaili state in Iran was a contributing factor in the birth of a more regionally focussed state in the northern provinces. The years between 504/1111 and 512/1118 were particularly devastating, as the armies of Shīrgīr, the amīr of Sāwa, systematically destroyed Nizārī areas around Alamūt and were on the verge of capturing Alamūt until the sudden death of Sultan Muḥammad I in 512/1118 compelled them to withdraw.[29]

In the years of the fiercest Saljūq attacks against Alamūt there was also Saljūq involvement in Bāwandid dynastic disputes in Ṭabaristān. After the death of Ḥusām al-Dawla in 503/1110, ʿAlāʾ al-Dawla ʿAlī and his brothers, Najm al-Dawla Qārin and Bahrām, as well as the descendants of Najm al-Dawla Qārin, fought a series of bloody wars with each other. Saljūq forces became actively involved in these battles and, finally, around 512/1118, ʿAlāʾ al-Dawla ʿAlī united Ṭabaristān with the active support of Sanjar, the Saljūq sultan of Khurāsān.

The third sub-period might be termed that of consolidation, when the Nizārīs and Bāwandids both began strengthening and extending their power again. The possible reason for these political changes was the rapid and spectacular weakening of Saljūq influence in northern Iran, which opened the way for local kingdoms to reinforce their authority. The western Saljūqs quickly lost their influence and even the eastern Saljūq branch, led by Sanjar, was not in a position to control remote areas such as Rūdbār. By the tail end of Kiyā Buzurg-Umīd's era in 530/1136 Alamūt was held in considerable prestige. The Bāwandids, also experienced a similar series of events and from around 514/1120 ʿAlāʾ al-Dawla ʿAlī extended his influence and hence Bāwandid power in the direction of Gurgān and Gīlān. Among the similarities between the early 6th/12th-century Nizārīs and Bāwandids, are their military and perhaps socio-economic structures. The strength of both states lay in their chains of castles and fortresses. The fortresses of Alamūt and Firīm, each the centre of each state, proved to be inaccessible during this period.

Regarding relations between Nizārīs and Bāwandids, Rashīd al-Dīn writes that according to the *Sargudhasht-i Sayyidnā*, between 473/1081 and 481/1088 Ḥasan-i Ṣabbāḥ stayed on two occasions in Firīm and Shahriyārkūh in the mountainous area of Ṭabaristān, the traditional political and dynastic strongholds of the Bāwandids. His main activity in Ṭabaristān seems to have been spreading the Ismaili *daʿwa*. He then left Ṭabaristān after four months and went to Khuzistān. From there he returned to Dāmghān and Gurgān, continuing the work of the *daʿwa* in these areas which later became important parts of the Nizārī Ismaili state, but which at times were also ruled by the Bāwandids in the 6th/12th century.

From Gurgān, Ḥasan-i Ṣabbāḥ returned to the area of Shahriyārkūh in Ṭabaristān for a second time, and from here he sent *dāʿīs* to Alamūt. Among the *dāʿīs* we find envoys from different places, such as Rayy, Qazwīn and Lārījān, and also a certain ʿAlī Namādgar Damāwandī, whose name suggests that the *daʿwa* led by Ḥasan-i Ṣabbāḥ in Ṭabaristān may have been a success.

It may be that Ḥasan-i Ṣabbāḥ's experiences in Shahriyārkūh and Firīm influenced his actions in the similarly mountainous area of Alamūt.[30] But although the geography of Firīm made it suitable place for locating the *daʿwa* it was already established as the centre of the Bāwandid dynasty. Ḥasan-i Ṣabbāḥ moved to Daylamān whose Zaydī rulers could muster less resistance to Ismaili ambitions.[31]

In the area of Girdkūh, in the vicinity of Qūmis, a number of fortresses also fell into the hands of the Ismailis. Of these, Girdkūh itself was the most important, though the fortresses of Ustunāwand and Manṣūrakūh were also of considerable strategic importance. They were all situated in the rich commercial centres of western Khurāsān and guarded the eastern gateway of the Alburz mountains and the Caspian highlands. This chain of castles also lay along the southern borders of the Bāwandid kingdom. With their strategic position guarding various trade routes, whoever held these fortresses was able to exert considerable influence over the Bāwandids even in periods of peace. This area had in fact been known to the Ismaili *da'wa* since the time of the *dā'ī* 'Abd al-Malik Kawkābī in the early 4th/10th century, and now Ḥasan-i Ṣabbāḥ continued the *da'wa* there visiting it on several occasions.[32]

According to an account given by both Juwaynī and Rashīd al-Dīn,[33] Ra'īs Muẓaffar (also known as Mu'ayyad al-Dīn Muẓaffar b. Aḥmad al-Mustawfī), the pro-Ismaili commander of Girdkūh, who as a Saljūq military leader had joined the Ismailis, supported Ḥasan-i Ṣabbāḥ by paying three thousand dinars for Alamūt. The date of Ra'īs Muẓaffar's arrival in Girdkūh, as a commander in the service of a Saljūq senior officer, Amīrdād Ḥabashī, was between 489/1096 and 493/1100. He had been converted by the *dā'ī*, 'Abd al-Malik b. 'Aṭṭāsh. After 489/1096 he managed to persuade his master, Amīrdād Ḥabashī, to appoint him as his lieutenant in Girdkūh in the service of Sultan Barkiyāruq. The former Saljūq governor of Girdkūh left the castle only reluctantly upon the orders of Amīrdād Ḥabashī. Ra'īs Muẓaffar rapidly transformed the fortress of Girdkūh into a self-sufficient military base. He ordered a very deep well to be sunk in the rock of Girdkūh, and although at first no water was found, following an earthquake a spring gushed out of the well, thereby making Girdkūh a highly resilient military base for many years.

In 493/1100 Ra'īs Muẓaffar joined the armies of Barkiyāruq and Amīrdād Ḥabashī against Sanjar who, however, had Ismaili warriors in his army. A battle was fought near Girdkūh and Sanjar eventually defeated his enemies, killing Amīrdād Ḥabashī too. Ra'īs Muẓaffar fled back to Girdkūh, where he assembled the treasure of his former patron. It was after this battle that, despite having fought for Barkiyāruq, he revealed his Ismaili adherence. Ra'īs Muẓaffar was succeeded as governor of Girdkūh by his son Sharaf al-Dīn Muḥammad, a former pupil of Ḥasan-i Ṣabbāḥ.[34]

The fact that the actions of the Nizārīs exacerbated the possibility of a military conflict with Bāwandids is attested by Ibn Isfandiyār, who mentions the first Nizārī-Bāwandid conflict. When the Bāwandid, 'Alā' al-Dawla 'Alī, was travelling to Iṣfahān around 501/1108 to visit the Saljūq court, his party was attacked by the Ismailis of Manṣūrakūh. However his statement regarding the Ismailis and Bāwandids is unique in all the historical texts, and it must be treated it with some caution for Mar'ashī, when recalling 'Alā' al-Dawla 'Alī's journey to Iṣfahān, largely relies on Ibn Isfandiyār, but removes all the anti-Nizārī passages, including the story of the Ismaili attack.[35]

On the other hand, when expedient, cooperation between Alamūt and Firīm took place. One example of this was a specific kind of military support which Ḥusām al-Dawla Shahriyār offered the Ismailis. When the armies of Sultan Muḥammad b. Malikshāh invaded the area of Rūdbār around 501/1108, local princes in Gīlān and Māzandarān were called upon to join his anti-Nizārī campaign. According to Ibn Isfandiyār and Marʿashī, the Saljūqs, who may have been angered by the ousting of their governors from Āmul and Sārī, despatched an insulting letter threatening the Bāwandids with loss of their kingdom should there be any failure to participate in the expedition against Alamūt. As a sign of his growing confidence and power, as well as being incensed by the threatening tone of the message,[36] Ḥusām al-Dawla Shahriyār refused to help the Saljūqs.[37] Sultan Muḥammad then sent a certain Amīr Sunqur Bukhārī with an army to besiege Ḥusām al-Dawla Shahriyār in Sārī, but the Saljūq army was routed by a foray led by Ḥusām al-Dawla Shahriyār's eldest son, Najm al-Dawla Qārin. Realising the difficulties the Saljūq army faced in Māzandarān, Sunqur sent a message to Sultan Muḥammad in which he clearly referred to the political reality in northern Iran: 'We do not gain anything in that province with force and violence, but with grace and pretence.'[38]

The Saljūq sultan now sent Ḥusām al-Dawla Shahriyār a conciliatory letter, apologising for the previous, insulting letter and Amīr Sunqur's attack. At the same time, he asked Ḥusām al-Dawla Shahriyār to despatch one of his sons to his court in Iṣfahān, where he created a dynastic link with the Bāwandids by marrying his sister to a Bāwandid prince.[39]

Saljūq policy was now to appease the Bāwandids instead of attacking them. It seems that the Bāwandids hesitated to attack the Nizārīs because they considered the Saljūqs the more dangerous and challenging threat to their kingdom, and their objective was to give tacit support to the less dangerous Nizārīs in their struggle against the mightier Saljūqs. No doubt Sultan Muḥammad saw the Bāwandids as a key northern ally against the Ismailis. But the dynastic marriage with the Bāwandid prince proved to be a sign of Saljūq weakness, as this was the union of a member of the staunchly Sunni dynasty and a

Twelver Shiʿi vassal. One must add here that, according our calculations, this marriage between the Saljūqs and Bāwandids must have taken place just weeks or a few months after the destruction of the Ismaili castle of Shāhdiz near Iṣfahān in 500/1107, which again shows Sultan Muḥammad's intention to destroy the Nizārīs within the framework of a broader coalition, one including the Bāwandids who who had military forces and knowledge of the lands in the vicinity of the Nizārīs' Caspian fortresses. After this marriage one might have expected active Bāwandid involvement in Sultan Muḥammad's military campaigns against the Nizārīs.[40] And indeed, in the *Sargudhasht-i Sayyidnā*, the name of Najm al-Dawla Qārin, the Bāwandid who married the Saljūq princess, does in fact appear in the list of princes who joined the Saljūq forces besieging Alamūt.[41]

However, there emerges here some serious doubt on chronological grounds about the actual participation of the Bāwandids. Whilst it is true that Rashīd al-Dīn also mentions Najm al-Dawla Qārin, in the month of Jumādā I 500/January 1107, as one of the besiegers of Alamūt,[42] according to Ibn Isfandiyār, Najm al-Dawla Qārin fought and defeated Sultan Muḥammad's amīr, Sunqur Bukhārī, in this same year. Therefore, Najm al-Dawla must have arrived at the Saljūq court in Baghdad no earlier than 502/1108 to marry the Saljūq princess. Ibn Isfandiyār says that Najm al-Dawla Qārin first rejected the Saljūq invitation to the court at Iṣfahān, fearing consequences arising from his anti-Saljūq raid; and he was replaced by his brother, ʿAlāʾ al-Dawla ʿAlī, who went there to pay homage in 502/1108. For this reason, Najm al-Dawla Qārin could hardly have been among the Saljūq-allied besiegers of Alamūt in Jumādā I 500/January 1107 since he defeated the Saljūq forces of Sunqūr Bukhārī near Sārī at around that time. It is important to note that both for that period and up until the end of ʿAlāʾ al-Dawla ʿAlī's rule in 536/1141 none of the sources refer to any major Nizārī-Bāwandid conflicts and in fact it would appear that the Nizārīs and Bāwandids were allies rather than enemies. Another indication of this state of affairs is the fact that in the sources there are no accusations against the Nizārīs regarding killing any of the Bāwandids or indeed any of their associates.

The same tacit logistical and military cooperation between the Nizārīs and Bāwandids more or less continued after 503/1110, the year of Ḥusām al-Dawla Shahriyār's death. Between 503/1110 and

510/1117, ʿAlāʾ al-Dawla ʿAlī defeated his relatives and, interestingly, with support from Sanjar became the new ruler of Ṭabaristān. ʿAlāʾ al-Dawla ʿAlī's victory over his relatives coincided with the westward military expansion of Sanjar. In this period, the Nizārīs were not actively involved in the affairs of the Bāwandids. This can be explained by the Saljūq attacks led by Anūshtigīn Shīrgīr against the Nizārī castles. Bāwandid reluctance to participate in these was probably caused by their fear that Saljūq authority might be re-established in the Caspian provinces.

According to Ibn Isfandiyār, in 512/1118 Bahrām tried to incite the Ismailis of Rayy to kill his brother ʿAlāʾ al-Dawla ʿAlī, but they turned down his request. Instead, it seems that the Ismailis supported ʿAlāʾ al-Dawla ʿAlī since, according to Ibn Isfandiyār, in 513/1119 the Ismailis murdered Unar (Öner) the Saljūq governor of Nīshāpūr, who was a supporter of Bahrām and had entertained him at his court in Nīshāpūr.[43] Thus it seems that the Ismailis very much reciprocated the support of Ḥusām al-Dawla Shahriyār and his son, ʿAlāʾ al-Dawla ʿAlī in their conflict with the Saljūqs. We can see that both Nizārī Ismailis and Bāwandids strove to keep the existing balance of power in northern Iran by supporting each other against the Saljūqs in the early decades of the newly founded Nizārī Ismaili state.

The idea that Nizārī Ismailis favoured certain of the Bāwandids, whom they considered more favourably inclined to the Nizārī cause, resembles the relationship the Nizārīs had had with the Zaydīs at the beginning of Ḥasan-i Ṣabbāḥ's time at Alamūt. Those groups that showed more understanding of the Ismailis were allowed to remain on their lands as allies or vassals, but those who resisted the Ismailis or allied themselves with the Ismailis' enemies naturally had to be opposed. In early Bāwandid-Nizārī contacts one can see parallel trends. Ḥusām al-Dawla Shahriyār and ʿAlāʾ al-Dawla ʿAlī may be considered pro-Ismaili. This support does not mean that they wished to build up a friendship or felt religious sympathies based on following a Shiʿi creed. There are no traces of mutual religious correspondence between them in this early period; however, the objectives of the pro-Ismaili Bāwandids and the first Nizārī rulers did coincide to a certain extent. Their actual opponents were the Saljūqs, and we can see that in 501/1108, 513/1119, 521/1127 and 525/1131 both Nizārīs and Bāwandids came under heavy pressure from the same invading Saljūq forces.

Nizārī and Bāwandid contacts with the Saljūqs in the time of Ḥasan-i Ṣabbāḥ (483–518/1090–1124)

Another interesting parallel between the two emerging states could be linked to the problem of Saljūq disintegration. Both the Nizārīs and Bāwandids pursued a very similar policy when dealing with the Saljūq armies.

As for Nizārī-Saljūq relations, they began in the expansionist period of the Nizārī Ismaili state, after 487/1094, when war broke out between Malikshāh's sons and successors. Barkiyāruq, Muḥammad Tapar and later Sanjar as well as others, for example, Tutush, the brother of Malikshāh, each endeavoured to become supreme sultan of the Saljūq-ruled lands. Eventually, all the aspirants failed to achieve their goals and the Saljūq empire fell apart. Although Barkiyāruq (r. 485–499/1092–1105) was recognised as the sole Saljūq ruler in the western parts of the Saljūq empire, he was generally regarded as weak and incompetent, someone whose authority was permanently challenged by his relatives and other local enemies, including the Nizārīs under Ḥasan-i Ṣabbāḥ.[44]

As Carole Hillenbrand has pointed out, it was owing to the political chaos in western Iran caused by the weakness of the Saljūqs, that the Ismailis managed to gain territory and in the reign of Barkiyāruq the influence of the Ismaili *da'wa* at the western Saljūq court attained its apogee.[45] The chroniclers, Ibn al-Athīr[46] and Ibn al-Jawzī,[47] held that Barkiyāruq himself had Ismaili sympathies. When Arghush and Surmuz, two notable Saljūq military leaders, were deemed to have been killed by the Nizārīs in 494/1101 their murder fuelled anti-Nizārī hysteria at Barkiyāruq's court, and he was compelled to root out allegedly pro-Nizārī individuals in his army.[48] As a result, hundreds of soldiers and courtiers were killed on his orders and the leader of the Nizārī Ismailis at his court was identified as a soldier from Yazd, Muḥammad b. Dushmanziyār.

In the same year, Sanjar, brother of Barkiyāruq and sultan of Khurāsān since 490/1097, sent one of his amīrs, Buzqush, to besiege the Ismaili fortress of Ṭabas Masinān in Quhistān, where the Ismailis had established themselves. However, the local Ismailis bribed the Saljūq forces to leave, and again, in 497/1104, when Buzqush mounted another attack, the Ismailis once again sent him gifts, and thus remained unharmed and in possession of Ṭabas Masinān. According to Ibn al-Athīr this provoked great anger among the local Sunnis.[49]

The reign of Barkiyāruq's successor Muḥammad I (r. 499–512/1105–1118) is generally characterised by his concerted attacks against the Nizārīs. His position was much more secure than Barkiyāruq's had been, and he enjoyed the support of the most powerful courtiers and the Saljūq military administration. What is more, Muḥammad acknowleged Sanjar as the ruler of the eastern Saljūq lands, and all of this paved the way for a more successful campaign against the Nizārīs.[50] Sultan Muḥammad captured the major Nizārī strongholds in Iran outside the Caspian and Quhistān regions. Most importantly, as we have seen, he conquered Shāhdiz, the great Ismaili castle outside Iṣfahān, and he also did away with the Nizārī groups based in Arrajān in the Southern Zagros[51] and in Kirmān, albeit details of these two latter campaigns remain obscure.

Indeed, evidence concerning Muḥammad I's anti-Nizārī campaigns and the number of expeditions in Arrajān and Kirmān undertaken by Saljūq armies during his reign is confused. As for the possible number of Saljūq attacks against Alamūt between 498/1105 and 512/1118, Juwaynī and Kāshānī mention eight, while Ibn al-Athīr claims there were only two occasions when Saljūq armies invaded the Alamūt region.[52]

One of two otherwise unsuccessful expeditions mentioned by Ibn al-Athīr was that led by Aḥmad b. Niẓām al-Mulk in 502–503/1109–1110.[53] Both Ibn al-Athīr[54] and Juwaynī[55] argue that the harsh winter weather took the army of Niẓām al-Mulk's son by surprise, and he was forced to retreat, while al-Ḥusaynī simply reports that the Saljūq army defeated a force of Nizārīs.[56]

The other expedition referred to by Ibn al-Athīr was the campaign led by the amīr of Sāwa, Anūshtigīn Shīrgīr, in 512/1118, which seems to have been a much more powerful attempt to wipe out the Nizārīs in their heartland. According to al-Ḥusaynī and Ibn al-Athīr, after laying siege for nine months, Anūshtigīn Shīrgīr was on the verge of taking Alamūt when news of Sultan Muḥammad I's death arrived, causing panic in the Saljūq camp.[57] As regards the veracity of this account, Hillenbrand claims that it shows striking similarities with the anti-Nizārī campaign led by a certain Qızıl Sārīgh, a local Saljūq leader in Quhistān, which was unexpectedly halted by the death of Malik Shāh.

It is likely that in both cases the same historical topos was used by the chroniclers to conceal the failure of both campaigns.[58] A more reliable and somewhat surprising element might be seen in the narrative of Ibn al-Athīr in connection with the siege of 512/1118.[59] He notes that the defenders of Alamūt had been informed of the death of Sultan Muḥammad I before the attack.[60] This is a reference to the highly efficient system of communication between the neighbouring fortresses of Alamūt, Maymūndiz and Lamasar which depended on their inter-visibility. Different means of sending messages, using fire, light and smoke (and possibly the use of homing pigeons) may have been deployed to relay information between the Daylamī castles of the Nizārīs.[61]

Hillenbrand gives credibility to Ibn al-Athīr's claims saying that as someone who constantly praised the Saljūqs, he would not have omitted to record any military action they undertook against the Nizārīs. Meanwhile, Juwaynī, in the service of the Īl Khān Hülegü, can be seen to have attempted to overstate Saljūq attempts to eliminate the Nizārīs in order to enhance the later success of the Mongols.[62] As David Morgan put it, Juwaynī 'was able to discern some silver linings in the Mongol clouds', in their destruction of the Ismailis.[63]

Then again, the phrase 'attack against Alamūt' does not necessarily refer to a direct siege of the castle since it could have referred to the valley of Alamūt being attacked and pillaged by invading armies. The same problem of interpretation of 'attack against Alamūt' might be put forward during the later Bāwandid-Nizārī wars when the armies of the Bāwandid *iṣfahbad*, Shāh Ghāzī Rustam raided Alamūt several times. Statements by Juwaynī, that eight successive military campaigns were undertaken by Saljūq armies, may be true if we see these as simply forays into the Alamūt valley.

But it should be noted that, although Ibn al-Athīr portrayed Sultan Muḥammad I as taking a committed anti-Nizārī stance, something that the campaigns would indeed seem to bear out, yet in his titles as seen in an inscription from Gulpāyagān there is no sign of anti-Nizārī sentiment. Ibn al-Athīr's words as quoted here may be more an expression of his own feeling on the matter:[64] 'When Muḥammad became Sultan and nobody opposed him any longer, there was no matter more important for him than attacking the Bāṭiniyya,[65] fighting them and exacting justice for the Muslims against their tyranny and oppression.'[66] Ibn al-Athīr further depicts this zealous hatred for the Ismailis on the arrest a certain Surkhān b. Kaykhusraw al-Daylamī, attributing to the sultan the following words: 'I have made a vow to God that I will not kill any prisoner. (But) if it is established that you are a Bāṭinī, then I will kill you.'[67]

On the other hand, there are signs of enduring contacts between certain of the Saljūqs and the Nizārīs when their interests coincided. A certain kind of pragmatism concerning common interests can be detected, especially on the disintegration of Saljūq power after the death of Malikshāh in 485/1092. Setting aside the idea of antagonism between Sunni Saljūqs and Nizārī Ismailis or other Shiʿi groups, despite the fact that the Saljūqs attacked the Nizārīs, it is clear from all the sources that both the Nizārīs and the Bāwandids often had expedient contacts with Sanjar and the eastern Saljūq sultanate.[68]

Signs of early interactions between the Nizārīs and Sanjar can be seen in the Nizārī take-over of Girdkūh in 493/1100, when Raʾīs Muẓaffar placed the castle at the disposal of Ḥasan-i Ṣabbāḥ, as mentioned earlier. According to Rashīd al-Dīn, Raʾīs Muẓaffar did not cut his ties with the Saljūqs and continued to maintain good relations with Sanjar, dividing revenues from the region with him. These good relations continued until Sanjar's death.

After 493/1110, pressure on the Nizārīs from the western Saljūqs increased but, conversely, Sanjar, sultan of the eastern Saljūq lands, saw the Nizārīs as a useful interim ally against his western Saljūq relatives, who were often in conflict with him. Rashīd al-Dīn says that Sanjar made an agreement of friendship[69] with the Nizārīs, and the documents of this agreement were held in the library of Alamūt at the time of the Mongol conquest, though the actual texts of these documents were not recorded in the sources.

Though we lack direct evidence for contacts between Sanjar and the Nizārī Ismailis that are recounted in Rashīd al-Dīn's quotations from *Sargudhasht-i Sayyidnā* and Qazwīnī Rāzī's *Kitāb al-Naqḍ*, yet, Juwaynī says that he saw the correspondence from Sanjar in the library of Alamūt before the documents were destroyed.[70] And quite apart from the material concerning Raʾīs Muẓaffar, there are a number of other references in the sources to Nizārī diplomacy at Sanjar's court in Marw. Although many of these episodes are imbued with a rather allegorical character, they nevertheless indicate that diplomatic exchanges took place whenever the political interests of the parties involved coincided.

Furthermore, there is evidence of the use of Ismaili auxiliary forces by the armies of the contending sons of Malikshāh. Barkiyāruq and two of his younger brothers, Muḥammad I and Aḥmad Sanjar, hired Ismaili mercenaries, sometimes in relatively high numbers. That the Nizārīs represented a significant military force is clearly reflected in the sources. Ibn al-Athīr mentions 5,000 Ismaili foot soldiers in Sanjar's battle against Barkiyāruq.[71] He says these Ismaili forces from Ṭabas in Quhistān were deployed or hired by Sanjar. It would seem to be further indication of agreements between Sanjar and the Nizārīs and against Barkiyāruq in 493/1100.[72] What is more, the *Kitāb al-Naqḍ* refers to a vizier of the western Saljūqs who, after many years, ventured to close the routes to Marw previously open to Ismailis, presumably to cut communications with Sanjar in the east. But we are also told that there were at least 5,000 Ismaili fighters in the army of Barkiyāruq against his brother Muḥammad.[73] Discounting the suspiciously similar number to that of the Nizārīs in Sanjar's army as a topos, nonetheless this is a significant indication of Ismaili interaction with Barkiyāruq and the Ismailis seem to have skillfully negotiated with both these Saljūq sultans, Barkiyāruq and Sanjar.

The existence of an Ismaili *daʿwat-khāna*, an Ismaili doctrinal and political centre, in Marw, as mentioned by Ghaznawī, and its discovery by Shaykh Aḥmad-i Jām in the *Maqāmāt-i zhanda pīl*, whether this is a strictly accurate account or not, indicates a relatively undisrupted Ismaili presence in the capital of the Eastern Saljūq empire. The *Maqāmāt-i zhanda pīl*, a work about the life and deeds of Shaykh Aḥmad-i Jām (d. ca. 532/1137), a Persian Sufi and an inveterate enemy of the Nizārī Ismailis, was written by one of his disciples, Muḥammad Ghaznawī, in the 6th/12th century, not long after the death of the shaykh. It has a very strong anti-Nizārī tone but in many cases its anecdotes reflect a memory of the influence of the Nizārī Ismailis in Khurāsān. The most well known of these tales concerns the discovery of a secret Nizārī Ismaili network operating among members of the Saljūq elite in the city of Marw during Sanjar's reign.[74] In the text, there is a brief story of wine-drinking ceremonies held by the Nizārī attackers before setting out on a mission, probably an early version of the Assassin legends.[75] In this context it should also be noted that recent scholarship has drawn attention to Muḥammad al-Shahrastānī's Ismaili affiliations. Al-Shahrastānī, author of various works including the encyclopaedic study of religions, *al-Milal wa'l-niḥal*, was *nā'ib al-sulṭān* at Sanjar's count in Marw from 514 to 536/1120 to 1141, and may well have been a vital figure in the negotiations between the Ismailis and Sanjar, although his possible Ismaili affiliation remained hidden.[76]

A recently discovered doctrinal source entitled *Qiṣṣa-i Malik-i Sīstān* also sheds some light on relations between Sanjar and the Nizārīs. In this text, preserved by the Ismaili communities of Badakhshān, Sanjar is characterised as a magnanimous, Ismaili friendly ruler suffering from a chronic illness. According to the *Qiṣṣa-i Malik-i Sīstān*, the Nizārīs offered to give him medication for this complaint on condition that he stop harassing the Nizārīs, to which he agreed.[77]

But all the evidence shows that Sanjar can hardly be regarded as pro-Ismaili, and in his interactions with the Ismailis he was simply following a medieval form of *Realpolitik*. When he had problems with his relatives in western Iran, in 493/1100 and in 513/1119, he recruited Ismaili soldiery, and possibly other local forces, to fight against them. This was the case in 501–502/1107–1108, when some 20,000 men were recruited in Khurāsān from among 'scattered groups of Kurds, Turks, Daylamīs and Arabs'.[78] The fact that there were Nizārīs among these rebellious groups is corroborated by Ibn al-Athīr, who speaks of a large number of Ismaili 'evil-doers' in the area of Bayhaq in 496–497/1103–1104 who pillaged the area, exploiting the unstable conditions caused by the war between the sons of Malikshāh. In 513–514/1119–1120, Sanjar once again relied on his local Nizārī allies in Quhistān when he led an expedition from Khurāsān to Rayy against his nephew, Maḥmūd b Muḥammad. Besides significant military help from other local rulers such as the Bāwandids of Ṭabaristān, Sanjar once again had Ismaili soldiers in his army. The leader of this contingent was called Ghuzzuglū according to Ibn al-Athīr, who he describes as the commander of the 'Ismaili Turks'.[79] One should note that the term 'Ismaili Turk' refers to an ethnic mixture of local Ismailis and to the successes of the local Ismaili *da'wa* in Saljūq military bases in Quhistān and Khurāsān. Ismaili names of the period suggest a vast majority of local Iranian-speaking communities (mainly from Daylam and Quhistān) but Turkic elements could occasionally have embraced the Ismaili faith, as in the case of Ghuzzuglū.

Sultan Sanjar's agreement with Ra'īs Muẓaffar and the Ismailis of Girdkūh around 493/1100 was entered into for both military and economic reasons. Regarding the financial parts of this agreement, the Persian chroniclers suggest that Sanjar permitted the Nizārīs to retain a sum of 3,000–4,000 dinars from the land tax (*kharāj*) on the lands they held around the city of Qūmis. Besides this, Sanjar allowed the Nizārīs to levy a toll on caravans and travellers passing near Girdkūh.[80]

This kind of pragmatic agreement between the eastern Saljūqs and the Ismailis, however, can be compared with the understanding with the Bāwandids. In the Bāwandid case, as well as many more mutual interests and regional similarities between the two states, there is a sense of being allied against a common enemy.

Whenever Aḥmad Sanjar managed to quell his disagreeable relatives, he routinely renewed his hostile policy against the Nizārīs, as in 521/1127, in 528/1134, when the defenders of Girdkūh bribed his army to raise their siege of the castle, or even later, in 545–546/1150–1151. And although he was an occasional ally of Alamūt and of the Ismailis of the Caspian provinces, Sanjar pursued a different and mainly belligerent policy against the Ismailis of Quhistān whom he routinely attacked even during periods of peace with Alamūt.

Political oscillations can also be observed in Saljūq-Bāwandid contacts, albeit with significant differences. The subtitle of a chapter of Ibn Isfandiyār's chronicle, 'Sultan Sanjar's change of mood towards the *iṣfahbad* and the Embassy of Arghash',[81] clearly indicates the changing dispositions of Sanjar's court towards the rulers of Ṭabaristān and, in particular, towards ʿAlāʾ al-Dawla ʿAlī, who until his accession had enjoyed Sanjar's support and had also made a good impression on the western Saljūqs, being offered a Saljūq princess in marriage by Sultan Muḥammad as we have seen. Although he cleverly distanced himself from this dynastic marriage out of fear of his elder brother, Najm al-Dawla Qārin, ʿAlāʾ al-Dawla ʿAlī became more less a protégé of the Saljūqs in Ṭabaristān. Indeed, when war broke out between him and Najm al-Dawla Qārin, ʿAlāʾ al-Dawla ʿAlī had the support of Sanjar. Sanjar's interest in his success cannot be separated from the fact that ʿAlāʾ al-Dawla ʿAlī's elder brother and rival, Najm al-Dawla, largely relied on the western Saljūqs, who opposed Sanjar's ambitions to rule over all of Iran. Furthermore, a Western Saljūq princess, Salgham Khātūn, was now the wife of Najm al-Dawla Qārin; so it can be argued that Sanjar recruited ʿAlāʾ al-Dawla ʿAlī against his Western Saljūq relatives just as he did the Ismailis of Alamūt and Girdkūh.

Once ʿAlāʾ al-Dawla ʿAlī had become the undisputed ruler of Ṭabaristān after 510/1117, he quickly turned into a reluctant ally of Sanjar. For this reason, Sanjar started to support ʿAlāʾ al-Dawla ʿAlī's brother, Bahrām; and when Bahrām was killed in 513/1120 (possibly at the instigation of ʿAlāʾ al-Dawla ʿAlī), Sanjar wanted to hand Ṭabaristān to one of his own nephews, Masʿūd. After the failure of his military campaign against Ṭabaristān in 521/1127, Aḥmad Sanjar found another pretext to invade. After 526/1132 when Salgham Khātūn, latterly the wife of ʿAlāʾ al-Dawla ʿAlī, died Sanjar laid claim to her estates and properties. However, once again he again failed to expel ʿAlāʾ al-Dawla ʿAlī from Ṭabaristān. On the other hand, ʿAlāʾ al-Dawla ʿAlī, seeking to appease Sanjar, sent his eldest son and heir, Shāh Ghāzī Rustam, to Sanjar's camp in order to participate in his campaigns against the Western Saljūqs (in 521/1127 and 525/1132). We also hear of another unsuccessful Eastern Saljūq invasion of Ṭabaristān in 533/1139.[82]

Sanjar's attitude towards the Bāwandid ʿAlāʾ al-Dawla ʿAlī was more or less the same as the one he took to the Nizārīs. When Sanjar needed ʿAlāʾ al-Dawla ʿAlī's help, he fostered cordial relations with him, though on other occasions when attempting to restored the unity of the Saljūq empire he also attacked the Bāwandids in Ṭabaristān. These similarities helps in understanding the logic of late Saljūq government. But despite this double-edged approach, Aḥmad Sanjar's actions in the Caspian provinces were not successful.

Nizārī-Bāwandid relations during the first years of Kiyā Buzurg-Umīd's rule

After these events concerning Sanjar and the Eastern Saljūq empire, we might mention another example of a specific kind of passive but conscious cooperation between the Nizārīs and the Bāwandids. In 519–520/1126–1127, a renewed Saljūq attempt to break Nizārī power in Northern Iran was initiated, and both the Saljūqs of ʿIrāq-i ʿAjām and Sanjar from Khurāsān attacked the Nizārīs in Rūdbār and

Daylamān. This was a military test of the new lord of Alamūt, Kiyā Buzurg-Umīd (518–532/1124–1138). That Nizārī power did not crumble under these combined attacks from both east and west demonstrates the strength of the Nizārī Ismaili state, both militarily and socially, that Ḥasan-i Ṣabbāḥ had established.

The western Iranian Saljūqs, under Maḥmūd II (r. 512–525/1118–1131), sent an army to Rūdbār commanded by Aṣīl, a nephew of Anūshtigīn Shīrgīr and a staunch enemy of the Nizārīs. The date of this expedition is not entirely clear but what is known is that his army suffered a heavy defeat at the hands of the Nizārīs, and the Saljūq soldiery fled. A second Saljūq army attacked Rūdbār but was likewise defeated by the Nizārīs, and one of the Saljūq amīrs, Tamurtughān, was taken prisoner and held in Alamūt for a while. Sultan Sanjar, now at the height of his power, invaded western Iran and despatched armies against Alamūt and Rūdbār. As his brother Muḥammad had done in 500/1107, Sanjar summoned the Bāwandid *iṣfahbad* to join him against the Nizārīs. Yet ʿAlāʾ al-Dawla ʿAlī, despite having been Sanjar's protégé, refused to accede to the order to attack Alamūt, just as his father had done nearly twenty years previously. Sanjar immediately despatched an army to Ṭabaristān but, with the help of 5,000 Zaydīs from Daylamān, ʿAlāʾ al-Dawla ʿAlī defeated the Saljūqs in various battles, again just as his father and brother had done in 502/1108.

Kiyā Buzurg-Umīd thus defended the area ruled by the Nizārīs and indeed extended it by capturing the castles of Manṣūra and some other, minor, places in Ṭāliqān. A most important military and strategic achievement was the construction of new Nizārī fortresses in Rūdbār, those of Saʿādatkūh and, notably, Maymūndiz; construction of the latter is said to have begun in Rabīʿ I 520/April 1126, though there is disagreement over this date in some of the Persian sources and archaeological surveys have not provided any solid evidence for any date.[83]

The last years of both Kiyā Buzurg-Umīd and ʿAlāʾ al-Dawla ʿAlī, were spent consolidating and extending their respective states. Kiyā Buzurg-Umīd's adoption of the role of a local Caspian territorial ruler and acceptance of his position as such by other local powers is demonstrated by the flight of a certain Saljūq amīr, Yaranqūsh, to Alamūt in 530/1136. Yaranqūsh was a former Saljūq governor and enemy of the Ismailis. He had been dislodged from his *iqṭāʿ* (an administrative grant of land) by the Khwārazmshāh, Quṭb al-Dīn Muḥammad (r. 490–521/1097–1127), and so sought help from the Ismailis at Alamūt.[84]

At the same time, after defeating the Saljūq armies sent by Sanjar in 521/1127, ʿAlāʾ al-Dawla ʿAlī also gave shelter to other princes seeking safety, including the Ghaznawid ruler, Shīrzād b. Masʿūd III (r. 509–510/1115–1116), after he had lost his throne to his brother, two sons of the Khwārazmshāh Quṭb al-Dīn Muḥammad and members of the Twelver Shiʿi Arab Mazyadid tribe of Ḥilla in southern ʿIrāq. Even a grandson of the Saljūq sultan Muḥammad I fled to Rayy and then Māzandarān where he stayed in the winter of 527/1132-33.[85]

The consolidation of the power of both the Nizārīs and the Bāwandids meant the gradual weakening of the Saljūqs in northern Iran. Besides political stability and providing refuge to deposed rulers, the Nizārīs and the Bāwandids began extending their respective territories. The Nizārīs conquered important new areas in Daylamān and Gīlān, while in the years before 534/1140 the Bāwandids tried to strengthen their influence in Rūyān, Gurgān and Hawsam. ʿAlāʾ al-Dawla ʿAlī spent his last years in Hawsam after he was forced to abdicate around 536/1142. The year of his abdication meant the end of a relatively long period of peace and stability in the Caspian provinces.

As far as the clashes between Nizārīs and Bāwandids during the era of Ḥasan-i Ṣabbāḥ are concerned, it seems there very few. In fact, it is only possible to give one clear example, occurring in the time of Kiyā Buzurg-Umīd in 532/1138, when according to Ibn Isfandiyār a certain Abū Jaʿfar Bāwandī, apparently a member of the Bāwandid family, was murdered by Nīzārī *fidāʾī*s.

Ibn Isfandiyār further relates that Shāh Ghāzī Rustam, the eldest son of ʿAlāʾ al-Dawla ʿAlī and the Bāwandid crown prince, then led a punitive expedition against the Nizārīs. Ibn Isfandiyār says that the people of Kīslīyān, Zangīān and Rukūna (around Lajīm in Sawādkūh, in the heartlands of the Bāwandid estates in central Ṭabaristān) had helped the Ismailis in Ṭabaristān and they were all slaughtered by Shāh Ghāzī Rustam.[86] The evidence in the sources suggests that the Bāwandids had various cadet branches which presided over small districts in Ṭabaristān. It is also important to note that the name 'Bāwand' is sometimes used as a synonym for the aristocracy of Ṭabaristān, which may indicate a high number of Bāwandid princes and a loose clan-like organisation of the kingdom.[87] It is possible that Abū Jaʿfar Bāwandī was governor of an area adjacent to Lajīm, close to the Bāwandid heartlands. The friendly attitude of the local inhabitants towards the Ismailis further indicates the *daʿwa* initiated by Ḥasan-i Ṣabbāḥ before moving to Alamūt was still active in Ṭabaristān.

The death of Abū Jaʿfar Bāwandī as reported by Ibn Isfandiyār points to the beginning of a deterioration in relations between the Bāwandids and the Nizārīs. We do not know exactly when the death happened, but Ibn Isfandiyār mentions it after the Saljūq attack on northern Iran, which took place in 521/1127. Following his failure to besiege Alamūt and the quarrel with his former protégé ʿAlāʾ al-Dawla ʿAlī, Sanjar despatched his nephew Masʿūd to invade Ṭabaristān. The province had been left largely undefended because Shāh Ghāzī Rustam was involved in a campaign against the Nizārīs in the region around Lajīm.[88] However, apart from this, there is no record of any hostility between these two neighbouring states.

By the end of Kiyā Buzurg-Umīd's life in 532/1138, the elimination of the Saljūqs and other major foreign threats in northern Iran had paved the way for a new era in which rivalry between the Nizārīs and Bāwandids emerged. The last decade before the deaths of Kiyā Buzurg-Umīd and ʿAlāʾ al-Dawla ʿAlī was devoted the consolidation and extension of their respective states.

Chapter 3

The Development of Local Powers in the Caspian during Saljūq Decline

Under Kiyā Buzurg-Umīd we can see the same practical approach to the political situation that operated in the era of Ḥasan-i Ṣabbāḥ. Diplomacy with the Saljūqs as practiced by the Bāwandids was not open to Kiyā Buzurg-Umīd. But, no doubt, relations with the Bāwandids, as well as the Saljūqs, were far more important in the eyes of the *dāʿīs* of Alamūt than those with the Zaydīs. However, the earlier successful policy in Daylamān against the Zaydīs, a policy which had already started before 518/1124, was continued.

But as well as these considerations, a shift from the idea of a greater Nizārī Ismaili state to a more localised Caspian state in Daylamān can be detected in the relocation of goods and finances by 518/1124 and the transfer of Nizārī treasure from Arrajān in the southern Zagros. Arrajān was ruled by the Nizārī Ismailis for only a brief period in the early years of Ḥasan-i Ṣabbāḥ's establishment of the Nizārī Ismaili state and was soon overrun by the Saljūqs. Studies dedicated to the early history of the Nizārī Ismaili state have largely failed to notice an event mentioned by Rashīd al-Dīn who writes that on 20 Ramaḍān 520/24 September 1126 a certain Amīr Sālārjūī came to Alamūt, possibly from Arrajān, in the southern Zagros. In Alamūt he became acknowledged as a *dāʿī* by Kiyā Buzurg-Umīd and was soon despatched to build a castle in Saʿādatkūh, reusing the goods accumulated in Arrajān.[1]

The most important event regarding the Zaydīs in this period was a religious debate with the Zaydī religious authority Abū Hāshim Jurjānī. As far as his background is concerned, according to Madelung Abū Hāshim Jurjānī was possibly related to Ḥasan Jurjānī;[2] and he may also have moved to Daylamān from Gurgān in the last years of Ḥasan-i Ṣabbāḥ, eventually claiming the Zaydī imamate for himself. Ḥasan

Jurjānī had fought the mighty local Zaydī leader, Abū Ṭālib Akhīr Yaḥyā, but was soon executed by his opponents. Thus, Abū Hāshim Jurjānī, a lesser-known Zaydī leader, could have been the son or close relative of this Ḥasan Jurjānī, but it is important to note that well-known Zaydī sources, such as the Letter of Yūsuf Jīlānī and *al-Ḥadāʾiq al-wardiyya*,[3] do not display any knowledge of him. Be that as it may, Abū Hāshim Jurjānī, whose Zaydī background is not clearly understood, i.e., whether he was a Qāsimī or a Nāṣirī Zaydī, became a committed enemy of the Nizārī Ismailis.[4]

According to Rashīd al-Dīn, in Muḥarram 526/December 1131 an Ismaili army was despatched to Gīlān, to the shores of the Caspian sea, to counter the advance of Abū Hāshim Jurjānī, who had revived the Zaydī *daʿwa* in Gīlān; but Abū Hāshim Jurjānī, here characterised as a Qāsimī Zaydī, sent envoys seeking help as far as Khurāsān. Kiyā Buzurg-Umīd tried to calm the belligerent Zaydī leader and sent him a letter of religious reconciliation, but Abū Hāshim Jurjānī refused any kind of cooperation, declaring: 'All your words are of unbelief, heresy and *zandaqa*.[5] If you are present, we will discuss it, and your unbelief will become clear.'[6] Following this failed attempt at reconciliation, Kiyā Buzurg-Umīd raided the areas of Tanhijān where Abū Hāshim Jurjānī was based. Abū Hāshim fled into the forest of Tanhijān but was captured. According to Rashīd al-Dīn, after a long theological debate he was executed.[7] It remains unclear, however, whether or not this Abū Hāshim Jurjānī is same as a certain Abū Hāshim Zaydī, who was called the Imam of the Zaydīs by Rashīd al-Dīn and who was killed by the Nizārīs in Jumādā II 525/May 1132.[8]

After Abū Hāshim's death, we hear no more about the *daʿwa* he set up or any other Zaydī anti-Nizārī actions during Kiyā Buzurg-Umīd's rule. Instead, the Nizārīs now took successful steps to extend their power into other parts of southern Daylamān, in the Ṭārum area. Rashīd al-Dīn wrote that in Jumādā II 530/March 1136 Ismaili forces were sent to besiege a castle in Daylamān called Daridiz, which was held by a local lord, Malikshāh Wakhsūdān. His name suggests that he may have had a connection with previous Justānid royal traditions when the name 'Wakhsūdān' was very popular. Another Ismaili attack occurred a month later, in Rajab 530/April 1136 against a village called Bul.[9] In 531/1137 the Ismailis attacked the area of Ṭārum, up to the village of Birak, where they took the castle of al-Baradayn.[10]

In the last months of his life, Kiyā Buzurg-Umīd sent his armies to the area of Tanhijān where they attacked Gurjīyān to the east of Rāmsar. This area is known as either Gurjīyān or Gurjistān in Rashīd al-Dīn,[11] though it has no connection with Georgia or the Georgian people.[12] Gurjīyān was on the border of Gīlān and north-western Ṭabaristān and thus could have been of strategic importance as it linked these two provinces. Rashīd al-Dīn's account suggests that Kiyā Buzurg-Umīd could not conquer Gurjīyān but, nonetheless, laid waste to much of the area. More intense military activity can be observed in this area after the death of Kiyā Buzurg-Umīd, ending eventually with the Nizārī Ismaili capture of the castle of Gurjīyān in 590/1194. The reason for these attacks against Gurjīyān was its geographical proximity to Tanhijān, where Abū Hāshim Jurjānī had been captured. Thus, one can speculate that Gurjīyān or Gurjistān, beyond its situation between Gīlān and Ṭabaristān, might also have acted as an important Zaydī military stronghold.

Rayy and Qazwīn

The two important urban centres of Rayy and Qazwīn, mercantile cities that lay on the western part the Silk Road, were in close contact with those areas in their vicinity ruled by the Nizārī Ismailis. The Nizārī Ismailis never fully controlled these cities but they remained of paramount interest for them.

Rayy was an important Twelver Shiʿi centre in the 5th–6th/11th–12th centuries. Ḥasan-i Ṣabbāḥ had been active there as an Ismaili *dāʿī*. Qazwīn was a predominantly Sunni and pro-Saljūq city in this period, though containing also different Shiʿi minorities and holy places.

The Ismaili presence was always strong in and around these cities, especially in Rayy where the heart of the Iranian Ismaili *daʿwa* was located from the 4th/10th century onwards. In the earliest days of the Nizārī Ismaili state, when moving from Ṭabaristān, Ḥasan-i Ṣabbāḥ and his *dāʿīs* travelled on the southern, secure road through Rayy and Qazwīn to reach the regions of Rūdbār and Alamūt.

The importance of Rayy and Qazwīn is strikingly demonstrated right after the capture of Alamūt, when in 485/1092 the first Saljūq assault against Alamūt took place. A local *dāʿī*, Abū ʿAlī Ardistānī (known as Dihdār) and based in Qazwīn,[13] recruited some 300 Ismailis from Rayy, Ṭāliqān and Qazwīn at Ḥasan-i Ṣabbāḥ's request. These Ismailis went immediately to Alamūt, bringing weapons and food for the few dozen Ismailis living there along with Ḥasan-i Ṣabbāḥ in those first months after taking over the castle.[14]

The Nizārīs quickly realised the strategic importance of the mountainous area north of Rayy and, according to Rashīd al-Dīn, started building fortresses there. When enumerating the various fortresses captured or constructed during the first years of Ḥasan-i Ṣabbāḥ, when Ismailis appeared in different areas of Persia exploiting the chaos in the Saljūq empire, Rashīd al-Dīn says that Ḥasan-i Ṣabbāḥ built a castle in the vicinity of Qazwīn.[15] Regrettably, he fails to mention the name of any Ismaili castle near Qazwīn.

Thus, Qazwīn and its area served as a permanent site for Ismaili military activity. As noted, substantial groups of Ismailis resided in and around Qazwīn; but it soon became clear that local forces were also actively involved in fighting against the Ismailis. In 486/1093, a large number of armed men, led by the son of al-Zaʿfarānī, who was the Sunni mufti of Rayy, invaded the area of Ṭāliqān and clashed with around a thousand Ismailis. After numerous bloody battles, the Ismailis succeeded in killing al-Zaʿfarānī and, according to Rashīd al-Dīn, about half the Sunni warriors were killed at Ṭāliqān. The Ismailis then raided the area of Qazwīn, where they occupied the village of Khaldīr, before returning to Alamūt and their other fortresses.[16]

Another event of importance occurred in 498/1105 when, as Rashīd al-Dīn claims, a group of Ismailis occupied areas around Rayy.[17] Hodgson attributed this attack to a group of Ismailis based in Turshīz which had raided Bayhaq in Khurāsān in the same year. Yet Rashīd al-Dīn says that a group of Ismailis left Turthith, which is the Arabised name of Turshīz,[18] and they raided the province of Bayhaq, and it was another group that occupied the vicinity of Rayy, blocking the roads there.[19] This does not suggest that both actions were carried out by the same group from Turshīz. In the light of the strengthened position of the Nizārī Ismailis in the vicinity of Ṭāliqān and Qazwīn, it is quite possible that an Ismaili group, despatched from Daylamān or Qazwīn, could have been responsible for this raid on Rayy in 499/1105.

According to Rashīd al-Dīn, in Jumādā I 523/May 1129, Kiyā Buzurg-Umīd sent an envoy to Iṣfahān to hold peace negotiations with the Saljūq sultan Maḥmūd II. But after his audience with the sultan the Nizārī envoy, Khwāja Muḥammad Nāṣiḥī Shahrastānī, was lynched by an angry mob. Furious, Kiyā Buzurg-Umīd sent his armies to Qazwīn where, according to Rashīd al-Dīn, the Nizārīs killed four hundred people, presumably in revenge.[20]

The presence of Ismaili forces in the Rayy area can be attested to by another interesting episode also noted by Rashīd al-Dīn, who mentions the relocation of the '*ra'īsān*' and the '*kadkhudāyān*' (leaders and landowners) of Shizr, persons who had converted to Ismailism and were harassed by their enemies, to a place called Manṣūrābād, near Rayy.[21] This event took place not long before the death of Kiyā Buzurg-Umīd in 532/1138.

By 532/1138, the Nizārī Ismaili state had extended its power in Daylamān and strengthened its positions around Dāmghān and Qūmis. No doubt the fragmentation of the different and mainly Zaydī Daylamī clans helped in the founding of a Nizārī-Ismaili state around Alamūt. In Rūdbār and Daylamān large portions of the local population, who formerly may have been Zaydīs, became followers of the Ismaili *da'wa* during these decades. Meanwhile, Ismaili successes in the area of Dāmghān and the acquisition of several important fortresses in the region were equally vital in providing secure finances for the Caspian Nizārī community.

The era of Ḥasan-i Ṣabbāḥ and Kiyā Buzurg-Umīd represents the initial phase of the Nizārī Ismaili state. Based on earlier *da'wa* successes, Ḥasan-i Ṣabbāḥ attempted to create a greater Nizārī Ismaili state in Kirmān, in the Southern Zagros, in Quhistān and in the Caspian provinces, quickly exploiting the chaos following the death of Malikshāh and his vizier Niẓām al-Mulk. After initial Ismaili successes, the Saljūqs led a concerted counterattack during the first years of the reign of Sultan Muḥammad I, and eliminated all the Ismaili strongholds in the southern Zagros and Kirmān. Significant but eventually abortive attempts were also made to destroy the Ismaili power-bases in Quhistān and in Rūdbār. Thus, after 498/1105, the idea of a greater Nizārī state was modified, and due to their largely inaccessible geographical position the Nizārīs more and more relied upon the Caspian provinces. It should also be borne in mind that both Ḥasan-i Ṣabbāḥ and Kiyā

Buzurg-Umīd were of northern Iranian origin and thus must have had an excellent knowledge of local circumstances as well as of the local terrain.

In the first decades of their state the Nizārī Ismailis saw the Saljūqs as their main opponents in the Caspian provinces, and so they tried to seek allies among those neighbouring principalities which, like the Bāwandids, felt threatened by the Saljūqs or, as with the Zaydīs, were subject to internal division.

The Bāwandids did not enjoy the cohesiveness of the Nizārīs, and evidently lacked the sort of ideological basis for their authority that the Nizārīs had, and were instead bedevilled by internecine conflict, much in the manner of the Saljūqs or the Zaydīs. But by exploiting the weakening of Saljūq power, these polities both achieved a prominent position in northern Iran. After 532/1138, there started an entirely new phase in Nizārī-Bāwandid relations and a struggle for hegemony in northern Iran.

Chapter 4

Nizārī-Bāwandid Competition for Hegemony, 534–565/1140–1170

By the last years of Kiyā Buzurg-Umīd's life, the Nizārī Ismaili state had become one of the strongest polities in northern Iran. The great majority of Nizārī castles in northern Iran had already been established by 532/1138, the year of Kiyā Buzurg-Umīd's death. Looking at a map of the Ismaili fortresses, it is evident that they were situated in three main areas: the area of Daylamān, the area of north of Rayy and the area around Girdkūh. These Ismaili castles made it easy to oversee the various routes that ran south of the Caspian range. As well as their strategic and military importance, these routes were part of a network of trade and travel that ran from Central Asia through to Anatolia and the Levant. In northern Iran these routes ran along the southern flanks of the Alburz mountains, passing through or near various towns and cities such as Qazwīn, Zanjān, Rayy, Simnān and Dāmghān.

The Nizārīs had also succeeded in eliminating the Saljūq menace by deploying a mixture of astute policies and tactics, supporting the diverse local powers and challenging the Saljūq force of arms as much psychologically as militarily. Furthermore, the Nizārīs now held significant areas of Daylamān that had been ruled previously by Zaydī Imams, which constituted the core of this new Ismaili state.

The prestige and strength of the Ismailis are clearly reflected in the contacts they held with the Saljūqs who were eventually forced to negotiate with them after a series of failed assaults against them. What is more the Nizārīs forged close contacts with the emerging Bāwandids, who also benefitted from the weakening position of the Saljūqs. The Bāwandids and Nizārīs gave tacit support to each other against the Saljūqs.

However, after 532/1138 a new generation of rulers appeared in both states, who were endeavouring to continue the expansionist ambitions of their predecessors. Muḥammad b. Buzurg-Umīd (r. 532–557/1138–1162) and Shāh Ghāzī Rustam b. ʿAlāʾ al-Dawla ʿAlī (r. 535–560/1142–1165),[1] the new rulers of the Nizārī Ismailis and Bāwandids respectively, acceded to power within three years of each other. In the case of Muḥammad b. Buzurg-Umīd, the succession took place smoothly. A similar approach can be seen in the case of Girdkūh after the death of Raʾīs Muẓaffar, where his family remained in command of the castle.

As far as Shāh Ghāzī Rustam's accession to power is concerned it was disrupted by the Saljūq sultan Sanjar, who supported his brother, Tāj al-Mulūk Mardāwīj.[2] Furthermore the notion of a peaceful accession is questioned by Marʿashī who claimed that ʿAlāʾ al-Dawla ʿAlī was forced to abdicate and then retreated to Tamīsha in Daylamān where he died some three years later in 537/1143.[3] However, other sources say that ʿAlāʾ al-Dawla ʿAlī was still an active ruler in 535/1141 when the Khwārazmshāh Atsız invaded Bāwandid-controlled Gurgān. Shāh Ghāzī Rustam acted there on behalf of his father ʿAlāʾ al-Dawla ʿAlī though without his official permission. It was after being rebuked by ʿAlāʾ al-Dawla ʿAlī for his presumption, that Shāh Ghāzī Rustam deposed his father.[4] Although the exact date of this is unknown, it must have occurred no later than 536/1142.

Thus, in the first years of his reign Shāh Ghāzī Rustam was forced to defend his kingdom against his brother, Tāj al-Mulūk Mardāwīj, who raised a rebellion in Ṭabaristān with the support of Sanjar. Having conquered Gurgān, which had been a Bāwandid province for a while during the reign of ʿAlāʾ al-Dawla ʿAlī, Shāh Ghāzī Rustam marched against his brother in Ṭabaristān. After various battles in Astarābād, Tamīsha and Juhayna, Tāj al-Mulūk now on the verge of victory laid siege to the castle of Dārā to which his brother had retreated with his followers. After eight months of siege, however, Tāj al-Mulūk failed to capture his brother. Despite this, he managed to hold on to his earlier conquests and Shāh Ghāzī Rustam had to concede many of his eastern provinces, including the whole of Gurgān, to his brother. So as to strengthen his claims and his Saljūqs links, Tāj al-Mulūk Mardāwīj married a Saljūq princess, who may have been a daughter or a niece of Sanjar.[5]

This situation changed dramatically after 548/1153, when Sanjar was defeated and captured by the Ghuzz Turks, being held their prisoner for three and a half years. Shāh Ghāzī Rustam exploited the fall of the eastern Saljūqs and his increased prestige is clearly reflected by the fact that in 549/1154, just a year after Sanjar's defeat, he entertained Sanjar's nephew, a son of Muḥammad Tapar, Sulaymān Shāh, who had proclaimed himself Sanjar's successor and attempted to take over the eastern lands of the empire. Sulaymān Shāh waited in vain for military help from Shāh Ghāzī Rustam, and a year later went to the court of his brother, Tāj al-Mulūk Mardāwīj, in Gurgān. However, in 550/1155 Shāh Ghāzī Rustam put an end to Tāj al-Mulūk's power in Gurgān and had him killed before Sulayman could reach Khurāsān.[6]

Shāh Ghāzī Rustam also acquired the services of able military leaders of the former eastern Saljūq empire, such as Sunqur Ināni and Sābiq Qazwīnī who had been important officers in Sanjar's army. After 548–550/1153–1155, both of them entered the service of Shāh Ghāzī Rustam, both married daughters of Shāh Ghāzī Rustam, and Sābiq Qazwīnī even married a Saljūq princess courtesy of Shāh Ghāzī Rustam.[7] Sābiq Qazwīnī became governor of Simnān, Dāmghān, Bisṭām and possibly other areas of Khurāsān for the Bāwandids, while after 550/1155 Sunqur Inānj governed Rayy and Qazwīn as well as the Jibāl in their name. Both of these men were actively involved in wars against the Nizārīs (see below): Sābiq Qazwīnī in the vicinity of Girdkūh, and Sunqur Inānj against Rūdbār and Alamūt.

After the fall of Sanjar, the Khwārazmshāhs, the Ghuzz and the Bāwandids, all aspired to fill the political vacuum in northern Khurāsān. The military strength of Shāh Ghāzī Rustam is clear from the fact that even his opponents, the Ghuzz Turks, and the former eastern Saljūq military leader Mu'ayyad Ayābā, who controlled vast areas of Khurāsān, sought to make peace with him.

One of the most notable steps in the increase of his power was taken by Shāh Ghāzī Rustam in 550/1155. The unfortunate Saljūq prince Sulaymān Shāh once again visited him in Āmul, seeking military support. Shāh Ghāzī Rustam, previously a Saljūq vassal, now had the upper hand in these dealings. According to Ibn Isfandiyār,[8] he was entertained by the Saljūq prince for two months, staging lavish ceremonies, and he asked for the wealthy towns of Rayy, Simnān and even the more remote Sāwa, in exchange for his military aid.

With the acquisition of Simnān, Rayy and Sāwa, the Bāwandid kingdom had expanded far beyond its traditional core areas. However,

Simnān and Rayy were also essential to the Caspian Nizārīs, a number of Nizārī fortresses having been built in these important regions. The rising ambitions of the *iṣfahbad* Shāh Ghāzī Rustam and the acquisition of these noteworthy cities enabled him to counter Nizārī influence there. The prospect of rich revenues from trade as well as the challenge of the widespread Nizārī presence there did not encourage him to pursue the Nizārī-friendly policies of his father and grandfather, and in fact, he sought to expand his territories at the expense of the Nizārīs.

There is little information relating to Bāwandid policy in the newly-acquired areas except for the fact that Shāh Ghāzī Rustam actively supported the Twelver Shiʿi *daʿwa* in these regions: for example, at some point after 550/1155 a Twelver Shiʿi madrasa was established by him in the Zādmihrān quarter of Rayy. Furthermore, Shāh Ghāzī Rustam was the unofficial dedicatee of the *Kitāb al-Naqḍ* of ʿAbd al-Jalīl Qazwīnī Rāzī, a well-known Twelver Shiʿi preacher and theologian in Rayy in this period. ʿAbd al-Jalīl Qazwīnī Rāzī completed the *Kitāb al-Naqḍ*, an important Uṣūlī Twelver Shiʿi treatise, in around 555/1160, when the Bāwandid state had reached its apogee. The *Kitāb al-Naqḍ* is considered a major source of information for northern Iran in the 6th/12th century, containing considerable material on historical, doctrinal and political concerns.[9]

The Nizārīs and Shāh Ghāzī Rustam

The Nizārīs had very strained relations with Shāh Ghāzī Rustam and he was their main local opponent in the 6th/12th century. Personal considerations and political ambitions both played a part in this. Shāh Ghāzī Rustam had engaged in actions against the Nizārīs before his accession to the throne 536/1142. According to Ibn Isfandiyār, it was Shāh Ghāzī Rustam who devastated the local population around Lajīm (in the villages of Kīsliyān, Rukūna and Zangiyān) as it was alleged that they had Nizārīs hidden there. As we have seen, Shāh Ghāzī Rustam led a punitive campaign against the Nizārīs, apparently to avenge the murder of his relative, Abū Jaʿfar Bāwand, as early as 532/1138.[10] However, in this context it should be noted that Rashīd al-Dīn and Kāshānī do not mention Abū Jaʿfar Bāwand in the list of supposed victims although other local individuals are included.

The next clash between Shāh Ghāzī Rustam and the Nizārīs may also have taken place before 536/1142, since Ibn Isfandiyār says that the Nizārī Ismailis attempted to murder Shāh Ghāzī Rustam when he was still crown prince and claims he was attacked at least twice. On the first occasion, a Nizārī *fidā'ī* rushed out of a workshop and attacked him as he came to a mosque in Zanagū, a settlement near Sārī.[11] But the entourage of the *iṣfahbad* managed to kill the *fidā'ī*.[12] Ibn Isfandiyār goes on to say that after the failure of the first attempt, two *fidā'ī*s then ambushed Shāh Ghāzī Rustam on the road between Sārī and Āmul, two of the most important Bāwandid towns in Ṭabaristān, so perhaps in an area where he might have felt he was safe, when he was having a drink of water before the start of the hunt. According to Ibn Isfandiyār, these *fidā'ī*s were men who had been in his service. One of them speared and deeply wounded Shāh Ghāzī Rustam in the back, while the other attacked the prince's companions.[13]

With the gradual weakening and disintegration of Saljūq power in the east, the rulers of the Nizārī Ismaili state realised that their most important enemy in northern Iran was now the Bāwandids who had already conquered many neighbouring provinces and had ambitions to expand their authority much further. Shāh Ghāzī had expanded his kingdom and had ambitions to extend his power. Thus, between 534/1140 and 560/1165, as the fortunes of the Bāwandid kingdom reached a peak, the most serious clashes between the Ismailis and the Bāwandids occurred.

Besides the personal antipathy and anti-Nizārī zeal of Shāh Ghāzī Rustam, there were other causes for conflict, the most important of them being that both states aspired to fill the vacuum left by the weakened Saljūqs. Secondly, there were already territorial disputes between the Nizārīs and their neighbours. Between the Bāwandid lands and the Nizārī lands lay various districts where there were various local dynasties, such as the Bādūspānids in Rūyān and several Zaydī rulers in Daylamān. These were usually considered vassals of the Bāwandids or were strongly linked to the Bāwandids through marriage. During the era of Muḥammad b. Buzurg-Umīd a conflict arose with the Bāwandids for authority over the remaining Zaydī kingdoms and for influence over Rūyān, where the Zaydī Bādūspānids ruled.

A third source of conflict between Nizārīs and Bāwandids can be detected in the area of Rayy, Girdkūh and Simnān. Here, besides territorial claims, a dispute arose over the division of trade income and revenues from levies on the main trading routes. With the elimination of the Eastern Saljūq empire, the agreement between the Nizārīs and Bāwandids mentioned by Rashīd al-Dīn was nullified, and given his antipathy to the Nizārīs, Shāh Ghāzī Rustam had no intention of seeing his claims challenged by them, above all when it came to these wealthy cities.

Nizārī-Bāwandid conflicts and the quest for hegemony between 536/1142 and 560/1165

The Nizārīs, under the leadership of Muḥammad b. Buzurg-Umīd, made various efforts to halt the expansionist actions of Shāh Ghāzī Rustam. After Shāh Ghāzī Rustam's accession to the throne in 536/1142, alleged Ismaili *fidā'ī*s killed his eldest, favourite son and designated heir, Girdbāzū, near Sarakhs, when he was en route to the court of Sanjar at Marw as a hostage. According to Ibn Isfandiyār, upon hearing of this Shāh Ghāzī Rustam immediately broke off all diplomatic ties with Sanjar, and despatched letters to the Khwārazmshāh Atsız and others, accusing both Sanjar and the Nizārīs of a plot against the Bāwandid crown prince and, as Ibn Isfandiyār notes, attacked Sanjar by using the derogotary term *mulḥid*, one applied primarily to the Nizārīs in this period:[14]

> One day Girdbāzū went to a hot bath in Sarakhs; he remained there for a while. Then he came to the hot bath's store house and stopped there till the steam settled (inside the hot bath). Two *mulḥid*s seized the opportunity and, entering there, killed Girdbāzū. When this news reached Shāh Ghāzī he lost the bridle of self-constraint and self-control in his intellect and patience and made complaints. After this event he called Sanjar a *mulḥid* all his life. He never sent an envoy or letter to that monarch. He wrote his memoirs about Sultan Sanjar, (addressing them) to those kings and suzerains who were his friends, saying that 'the *mulḥid* Sanjar ordered the assassination of my son'.[15]

It must be acknowledged that it is rather curious to see the term *mulḥid* apparently used by pious Twelver Shiʿi ruler, who generously supported Twelver Shiʿi *waqf*s and madrasas in Mashhad and Rayy, in reference to one of the Saljūq sultans, ostensibly a Sunni.

Given his use of the word *mulḥid*, it appears that Shāh Ghāzī Rustam suspected that Sanjar had also become involved with the Nizārīs, or at least felt some sympathy towards them. It is not completely clear why Sanjar would have cooperated with the Nizārīs against Shāh Ghāzī Rustam although two facts are apparent from previous years: first, the brother of Shāh Ghāzī Rustam, Tāj al-Mulūk Mardāwīj, was a protégé of Sanjar and the sultan had actively supported Tāj al-Mulūk Mardāwīj in Gurgān and Ṭabaristān against his elder brother after the death of their father. Sanjar continued the Saljūq policy of previous decades, when he attempted to create a schism in the Bāwandid royal family of Ṭabaristān. Secondly, it seems that Sanjar had established connections with the Nizārīs, as discussed previously. The division of the revenues of Girdkūh and the alleged Nizārī military support for Sanjar against his Saljūq relatives in western Iran also attest to his ambiguous attitude towards the Nizārīs. Shāh Ghāzī Rustam's accusation is therefore not at all unfounded for although Sanjar was hardly a supporter of the Nizārīs in his personal beliefs, he was pragmatic about making temporary coalitions, even with his most feared adversaries, if that served his interests.

From this event it is again quite evident that, after 536/1142 and the accession of Shāh Ghāzī Rustam, the Bāwandids were considered far more dangerous than the Saljūqs as far as the Nizārīs were concerned and thus they were repeatedly induced to cooperate with the diminishing Eastern Saljūq state of Sanjar.

Shāh Ghāzī Rustam faced a double threat from the western and eastern borders of his kingdom. Sending his eldest son and crown prince as a hostage to Sanjar's court was doubtless meant to appease the Saljūqs; but after the murder of Girdbāzū, relations with Sanjar went downhill — and with the Ismailis they became even more hostile. The sudden fall of Sanjar in 548/1153 eliminated one threat. However, in the south and west of the Caspian, Shāh Ghāzī Rustam had to face fierce Nizārī resistance to his power.

The last Saljūq assaults against the Nizārīs

Before discussing the complex history of Bāwandid-Nizārī wars in the mid-6th/12th century, mention must be made of the last Saljūq attempts to overthrow, or at least to weaken, the Nizārīs.

In 533/1139, the Nizārīs raided the area of Rayy and captured ʿAbd al-Malik Qaṣrānī, the amīr of Qasrān, a city near Rayy. According to Rashīd al-Dīn, in 535/1141 the Nizārīs murdered Jawhar, a Saljūq amīr in Sanjar's camp in Khurāsān. Shortly after this, ʿAbbās, the Saljūq amīr of Rayy in the service of Sanjar, massacred a large number of Nizārīs in reprisal. The same Saljūq governor also raided Nizārī outposts near Alamūt. His military activities against the Nizārīs became more frequent, so they despatched an emissary to Sultan Sanjar in 541/1146, seeking his intervention in the matter. It appears that ʿAbbās did not cease his hostilities despite several attempts by Sanjar to restrain him. A few months later, ʿAbbās was executed whilst on a visit to Baghdad, on the orders of the Saljūq sultan Masʿūd (r. 528–547/1133–1152) and, it seems, at Sanjar's request, and his head was sent to Khurāsān. The elimination of the reluctantly loyal Saljūq governor apparently led to another period of truce between the Nizārī leadership and Sanjar.[16]

As far as the Nizārīs relations with the western Saljūqs are concerned, Rashīd al-Dīn informs us that, in 537/1143, they repelled an attack against Lamasar and other places in Rūdbār launched by the Saljūq sultan, Masʿūd b. Muḥammad.[17]

In 544/1149, Sanjar himself came to Rayy where, Rashīd al-Din says, he was involved in doctrinal discussions with the Nizārīs. Sanjar sent an envoy to Alamūt to obtain more knowledge about the beliefs of the Nizārīs, and they replied to the messenger thus:

> It is our principle to believe in the grandeur and greatness of God, to obey His ordinances, to act on the *sharīʿa* as shown by God in the Qurʾan and by His Prophet, and to believe in the Day of Judgment, the reward and the punishment of deeds. No one is authorised to alter these ordinances according to his will. Tell your king that these are our beliefs. It is well if he is satisfied, otherwise send his scholar, so that we may debate with him.[18]

This wording suggests an amicable or pragmatic approach by both sides. The first contact between Sanjar and Nizārīs had probably occurred five decades earlier and, as noted above, both sides had good reasons for occasionally cooperating with each other. Relations were sometimes briefly tense, but Nizārī dealings with the eastern Saljūqs were far more cordial than those with the western Saljūqs. As stated above, Sanjar had occasionally recruited Nizārī military forces against his Western Saljūq relatives, and we have already mentioned that Sanjar made a pact with the Nizārīs of Girdkūh over the division of revenue.

The attitude of Sanjar towards ʿAbbās, his governor of Rayy, is described in the very intricate story reported by Rashīd al-Dīn, referred to above, which casts an interesting light on the internal conflicts of the Saljūq state as its power was fading. ʿAbbās acted on his own against the Nizārīs, not following the orders of Sanjar and, as Rashīd al-Dīn suggests, it is likely that Sanjar was involved in his death.[19] ʿAbbās can be seen as one of those military leaders who were on the verge of deserting Sanjar's camp. Had he not been killed by Sanjar he might have had a career similar to that of Sābiq Qazwīnī or Sunqur Inānj, either as a pro-Bāwandid military commander or as an independent ruler of a province.

After 544/1149, the sources do not mention any further conflict between the Nizārīs and the Saljūqs. After Sanjar's defeat by the Ghuzz Turks the decades of Saljūq involvement in the affairs of the Nizārīs, direct and indirect, friendly or aggressive, came to an end.

The Khurramī interlude, 536/1142

Alongside the major events seen in the last Saljūq incursions and Bāwandid military expeditions, mention must also be made of an episode that sheds some light on the inner circles of the Nizārī Ismailis in the first decades of their rule in the Caspian region and also on their governmental structure. In an account attributed to a certain Dihkhudā b. ʿAbd al-Malik b. ʿAlī and preserved by both Rashīd al-Dīn and Kāshānī, there is material relating to the conversion of a group of persons referred to as 'Pārsīs'. This group, according to Madelung, belonged to a once popular socio-religious movement, the Khurramiyya;[20] which adhered to a mixture of religious beliefs and teachings, wherein elements of early Shiʿi *ghulāt* (extremism) and Imami beliefs along with strong Persian national sentiment can be detected, albeit with certain inconsistencies. Their popularity reached its zenith in the 2nd–3rd/8th–9th centuries under Bābak Khurramī. After the fall of Bābak Khurramī (223/838), we do not hear of any Khurramī groups, apart from that of Dihkhudā b. ʿAbd al-Malik b. ʿAlī. The author of this report could have been identical with a certain

Dihkhudā b. ʿAbd al-Malik Fashandī, a possible chronicler of Nizārī-related events under Muḥammad b. Buzurg-Umīd, who was appointed as commander of the Ismaili fortress of Maymūndiz in Rabīʿ I 520/April 1126. It was this account of Ismaili-Khurramī interactions that was preserved by later authors, such as Rashīd al-Dīn and Kāshānī.[21]

According to Dihkhudā b. ʿAbd al-Malik b. ʿAlī, a group of 'Pārsīs' converted to Nizārī Ismailism some time before 513/1119, and a certain Dihkhudā Kaykhusraw, himself a former Khurramī, was despatched by Ḥasan-i Ṣabbāḥ to teach them Ismaili beliefs. The location of this group is not exactly known, they may either have come from Ādharbayjān or have lived somewhere in the province of Ādharbayjān. However, as Rashīd al-Dīn notes, 'whenever a faith or religious doctrine became dominant, they [the Pārsīs] would pretend to back it while keeping their true beliefs concealed.'[22]

When Dihkhudā Kaykhusraw died in Muḥarram 513/April-May 1119, the leadership and religious education of the group was taken over by his sons, Abu'l-ʿAlā' and Yūsuf. Yet it is related that they were more interested in their own prestige and wealth, and neglected their responsibilities as Nizārī Ismaili leaders of this new community. After the death of Ḥasan-i Ṣabbāḥ, a certain Budayl started to preach against the Ismailis in the 'Pārsī' community. According to Rashīd al-Dīn, Budayl, who was a weaver, declared that 'the truth is with the Pārsīs, the Ismailis are people clinging to the exterior of religion (*mardum-i ẓāhirīand*), the esoteric truth is that Abu'l-ʿAlā' and Yūsuf are now in the position of Muḥammad and ʿAlī. Muḥammad, ʿAlī and Salmān were all three Gods, for He appears at one time in a single person, at another in two, and at another in three persons. The law of the *sharīʿa* is only for those adhering to the exterior of religion [. . .] Prayer and fasting must therefore be abandoned.'[23]

When reports arrived at Alamūt about the apostasy of this community, some of them were imprisoned and interrogated by the soldiers of Muḥammad b. Buzurg-Umīd to make them confess their true beliefs. Their leaders, Abu'l-ʿAlā' and Yūsuf, who had gone along with Budayl's teachings, were also arrested in Rabīʿ II 537/October 1142, and both were put to death. Within a year, all members of the group had been eliminated by the Nizārīs.

Madelung argued that apart from theological disputes, which completely alienated the group from the Nizārīs, the main concern could have been the division of income between the Nizārīs and the leaders of the new group.

There is a final charge made by the Ismaili author against the heretics, the significance of which is more obscure. It was held that their doctrine was that everyone who possesses wealth and prestige will be rewarded, on which basis, prophets and saints would be punished, while evil men and criminals would be rewarded. This is evidently to be connected with the accusation made earlier against Abu'l-ʿAlāʾ and Yūsuf, that they aspired to wealth and power while abandoning Ismaili beliefs, apparently, and were reprimanded for this by Ḥasan-i Ṣabbāḥ.[24] Hodgson argued that this was an internal Nizārī dispute that revealed some aspects of the 'strict internal conformity' to rules required by the state Ḥasan-i Ṣabbāḥ had established.[25] Thus, the reluctance of Abu'l-ʿAlāʾ and Yūsuf to send revenues to Alamūt may have contributed to the end of the group as much as any apostasy.

Shāh Ghāzī Rustam in Rūyān and Daylam

Shāh Ghāzī Rustam had expanded his realm beyond the traditional borders of the Bāwandid kingdom into Khurāsān, using military as well as diplomatic means. Similarly, and as discussed previously, Nizārī influence had grown rapidly in western Ṭabaristān (Rūyān), in eastern Daylamān and Gīlān in earlier decades. The local Zaydī polities in eastern Daylamān and Gīlān were defeated several times and had to concede towns and fortresses to the Nizārīs while a major portion of the local population in these provinces converted to Ismailism.

These disagreements were so serious that they should in fact be seen as wars.[26] The conflict between Nizārīs and Bāwandids in western Ṭabaristān and Daylamān became intense in the second half of Shāh Ghāzī Rustam's reign, i.e. after 550/1155, when the Bāwandid *iṣfahbad* was freed from the threat of Sanjar, and it took some time before the Nizārīs could achieve a counterbalance to his actions.

Shāh Ghāzī Rustam pursued two principal objectives in western Ṭabaristān (Rūyān) and Daylamān: he intended to strengthen his suzerainty over the Zaydī Bādūspānid dynasty in Rūyān as well as strengthening himself against the Zaydī Imams in Daylamān, both of these having been considered long-standing Bāwandid vassals and opposed to the Nizārīs. Yet, at the same time, it appears that Shāh Ghāzī Rustam attempted to conquer the whole of Gīlān and Māzandarān, to take control of, and incorporate, both the vassal polities and the Nizārī-controlled areas; so his attempts posed a direct threat to the existence of the Nizārīs. After 550/1155, emboldened by the disappearance of both his brother and Sanjar, Shāh Ghāzī Rustam now felt free to invade the Alamūt region.

Zaydī-Bāwandid political and dynastic relations were established long before Shāh Ghāzī Rustam's time. The Twelver Shiʿi Bāwandids apparently acted as patrons of the Zaydī Imams, and then, from the reign of Ḥusām al-Dawla Shahriyār, they built strong ties with both the Qāsimī and Nāṣirī Zaydī Imams. Religious or doctrinal considerations evidently played a smaller role in the making of coalitions than did political advantage. After 465/1073 the Zaydī Imam in Daylamān, Ḥusayn b. Jaʿfar Nāṣir, married a Bāwandid princess, who was probably the daughter of Ḥusām al-Dawla Shahriyār. In later periods, Daylamī soldiers appeared regularly in the armies of the Bāwandids, as in 517/1123, when the Saljūqs attacked Ṭabaristān.

Less clear is when and how the Bādūspānids succumbed to Bāwandid overlordship. The early history of the Bādūspānid dynasty in Rūyān, that is before 493/1100, is not especially well known. However, their lands were closer to the Bāwandid heartlands than those of the Zaydī Imams of Daylamān. Since in this period the Zaydī Imams seem to be Bāwandid protégés, the Bādūspānids in Rūyān might also have been controlled by the Bāwandids in the first decades of the 6th/12th century.

We learn from Rashīd al-Dīn[27] that after the accession of Muḥammad b. Buzurg-Umīd, beginning in Rajab 536/February 1142 the Nizārīs again raided parts of Gurjīyān which was populated mainly by Zaydīs. The local Zaydī forces requested help both from Daylamān and from Ṭabaristān. Rashīd al-Dīn says that the Zaydīs in Gurjīyān split, and some local Zaydī circles led by Amīr Tarasf b. Malikshāh Gurjī sought reconciliation with the Nizārīs, while his brother Kirshāsf was in correspondence with an anti-Nizārī Daylamī whose title was the Dāʿī Pādishāh Daylamān, and also with ʿAlāʾ al-Dawla ʿAlī, the Bāwandid *iṣfahbad* of Ṭabaristān (a clear reference to the fact that in the first months of 536/1142, ʿAlāʾ al-Dawla ʿAlī, and not his son, Shāh Ghāzī Rustam, was the ruling *iṣfahbad* of Ṭabaristān).[28]

According to Rashīd al-Dīn, Kirshāsf described the miserable situation caused by the Nizārīs and came to an agreement with both the Bāwandid *iṣfahbad* and the anti-Nizārī Daylamī leader. Kirshāsf sent his nephew Amīr Lashkargīr to Ṭabaristān although specifically why is not known. We are not given any further details of this Zaydī-Bāwandid alliance, however Rashīd al-Dīn's wording suggests that the Gurjīyān area was annexed by the Nizārīs, where they then built two fortresses: Saʿādatkūh and Mubārakkūh. These names may suggest some sort of ideological approach by the Nizārīs. The original name of Mubārakkūh was Mārkūh, that is, 'hill of the snake'. This Nizārī practice of giving old castles new ideologically charged names is reflected in these two examples. Similar practices can be detected in a few cases in the area of Qazwīn, where in the time of Kiyā Buzurg-Umīd the Nizārīs also renamed old castles.

Zaydī resistance to the Ismailis however did not end with the battles in Gurjīyān. According to Rashīd al-Dīn, a group of Daylamī aristocrats led by a certain Sīyāwush b. Khalīl (who may have belonged to the former dynasty, the Justānids) plotted against the Nizārīs. Yet one of the conspirators betrayed the plot to the Nizārīs, who thereupon arrested all the Justānids and brought them to Alamūt, where they were interrogated one after the other by the Nizārīs and then imprisoned there.

As far as Bāwandid involvement in actions against the Nizārīs in Daylamān is concerned, direct evidence can be found in Ibn Isfandiyār's account. Interestingly, he does not mention the persons who defended the castles of Gurjīyān against the Nizārīs and sought military aid from Ṭabaristān; nor does he refer to the anti-Nizārī Daylamī conspirators. However, Ibn Isfandiyār, Āmulī and Marʿashī all refer to a certain Kiyā Buzurg Daylamānī, or Kiyā Buzurg al-Dāʿī ila'l-Ḥaqq Riḍā b. Hādī.[29] He was the son of Hādī Ḥuqaynī, the vehemently anti-Nizārī, Nāṣirī Zaydī Imam who had been killed by them in 490/1097. Ibn Isfandiyār says that Kiyā Buzurg Daylamānī was first heard of as coming with 5,000 Daylamīs to the aid of ʿAlāʾ al-Dawla ʿAlī, when the latter was attacked by the western Saljūq sultan, Masʿūd, in around 522/1128. Under ʿAlāʾ al-Dawla's son and successor, Shāh Ghāzī Rustam, this Kiyā Buzurg Daylamānī held the area of Rūdbast as an *iqṭāʿ* from his father-in-law, the Bāwandid king, and was in command during the war against the Ismailis in Daylamān.

Unfortunately, details of the course of this war are unknown. According to Rashīd al-Dīn, Kiyā ʿAlī, possibly a son of Kiyā Buzurg-Umīd, was also involved in military campaigns against the Nizārīs as early as Dhu'l-Qaʿda 535/June 1141. Together with Qutlugh Ābā the Saljūq governor of Qazwīn, Kiyā ʿAlī attacked the Alamūt region. This concerted attack failed and the attackers were quickly scattered by the Nizārīs. Again according to Rashīd al-Dīn, the attackers lost 150 soldiers.[30]

This Zaydī Kiyā ʿAlī married another daughter of Shāh Ghāzī Rustam, while Kiyā ʿAlī's daughter was married to the Bādūspānid Hazārasf, another vassal of the Bāwandids in this period. Taken with the marriages of Sunqur Inānj, and Sābiq Qazwīnī to Bāwandid princesses, it is reasonable to see these alliances as a strategy to strengthen Bāwandid control of the region and challenge the Nizārīs.[31]

The Bādūspānids, the rulers of Rūyān, were strongly linked to the Bāwandids and their role became more important in course of the 6th/12th century. A local Zaydī family of unknown origin, at the end of the 5th/11th century the Bādūspānid *ustāndār*s were vassals of the Saljūqs.[32] Later they became Bāwandid vassals, perhaps in the reign of Bāwandid ʿAlā' al-Dawla ʿAlī (r. 514–535/1120–1141), one of whose daughters became the wife of the Bādūspānid *ustāndār*, Kay Kā'ūs. Kay Kā'ūs's mother was a sister of Kiyā Buzurg Daylamānī, another vassal of the Bāwandids who had also married a Bāwandid princess, alliances that served to reinforce the authority of the Bāwandids in their conflict with the Nizārī Ismailis.

Unlike the Zaydī Imams of Daylamān, the populous Bādūspānid clan tended to be reluctant and divided when it came to supporting the Bāwandids. Perhaps they felt uncomfortable at being subordinate to them. Specifically, the Bādūspānid Kay Kā'ūs's elder half-brother, *ustāndār* Shahrnūsh, was a far less enthusiastic supporter of Shāh Ghāzī Rustam than Kay Kā'ūs. He was not the son of Kiyā ʿAlī's daughter and he did not readily accept the authority of the Bāwandids. Prompted by Sanjar, he attacked Shāh Ghāzī Rustam after his accession to power in 535–536/1141–1142, and first allied himself to Tāj al-Mulūk Mardāwīj, Shāh Ghāzī Rustam's brother and rival. Shāh Ghāzī Rustam therefore supported Shahrnūsh's brother, Kay Kā'ūs. Under such pressure, Shahrnūsh was forced to accept the suzerainty of Shāh Ghāzī Rustam in order to hold onto his kingdom. For this reason, he was also given the hand of a Bāwandid princess. However, Kay Kāʾūs remained the personal favourite of Shāh Ghāzī Rustam.

It is unclear when Shahrnūsh died. According to Marʿashī, it was in 563/1168 after he had reigned for thirteen years, yet this is highly unlikely when we look at the chronology.[33] Doubts about the length and the end of his reign indicate Bāwandid influence and are further reinforced by the fact that after his demise his sons were excluded from the Bādūspānid line of succession and it was Kay Kāʾūs who became the new *ustāndār* of Rūyān, possibly with strong Bāwandid backing. The half-Bāwandid–half-Bādūspānid Kay Kāʾūs, both before and after his accession, actively fought the Nizārīs together with his maternal uncle, the above-mentioned Zaydī Imam, Kiyā Buzurg Daylamānī.

Kiyā Buzurg Daylamānī himself was undoubtedly able to play an important role in the wars of Shāh Ghāzī Rustam against the Nizārīs. He was generally active in Rūdbast and in Daylamān in the west, yet there is also mention of his participation in the siege of Mihrīn castle near Girdkūh, in the south-east.[34]

Shāh Ghāzī Rustam led several raids into Daylamān against the Nizārīs. According to Ibn Isfandiyār[35] and Āmulī,[36] he attacked Alamūt several times to avenge the murder of his eldest son, as we have seen, while Marʿashī[37] says that it was his vassal, the Bādūspānid Kay Kāʾūs, who besieged Alamūt. One of Shāh Ghāzī Rustam's attacks against Alamūt in 552/1157 is recorded by Ibn al-Athīr also who says he raided the region.[38] However, Ibn al-Athīr's statement is rather brief and, moreover, the fact is that Shāh Ghāzī Rustam failed to take the castle itself. But it is possible that he pillaged the valley of Alamūt, destroying villages around the castle. According to all the Caspian chronicles, Shāh Ghāzī Rustam and his vassal Kay Kāʾūs caused the Nizārīs so much trouble that they did not dare to come out from their castles during these years. In the Caspian chronicles, a letter is preserved, addressed to the Nizārī *dāʿī*, Muḥammad b. Buzurg-Umīd. Ibn Isfandiyār and Āmulī claim that this letter was written at the court of Shāh Ghāzī Rustam, while Marʿashī argues that it was written by the Bādūspānid Kay Kāʾūs:[39]

> Shāh Ghāzī did not rest for a minute in the holy war against the *mulḥids*. He conducted raids a few times against Alamūt. At this time none of the *mulḥids* was able to appear outside Alamūt.

> Once, Shāh Ghāzī wrote a letter to Kiyā Kūr Muḥammad.[40] Its text is as follows:
>
> 'Let the evil-spirited life of all damned, corrupt, unclean apostates of this hopeless Muḥammad be short on the earth. Stretching your legs into the four parts of the walls of Alamūt, you have sat here and, like a fox, you have put your head into the depths of the cave. I have occupied all positions without either a military commander, a confidante, a deputy commander or an assistant (around your fortress). Throughout the world there is nobody who is more hostile to you than me.'
>
> They (the Nizārīs) wrote in reply: 'We read your letter, it was a great insult; and one insult generates another insult.'[41]

The offensive tone of the letter and the antipathy to the Nizārīs are in fact more important than its actual contents. It might be conceived rather as a product of an ideological stance rather than as an example of any actual correspondence between the Bāwandids and Nizārīs; though Ibn Isfandiyār does identify the writer as a scribe called Kāfī Abu'l-Qāsim.[42] Whatever the case, later Bāwandid tradition held this, probably fictitious, letter in high esteem, for all the main sources carefully preserved it.

The Nizārī-related sources, Rashīd al-Dīn and Kāshānī, are usually silent about these battles or only briefly refer to any of these events. It has been argued that their brief accounts tend to glorify the Nizārīs, commemorating their raids on Qazwīn and Rayy during these years.[43] Conversely, Ibn Isfandiyār mentions various military expeditions against Daylamān led by the Bāwandid vassals or by Shāh Ghāzī Rustam himself. Unfortunately, he never gives the years in which these expeditions took place. The expeditions did not necessarily target Nizārī castles but Bāwandid raids into the province could only have had a painfully negative effect on the Nizārīs.

We learn from Ibn Isfandiyār that, both during and after the failed siege of Girdkūh, Bāwandid forces were twice despatched to Daylamān, which resulted in the capture of Chināshak, an important place close to Alamūt.[44]

Some of the Bāwandid attacks enumerated by Ibn Isfandiyār are also briefly mentioned by Rashīd al-Dīn. In Ṣafar 545/April 1151, a certain Hādī son of Abū Hāshim, summoned the Gilite and Daylamī forces of Gurjīyān, Sījān and Awsān, and besieged the Nizārī fortress of Barkawān. Here, two facts are particularly interesting. Hādī's name suggests that his father was Abū Hāshim Jurjānī, who is mentioned both by Zaydī sources and Rashīd al-Dīn, and was a fiercely anti-Nizārī, Zaydī leader. He had led a Zaydī uprising against the Nizārīs and was killed by them in 526/1132.[45] Furthermore, the population of Gurjīyān had already asked for military aid from the Bāwandids when Nizārī forces appeared there in around 533/1139. Given these connections, it is highly probabile that Hādī b. Abū Hāshim Jurjānī led a revolt in Gurjīyān at the instigation of Shāh Ghāzī Rustam.

As for as other attacks conducted by the Bāwandids in Muḥarram 555/February 1160, the forces of Sābiq Qazwīnī made a relatively successful raid on the important Nizārī castle of Lamasar. Besides killing a group of Nizārīs they captured a certain Bu'l-Qāsim Shamshīrzan and brought him to Qazwīn. It is not fully understood what position he may have held, but he was considered by the Qazwīnīs to be an important source of information about the Nizārīs. His captors tried to force him to reveal Nizārī military information, but Bu'l-Qāsim Shamshīrzan refused to do so and was eventually executed. The situation for the Nizārīs around Lamasar must have been bleak as only a month after this raid Muḥammad b. Buzurg himself arrived there and despatched an army against Qazwīn, killing thirty local people in retaliation for the losses the Nizārīs had previously suffered.[46]

Another anti-Nizārī campaign was led by Sunqur Inānj and a certain Qaymaz Khurramī, who may have been someone related to the Khurramī-Ismaili episode of 536/1142 described earlier, who 'suddenly' (*nāgāh*) attacked the area of Rūdbār on 21 Jumādā I 553/25 June 1158. According to the pro-Nizārī sources used by Rashīd al-Dīn, the watchful Nizārīs repelled this attack.[47] Another attack by Qazwīnī forces against Rūdbār in 555/1160 is referred to briefly by Rashīd al-Dīn.[48]

A further and perhaps more serious Bāwandid confrontation led by Sunqur Inānj took place on 20 Shaʿbān 556/2 August 1160, when he was governor of Rayy and *iṣfahbad* of Jibāl, invading the area of Kay and Sīra, causing great damage to the Nizārīs, as also acknowledged by Rashīd al-Dīn's Nizārī source.[49]

Possible evidence of a troubled Nizārī defence system might be detected in our sources, when Rashīd al-Dīn speaks of the absence of Muḥammad b. Buzurg-Umīd from Alamūt. In 544–545/1150–1151, Muḥammad b. Buzurg-Umīd twice left Alamūt and visited a series of Nizārī fortresses near Ṭalīqān, north of Rayy and west of Mount Damāwand, such as Arzhang, Lurā, Darband, Karīm, Manṣūrābād Sarbashm and Kahūr; and he journeyed as far as the vicinity of Rayy. According to Rashīd al-Dīn he was supervising the construction of new fortresses, such as that of Arzhang in Ṭalīqān. The mounting pressure of allied Zaydī, Bādūspānid and Bāwandid forces can be seen as at least one reason for these journeys.[50]

The region of Girdkūh under Shāh Ghāzī Rustam

According to the Caspian chronicles, over this same period Shāh Ghāzī Rustam had more success against the Nizārīs in the region of Girdkūh and Dāmghān. Here, there were at least four important Nizārī castles, namely Ustunāwand, Mihrīn, Manṣūrakūh, Fīrūzkūh, that were taken from the Nizārīs, but a siege of the main seat of the Nizārīs in Dāmghān, Girdkūh was unsuccessful. The loss of these castles constituted a serious blow to the Nizārīs.[51] However, it should be pointed out that these events are only recounted in pro-Bāwandid chronicles; no other sources, whether Nizārī, Sunni or Zaydī, mention them.

The fortress of Ustunāwand was taken from the Nizārīs some time before 542/1147 by ʿAbbās, the Saljūq governor of Rayy, though it is said that he was later killed by them. It is not known when Shāh Ghāzī Rustam came into possession of such an important fortress, but after the death of ʿAbbās it had a Turkic governor who was still in the service of the eastern Saljūqs, and Shāh Ghāzī Rustam simply purchased the castle from this unknown Saljūq governor. The death of Sanjar and the disintegration of the Eastern Saljūq empire can help in defining the date of acquisition. Since Sunqur Inānj joined Shāh Ghāzī Rustam in around 550/1155; consequently, Ustunāwand must have come into the possession of the Bāwandids in around 550/1155.

The next important conflict took place at Fīrūzkūh, the major easternmost fortress of the castles near Girdkūh. According to Willey:

> The Firuzkuh road skirts the extinct volcano of Damavand, and the landscape here is really magnificent. Firuzkuh itself is strategically placed at the entrance to a narrow gorge and the mountain peaks around are topped with many forts. Some of

> them were built in Daylamite times and were later taken over and enlarged by the Ismailis. One guards the entrance to the gorge. Firuzkuh was always an important stronghold because of its strategic position. The castle goes back to Sasanid times.[52]

As far as Fīrūzkūh, which lay near Mount Damāwand, is concerned, Ibn Isfandiyār says it was besieged by Shāh Ghāzī Rustam, but from the context in his account it is not entirely clear whether the defenders of the castle of Fīrūzkūh were the Nizārīs or Saljūq amīrs. The possibility that Fīrūzkūh was still in possession of a Saljūq amīr is further suggested by a statement from Ibn Isfandiyār: 'When the defenders realised that they could not hold the fortress of Fīrūzkūh, they sold it to the *iṣfahbad*, and all of Damāwand was given back by the amīrs of 'Irāq (to Shāh Ghāzī Rustam).'[53] However, the names of these amīrs were unknown to the sources.

Manṣūrakūh and Mihrīn were taken by Shāh Ghāzī Rustam after a disastrous military adventure in Dihistān. He retreated to Ṭabaristān and reorganised his forces, and soon had recruited 12,000 soldiers. He then attacked these two Nizārī castles. According to Ibn Isfandiyār, the Zaydī Kiyā Buzurg Daylamānī joined the campaign against Mihrīn and Manṣūrakūh.[54] The sieges lasted eight months before they were finally captured.[55] After this raid Shāḥ Ghāzī Rustam also occupied the important commercial centres of Dāmghān and Bisṭām.

There were other fortresses in the area about which the sources say little. As Willey points out,[56] the histories of the castles of Greater and Lesser Surū, at Shāhmīrzād near Chashma, as well Sarā Anzā, Lājiwardī and Kalār Khān are completely omitted from the medieval chronicles.[57] It is not known whether these castles remained in Nizārī hands or were besieged and captured by Saljūq or Bāwandid armies in the years between 535/1141 and 560/1165.

The fortress that had a pivotal role in controlling the area of Dāmghān was undoubtedly Girdkūh, situated some 18 kilometres west of Dāmghān. Girdkūh was especially heavily fortified and virtually inaccessible to any invader. It was besieged by the Mongols for seventeen years from 651/1253 to 669/1270 and was the last Nizārī fortress to surrender to them. According to Daftary, Girdkūh was 'self-sufficient and as impregnable as possible. It was a strongly fortified castle with ample water and food storage facilities, capable of withstanding long sieges when it came into the possession of the Nizārī

Ismāʿīlīs.'[58] Girdkūh was termed 'a fortified mountain' by Willey, as indeed its appearance makes plain and its name suggests.[59] Thus, the difficulties in besieging this enormous fortress, which was the core of the eastern Nizārī areas, proved to be far more challenging than attacking any other castle in the region. The buildings, walls and ditches constructed by the Mongols in order to conquer Girdkūh are still visible.[60]

Shāh Ghāzī Rustam obviously realised the difficulties, as well as the importance, of capturing Girdkūh. According to Ibn Isfandiyār, he made enormous preparations before embarking on the seige:

> And Shāh Ghāzī Rustam came to Māzandarān as far as Dīnārjārī and Jājarm and Sabinqān and Ṭarmaghān, and summoned an army for six months and ordered that trees be cut from Lund and Burd and from other residences. After six months, he went to the foot of Girdkūh with 200,000 horse-loads of trees and he built (his own fortresses) patiently and able-mindedly around the castle of Girdkūh.
>
> The *mulḥid*s sent him a message: 'You came too late, you should have come here more quickly and in due time.' The *iṣfahbad* Shāh Ghāzī Rustam replied: 'If this year I came late, next year we will come more quickly.' And the whole population of Māzandarān was involved in the preparations to lay siege to the castle for a two-month period. And eight months was spent this way (with the besieging).
>
> The *mulḥids* sent a few *kharwār*s of gold to Bughrātigīn[61] in Khurāsān until this 'damned evil and intellectually weak' apostate (Bughrātigīn) had prepared the entire army of Khurāsān and brought it up to the *iṣfahbad*.[62] The *iṣfahbad* was unaware of the threat and his army, which had been sent to raid Alamūt, was absent. It was unprecedented that a Muslim had carried out a raid with such aggressive haste (i.e. Bughrātigīn); and Bughrātigīn rapidly reached the camp of the *iṣfahbad*; the *mulḥids* beat the drums with their hands from the fortress of Girdkūh and attacked the name and the servants of Shāh Ghāzī.
>
> The *iṣfahbad* was informed about the arrival of the Turk. He said: 'Bring my throne!' The throne was brought there and he sat on his throne, but the army of Bughrātigīn was raiding the edges of his camp. Then the army of Bughrātigīn hastily retreated from there. All the people of Shāh Ghāzī Rustam were dispersed. Shāh

> Ghāzī Rustam marched to Zaram and Ajurrūd, but his besieging system had been demolished. Local people sent the *iṣfahbad* several thousand dīnārs and a thousand pieces of clothing as a sign of gift and service. The *iṣfahbad* said, 'Because of the respect shown towards Muslims I will strive to annihilate the *mulḥids*, as such a thing is a Muslim endeavour — so what can I do?' And he ordered the burning of all wooden material (for the siege of the castle). Then the *mulḥids* sent him an envoy, who said, 'In so far as you wish to, please sell this wood to us!' The *iṣfahbad* replied, 'It would be unjust since I did not confer a fortress on these dishonoured Muslims — for this reason I will not increase their supplies by selling [them] wood!' And the *iṣfahbad* ordered it all to be burned, and, furthermore, ordered the army of Bīrūn Tamīsha to conquer the area of Janāshak.[63]

This episode from Ibn Isfandiyār is a detailed account of Shāh Ghāzī Rustam's operations at Girdkūh. It was one of the key objectives of the Bāwandid *iṣfahbad*, who could then have controlled the southern slopes of the south-eastern Alburz entirely as all the other important locations around the castle had fallen into his hands. The large-scale preparations before the siege by Shāh Ghāzī Rustam and the cutting down of forests around Girdkūh suggest a major military operation, though lacking the technical and engineering sophistication of the Mongols a hundred years later.

One cannot estimate the problems the *iṣfahbad* was able to cause a highly fortified castle such as Girdkūh. It appears from this brief account that Shāh Ghāzī Rustam may have intended to isolate Girdkūh with an extended siege. The fact that he recruited Māzandarānīs every two months to continue the fight suggests that he had also foreseen the difficulties that his army might encounter. Despite the failure of the siege, Ibn Isfandiyār gives more space to recounting the course of events at Girdkūh than to accounts of attacks on other fortresses in the vicinity.

After a relatively long siege, the Nizārīs felt the need to seek help and paid for the services of the Sunni amīr Bughrātigīn of Khurāsān, a former eastern Saljūq military leader. Bughrātigīn is also mentioned by Ibn al-Athīr in the middle of Shaʿbān 1160/August 1160, but he does not refer to his expedition against the Bāwandids and makes no mention of the Ismailis or Girdkūh; yet it seems clear from the context of these accounts that Bughrātigīn was one of the Bāwandids' enemies since Ibn al-Athīr relates that he first fought Ay-tāq, the Turkish governor of Gurgān and Astarābād, a vassal of Shāh Ghāzī Rustam, and that, after being defeated, sought refuge in Nīshāpūr at the court of Mu'ayyad Ayābā, another former Saljūq amīr.[64] From Ibn al-Athīr we see that Sunqur Inānj, Ay-tāq and Sābiq Qazwīnī all sided with Shāh Ghāzī Rustam, while Bughrātigīn and Mu'ayyad Ayābā opposed him. It seems that the Nizārīs of Girdkūh followed closely events after the fall of Sanjar, and they built up good contacts with those Khurāsānī, formerly Saljūq, military forces who had not joined the Bāwandids. This is another instance of the Nizārī policy of finding a way of counterbalancing their opponent's forces by taking the conflict to the enemy's sphere of influence, politically and militarily, through alliances with other opponents of their enemy, who in this case was Shāh Ghāzī Rustam.[65]

The insulting adjectives applied to Bughrātigīn in Ibn Isfandiyār's account indicate the anger that was felt at the Sunni-Nizārī cooperation around Girdkūh. The forces of Bughrātigīn defeated the Bāwandid army and destroyed the wooden structures used for the siege. However, despite the damage caused there remained sufficient forces in Shāh Ghazi Rustam's camp to continue his campaign in Daylamān, and he invaded Chināshak, not far from Alamūt. Another interesting element of this account is a brief reference to a Bāwandid raid conducted against Alamūt during the siege of Girdkūh. The details of this second putative Bāwandid attack against Alamūt, possibly around 555/1160, are obscure as Ibn Isfandiyār's references to it are very brief.

After the unsuccessful attempts to capture Girdkūh, Shāh Ghāzī Rustam sent his son-in-law, Sābiq Qazwīnī, to govern the newly-acquired areas of Bisṭām, Dāmghān and Simnān; and as a result the Nizārīs of Girdkūh were unable to leave their castle during the last years of his reign.[66]

The Nizārī response

There is not a great deal of information in the sources concerning Nizārī resistance to the Bāwandids during Shāh Ghāzī Rustam's reign. The Nizārī sources do not usually mention either the Bāwandids or any military defeats during the time of Muḥammad b. Buzurg-Umīd. On the contrary, the Nizārī narrative suggests rather a chain of unbroken successes against neighbouring principalities. As we have seen, the first years of Muḥammad b. Buzurg-Umīd's reign can perhaps be viewed as a successful period when there were new territorial gains in Gurjīyān. However, after this brief initial period the sources do not mention any further territorial advances by the Nizārīs.

The military operations undertaken under Muḥammad b. Buzurg-Umīd were of two types: the well-documented establishment of fortresses and the campaigns against areas around Rayy and Qazwīn. Yet the number of newly established castles in this period was lower than in preceding periods. According to Rashīd al-Dīn, the Nizārīs founded a castle near Qazwīn in a place called Lār, in 538/1144.[67]

Between 544/1150 and 560/1165, the Nizārīs had to confront numerous attacks against their central regions in Daylamān. As Daftary has noted: 'By the time of Muḥammad b. Buzurg-Umīd, many Nizārīs doubtless looked back to the glorious past and the campaigns of Ḥasan-i Ṣabbāḥ.'[68] In spite of the serious setbacks they suffered both in the lands they controlled and possibly in the *daʿwa* too, they nevertheless put up a fierce resistance to enemy attacks, and their opponents lacked the means and the ability to destroy the Nizārī Ismaili state in the Caspian provinces. According to Rashīd al-Dīn, the Nizārīs tried to counterattack, and their response was to cause as much damage as possible to the areas of Rayy and Qazwīn after each incursion into Nizārī areas by Bāwandid forces.

Another element of Nizārī resistance during the time of Muḥammad b. Buzurg-Umīd was the support they gave to some of the Bādūspānids who had rejected Bāwandid rule in Rūyān. Although the Bādūspānids were Zaydīs, and many of them had opposed the Nizārīs, they were deeply divided and whilst there were those who acknowleged Bāwandid suzerainty and joined their military campaigns, there were others who were more reluctant to participate in a campaign against the Nizārīs. Furthermore, they were based in Rūyān, near Rūdbār and so near Alamūt. From the sources it is evident that the Bāwandids regarded the Bādūspānids as their protégés.[69] Yet the Bādūspānids, on various occasions rebelled against Bāwandid rule. Thus, their stance was unique in terms of local policy in Rūyān.

The first attested rulers of the Bādūspānids were thought to be Saljūq allies.[70] Before Sultan Muḥammad b. Malikshāh died in 512/1118, it was the norm for local dynasties in northern Iran to acknowledge the suzerainty of the Saljūqs. The Nizārīs, uniquely and for very specific reasons of faith above all, went against the grain in this respect but at times also showed a willingness to consolidate their power by making temporary agreements with the Saljūqs.

The Bādūspānids acted as a counterbalance to the increasing Bāwandid influence in northern Iran, and their alliance with the Saljūqs was similar to the Bāwandid-Nizārī cooperation during the period; both were based simply on pragmatic and military considerations. With the spectacular weakening of the Saljūqs after the death of Sultan Muḥammad I, the foundations of Bādūspānid-Saljūq cooperation were severely damaged and the commitment of the Bādūspānids to the Saljūqs gradually became questionable. According to Marʿashī, ʿAlāʾ al-Dawla ʿAlī persuaded the Bādūspānid, Shahrnūsh b. Hazārasf to abandon Amīr ʿAbbās's camp when he was campaigning against the Bāwandids.

Things changed slowly, however, and even after the death of ʿAlāʾ al-Dawla ʿAlī, the Bādūspānid Shahrnūsh b. Hazārasf still supported Tāj al-Mulūk Mardāwīj, the pro-Saljūq Bāwandid prince, brother and rival of Shāh Ghāzī Rustam; but this was the last occasion on which the Bādūspānids openly served Saljūq interests. After this, they began to develop an independent strategy. Indeed, after the fall of the Saljūq protégé, Tāj al-Mulūk Mardāwīj, Shahrnūsh b. Hazārasf allied with Shāh Ghāzī Rustam, and married a Bāwandid princess who was possibly a daughter of Shāh Ghāzī Rustam.[71] Shahrnūsh b. Hazārasf's pro-Bāwandid policy was warmly welcomed by the Bāwandids and he was not only rewarded with the hand of a Bāwandid princess but the towns of Nātil and Sīyāhrūd were also conferred on him.

The mention of Sīyāhrūd is particularly interesting here. It lies in Gīlān, very close to the Nizārī heartlands and is mentioned by Rashīd al-Dīn and Āmulī as the seat of power of an obscure figure and alleged member of the Bādūspānid dynasty, someone called Nāmāwar. It is said that this Nāmāwar had already donated the fortress of Sīyāhrūd to the Nizārīs in around 533/1139 and although it is not known precisely when Shāh Ghāzī Rustam gifted Nātil and Sīyāhrūd to Shahrnūsh b. Hazārasf, these places were at the forefront of Nizārī activities in Gīlān at the time. They were therefore especially important in the eyes of the Bāwandids, since they sought to put an end to further Nizārī territorial expansion.

Shahrnūsh and his half-brother Kay Kāʾūs, had major disputes over control of Rūyān. Kay Kāʾūs, who was the maternal nephew of the pro-Bāwandid Zaydī, Kiyā Buzurg Daylamānī, played a large role in organising campaigns against the Nizārīs following his death. We do not know the dates of these expeditions, but they must have been conducted in the second half of the 530s/1140s. Besides military force, Bāwandid family links and clan considerations played a key role in the selection of new Bādūspānid ruler since Hazārasf, unlike his half-brother, was not a nephew of the Zaydī Kiyā Buzurg Daylamānī. The loyalty of Shahrnūsh, and later that of his sons, remained suspect to Shāh Ghāzī Rustam. Thus when Shahrnūsh died he made the loyal and openly pro-Bāwandid brother, Kay Kāʾūs, the *ustāndār* of Rūyān, instead of one of Shahrnūsh's sons.

Yet things became more complicated when a hitherto obscure Bādūspānid suddenly appeared and claimed the throne of Rūyān for himself. The year of Shahrnūsh's death is not given in the sources, but it must have occurred before 546/1152, since it is in that year that his half-brother Kay Kāʾūs is referred to by Ibn Isfandiyār as the new ruler of Rūyān. The name of the new claimant was Nāmāwar. His Bādūspānid origins are openly questioned by Marʿashī, but it is clear some local groups in Rūyān supported his claim. According to Āmulī, Kay Kāʾūs had the 'usurper' arrested and imprisoned in the castle of Nūr. As a reward Kay Kāʾūs was given the areas between ʿAlīshāhrūd and Sīyāhrūd by the Bāwandids for his loyalty, and apparently began to send 24,000 dinars every week to the treasury of Āmul, the capital of Shāh Ghāzī Rustam.[72] This Nāmāwar may be the pro-Nizārī local ruler mentioned above. Rashīd al-Dīn relates a different series of events in which a certain Nāmāwar b. Kay Kāʾūs came to Gīlān in 533/1139 and built a fortress at a place called Sīyāhrūd which he then gave to the Nizārīs.[73] There are two points of similarity in the accounts by Āmulī and Rashīd al-Dīn. The two rulers' names are the same, and the place in Gīlān, which was acquired by this mysterious Nāmāwar, is called Sīyāhrūd by Rashīd al-Dīn, and Sīyāhkīlrūd by Āmulī.[74] Though we cannot prove that these Nāmāwars were one and the same person, yet if we do accept this identity, he can be seen as a pro-Nizārī local Bādūspānid prince since he invited the Nizārīs into his castle. Nāmāwar may have had quite a number of followers in Rūyān because many years later a certain Bīsutūn b. Nāmāwar, who may well have been his son, successfully laid claim to power in Rūyān.

However, not only Nāmāwar opposed Bāwandid rule in Rūyān. To further complicate the matter, the sons of Shahrnūsh were also believed to support the Nizārīs, since they had been removed from power by the Bāwandids after the death of their father. Yet, after the reign of Kay Kā'ūs, the eldest son of Shahrnūsh, Hazārasf, upon his accession to the throne, immediately reverted to the anti-Nizārī policy of his uncle. Thus, the Bādūspānids were changeable allies of the Bāwandids in their conflict against the Nizārīs; some of them were more motivated to cooperate with the Bāwandids, but a preference for alliances with the Nizārīs is also apparent among them as early as in the time of Shāh Ghāzī Rustam, which marked the height of Bāwandid power in northern Iran.[75]

Yet Kay Kā'ūs himself can hardly be thought to have been a supporter of the Nizārīs, as before his accession he had displayed fierce anti-Nizārī sentiments, had fought the Nizārīs for many years and could have continued doing so after gaining power in Rūyān. The chronology of his campaigns against the Nizārīs is not well documented. However, his later plotting and revolts against the Bāwandids may have unwittingly assisted the Nizārīs, and provided the lords of Alamūt with a relief from the years of conflict with the Bāwandids who were now engaged elsewhere. The Bādūspānids can be said to have constituted a buffer or neutral zone for the Nizārīs against Bāwandid raids and this, albeit unwitting, common interest brought positive results for the Nizārīs in later decades.

Chapter 5

Bāwandid-Nizārī Confrontation in the Late 6th/12th Century

The doctrinal opposition of the Bāwandids and the Nizāris

There are a number of doctrinal works that Bāwandid rulers directed against the Nizārīs between 486/1093 and 655/1257. The extensive loss of Nizārī Ismaili writings limits any analysis of Nizārī thinking about their doctrinal opposition to the Bāwandids. Only these sources that support the position of the Bāwandids, their main opponent among the Caspian dynasties of the age, can be readily subjected to analysis.

Of the anti-Nizārī polemical sources stemming from Bāwandid circles, one can mention first of all the local medieval historiography of the Caspian region, such as the works of Ibn Isfandiyār, Āmulī and Marʿashī, which often reflected the ideology of the local post-Sasanian kings of the Caspian region. Apart from these sources, several religious and literary sources of the 6th/12th century contain material useful for the study of Nizārī-Bāwandid relations. In this sense, the *Kitāb al-Naqḍ* by ʿAbd al-Jalīl Qazwīnī Rāzī written in the second half of the 6th/12th century, is of considerable importance. In his writings, Qazwīnī Rāzī advocated a conciliatory attitude between Twelver Shiʿi and Sunni groups in order to unite them against the Nizārīs, muting Shiʿi criticism of the Companions of the Prophet, and stressing ʿAlid sympathies found among the Sunni *ʿulamāʾ* and ascetics. In particular, Rāzī favoured friendly ties with the Ḥanafī *madhhab*, which was generally followed by the Saljūqs including Sanjar, and emphasised Twelver doctrinal agreement with Muʿtazilī and Māturīdī theology and also the general pro-ʿAlid sentiment of the Saljūq Turks, something not unusual in medieval Iran.[1] Apart from this important polemical source, a few of the *qaṣīdas* of Muʿizzī, an important poet of the Saljūq era who was clearly a Sunni in his beliefs, where Bāwandid princes are described as 'the praised ones (sing. *mamdūḥ*)', thus also hint interestingly about the ideological background of the Bāwandids.[2]

As for the role of the Nizārī Ismaili state, its opposition to the Saljūqs and, later, to the influence of the Khwārazmshāhs, is well known. Daftary notes that there was a clear element of Turco-Iranian rivalry in this stance.[3] Indeed, according to Kāshānī in the *Sargudhasht-i Sayyidnā* and also in a later Nizārī text of the Alamūt era, the *Haft bāb* of Ḥasan-i Maḥmūd-i Kātib, Ḥasan-i Ṣabbāḥ is credited with calling Turks ignoramuses and enemies of the Persian-speaking world, above all of the Nizārī Ismailis.[4] But conditions in the Caspian region were far more complex than simple binaries of Nizārī-Saljūq, Ismaili-Sunni or Persian-Turkic animosities since, at the local level, the Ismailis had non-Turkic belligerent neighbours, the Twelver Shiʿi Bāwandids, who viewed them as their main rivals in the Caspian provinces.[5]

The three main powers in the Caspian region were the Ismailis, the Bāwandids and the Bādūspānids. These groups considered themselves foes and rivals for control of lands in northern Iran. Besides military action (already discussed) ideological weapons were also used targeting each other's identities. A hitherto unstudied phenomenon is the fact that the Bāwandids used the same ideological weapons against the Nizārī Ismailis as the Nizārī Ismailis used against the Saljūqs. In the eyes of the Bāwandids, the Nizārī Ismailis were outsiders, as were the Saljūqs in the eyes of the Ismailis. Thus, there was a twofold approach by the most formidable anti-Nizārī groups: a unique combination of traditional elements whose history went back, it was claimed, to a pre-Islamic aristocracy combined with a Twelver Shiʿi doctrinal attitude.

The polemic against the Nizārī Ismailis in the *Kitāb al-Naqḍ*

The author of this doctrinal work attempted to reconcile the Uṣūlī Twelver Shiʿis with the Ḥanafī Sunnis, both groups opposed to the Ismailis. Given what he says, he must have been an enthusiastic supporter of the Saljūq-Bāwandid alliance against the Ismailis. So, the main reason behind promulgation of this unusual Twelver Shiʿi-Sunni alliance was probably Qazwīnī Rāzī's vehement rejection of the Nizārīs. Although of Qazwīnī origin, he in fact spent most of his life in

Rayy. But both these cities were at the forefront of military confrontations between the Nizārīs and their opponents. As a Twelver Shiʿi scholar, Qazwīnī Rāzī would have had direct experience of the decline of the Twelver Shiʿi educational centres in Rayy, which he probably attributed to the threat represented by the Nizārīs.

Anti-Nizārī rhetoric in this period was hardly a rare phenomenon but the novelty in Qazwīnī Rāzī's argument is his attempt to link his own views with support for the Bāwandids. Qazwīnī Rāzī lived during the reign of the Bāwandid *iṣfahbad* Shāh Ghāzī Rustam when the Bāwandids were at the height of their power and had taken over many areas of Ṭabaristān, including Rayy and Qazwīn. In the second half of his reign, after 549/1154, Shāh Ghāzī Rustam had aspirations also to replace the Saljūqs in northern Iran generally and even in Khurāsān. In this, the Nizārīs were his main opponents. Shāh Ghāzī Rustam's attempts to conquer Nizārī-controlled areas were only successful to a limited degree, and he was ultimately unable to capture the key fortresses of the Nizārīs, Alamūt, Lamasar and Girdkūh. Of all of this, Qazwīnī Rāzī must have been acutely aware.

In his writings, Qazwīnī Rāzī gave clear doctrinal support to the Bāwandid-Saljūq alliance. There are many passages in which he lays great emphasis on conciliatory ideas developing between the Bāwandids and Saljūqs. However, in some cases the *Kitāb al-Naqd* includes past events, and these passages re-interpret well-known facts for a contemporary audience. In many cases, Qazwīnī Rāzī's logic lies in the fact that he seeks to establish a new Twelver Shiʿi-Sunni doctrinal and theological accord by recounting military campaigns led by the Bāwandid armies and former Saljūq military leaders, such as Sunqur Inānj and Sābiq Qazwīnī. Though he does not mention many political events in great detail, it is clear that he followed the events of Shāh Ghāzī Rustam's reign including his actions against the Nizārīs very closely:

> The kingdom of Māzandarān became ruled by Rustam b. ʿAlī b. Shahriyār and 27,000 *mulḥid*s, of whom there is credit and information, were killed by his sword, besides that group of *mulḥid*s of whose massacre there is no information. And none of the sultans and amīrs of the world had made similar conquests, and if somebody had made them, it would not have remained uncovered that everybody should know that it is Sārī and Uram[6]

> that are the *qiblas* of Islam (*qiblat al-Islām*) and not the demons of Alamūt.[7]

In his narrative Qazwīnī Rāzī constructs the idea of the Muslim champion embodied by Shāh Ghāzī Rustam, who was much praised for his piety and courage and for the support offered to Twelver Shiʿi *sayyids* during his reign. In his book, Sārī and Uram the heartlands of the Bāwandid kingdom were, as seen in the quote above, hailed as the new centres of Islam. The notion of comparing the chief urban areas of the Bāwandids with the holiest site of Islam is perhaps the most notable element in this account. In this one can see the possible influence of some kind of Bāwandid propaganda.

From time to time, Qazwīnī Rāzī glorifies Shāh Ghāzī Rustam's military prowess against the Nizārīs, giving numbers of them killed and fortresses conquered. In addition, he declares with satisfaction that the Bāwandid ruler left the bodies of the massacred Nizārīs for the dogs. Elsewhere, he praises the dynastic connections between the Saljūqs and the Bāwandids responding thereby to criticism of a marriage between a Sunni and a Twelver Shiʿi. Furthermore, Qazwīnī Rāzī dismisses the notion of any similarity or links between the Ismailis and Twelver Shiʿis, that is, between two branches of Shiʿi Islam; he praises rather the common moral and religious values of the Saljūq and Bāwandid rulers. In his eyes the shared concepts of justice and religious piety between Sunni and Twelver Shiʿi princes are of greater worth than theological similarities between the various communities of Shiʿi Islam.

> It is known that Sārī and Uram were always the capital of the kingdom (*dār al-mulk*) and the seat of the kings of Māzandarān (*sarīrgāh-i mulūk Māzandarān*). Foreigners and merchants were safe there, and the voices of the Muslims sounded from their communities, mosques, madrasas and assemblies. And nowadays, during the rule of the King of Kings, Rustam b. ʿAlī, may God endorse his victory, and during the time of his father, the king of Māzandarān ʿAlī b. Shahriyār, may God be merciful to him, this kingdom was the *qibla* of Islam (*qiblat al-Islām*), and each year thousands of *mulḥids* and *bāṭinīs* (Nizārī Ismailis) were left as food for the dogs (*taʿma-i sagān*) in these provinces.[8]

In the following passage there are further elements in praise of the Bāwandids for the long-lasting peace, cooperation and harmony between the Bāwandids and the Saljūqs, though this is something of a polemical exaggeration by the author. Qazwīnī Rāzī's account would appear to have been greatly influenced by the attacks against the Nizārīs mounted by the armies of Shāh Ghāzī Rustam once former high-ranking Saljūq officers joined him after the disintegration of Sanjar's empire in 548/1154. Qazwīnī Rāzī's statement that the Bāwandids were the favourites of the Saljūqs certainly indicates that his work was composed no earlier than the second half of Shāh Ghāzī Rustam's reign, and possibly after 548/1154, when major anti-Nizārī operations were initiated by the Bāwandids:

> *Iṣfahbad* ʿAlī was a Shiʿi and a thoughtful individual, and a Twelver Imāmī (*Shiʿi va muʿtaqad va dawāzdah Imāmī*), in contrast to Khwāja,[9] who had said in this book a few times that there was neither power nor place for the Twelver Shiʿis; for he explained that the Twelver Shiʿi and *mulḥid* (Nizārī Ismaili) are the same and on one occasion he said the following: 'A sultan such as Malikshāh gave his daughter to a Twelver Shiʿi, meaning that he handed her over to uncertainty, malevolence and evil faith', and these claims were ground down to nothing, the sultan being wise, just, a believer; and the *iṣfahbad* ʿAlī, who was his son-in-law, is also a believer, thoughtful, a Shiʿi, Imāmī and Uṣūlī.[10]

In the following excerpt Qazwīnī Rāzī repeats his argument that the priorities and common values for the Saljūq-Bāwandid coalition were piety, justice, prudence, but above all decisive action against the Nizārīs. He stresses the magnanimity of the Bāwandid dynasty, underlying their active support for the leading *sayyid* families. Similar passages can also be found in the *Tārīkh-i Ṭabaristān* of Ibn Isfandiyār, where there are accounts of lavish ceremonies held by Shāh Ghāzī Rustam in honour of the *sayyids*:[11]

> The kings of Māzandarān (*mulūk-i Māzandarān*) such as Shahriyār, Qārin, Girdbāzū, the *iṣfahbad* ʿAlī and the martyr Rustam b. ʿAlī are more renowned than the sun in ruling the world, in capturing castles, in leading military campaigns, in killing enemies, in eloquence, in intelligence, in justice and in massacring, and are the favourites of Their Majesties the Sultans, and these sultans are from the Saljūq dynasty. And that family is more renowned than the sun in their homeland and province,

> may God grant them life in posterity. And the fact that the *sayyids* of Sārī, Sayyid al-Ḥasan and his sons Sharaf al-Dīn, Tāj al-Dīn, Quṭb al-Dīn and Bahā' al-Dīn, all possessed learning, eloquence, nobility and prominent descent and virtue, which existed and still exists, has not remained hidden from us.[12]

Whilst the main emphasis is on the Bāwandids in the next passage, there are also references to the Saljūqs and their Nizārī policy. Qazwīnī Rāzī acknowledges that the Saljūqs had had relations with the Nizārīs. But by Qazwīnī Rāzī's time the Saljūqs, under the vizierate of Khwāja Mu'īn al-Dīn Kāshī, had cut all ties with them. This Saljūq statesman was killed, it has been presumed by the Nizārīs, after having fought them and was highly praised in the *Kitāb al-Naqḍ* as a martyr by dint of his actions against them:

> That Khwāja *shahīd* Mu'īn al-Dīn Kāshī, when he became vizier of the great Sultan Sanjar, May God's mercy be upon them both, rejected Sanjar's advisors concerning peace with the *mulḥids*, he closed the way to the *mulḥids* and levied heavy taxes on them. Thousands of them were taken prisoner and killed by him until he was finally killed by the sword of a *mulḥid* in the capital of Khurāsān, when he had become an old, just man.[13]

Shāh Ghāzī Rustam, who was probably Qazwīnī Rāzī's patron, is often portrayed by him as an ideal Muslim ruler and a true Muslim warrior. He championed Shāh Ghāzī Rustam in a practical fashion, declaring that no Sunni ruler had achieved as much military success. He argued that since Shāh Ghāzī Rustam, as a Twelver Shi'i ruler, had proved to be far superior in his fight against the *mulḥids* than any Sunni ruler, the Sunnis should also favour him as their righteous leader. This refers explicitly to the period between 548/1154 and 560/1165, when the armies of Shāh Ghāzī Rustam carried out a concerted campaign against the Nizārīs:

> Which of the Sunni rulers did the same with the *mulḥids* as that done by the Shi'i King of Kings, Rustam b. 'Alī b. Shahriyār, in all the world and in Sunni Muslim territories? He captured castles and took and killed, nay exterminated, the *mulḥids*, [the logic of] which [action] is clearer than the sun as it becomes evident that is how the Shi'a treat the infidels and enemies of their faith through Holy War.[14]

Another aspect of Bāwandid political propaganda in the *Kitāb al-Naqḍ* is the strict denial of any kind of contact between the Nizārīs and Twelver Shiʿis both in terms of political connections and of shared religious values. Yet, in fact, there was contact including peaceful alliances between the Nizārīs and the Bāwandids when both local states were threatened by Saljūq invasion, as we have seen. Despite denials made in the *Kitāb al-Naqḍ*, there were Nizārī groups operating in Bāwandid provinces as well. Furthermore, from Ibn Isfandiyār we learn about the operations of Nizārī groups in the principal cities of Ṭabaristān as well as in some of the mountain areas around Lajīm, for some twenty years, 514–535/1120–1141. It is quite conceivable that these Nizārīs remained active even under Shāh Ghāzī Rustam, providing valuable information to their co-religionists about political and military plans against the Nizārī fortresses.

When Qazwīnī Rāzī takes pains at various points to refute any idea of cooperation between the Nizārīs and the Twelver Shiʿis during Shāh Ghāzī Rustam's reign these are passages addressed perhaps to a contemporary Sunni audience which seek to recruit support for Shāh Ghāzī Rustam. Indeed, after the fall of Sanjar many former Saljūq amīrs joined Shāh Ghāzī Rustam and many of them became prominent at his court and in his army:

> And it was said: 'And there was another traitor (*khabīthī*), named Bilʿamīd Munāqibī, who gave voice to the same absurdities, and he fled to Sārī from Rayy, being accused of heresy, and he settled there and he was treated well by the *mulḥid*s of Sārī and Uram, but, finally, at the end of his life, he was arrested and his head became like the head of pigs and he died.' But the reply to these words of absurdity and madness which were uttered because of vengeance, accusation and absurdity is this: When did this man flee from Rayy to Sārī!? Intelligent persons do not believe that in these thirty years any renowned *mulḥid*, hiding himself in the area of Girdkūh or the Ṭabas of Gīlakī (?), or in the district of Alamūt or in the castles of Ṭāliqān, when these fortresses were surrounded (by the forces of the Bāwandids), found his way to Sārī or Uram against the spears of the King of Kings, the ruler of Māzandarān; thus the bodies of these *mulḥid*s became the food of dogs.[15]

In many ways, the *Kitāb al-Naqḍ* reflects the image the Bāwandids had of themselves, as reflected also in the local chronicles. There is no exact date of composition for this polemic. At one point, the text hails Shāh Ghāzī Rustam as a *shahīd* or martyr, which is surprising. It is true that Ibn Isfandiyār says he was attacked and wounded several times by *fidā'īs*, and Ibn Isfandiyār was as hostile as Qazwīnī Rāzī towards the Nizārīs and never missed an opportunity to report a Nizārī attack against the Bāwandids, but in fact Shāh Ghāzī Rustam died from an illness on 8 Rabīʿ I 560/23 January 1165 when he was nearly sixty years old. In other passages, however, Qazwīnī Rāzī promotes Shāh Ghāzī Rustam as his contemporary. It can thus be said that this important ideological source was most likely written towards the end of Shāh Ghāzī Rustam's reign.[16]

In these two Bāwandid-related sources a certain element of pre-Islamic heritage co-exists with Twelver Shiʿi ideas as can be seen in selecting Bāwandid ideas of themselves as well as their attitude to the Ismailis. However, it is clear that these elements were often combined with pro-Sunni and pro-Saljūq sentiments in an attempt to further strengthen the image of the Nizārī Ismailis as alien. But if the Nizārī Ismailis were regarded as 'intruders' by pro-Bāwandid writers, the also alien Saljūqs were treated more positively, doubtless a result of the mercurial nature of alliances during the fragmentation of the Saljūq empire.

Qiyāma in heaven and *Qiyāma* on earth: the Nizārī-Bādūspānid-Khwārazmian alliance against the Bāwandids (560–607/1165–1210)

The short reign of Ḥasan II (r. 557–561/1162–1166) was characterised by one event, that of the proclamation of the *qiyāma* in 559/1164. In the brief report on Ḥasan II by Rashīd al-Dīn, the announcement of the *qiyāma*, the great resurrection, predominates. Except for the last months, his reign coincided with that of the Bāwandid Shāh Ghāzī Rustam, who, as seen, led routine attacks against Nizārī lands. These attacks constituted serious setbacks for the Nizārīs, for they lost control of great fortresses around the Damāwand district and as a result their wider influence was weakened too. The regular depredations of Bāwandid military campaigns may well have continued up until the last years of Shāh Ghāzī Rustam's reign.

According to Juwaynī, in 557/1162, three years before the death of Muḥammad b. Buzurg-Umīd, Ḥasan II was 35 years old, and he describes him as having a favourable appearance, a very charming and eloquent personality and says this had already attracted many followers to him. Juwaynī claims that many had already regarded Ḥasan II as the Imam when he was younger, causing outrage at Muḥammad b. Buzurg-Umīd's court and as a result some 250 of his followers were killed and another 250 had to leave the Nizārī-controlled regions of Daylamān, compelling him to temporarily recant his views.[17] However, given Juwaynī's own anti-Nizārī zeal, the story as he relates it must be regarded as dubious. Perhaps it reveals some internal conflict between Ḥasan and Muḥammad b. Buzurg-Umīd and also between different groups of Daylamī Nizārīs, but the exact nature of this dispute is not well understood. The fact that Ḥasan II was killed less than four years after acceding in 561/1166 should indicate that disputes over the nature of authority within the Nizārī ruling elite lay behind these events.

Ḥasan II therefore had a short but very eventful reign, dominated by the declaration of the *qiyāma*. Though it appears to be a unique event in the history of the Nizārī Ismaili state, one can however detect earlier preparations for this declaration. Ḥasan II was a contemporary of Rāshid al-Dīn Sinān, the leader of the Syrian branch of the Nizārī Ismailis, and the two men were probably educated together at Alamūt. Then when he succeeded Muḥammad b. Buzūrg-Umīd, Ḥasan II chose Rāshid al-Dīn Sinān to be the new leader of the Syrian Nizārīs and sent him to the community there in 557/1162. In 559/1164, Ḥasan II sent him a letter which anticipates the announcement of the *qiyāma*. An eschatological message and repeated calls for unity are paramount in the letter where the need for unity among the believers according to the teaching of a person appointed by God and his *wālī* is emphasised.[18] In the letter, Ḥasan talked about an imminent preparation for the Hereafter, and paraphrased the Qur'an, announcing that 'in a little while they will come to the Hereafter'.[19] As Delia Cortese has argued, the phrase 'in a little while they will come to it', could be a reference to the declaration that was made on 17 Ramaḍān 559/8 August 1164. The choice of this particular day points to a major astrological event and has been thought to refer to the day of Imam ʿAlī b. Abū Ṭālib's martyrdom,[20] though this has been recently disputed by Badakhchani.[21]

The subsequent influence of the *qiyāma* on the wider Nizārī Ismaili community is beyond the scope of this study.[22] There is a rich secondary literature focussing on the theological impact of the *qiyāma* on later

Nizārī traditions and thought.[23] However, it is important to stress the fact that, as Daftary points out, the *qiyāma* was not noticed in the wider Islamic world in the years after 559/1164 and none of the contemporary non-Ismaili sources mention it. Even local historians such Ibn Isfandiyār, and Āmulī, are silent about this event. As Daftary says, 'It was, in fact, only after the fall of Alamūt that Persian historians and the outside world in general became aware of the Nizārī declaration of the *qiyāma* that had taken place almost a century earlier.'[24] Even in the *Kitāb al-Naqḍ*, which is regarded as a major contemporary anti-Nizārī doctrinal work, thought to have been compiled before 565/1170, there is no reference to, or evidence for a direct knowledge of the *qiyāma* declaration of 559/1164.

Although an event not known to non-Nizārīs and primarily a doctrinal decision, it is possible that the *qiyāma* triggered a reconsideration of the Nizārīs in the Caspian area. As Daftary notes: 'This announcement of the *qiyāma* was in fact a declaration of independence from the larger Muslim society. The Nizārīs now envisaged themselves in spiritual Paradise, while condemning the non-Nizārīs to spiritual non-existence. Now the Nizārīs had the opportunity of being collectively introduced to Paradise on earth, which was the knowledge of the unveiled truth.'[25]

Rendering the outside world irrelevant made the *qiyāma* declaration an important pragmatic change as well as a doctrinal one. The stronger emphasis on the spiritual rather than the material might suggest a brief hiatus in the expansion of the Nizārī *daʿwa* and a reshaping of the objectives and outlook of the Nizārī Ismaili community as a whole.

In terms of theology, therefore, in later sources the announcement of the *qiyāma* has three main messages which were embraced by the later Nizārīs and to a certain extent by other spiritual communities. According to post-Alamūt interpretations, by announcing the *qiyāma*, Ḥasan II proclaimed the resurrection, claiming that the end of the world had now in fact happened and proclaimed himself no longer the *dāʿī*, but God's deputy (*khalīfa*) on earth as well.[26]

Examining the sources, one can surmise various possible political motives in addition to the religious ones that are evident in the *qiyāma* announcement. These other reasons can be seen to have had an impact on the political approach of the Nizārīs, and taken all together may have contributed to the decision to make the announcement.

Two important sources relating to the *qiyāma* as a historical event are Rashīd al-Dīn's *Jamiʿ al-tawārīkh* and a 7th/13th-century Ismaili treatise, the *Haft bāb* of Ḥasan-i Maḥmūd-i Kātib.[27] But first the earliest surving Ismaili account by Abū Isḥāq follows:[28]

> On the 17th day of the month of Ramaḍān 559 [8 August 1164], under the sign of Virgo (*Sunbula*), while the Sun was rising in the constellation of Cancer (*Saraṭān*), by his order on the square of Alamūt a pulpit (*minbar*) was set up, facing west. Four flags were raised, one on each corner of the pulpit. The followers from Khurāsān were placed at the right of the pulpit; those from the Persian Iraq took their place to the left; the Daylamites and the followers from Rudbar were located immediately in front. In the middle, facing the pulpit, they set up a platform, and the *faqīh* (jurist) Muḥammad-i Bustī received a command to take his place on this platform.
>
> Around noon, the Lord (*khudāwand*) [Ḥasan II] *ʿalā dhikrihi'l-salām*, who had dressed in a white cloak with a white turban, came down from the castle. He approached the pulpit from the right side and climbed its steps slowly and majestically. Three times he expressed his greetings: first to the Daylamites, then a second time, turning to the right, and a third time, turning to the left. For a moment, he remained seated on his heels. Then he stood up, while having his sword hanging diagonally on his shoulder-belt, and read [in Arabic the following proclamation] in a loud voice:
>
> 'Stand, for the Day of Resurrection has risen! From now on the waiting for the signal is fulfilled. This is the rising of the Resurrection (*qiyamat*) which is the culmination of all the Resurrections. Today there is no longer any need to search for proofs or indications; today true knowledge no longer depends on the signs [i.e. the verses of the revealed book], nor words, nor symbols, nor acts of devotion bending the body. Today those acts and words, those signs and symbols, have reached the end of their appointed time. He who with his own eyes has contemplated the essence (*dhāt*) in person has contemplated with his own eye the totality of signs and indications of all the revelations; whereas what he knew of it by means of names and descriptions was outside and the inverse aspect, what was still hidden beneath the veil.
>
> 'O you, you beings who fill the universe! You men and angels know that Mawlānā is the inaugurator of the Resurrection

> (*Qā'im-i qiyāmat*). He is the lord of [all] the beings. He is the lord who is absolute existence (*wujūd-i muṭlaq*), thereby excluding every existential determination, since he transcends them all. He opens the gate of his mercy, and by the light of his knowledge he causes each being to be seeing, hearing, speaking, living for all eternity. It behoves the one knows to praise him and give him thanks, even though he transcends all that, since it is he who in himself is the knowing one by his very essence.'
>
> After that the Imam delivered the first exhortation. Then he read out aloud a copy of the epistle beginning with these words: 'We are that which is always existing in the present. . .' Next he gave the first sermon. Then he sat down for a moment, again stood up and delivered the second sermon. After that, the *faqīh* Muḥammad-i Bustī stood up on his platform, facing the pulpit, and read the translation of these sermons and of the great epistle from beginning to end. Throughout the course of that reading, the grand master himself remained standing. When the reading was finished, he came down from the pulpit and recited the liturgical prayer comprising two successive inclinations (*rakaʿat*) as is the usual practice on the official feast-days.[29]

According to Rashīd al-Dīn, the announcement of the *qiyāma* went as follows:

> On the 17th of Ramaḍān of the year 559 (8 August 559/1164) he (Ḥasan II) ordered the people of these lands, whom he had caused to be present in Alamūt at that time, to gather in those public prayer grounds. They set up four large banners of four colours, white, red, yellow and green, which had been arranged for the affair at the four corners of the minbar.[30]
>
> He [Ḥasan II] mounted the pulpit, which faced the *qibla*, and declared to the comrades that someone had come to him in secret from the leader that is the supposed Imam, who was missing and non-existent,[31] and had brought an address, for their enlightenment, setting forth the doctrines of their faith. From the top of the pulpit he presented a clear and eloquent epistle, and at the end of the address he said, 'The Imam of our time sends you blessings and compassion, calling you his specially selected servants. He has lifted from you the burden of the obligation of the *sharīʿa* and has brought you to the Resurrection [*qiyāma*].' Then he delivered an address in Arabic, such that those there

> became ashamed, alleging that it was the word of the Imam. He had posted someone [the legist Muḥammad Bustī] who knew Arabic at the foot of the pulpit, to translate those words into Persian to those present. The sense of the address was along these lines: 'Ḥasan b. Muḥammad b. Buzurg-Umīd is our representative [Caliph], our *dāʿī*, our *ḥujja*; our Shiʿa must be obedient and submit to him in the affairs of this world and the next, considering his command incontrovertible and knowing his word to be of our word. They must know that our Lord [*mawlānā*] has interceded on their behalf and has brought you to God.' He read an epistle packed full of such words; after its recitation he came down from the pulpit and performed the two prostrations of the festival [*ʿīd*] prayer. Then he set up a table and seated people to break the fast; they made merry and exulted in the manner of the ritual festivals. He said, 'Today is the festival [of the end of the fast — usually held at the end of the month].' Ever after that the *malāḥida* called the 17th of Ramaḍān the festival of the *qiyāma*; upon that they showed their joy with wine and repose, and played and made entertainment openly.[32]

In the above declaration, Ḥasan II is not referred to as the Imam but speaks in the name of the Imam. Furthermore, according to both the *Haft Bāb* and Rashīd al-Dīn, he is known as a *dāʿī*, *ḥujja* and caliph, but not as the Imam. Caliph is coupled with two other titles, *dāʿī* and *ḥujja*, so it refers to the position of the Imam's representative. This meaning of caliph in the *qiyāma* declaration is further confirmed by later Persian sources when Ḥasan II is spoken about as the *nā'ib-i munfarid*, 'the unique deputy' of the Imam.[33]

However, Ḥasan II could have been following the practice of the Fatimids of Egypt. In this sense, by claiming the status of caliph for himself, he also considered himself the Imam. Furthermore, Abū Isḥāq Quhistānī in the *Haft bāb* makes it plain that Ḥasan II remained standing during the announcement of the *qiyāma* which perhaps might indicate his greater role in the concept of the *qiyāma* confirming perhaps the concept of his own imamate.[34] Then again, Juwaynī's account mentioned above, suggests that many of his followers already thought that Ḥasan II was the Imam when Muḥammad b. Buzurg-Umīd was still alive. The theory of imamate was further confirmed by epistles, or *fuṣūl* sent confidentially by Ḥasan II after the *qiyāma* declaration, in which he laid claim to a spiritual imamate in *ḥaqīqa*. In these *fuṣūl* Ḥasan declared that he was the spiritual descendant of Nizār of Egypt, the son of al-Mustanṣir.[35] In the *Haft bāb* of Ḥasan-i Maḥmūd-i Kātib[36] it is stated that Ḥasan II did not completely reveal his imamate therefore, suggesting rather a developing concept of imamate.[37]

Ḥasan II's thoughts about his role are further attested to in a letter held in the Ismaili Special Collections Unit of the Institute of Ismaili Studies in London. Though the authenticity of this document is partly open to question, its contents support the idea of a relatively early origin for his claim to the imamate. In this letter, which was written to a certain Dihkhudā ʿAlī Abū Shujāʿ, commander of the castle of Sar-i Kūshk, Ḥasan II emphasises his own role as an envoy of the Imam: 'Who is more reliable, the messenger from the sultan, or myself [sic] who comes [sic] from the court of *mawlānā* (that is the Imam), and brings you information on infinite grace and eternal life?'[38]

As for later events related to the *qiyāma*, we know that the ceremony of the declaration was repeated approximately two months later, shortly before the start of the *ḥajj*, in Dhu'l-Qaʿda 559/October 1164, at the fortress of Mu'minābād, for the Nizārīs of Quhistān. Ḥasan II himself did not leave Alamūt but sent the *khuṭba*, an epistle and a copy of the declaration he had made in Alamūt, to Ra'īs Muẓaffar, who had been the Nizārī *muḥtasham* (governor) of Quhistān since 555/1160.[39] Ḥasan II's representative reading out the declaration was a certain Muḥammad Khāqān, apparently one of the local Nizārī community. In his message to the Nizārīs of Quhistān, Ḥasan II emphasised the point that just as the Fatimid Imam-caliph al-Mustanṣir (r. 427–487/1036–1094) had been God's *khalīfa* or representative on earth in his time, so now Ḥasan II himself was the *khalīfa* of God. Following this declaration, the local Nizārīs celebrated the event at a sumptuous ceremony, and similarly in Syria the Nizārīs there held lavish ceremonies to celebrate the announcement of the *qiyāma*.[40]

In terms of policy, the foremost factor to influence the announcement of the *qiyāma* may well have been awareness of the decline of the Fatimid caliphate. By announcing the *qiyāma*, and possibly his imamate, indicating a descent from Nizār b. al-Mustanṣir therefore, Ḥasan II claimed leadership of the entire Ismaili community, including those in the Fatimid caliphate now led by the successors to Nizār's younger brother, and sought to strengthen and unite the Ismaili *daʿwa* under his authority.

As regards any link to the Fatimid caliphate, which was on the verge of collapse in 559/1164, the yellow flag was its traditional symbol.[41] Thus the use of the yellow flag at the *qiyāma* may have been symbolic of a claim to supplant, or to have supplanted, what the Nizārīs would have regarded as the illegitimate caliphate in Egypt. Rashīd al-Dīn says that Ḥasan II was entitled to be caliph after the *qiyāma* but by this he could have meant that Ḥasan II aspired to supplant the Abbasid caliphate, something which the Fatimids had always sought to do. The presence of "Irāqī' emissaries at the announcement of the *qiyāma* at Alamūt also suggests the arrival of Ismailis from communities in lands further west.

The other flags (red, white and green) used during the announcement of the *qiyāma* also had important meanings, ones symbolising the millenarian claims of Ḥasan II. The white flag possibly refers to the Nizārī Imams themselves since, according to the *Haft bāb* of Abū Isḥāq Quhistānī, Ḥasan II was dressed entirely in white. The green and red flags can be interpreted possibly as the traditional colours of Islam, and especially Shiʿi Islam.[42] However, as regards the colours, Cortese offers an entirely different explanation of the symbols. Based on ideas put forward by Corbin, she argues these colours have an eschatological message linked to the figures of the archangels. According to a *ḥadīth* found in Abū Jaʿfar Muḥammad Kulaynī's *Kitāb al-Kāfī*, a *ḥadīth* collection of the 4th/10th century, white is the top right column of the Throne of God, representing the world of intelligences as symbolised by the archangel Seraphiel; yellow is in the bottom right, meaning the world of the spirit, as symbolised by Michael; green is top left, referring to the world of the soul, as personified by Azrael; and red in the bottom left is the natural world of God, a symbol of the archangel Gabriel.[43]

Thus, Ḥasan II was seeking to restore the Nizārī Ismaili state from the position of a local kingdom constantly under attack by other local forces, obliged to make major compromises, to a more prominent role in a broader Ismaili and generally Islamic context. The emphasis on a Fatimid genealogy altered Ḥasan's position. By the use of the title caliph, as Daftary explains, 'Ḥasan II was claiming a specific position, one evidently superior to the ranks of *dāʿī* and *ḥujja*. Our Persian historians explain that Ḥasan II claimed to be the Imam's sole vice-regent and deputy (*qā'im maqām va nā'ib-i munfarid*). At Mu'minābād, Ḥasan's status as *khalīfa* was explicitly equated with God's *khalīfa* and identified with the rank held by the Fatimid caliph al-Mustanṣir, who had been the Imam.'[44] Indeed in his subsequent epistles and addresses, Ḥasan claimed the imamate for himself along with the concept of the *qā'im al-qiyāma*[45] a term referring to his own eschatological importance as a descendent of Nizār b. al-Mustanṣir.

Apart from the decline of the Fatimid caliphate, there were other influencing factors. By 559/1164, the collapse of the eastern Saljūq empire of Sanjar, which had been devastated by the Ghuzz tribes, had resulted in tremendous damage to the urban society and the social and religious institutions of Khurāsān.[46] The captivity and death of Sanjar led to the imminent fall of the last real stronghold of the Saljūqs on Iranian soil. Besides this, not only the Eastern Saljūqs but the ʿIrāqī Saljūqs also showed signs of disintegration and their influence was becoming ever more limited until they were finally replaced by the Khwārazmshāhs in 590/1194. During the last fifty years of their state, the ʿIrāqī Saljūqs did not represent any kind of threat to the Nizārīs. In this context, Ḥasan II's declaration of the *qiyāma* can be perceived as a bold step and perhaps an attempt to increase his political standing by reinforcing his position in both the Caspian area and Quhistān (which was nominally ruled by the Saljūqs), since Sanjar's death marked the end of a serious threat from an important polity on the Iranian plateau.

Thus, the decline of the Fatimids and the Saljūqs might also have been seen as an opportunity for a broader Shiʿi Ismaili resurgence to fill the spiritual and political vacuum these two empires had left.

Other more local concerns may have influenced the timing of the announcement, for instance rivalries and hostilities in the Nizārī community in the Daylām, which it may have sought to quell. There were clearly sources of dissent and opposition to Ḥasan II and these came out into the open in 562/1166 when he was killed in the castle of Lamasar. According to Rashīd al-Dīn, the individual who killed him was his brother-in-law, Ḥasan b. Nāmāwar. it appears that Ḥasan b. Nāmāwar came from a branch of the Būyids and represented a local and influential Daylamī clan of Caspian origin, one that presumably had been adherents of Twelver Shiʿism in the past and had converted to Ismailism. The causes of the conflict, however, are not well understood.

The first of these may be simply dynastic. Declaring the *qiyāma* and repeating the ceremony in more distant Ismaili communities in the following months, was a means also of strengthening his position against potential opponents in the local community, including his closest relatives, members of the local Daylamī aristocracy who might have thought him too young, inexperienced and volatile to lead the Nizārīs.

Additionally, Juwaynī hints at the fact that there was a certain sense of frustration and unrest among some Nizārī Ismailis circles in Daylam following the *qiyāma* declaration, and there were Nizārīs who chose to leave Daylam after the declaration.[47]

Any possible revolt was immediately suppressed and Ḥasan b. Nāmāwar and his followers were almost immediately executed. As far as the historicity of Ḥasan b. Nāmāwar is concerned it has proved impossible to identify much about his origins, simply that he was the lord of Lamasar and brother-in-law of Ḥasan II. The name Nāmāwar is not uncommon in the onomastics of medieval Persia and there was the Nāmāwar b. Kay Kāʾūs whose activities in 533/1139 in Gīlān and Rūyān, were discussed above. He was described in the sources as being a pro-Ismaili local prince of the Bādūspānid family. The Bādūspānid lineage of this Nāmāwar was disputed by later chroniclers, but nevertheless it is clear that he managed to gain the support of pro-Ismaili clans in Rūyān after 534/1140. It should be remembered that he built a castle at a place called Sīyāhrūd which he handed over to the Nizārīs.[48]

From Ibn Isfandiyār and Marʿashī we hear about a certain Bīsutūn b. Nāmāwar who was active in Rūyān at around 575/1180, being a Bādūspānid claimant enjoying the military support of the Nizārīs. Bīsutūn may have been another son of the same Nāmāwar who had been the Nizārīs' protégé, although it should be pointed out that Rashīd al-Dīn says all Ḥasan b. Nāmāwar's relatives were put to death immediately after the murder of Ḥasan II.[49]

The role that Ḥasan b. Nāmāwar and his clan played after 559/1164 is somewhat similar to that of the early Būyids and other Daylamī clans who were in the service of Zaydī shaykhs in the second half of the 3rd/9th century or at the beginning of the 4th/10th century. These Daylamī *condottieri* played an essential role in Zaydī successes in Gīlān and Ṭabaristān. However, they later turned away from their Zaydī masters and the surviving Daylamī warlords offered their military services to the Nizārī Ismailis at the beginning of the 6th/12th century.

Returning to the declaration of the *qiyāma*, it can also be seen as a response to a local rival among the enemies of the Nizārīs in the Caspian provinces. Their most formidable and effective local opponent was the Bāwandid kingdom, which routinely attacked Ismaili strongholds in northern Iran in the mid 6th/12th century. Bāwandid power had reached a height under Shāh Ghāzī Rustam and the end of his reign coincided with the declaration of the *qiyāma*. The long-lasting state of conflict with intermittent skirmishing must have disrupted the daily life of the Nizārī communities in the region. Whilst there is no doubt that the declaration of the *qiyāma* was solely an internal Nizārī issue, as far as its roots are concerned the chaos of war over the preceding decades and the apparent failure to challenge the major states of the Iranian plateau can all have fed into Ḥasan II's decision.

Thus the aim of the declaration of the *qiyāma* was to reinforce the spiritual life of the Nizārīs. Bearing in mind that the declaration of the *qiyāma* nearly coincided with the last years of the weakened Fatimid caliphate in Egypt and of the Saljūqs in the Iranian lands as well as with the heaviest Bāwandid anti-Nizārī attacks in Daylamān and around Girdkūh, it had both a universal and local message for non-Caspian and the Caspian Nizārī Ismailis alike.

Few other facts of Ḥasan II's brief reign are recorded. Mustawfī Qazwīnī says that he was known as *Kūra Kiyā*, lord of the villages, among the Qazwīnīs in the local Gīlakī dialect, though without any elaboration.[50] As regards the city of Qazwīn, Ibn al-Athīr says that the Nizārīs built a fortress in the vicinity in 560/1165. However, neither the name nor the precise locality of this new fortress are given in this brief notice.[51]

The local approach of Nūr al-Dīn Muḥammad II (r. 561–607/1166–1210)

Following the deaths of Ḥasan II (561/1166) and Shāh Ghāzī Rustam (560/1165), new rulers appeared on the scene in northern Iran. In Alamūt, the 19-year-old Nūr al-Dīn Muḥammad acceded to the imamate as Muḥammad II, while in Ṭabaristān 'Alā' al-Dawla Sharaf al-Mulūk Ḥasan emerged as the new *iṣfahbad* of the Bāwandid kingdom.

The long reign of Muḥammad II is often termed 'uneventful' in secondary sources. In the primary source material only a few events are mentioned in connection with it. In fact, his era should be understood as the age of the implementation and refinement of the teachings related to the *qiyāma*.[52] Muḥammad II is said to have been a prolific author of various doctrinal treatises and seems to have been an energetic leader. He strengthened the doctrinal fundamentals laid down by his father, putting the concept of the Nizārī imamate at the heart of *qiyāma* teachings.

But even though what the sources say about this reign is very limited, it does include some important events concerning the politics of the period. Assessing the material in the medieval histories, it can be said that there were three main directions for Nizārī activity in the Caspian provinces. The first was participation in the Bādūspānid-Bāwandid wars, which can be seen as a purely local Caspian issue. The second can perhaps be seen as a neighbour-related issue: the relationship of the Nizārīs with the Īldigüzid *atabeg*s of the Jibāl; and last but not least, mention should be made of Nizārī-Khwārazmian contacts, which can be seen as an important macropolitical issue of the period.

Regional issues in the time of Nūr al-Dīn Muḥammad II

As has been noted, the last years of Shāh Ghāzī Rustam's rule saw the emergence of the Bādūspānids in Rūyān in western Ṭabaristān. The Bādūspānids, whose territory was situated between that of the Nizārīs and the Bāwandids, were divided politically and showed much ambiguity regarding whom to support. Undoubtedly, they had their own concerns, and, as we have suggested, the creation of their polity might be attributed to the Saljūqs at the beginning of the 6th/12th century as part of an effort to undermine anti-Saljūq resistance in the region of the Nizārī and Bāwandid states.

The Nizārīs followed these events, and their involvement is undeniable, although as has been stated, there are only limited accounts at our disposal with which to evaluate the role they played in these Bādūspānid-Bāwandid clashes, a deeply regrettable fact since it is quite possible that it was not insignificant. The Bāwandid kingdom was finally crushed at the end of Muḥammad II's reign, and the

Nizārīs, along with the Khwārazmians and the Bādūspānids, played an active part in extirpating the main Iṣfahbadiyya branch of the Bāwandids.

As far as the beginning of these highly complex events is concerned, we know that, at the time of death of Shāh Ghāzī Rustam, the head of the Bādūspānid dynasty was the *ustāndār* Kay Kā'ūs. He received the Bāwandid crown prince, Sharaf al-Mulūk Ḥasan, at his court and it was with his support that Sharaf al-Mulūk Ḥasan returned to Ṭabaristān and killed many of his relatives who had contested his right to the throne. During the reign of Sharaf al-Mulūk Ḥasan (560–568/1165–1173), the influence of Kay Kā'ūs reached its zenith. During this relatively brief period Sharaf al-Mulūk Ḥasan maintained the borders his father had delineated and the wars he waged were of a defensive nature. In 562–563/1167–1168, Sharaf al-Mulūk Ḥasan fought the Īldigüzids, the important Turkic *atabegs* of the Jibāl and Ādharbayjān, who had tried to take Rayy, Simnān and Dāmghān from the Bāwandids. In these battles his old ally and brother-in-law, Sunqur Inānj, lost his life, but Sharaf al-Mulūk Ḥasan defended these rich cities. According to a short piece in the *Qiṣṣa-i Malik-i Sīstān*, a recently discovered Ismaili doctrinal source, the death of Sunqur Inānj is attributed to the Nizārīs, though there is no evidence for this in other sources.[53] But in 567/1172 Sharaf al-Mulūk Ḥasan was less fortunate against Mu'ayyad Ayābā, the new ruler of Khurāsān after the Saljūq collapse, when he attacked Ṭabaristān. Mu'ayyad Ayābā's forces reached the Bāwandid capital Sārī and pillaged it, but Sharaf al-Mulūk Ḥasan was able to flee to Firīm, the ancient homeland of the Bāwandids. Later, he reorganised his troops and defeated Mu'ayyad Ayābā, but before he could consolidate this success he was murdered by his soldiers, according to Ibn Isfandiyār because of his intolerable behaviour.[54] During Sharaf al-Mulūk Ḥasan's reign we are not informed about any Nizārī actions against the Bāwandids and none of our sources mentions their involvement in these wars in Khurāsān.[55]

As for the western neighbours of the Bāwandids, one might surmise that during these years the Bāwandid *iṣfahbad* exerted only nominal overlordship in the Bādūspānid kingdom. The fact that after 568/1173 Kay Kā'ūs was greatly annoyed by the restoration of the Bāwandid administration in Rūyān suggests that he had acted independently between 560/1165 and 568/1173. This may also indicate that concomitantly the pressure on the Nizārīs was lessened during the reign of Sharaf al-Mulūk Ḥasan.

After 568/1173, however, the political climate changed dramatically when Ḥusām al-Dawla Ardashīr I (569–603/1173–1206), the son of Sharaf al-Mulūk Ḥasan, made significant efforts to restore the pre-560/1165 conditions in northern Iran. But his attempts to reinstate direct military and administrative measures met with opposition in the Bādūspānid kingdom. Ḥusām al-Dawla Ardashīr initially confirmed Kay Kāʾūs in his estates, though a while later he reclaimed lands in Rūyān and Daylamān that had been granted to Kay Kāʾūs by Shāh Ghāzī Rustam. For reasons which are unclear, it seems Ḥusām al-Dawla Ardashīr had lost faith in his Bādūspānid vassal and despatched a governor to Rūyān to replace him.

However, Kay Kāʾūs once again avoided a reverse, perhaps due to strong local support. At the end of his life, the experienced Bādūspānid ruler even married the daughter of Ḥusām al-Dawla Ardashīr. Kay Kāʾūs died in 580/1184.[56]

Upon the death of Kay Kāʾūs, however, major changes occurred in Rūyān, a place where Nizārī activity is recorded by the sources. The dynastic situation among the Bādūspānid princes in Rūyān during this period was relatively troubled and in the second half of the 6th/12th century three main branches of the Bādūspānids can be distinguished.

When Kay Kāʾūs died in 580/1184, all three lines of the Bādūspānids vied for power in Rūyān. Shahrnūsh and Nāmāwar were hostile towards the Bāwandids, and in the reign of Shāh Ghāzī Rustam they built up contacts with the Nizārīs, who supported these local figures against the more dangerous Bāwandids. With Nāmāwar, we find strong evidence in some sources for the fact that this same (assumed) Bādūspānid Nāmāwar, who seriously challenged the power of other Bādūspānids in Rūyān, and gave the fortress of Sīyāhrūd to the Nizārīs in around 533/1139. Furthermore, as seen, it is possible that his family was involved in the internal Nizārī clashes of around 559–562/1164–1166. After the death of Kay Kāʾūs, whose only son predeceased him, his grandson Zarrīnkamar was not able to inherit his grandfather's kingdom. Instead, Zarrīnkamar spent his childhood at the Bāwandid court where the new *ustāndār* was Hazārasf, one of the sons of Shahrnūsh.[57]

As mentioned, Hazārasf and his brother Khalīl were excluded from inheriting Rūyān after their father's death. Their whereabouts remain obscure during the long reign of their uncle Kay Kāʾūs. It is not unreasonable however to assume that the two Bādūspānids fled to Nizārī-controlled areas since, upon his accession to power, Hazārasf ended the anti-Nizārī policy of his uncle and, according to Ibn Isfandiyār, made important territorial concessions to them, notably the area between Sakhtsar and Malāt.[58] These events suggest that he had maintained good relations with the Nizārīs before 580/1184, though the details are unknown. Marʿashī's account, too, presents Hazārasf as friendly to the Ismailis:

> Hazārasf became the governor of Rūyān. The noblemen and ordinary people became obedient to him. Before this, Kay Kāʾūs had had antagonisms with the *mulḥid*s every day. Kay Kāʾūs did not dismount from his horse at any time, and in none of his territories did the *mulḥid*s dare to rule. Hazārasf changed this manner, and he sent his envoys to the *mulḥid*s, making peace with them and asking them for their support. He gave them back the majority of his fortresses and spent most of his time drinking wine.[59]

One cannot judge the amount of Nizārī support given to Hazārasf in return. It seems evident that the Nizārīs were his allies but the sources do not contain evidence of any of their actions during Hazārasf's reign. However, any mention of them in the sources is an indication of political instability with which they may or may not have been associated.

The statements in the local histories that Hazārasf had good relations with the Nizārīs should be accepted with some reservations, for instance in Ibn Isfandiyār's account one can discern an element of exaggeration as born of his anti-Nizārī zeal.[60] Not long after Hazārasf's accession to the throne a group of local nobles led by a certain Zarmīwand Mānīwand fled Ruyān for the Bāwandid court and made accusations against Hazārasf there, claiming that he was allied to the Nizārīs. That their accusations were grounded in their own ambitions became clear after the death of Hazārasf, when Zarmīwand Mānīwand revolted against the pro-Bāwandid Zarrīnkamar. However, the Bāwandid, Ḥusām al-Dawla Ardashīr (569–603/1173–1206), remained firm in his support of Zarrīnkamar b. Justān and executed Zarmīwand Mānīwand and his entire family. This later incident somehow weakens the strength of the Bāwandid accusations against Hazārasf and his presumed Nizārī connections, suggesting that pro-Nizārī accusations were occasionally used as a pretext for actions and objectives. Furthermore, one must bear in mind that Hazārasf in fact made overtures to the Bāwandids. For instance, after acceding to the throne, he despatched his brother Khalīl to the Bāwandid court with official greetings.[61]

Thus it can be said, that the concession of fortresses by Hazārasf to the Nizārīs is greatly emphasised in our pro-Bāwandid sources. Ibn Isfandiyār says the Nizāris gained control of a few strategically important castles, which were then overrun by Ḥusām al-Dawla Ardashīr at the instigation of elements in Rūyān opposed to the Nizārīs. These castles were Walīj (perhaps the most important fortress, Ḥusām al-Dawla only captured it on the second assault), Nūr, Najūr, Kalār and Uzbulū.[62] There may of course have been others. However, these five castles were reconquered by the Bāwandids in 582/1186. Although the defenders of these castles are not described as Ismailis, the sources do give a relatively detailed account of the history of the Bāwandid conquests suggesting that this campaign was intended to halt Ismaili expansion in Rūyān.[63] Since Zarrīnkamar, the grandson of Kay Kā'ūs, was still very young, Ḥusām al-Dawla despatched Mubāriz al-Dīn Arjāsf, a Bāwandid relative, to take over Rūyān and expel the rebellious pro-Ismaili forces of Hazārasf.

Ḥusām al-Dawla Ardashīr also revived relations with the local Zaydī elite of Daylamān and he donated the area of Daylamān, presumably those parts which had not been conquered by the Ismailis, to a certain al-Dāʿī ilā'l-Ḥaqq al-Riḍā.[64] This local Zaydī Daylamī ruler, as his name suggests, may have belonged to the same family of Zaydī rulers who had been attached to the Bāwandids both dynastically and politically for nearly a century. As has been shown, this eminent Zaydī family had built up close contacts with the Bāwandids from the time of Ḥusām al-Dawla Shahriyār, and this alliance was regularly renewed during later generations. Under Shāh Ghāzī Rustam, this Zaydī clan became related dynastically with the Bādūspānids, and members of both families played a prominent role in the fight against the enemies of the Bāwandids, including against the Ismailis.[65]

The deposed Bādūspānid Hazārasf fled to the Ismailis and within months, in 582/1186, he reappeared in Daylamān with Nizārī military forces and succeeded in killing al-Dāʿī ilāʾl-Ḥaqq al-Riḍā. At that point, Ḥusām al-Ardashīr himself felt the need to intervene personally, leading a punitive expedition to Rūyān to avenge the death of the Zaydī prince who may, what is more, have been closely related to him. Ḥusām al-Dawla Ardashīr drove Hazārasf and the Nizārīs from Rūyān, and allowed a local pro-Bāwandid nobleman, Hizabr al-Dīn Khūrshīd, to govern the Bādūspānid lands. Hazārasf and his brother now found their way to the court of Ṭughril III, the last Saljūq ruler of Iran. However, Ṭughril III and Ḥusām al-Dawla Ardashīr were on good terms, and the Bādūspānid princes' request for support proved unsuccessful.[66] This was the start of a fugitive adventure which ended some four years later with Hazārasf submitting to Ḥusām al-Dawla, only to be executed by the governor of Rūyān, Hizabr al-Dīn Khūrshīd.[67]

Rūyān became a major battlefield between various local clans in the final decades of the 6th/12th century. There were no less than four clans contending for power: the parties of Hazārasf, Hizabr al-Dīn Khūrshīd, Zarmīwand Mānīwand and Bīsutūn b. Nāmāwar. Besides these, the Bāwandids and, presumably, the Nizārīs also had a significant degree of influence in the province. The fragmentation of power and the constant fighting between these forces over these years helped eliminate any threat of a resurgence of the Bāwandid-Bādūspānid coalition against the Nizārīs that had existed some thirty years earlier. The Nizārī role in Rūyān during the imamate of Nūr al-Dīn Muḥammad II in these times of chaos is only partially understood but their ultimate goal was still the weakening of Bāwandid influence there.[68]

The Bāwandids made serious efforts to pacify Rūyān and to eliminate any challenge to their power. However, their efforts met with fierce resistance from the local forces who were strongly opposed to the establishment of Bāwandid power in Rūyān and Daylamān.[69] It is clear that, in Rūyān, pro-Bāwandid and pro-Nizārī groups continued to fight up until 607/1210, when the Iṣfahbadiyya line of the Bāwandids became extinct. This event stunned contemporaries and paved the way for an openly pro-Nizārī Bādūspānid regime in Rūyān.

As far as the pro-Bāwandid Bādūspānids are concerned, they were now led by the young Zarrīnkamar b. Justān b. Kay Kāʾūs.[70] His leadership may have been only nominal for many years. Ḥusām al-Dawla Ardashīr, feeling that the young Zarrīnkamar would be unable to govern the volatile province of Rūyān, sent another member of his family to exert control over Rūyān in his name. Thus, a Bāwandid prince called Pāshā ʿAlī was entrusted with the education of the young Zarrīnkamar. This cousin of Ḥusām al-Dawla Ardashīr was a nephew of Mubāriz al-Dīn Arjāsf, who was in charge of Rūyān for the Bāwandids after 582/1186, and the Bāwandids now aimed at complete control of Rūyān. They not only extirpated the line of Shahrnūsh but also removed their local supporter, Hizabr al-Dīn Khūrshīd. He had killed Hazārasf without the consent of Ḥusām al-Dawla Ardashīr, thereby arousing some suspicion in the Bāwandid court regarding his trustworthiness.[71]

On the other hand, after the death of the pro-Nizārī Hazārasf there were still members of the Bādūspānid clan who enjoyed the support of the Nizārīs. Since neither Hazārasf nor his brother Khalīl had descendants, the eldest line of the Bādūspānids became extinct upon Hazārasf's death. The anti-Bāwandid groups therefore had to look for another potential Bādūspānid candidate after 582/1186. The Nizārīs and other local anti-Bāwandid circles started supporting an alleged cadet branch of the Bādūspānids, one led by a certain Bīsutūn b. Nāmāwar. He took over leadership of the anti-Bāwandid forces in Rūyān after the execution of Hazārasf b. Shahrnūsh, and at that time he was unanimously accepted as a legitimate Bādūspānid. Of his origins, however, little is known; he was perhaps a son of Nāmāwar b. Kay Kā'ūs, who had attempted to take over control of Rūyān in around 533/1139, and whose Bādūspānid lineage was questionable. This alleged cadet branch of the Bādūspānids played a notable role in the battles in Rūyān after 582/1186.

The second half of Nūr al-Dīn Muḥammad II's reign, between 582/1186 and 607/1210, was therefore marked by intense fighting between pro and anti-Nizārī groups in Rūyān. Using the chronicles of Āmulī and Marʿashī it is possible to reconstruct events though, as ever, some details remain confused, in particular the sequence of events in times of major political strife is not well understood.

The first problem in the chronology is how to fill in the gap between 582/1186 and 596/1200. In 582/1186 Zarrīnkamar was certainly too young to govern Rūyān. The earliest date possible, i.e., when he reached adulthood, would be, as Madelung has calculated, around 596/1200.[72] At that time, Zarrīnkamar may have been eighteen years old and ready to take power in Rūyān. Our sources, however, remain silent about the years between 582 and 596/1186 and 1200. Based on our calculations, we shall try to offer a reconstruction of these fourteen years as follows:

Rūyān was ruled in the name of Zarrīnkamar after 582/1186, and the governor was Pāshā ʿAlī, the Bāwandid prince mentioned earlier. However, somewhere around 586/1190 Pāshā ʿAlī was killed by the Nizārīs, and Bīsutūn b. Nāmāwar invaded Rūyān with the help of the Nizārīs. Therefore, the contradictory statements of Ibn Isfandiyār and Marʿashī might be compatible and reconcilable. According to Ibn Isfandiyār, Bīsutūn b. Nāmāwar preceded Zarrīnkamar b. Justān whereas Marʿashī claims[73] that Zarrīnkamar and his supporters were expelled from Rūyān by the Nizārīs and Bīsutūn b. Nāmāwar. However, if we accept that Zarrīnkamar was only nominally the ruler of Rūyān after 582/1186, as he was indeed too young to have the burden of government on his shoulders, then Bīsutūn b. Nāmāwar must have ousted the supporters of Zarrīnkamar from Rūyān in around 586/1190.[74] The nominal leadership of Zarrīnkamar helps to explain the controversy and *lacunae* in the sources.

Bīsutūn b. Nāmāwar did not retain power for long after the death of Pāshā ʿAlī. Ḥusām al-Dawla Ardashīr again restored Zarrīnkamar's rule in Rūyān. It can be argued that this Bāwandid interference could have taken place around 596/1200, when the young Zarrīnkamar was already able to participate personally in a campaign and join the forces of Ḥusām al-Dawla Ardashīr. At any event, according to the brief accounts by Āmulī and Marʿashī, Bīsutūn b. Nāmāwar was ousted from Rūyān and took shelter among the Nizārīs at Kharraqān, near Qazwīn. In Kharraqān local Nizārīs seized the opportunity to contact Ḥusām al-Dawla Ardashīr. According to Āmulī and Marʿashī, the Nizārīs of Kharraqān were ready to extradite Bīsutūn b. Nāmāwar to the Bāwandids in exchange for an area called Qirya Harjān, presumably a village or settlement of some kind. If it is the same as modern Harījān, then it lay at a high point on a route between Rayy and the Caspian sea to the east of Alamūt and represented an important extension of the lands the Nizārīs controlled. Yet, perhaps unsurprisingly in light of the above, Ḥusām al-Dawla Ardashīr rejected their offer, denouncing the lowly origins of Bīsutūn b. Nāmāwar and hinting at his dubious Bādūspānid lineage; after this episode no more is heard of Bīsutūn b. Nāmāwar.[75]

After the end of the Bāwandid dynasty in 607/1210 there are interesting passages in Āmulī's history where the author laments their downfall, perhaps echoing the views of Zarrīnkamar's court in Rūyān.[76] According to both Āmulī and Marʿashī, Zarrīnkamar ruled until 610-11/1213-14. Thus he survived the lapse of Bāwandid power in Ṭabaristān in 607/1210. Material concerning Zarrīnkamar's rule is, over all, very sketchy. Though he withstood the Nizārīs and relied heavily on the Bāwandids, the general decline of the Bāwandids after 590/1194 had a deleterious effect on his kingdom with the effect that around 605/1209, he was obliged to concede significant areas of Rūyān to the Nizārīs.

The influence of the Nizārīs was thus further strengthened by the fall of the Bāwandids, their main enemies. Though the Bādūspānids remained independent, Zarrīnkamar's successors, perhaps even Zarrīnkamar himself in his later years, had to accept the suzerainty of the Nizārīs. Thus the fall of the Bāwandids was a momentous event in the history of the Nizārī Ismaili state in northern Iran. Even though it was not entirely due to the Nizārīs, the long reign of Nūr al-Dīn Muḥammad II had ended with the complete elimination of their most feared enemy. The state of affairs in northern Iran after the fall of the Bāwandids (607/1210) and before the appearance of the Mongols gave unprecedented space and influence to the Nizārīs. They had managed to outlast all the local kingdoms and their state had achieved a greater degree of eminence in northern Iran. All this occurred during a period when they had apparently withdrawn from the wider world and had taken refuge in the ultimate reality of the *qiyāma*. Clearly, any understanding of the effect of the declaration of Ḥasan II *alāʾ dhikrihiʾl-salām* is a complex and varied matter.

The Nizārīs and Bāwandids in the reign of Nūr al-Dīn Muḥammad II — the last decades of a long conflict

The Bāwandid dynasty remained a significant power during the reign of Ḥusām al-Dawla Ardashīr, although their influence and efficacy had declined from that of Shāh Ghāzī Rustam's era. There is no record of concerted attacks against Alamūt or other core areas of the Nizārī Ismaili state, but before 601/1205 the Bāwandids still were able to exert their control over areas adjacent to Nizārī lands. Ḥusām al-Dawla Ardashīr's efforts to reinstate control over fortresses acquired by the Nizārīs in Rūyān were relatively successful, and he was able to strengthen Bāwandid suzerainty up until the last decade of his life. However, after 590/1194 there occurred enormous changes in the history of northern Iran which led to decisive steps being taken in Nizārī policy. Due to the paucity of the material in the local sources we have to look at those sources which deal with the major events in north-eastern Iran in the last decade of the 6th/12th century.

Undoubtedly, the most significant of these was the destruction of the last Saljūq state in Iran by the Khwārazmshāhs which occurred 590/1194. This event had enormous consequences both in the imperial policy of the major powers of the time as well as at a local level. Northern Iran and the Caspian provinces now fell under the shadow of the expansionist Khwārazmshāhs who proceeded westwards with much speed. This Central Asian Turkic dynasty aimed at filling the political and geographical vacuum left by the Saljūqs and successor polities.

Nizārī-Khwārazmian connections before 596/1200 are not well understood owing to the limited number of relevant sources. But, as has been demonstrated, the Nizārīs always supported a strong power in the east to counter that of the Bāwandids. Regrettably, the years of Nūr al-Dīn Muḥammad II's reign are sparsely documented, Juwaynī and Rashīd al-Dīn providing only scant details. Other chronicles of the period, such as Ibn al-Athīr's, as well as the historiography of Ṭabaristān, are of more use, albeit they are not always reliable.

As far as political events in northern Iran are concerned, the years before and after 590/1194 are significantly different. The major difference between Sanjar's era and that of the early Khwārazmshāhs is that Sanjar represented a slowly declining power, while the Khwārazmshāhs constituted a rapidly emerging, new and powerful kingdom. The difference in imperial dynamics between the last Saljūqs and early Khwārazmians was decisive in the elimination of the Bāwandids.[77]

At the beginning of this new period, and until 567/1172, relations with the Khwārazmshāhs as well as Bāwandid acquisitions in western Khurāsān remained largely intact.

The new *iṣfahbad*, Ḥusām al-Dawla Ardashīr formed an alliance with the new Khwārazmshāh, ʿAlāʾ al-Dīn Tikish, whose two-year-old daughter was betrothed him.

However, subsequent years saw a worsening of Bāwandid-Khwārazmian relations. In the end, Ḥusām al-Dawla Ardashīr decided to join the powers opposed to Khwārazmian expansion, the last of the Iranian Saljūqs, Ṭughril III, the Abbasid caliph, al-Nāṣir li-Dīn Allāh and the Īldigüzid *atabeg* in Ādharbayjān, Muḥammad Pahlawān.[78]

Yet the Khwārazmshāhs proved to be unstoppable in their expansion into northern and western Iran and for four years from 586 to 590/1190 to 1194 fought successfully against the Saljūqs and Bāwandids.[79] In 590/1194, Ṭughril III lost his life in a decisive battle against the Khwārazmshāh, thus ending the history of the Iranian Saljūqs. After this disaster, the Bāwandid *iṣfahbad* decided to surrender to the Khwārazmshāh, promising to send him military aid once again. But the Khwārazmshāh, who suspected that the Bāwandid ruler had been the mastermind of the anti-Khwārazmian coalition, rejected Ḥusām al-Dawla Ardashīr's request for reconciliation. Instead, Khwārazmian forces marched into Ṭabaristān, as far as Sārī, pillaging the Bāwandid capital and occupying areas east of Tamīsha, thus causing the Bāwandids further territorial losses.

In 595/1199, ʿAlāʾ al-Dīn Tikish led another military campaign against Ṭabaristān, capturing key fortresses such as Fīrūzkūh, Ustunāwand and Fulāl, and the cities of Sārī and Āmul; and he also took hostage Sharaf al-Mulūk Ḥasan, the eldest son of Ḥusām al-Dawla Ardashīr. The area of Fīrūzkūh was a major loss for the Bāwandids since, as recounted earlier,[80] it was the site of a victory in 552/1157 before which it had been owned by the Nizārīs, who had controlled the area north of Rayy from this fortress.[81]

The Bāwandid kingdom was thus on the verge of total collapse and only the sudden death in 596/1200 Khwārazmshāh ʿAlāʾ al-Dīn Tikish prevented it. Following this unexpected event, Ḥusām al-Dawla Ardashīr was able to rally himself and defeat some of the Khwārazmian forces as they withdrew and restore his suzerainty over much of the provinces they had conquered, retaking Dāmghān, Fīrūzkūh, Fulāl and Ustunāwand.

The ageing Ḥusām al-Dawla Ardashīr was aware that his kingdom had little chance of surviving without acquiring notable allies against the new Khwārazmshāh, ʿAlāʾ al-Dīn Muḥammad. In 601/1204 the Ghūrids, a dynasty whose capital lay at Ghūr in the mountains of central Afghanistan, sent an envoy to the Bāwandid court for negotiations about an alliance against the Khwārazmshāh. The Ghūrid sultan, Shihāb al-Dīn (r. 598–602/1202–1206), did in fact attack the Khwārazmshāh in 601/1205 but suffered a humiliating defeat. Shihāb al-Dīn himself was said to have been killed by the Nizārīs of Qūhistān whom he had also attacked around this time. According to al-Nasawī and Juzjānī, contemporaries of these events, the Nizārīs of Qūhistān had sought to please the Khwārazmshāh by killing the Ghūrid sultan.[82] Not long after these events, Ḥusām al-Dawla Ardashīr died and his two surviving sons, Shams al-Mulūk Shāh Ghāzī Rustam (Shāh Ghāzī Rustam II) and Rukn al-Dawla Qārin, immediately clashed over control of Ṭabaristān. This internecine conflict precipitated the fall of the already mutilated Bāwandid state because it led to further territorial division. Regrettably, the accounts in the Caspian sources about the last years of the Iṣfahbadiyya branch of the Bāwandids are sparce, so not all details can be studied properly.[83]

The final years of the Iṣfahbadiyya Bāwandids are thus seen as ones of increasing chaos. In 605/1208, another Khwārazmian military expedition pillaged Ṭabaristān, when ʿAlāʾ al-Dīn Muḥammad sought to punish Shāh Ghāzī Rustam II for supporting ʿAlī Shāh, ʿAlāʾ al-Dīn's rebellious brother. The Khwārazmian forces occupied a great deal of the Bāwandid kingdom, and the provinces east of Tamīsha came under direct Khwārazmian control from then on.

Marʿashī says that after the division of power between the sons of Ḥusām al-Dawla Ardashīr the Nizārīs became active, and so they may have conquered former Bāwandid areas and have killed Rukn al-Dawla Qārin. It is not known where and how this happened or what areas the Nizārīs occupied but, based on parallels from Ḥusām al-Dawla Ardashīr's time, one can assume that this all concerned control of Rūyān.[84] Backed by the Khwārazmshāhs, Rukn al-Dawla had acquired areas of western Ṭabaristān, which may well have included Rūyān. The Nizārīs probably reconquered the same fortresses in Rūyān that they had held temporarily in the early years of Ḥusām al-Dawla Ardashīr's reign.

It is also known that Nizārīs had already clashed with Khwārazmians in northern Iran in 601/1205, which means that the Khwārazmshāhs had already replaced the Bāwandids in some parts of northern Iran after the death of Ḥusām al-Dawla Ardashīr.[85] Perhaps it was Rukn al-Dawla Qārin who acted as a Khwārazmian officer, commanding both local and Khwārazmian forces in Rūyān and in western Ṭabaristān. Sadly, though, details of his biography are not recorded in any of sources.

After the death of Rukn al-Dawla Qārin, the Iṣfahbadiyya line had only one male member living, Shāh Ghāzī Rustam II; yet he had no opportunity to restore his power since a year later he was also killed. It is conceivable that Shāh Ghāzī Rustam II was involved in the killing of his brother, and that later the pro-Bāwandid sources simply blamed the Nizārīs. The fact that he himself was also killed only a year after Rukn al-Dawla Qārin's death raises possibility that he was involved in a plot to kill his brother. According to Ibn Isfandiyār and Marʿashī Shāh Ghāzī Rustam II's murderer was a Zaydī aristocrat, Abū Riḍā Ḥusayn b. Muḥammad Abu'l-ʿAlawī al-Māmṭīrī.[86]

After the death of Shāh Ghāzī Rustam II, the Khwārazm-shāh incorporated Ṭabaristān into his realm. The anti-Khwārazmian revolts and military coalitions organised by Ḥusām al-Dawla Ardashīr and Shāh Ghāzī Rustam II had led to the complete elimination of the Iṣfahbadiyya branch of the dynasty.

Yet the Bāwandids did not disappear from the scene; the situation was now perhaps similar to that in the early 5th/11th century when different Bāwandid cadet branches claimed the kingdom. Various Bāwandid families continued to live in and maybe govern parts of Ṭabaristān under Khwārazmian suzerainty even after 607/1210. Then the fall of the Khwārazmshāhs to the Mongols opened the way to a third Bāwandid restoration, that of the Kīnkhwāriyya branch, albeit on a limited scale, after 638/1240.[87]

The Nizārī Ismaili state undoubtedly looked positively on the disintegration of its most formidable local enemy. As we have seen, there were earlier periods when the two states allied themselves against the Saljūqs, but from the time of Shāh Ghāzī Rustam, when the Bāwandids attempted to expand their kingdom and build a greater state in northern Iran on the ruins of the declining Saljūq empire, there were no more such alliances with the Nizārīs. Instead, their ruthless attacks caused significant damage and setbacks for the Nizārīs, who were obliged to seek out new allies against them. Yet, in immediate terms, it was the Khwārazmshāh who benefitted from the end of the Bāwandid kingdom since alongside territorial gains, one of the main obstacles standing in the way of westward expansion had disappeared.

Ḥasan-i Maḥmūd-i Kātib and the *Dīwān-i Qā'imiyyāt*

As noted, our knowledge of the events of Nūr al-Dīn Muḥammad II's reign is inadequate due to a lack of anything but the slightest of source material. However, mention must be made of a poem written by Ḥasan-i Maḥmūd-i Kātib,[88] an influential intellectual figure in the last decades of the Nizārī Ismaili state. Ḥasan-i Maḥmūd-i Kātib was a Nizārī Ismaili writer of the first half of the 7th/13th century and two important works, the *Haft bāb*[89] and the *Dīwān-i Qā'imiyyāt*, are ascribed to him. His authorship of the *Haft bāb* may not be in doubt but not all the poems in the *Dīwān* can be regarded as by him, as later additions were made over the subsequent centuries. Ḥasan-i Maḥmūd-i Kātib is mentioned several times in different medieval sources. His name occurs in various forms such as Jalāl al-Dīn Ḥasan,[90] Malik al-Kuttāb Ṣalāh al-Dīn Ḥasan,[91] Ra'īs Ḥasan-i Ṣalāḥ-i Munshī[92] and Ḥasan-i Ṣalāh-i Bīrjandī.[93] He was born in Quhistān, but the exact date of his birth is unknown, although he was already a mature individual around 596/1200 when he completed the *Haft bāb*. At that time, he could have been in the service of the Nizārī Ismaili *muḥtasham* (governor) of Quhistān, Shihāb al-Dīn. After 615 or 619/1218 or 1222 he moved to the fortress of Girdkūh perhaps as a consequence of the Mongol invasion of Iran, when he was still secretary to the *muḥtasham* of Quhistān. Ḥasan-i Maḥmūd-i Kātib arrived at Alamūt in 634/1237 in the company of Naṣīr al-Dīn al-Ṭūsī, the great polymath of 7th/13th century Iran, who was currently working for the Nizārīs. The last precise date regarding Ḥasan is a Tuesday, 15 Shawwāl 640/7 April 1243 when al-Ṭūsī refers to him in the *Rawḍat al-taslīm*,[94] though he was perhaps still alive as late as 647/1250.

As for the *Dīwān-i Qā'imiyyāt*, the core of the poems in it were composed by Ḥasan-i Maḥmūd-i Kātib before 641/1243, in a period when the doctrinal importance of the declaration of the *qiyāma* was reinstated after nearly three decades of reconciliatory politics by

Ḥasan III towards the Sunni world, a period considered by the Ismailis as a time of observing *taqiyya*.[95] The *Dīwān-i Qā'imiyyāt* includes poems by several authors, but it was Ḥasan-i Maḥmūd-i Kātib who composed or edited most of the *qaṣā'id*. The bulk of the work praises the 559/1164 declaration of the *qiyāma*. However, apparent historical fact can occasionally be found in some of these poems, often blended with eschatological and doctrinal elements. Regarding the reign of Nūr al-Dīn Muḥammad II, in *qaṣīda* no. 75, there are references to three Khurāsānī *fidā'īs* killing the Īldigüzid Muẓaffar al-Dīn Qızıl Arslān, in 587/1191. This *qaṣīda* was published in 1938 by Wladimir Ivanow. In the introduction to the recently published edition of the *Dīwān*, Jalal Badakhchani attributes its authorship to Ḥasan-i Maḥmūd-i Kātib saying that the poem was written in November 637/1234.[96] Muḥammad Shafī'ī-Kadkānī in the Persian foreword of the *Dīwān-i Qā'imiyyāt* argues that authorship of *qaṣīda* 75 cannot be readily resolved.[97]

As regards importance, the *qaṣīda* appears to be an unusual piece of work since it is a rare source on the *fidā'īs* from a Nizārī point of view. Anti-Nizārī sources regularly use a pejorative characterisation of the Nizārī *fidā'īs*, and there is almost nothing that elucidates the Nizārī view of this subject.

The *qaṣīda* is structured in four main parts. The first stanzas lionise the three heroes for their bravery, while the second part contains descriptions of the attack on the Ildigüzid, whose arrogance, the poem says, had greatly offended the Lord of Alamūt. This is followed by passages again praising the three *fidā'īs* along with the Nizārī Ismaili Imām-Qā'im; and the poem concludes with self-reflection along with an apocalyptic message and a call for repentance.

The Īldigüzids were a dynasty in north-western Iran which rose to power in the mid 6th/12th century and ruled in northern Iran for ninety years between 529/1135 and 622/1225. As in the case of many post-Saljūq kingdoms, Shams al-Dīn Īldigüz, the first ruler of the dynasty, was the *atabeg*, or guardian, of a minor Saljūq prince. By the end of the 6th/12th century his successors controlled much of Ādharbāyjān.[98]

Ibn Isfandiyār[99] also refers to the alleged '*mulḥid*' killers of the Īldigüzid ruler. Although it has been established that it was customary in the 6th/12th century to accuse the Nizārīs of killing prominent persons and these accusations were often entirely unfounded the actual cause or perpetrators of death being quite different, in this instance it appears this was not the case.[100]

From our point of view, one needs to understand the actual reasons for Nizārī participation in a plot against Qızıl Arslān. Before 582/1186 Qizil Arslān was the ruler of the north-western regions of the Īldigūzid state and, as governor of Ardabīl, his influence reached as far as Gīlān, which meant he could have been able to do some harm to the Nizārīs. At the height of their influence, the Īldigüzids perhaps had intentions to invade Gīlān or to control the area north of Qazwīn. We have demonstrated previously that the first Īldigüzid ruler had shown a strong interest in controlling the areas of Dāmghān, Rayy and Qazwīn in the last years of Shāh Ghāzī Rustam's reign.[101] This policy led to a military confrontation between Sunqur Inānj, the Bāwandid governor of Rayy, and the Īldigüzids.

The Īldigüzids made a second attempt to capture these wealthy cities from the Bāwandids in around 562–563/1167–1168, but the Bāwandid ruler, Sharaf al-Mulūk Ḥasan, made successful efforts to defend them. In this second Īldigüzid-Bāwandid conflict, Sunqur Inānj lost his life. A third Īldigüzid attempt to interfere in the affairs of northern Iran was led by Sirāj al-Dīn Qaymāz, the Īldigüzid governor of Rayy in 582/1186, when he endeavoured to give military support to the expelled Bādūspānid ruler, Hazārasf b. Shahrnūsh, against his pro-Bāwandid rivals. This also meant that Rayy was firmly in the hands of the Īldigüzids by 582/1186. Thus the Īldigüzids were now in areas close to those around Rayy and Qazwīn controlled by the Nizārīs in around 582/1186.[102] Although the Īldigüzids supported the same Bādūspānid, Hazārasf b. Shahrnūsh, who also enjoyed the sympathy of the Nizārīs, this does not point to any obvious friendship between the Nizārīs and the Īldigüzids. The growing influence and active military presence of the Īldigüzids was established sufficiently to be considered dangerous by the Nizārīs.

Qızıl Arslān was killed soon after he officially took over the title of sultan and at the same time imprisoned Ṭughril III, the last Saljūq ruler in Iran. Furthermore, Qızıl Arslān preferred the Khwārazmshāhs over the Saljūqs as his natural allies, perhaps because the Saljūqs were on his doorstep and the Khwārazmshāhs were not.[103] The Nizārīs, seeing the reinvigorated position of the ambitious Īldigüzid ruler, may have decided to eliminate this menace following their tried and tested tactic of supporting the weaker political group (in this case the Saljūqs) against the mightier. If this happened, this may be a clue to the otherwise lesser-known Nizārī attitude towards the Khwārazmshāhs before 601/1205, supporting the Saljūq-Bāwandid coalition against the expansion of the Khwārazmshāhs; thus by eliminating Qızıl Arslān, they could remove a key Khwārazmian ally in western Iran and give support to the foes of the Khwārazmshāhs. Another consequence of the murder of Qızıl Arslān was the swift disintegration of the Īldigüzid amirate between three rival princes Abū Bakr, Qutluq Inānj and Amīr-i Amīrān. The weakened Īldigüzid state, where these princes were fighting for power, was hardly in a position to harass Nizārī areas.

However, there does not seem to have been any enduring hostility between the Nizārīs and the Īldigüzids, something that is reinforced by the fact that, after Nūr al-Dīn Muḥammad, the new Imam, Jalāl al-Dīn Ḥasan III (r. 607–618/1210–1221), built up relations with them and supported the Īldigüzid amīr against two rebel governors, Mingli and Īlghamīsh. During the military campaign against Minglī, in 611–612/1214–1215 Jalāl al-Dīn Ḥasan himself appeared with his soldiery in northern ʿIrāq and spent over a year away from Alamūt. It is also reported that in 614/1217 Jalāl al-Dīn Ḥasan despatched *fidāʾī*s to kill Īlghamīsh at the bequest of the Abbasid caliph al-Nāṣir but although the sources mention this event, the details are not specified.

Chapter 6

The Last Decades of the Nizārī Ismaili State

After 586/1190 the empire of the Khwārazmshāhs became the most significant political power in the Iranian world until its destruction by the Mongols in 616–617/1219–1220. Khwārazmian expansion was rapid and seemed to be unstoppable. Instead of imposing vassal statehood on the principalities and polities they conquered, the Khwārazmshāhs tended to introduce direct administration. For example, after the death of Shāh Ghāzī Rustam II and the end of the Iṣfahbadiyya line of the Bāwandids, the Khwārazmshāh ʿAlāʾ al-Dīn Muḥammad did not aim to restore the Bāwandids by supporting one of its cadet branches; rather, he despatched his own governors to rule Ṭabaristān.

The areas around Girdkūh as well as Rūyān ruled by the Bādūspānids (who, unlike the Bāwandids, managed to retain a certain amount of autonomy and continuity even under the Khwārazmshāhs) came under direct Khwārazmian control possibly as early as 601/1205, after the death of Bāwandid ruler Ḥusām al-Dawla Ardashīr, or may be later in 607/1210. Khwārazmian governors were also despatched to more western areas around Qazwīn. At any rate, by 601–606/1205–1210 the Khwārazmshāhs had taken over nearly all the Nizārī-controlled areas in the Caspian provinces except for those in western and northern Gīlān.

Documents before 601/1205 relating to Nizārī-Khwārazmian relations are extremely rare; our sources do not mention the Nizārī attitude towards the expansion of the Khwārazmshāhs' power. However, there is no doubt that the Nizārīs were well informed of the wider political situation and even of the slightest political changes in their region. It is possible that the Nizārīs had been in touch with the Khwārazmshāhs, given the Nizārī tactic of supporting the enemies of their enemies. Considering that the Bāwandids had been the main rivals and opponents of the Nizārīs for decades and that the Khwārazmshāhs strongly opposed the Bāwandid ambition of building up a northern Iranian empire there seems little doubt that the Nizārīs would not have opposed the Khwārazmshāhs in their anti-Bāwandid policy.

However, the only episode known to us relating to Nizārī-Khwārazmian relations before 601/1205 slightly contradicts the idea of a pro-Khwārazmian attitude on the part of the Nizārīs, found in a single source, the *Āthār al-bilād* of Zakariyā᾽ al-Qazwīnī which mentions a skirmish between them. According to Zakariyā᾽ in 595/1199 the Nizārīs seized a fortress near Qazwīn called Arslān Qushād. The efforts of the Qazwīnīs to regain this strategic point proved fruitless, so a local Sunni shaykh, ʿAlī al-Yūnānī, invited ʿAlā᾽ al-Dīn Tikish to oust the Nizārīs from Arslān Qushād.

Upon the arrival of the Khwārazmians, the Nizārīs abandoned the fortress. However, they soon returned using a secret route into the fortress and reoccupied it. ʿAlī al-Yūnānī sent a second letter to ʿAlā᾽ al-Dīn Tikish, and, according to the *Āthār al-bilād*, he reappeared with his armies before the walls of the fortress. The Nizārīs, realising that he was stronger than them, soon came to an agreement with him, asking for safe passage in order to withdraw their forces in two phases. The Khwārazmshāh accepted these conditions and the first group of Nizārīs left the fortress. Later, it turned out that the fortress was empty, meaning that all the Nizārīs had departed with the first group. The Khwārazmians then razed the fortress to the ground.[1]

Then in 601/1205, according to al-Rāwandī, a powerful and influential Khwārazmian amīr called Mīyājīq, presumably a Central Asian nomad given his name, pillaged Nizārī areas north of Qazwīn not long after his arrival in Rūdbār.[2]

Amīr Mīyājīq had been appointed as a governor in northern Iran, but his independent attitude aroused the anger of Tikish's successor, ʿAlā᾽ al-Dīn Muḥammad. Al-Rāwandī says[3] that Mīyājīq lost the support of ʿAlā᾽ al-Dīn Muḥammad and fled to the Nizārīs. Apparently, his involvement in the Jibāl with the Īldigüzids had made him the object of suspicion. Al-Rāwandī says that on arriving in Rūdbār (the exact place is not known), Mīyājīq explained that he could not return to Khwārazm and that he was being threatened by Uzbak, the Īldigüzid ruler in Ādharbayjān. At first, he was able to ingratiate himself with the Nizārīs and he received the lordship of a few villages and some provisions from them. Al-Rāwandī says that the Nizārīs 'ate' (*bikhūrdand*) his words, suggesting that his story was less than truthful.[4]

It is not clear why Mīyājīq attacked his hosts but not long after he left Rūdbār and returned to Khwārazm, where he was swiftly arrested. His supporters, presumably in the region, were killed by *fidā'īs*, according to al-Rāwandī at the instigation of 'Alā' al-Dīn Muḥammad, although the details of this event and the role of the *fidā'īs* in it are unclear. Perhaps in 601/1205 when the Bāwandid kingdom was still in existence, the Nizārīs found it more important to maintain good relations with the Khwārazmshāh, than to support a rebellious Khwārazmian amīr. Parallels with the accounts about other figures who sought asylum among the Nizārīs in previous decades can be seen in the career of Mīyājīq.

This pro-Khwārazmian policy slowly began to change around 601/1205 after the fall of the Bāwandids, when the Nizārīs in Daylamān felt a need to seek a new counterbalance against the growing power of the Khwārazmshāh.

In 600/1204, the Ghūrid, Shihāb al-Dīn, sent an envoy to the Bāwandid court at the end of the war that the Bāwandids had waged against the Khwārazmshāhs. The purpose of the Ghūrid envoys was to undermine the authority of the Khwārazmshāh on the Iranian plateau. A similar anti-Khwārazmian alliance, as a common political goal, may have been a possible motive for the increased number of visits between the Nizārī communities of Alamūt and Quhistān, including that of Ḥasan-i Maḥmūd-i Kātib, or Rā'is Ḥasan, to Alamūt. It is possible here that the Quhistānī Nizārīs were acting as mediators between the Ghūrids and Nūr al-Dīn Muḥammad.

Perhaps it was the fact that Ghūrids also sought out the Bāwandids that induced the Nizārīs to build up comparable relations with them. According to Jūzjānī, Nizārī *dā'īs* arrived in Ghūr at the request of the Ghūrid rulers.[5] It seems unlikely that Ghūrid rulers wished to become Ismaili, so this invitation should be seen in the light of countering the threat the Khwāramshāhs posed to both the Ghūrids and the Nizārīs.

The reign of Jalāl al-Dīn Ḥasan III lasted for just over a decade between 607/1210 and 618/1221 and he is credited with achieving a rapprochement with Sunni Muslim rulers and, for this, according to Sunni sources, he was awarded the title Naw-Musalmān.[6] Indeed, his efforts to gain wider acceptance in the Islamic world, and especially from the Abbasid caliph, were remarkably successful. Jalāl al-Dīn Ḥasan III was a significant and talented leader who did his utmost to reposition the Nizārī Ismaili state both internationally and locally.

The Nizārīs were extremely flexible in their local and regional policies, usually making agreements with every possible local polity or dynasty which could serve their interests. Thus, we see Nizārī-Twelver Shiʿi, Nizārī-Sunni and Nizārī-Zaydī alliances, which fluctuated according to the needs of the Nizārī state.

Jalal-al-Dīn Ḥasan's rapprochement with the Abbasids and Sunni Islam is another part of this pragmatism; but there were also exceptions to this during his reign. His decision was widely publicised in the Sunni world by both contemporary and later Sunni chroniclers.[7] Unlike the dealings of his predecessors with various local and major powers which are either neglected or suppressed in most medieval sources, the decision of Jalāl al-Dīn Ḥasan III to acknowledge the Abbasid caliphate is generally recorded.

The increasing isolation of the community has been convincingly presented as a possible reason for Ḥasan III's decision to accept, at least nominally, Sunni Islam.[8] It has been has pointed out that Ḥasan III was perhaps the most versatile Nizārī ruler, one who did not hesitate to create a coalition with any possible partner who might serve his interests.[9] Thus, his followers regarded his 'new' policy simply as another instance of *taqiyya*.

As for the Khwārazmshāhs, it should be noted that Juwaynī,[10] who occasionally praises Ḥasan III for his turn towards Sunni Islam, also says that at the beginning of his reign he sent envoys to Gurgānj and had the *khuṭba* recited in the name of the Khwārazmshāhs. Al-Nasawī[11] records that later, they reproached Ḥasan III's successor for abandoning the custom of reciting the *khuṭba* in the name of the Khwārazmshāh and ʿAlāʾ al-Dīn Khwārazmshāh demanded it be reinstated as a precondition for establishing relations once again.[12]

While Ḥasan III could make overtures to the Khwārazmshāhs, in reality he had clearly allied himself with the Abbasids. According to Juwaynī, Ḥasan III sent secret envoys to Nizārī communities living under Khwārazmian rule in Central Asia as early as 616/1219 to warn them of the arrival of the Mongol army.[13] And it was Ḥasan III who was the first Muslim ruler to send ambassadors to Chingiz Khān in Jumādā I 616/August1219 when the Mongols crossed the Oxus river.[14] These two reports demonstrate the flexibility of Nizārī policy under Ḥasan III.

The caliph al-Nāṣir li-Dīn Allāh (r. 596–622/1200–1225) was as ready to acknowledge this novel rapprochement as was Ḥasan III. Al-Nāṣir had supported and developed the *futuwwa* movement, a series of Sufi-based brotherhoods, as a means of restoring the authority of the Abbasid caliphate which was flexible in avoiding specific adherence to any school of Islam.[15] His construction of the Talisman Gate in Baghdad with its inscription referring to *al-daʿwa al-hādīya* displays a possible Shiʿi influence or at least an appropriation of some Shiʿi terminology and concepts.[16] The influence over the caliph of Shihāb al-Dīn al-Suhrāwardī, a leading mystic of the age, who was apparently attracted to elements of Ismaili thought,[17] has also been cited as an element in this rapprochement. Al-Suhrāwardī was accused of adherence to Ismailism by ʿAlāʾ al-Dīn Muḥammad when he was sent as an envoy to the Khwārazmian camp in Hamadān in 615/1218.[18] However, accusations of adherence to Ismailism were quite widespread before the Mongol period as a means of denigrating individuals or communities.[19]

Abbasid-Nizārī cooperation thus quickly evolved into a relatively strong anti-Khwārazmian military and political coalition. Ḥasan III, as an ally of al-Nāṣir, acted relatively freely, with the blessing of the Abbasids.[20] Within the framework of this cooperation, Ḥasan III and al-Nāṣir intervened in support of the last Īldigüzid ruler, Muẓaffar al-Dīn Uzbak (r. 607–622/1210–1225), the ruler of Ādharbayjān and northern ʿIrāq, when Minglī, the Īldigüzid governor of northern ʿIrāq and western Iran, rebelled against his overlord. In an exceptional military venture organised by al-Nāṣir, forces from Baghdad, Syria and Alamūt joined against the rebellious Minglī, who suffered a humiliating defeat. The expedition lasted two years from 610 to 612/1214 to 1215. During this time, Ḥasan III left Alamūt and enjoyed the hospitality of Muẓaffar al-Dīn Uzbak. The decisive battle of this campaign was fought near Hamadān in 612/1215 when the alliance defeated Mingli.[21] Following this Hasan III was rewarded with the cities of Abhar and Zanjān in the south of the Alburz for his military services. Rashīd al-Dīn says that Abhar, a former Sunni and pro-Saljūq stronghold, as well as Zanjān, remained in Nizārī possession for a few years under Ḥasan III, perhaps implying that these were probably lost to the Nizārīs before the end of Ḥasan III's reign in 618/1221.[22] But nonetheless, the Nizārī acquisition of these two cities was of importance both in terms of the economy and of strategy. The Nizārī Ismaili state already possessed important sites and locations around Dāmghān and Bisṭām, and it could have derived revenue from taxes levied on merchants and caravans along northern Iranian trade routes. During Sanjar's reign in Khurāsān there had also been economic agreements between the Nizārīs and Sanjar about the division of revenue most importantly from *kharāj*, land tax, which indicates a settled ordered state, or at the very least an aspiration to such.[23] From this point of view the Nizārī acquisition of Abhar and Zanjān was a logical step as regards a broadening of the region for revenues in the area of the Alburz mountains.[24]

After the victory of the allied Nizārī-Sunni forces, Muẓaffar al-Dīn Uzbak appointed a certain Ighlamīsh as the new governor of ʿIrāq-i ʿAjam. Ighlamīsh received the bulk of the areas that Minglī had formerly possessed, including Hamadān, Rayy and Iṣfahān. However in 614/1217, Ighlamīsh also rebelled against his master. At this time there was no serious military intervention but the sources say that Ḥasan III was asked by Muẓaffar al-Dīn Uzbak and al-Nāṣir to despatch *fidāʾī*s against him.[25]

Control over Abhar and Zanjān helped the Nizārīs to weaken and isolate Qazwīn, which had steadfastly resisted them. Nevertheless, Ḥasan III made some efforts to convince the Qazwīnīs of the sincerity of his conversion to Sunni Islam, and it is said that he invited a delegation of devout Sunni Qazwīnīs to Alamūt to participate in the burning of books deemed heretical by this delegation.[26]

As far as local history is concerned, these events have their own significance and implications. Firstly, the strong support of al-Nāṣir helped to legitimise the Nizārī Ismaili state in the eastern lands of the caliphate. Al-Nāṣir, for instance, stipulated that local Sunni clans of Gīlān should send their daughters for marriage to Ḥasan III, which would have greatly enhanced the acceptance of the Nizārī Ismaili state. We do not know the nature of relations between these Sunni clans and the Nizārīs, but they accepted the caliph's command to marry relatives of Ḥasan III. This step perhaps helped to lessen the isolation and anti-Nizārī feelings in Gīlān.[27] One must note, however, that Ḥasan III's mother was also said to be a local Sunni, and this fact suggests that there had been relations with local Sunni clans long before 607/1210.

The campaign in ʿIrāq-i ʿAjam greatly enhanced the international prestige and acceptance of the Nizārīs. The reasons for Ḥasan III's involvement in the campaign must have surely been based in his desire to make the Nizārīs and himself as their Imam acceptable to the wider Islamic world. But other factors should not be ignored including a coalescence of the interests of al-Nāṣir and Ḥasan III and their concerted effort to suppress any kind of disunity given possible Khwārazmian military intervention in northern and western Iran.

It is clear that the Abbasid caliphate underwent notable ideological-doctrinal developments driven by the innovative outlook of al-Nāṣir, with the deployment of a range of methods to increase his authority. As with Ḥasan III, in the case of al-Nāṣir there were doctrinal concerns that actively shaped al-Nāṣir's perception of Islam. The apparent theological rapprochement between these two religious leaders served the objectives of both of them, for the one to end the isolation of the Nizārī community and seek alliance with the spiritual head of the Sunni world and for the other to enhance the authority of the Abbasid caliphate.[28]

It is also important to note that al-Nāṣir's attempts to foster good relations with the Shiʿi rulers of northern Iran were not restricted to Ḥasan III. According to Ibn Isfandiyār, al-Nāṣir had previously sent robes of honour to Ḥusām al-Dawla Ardashīr I, the Bāwandid ruler in 591/1195, following the Abbasid occupation of Rayy by Ibn al-Qaṣṣāb, an Abbasid military leader. It appears that al-Nāṣir endeavoured to fill the political vacuum left by the Saljūqs. However, in Abbasid connections with the Bāwandids it is not possible to identify any personal episode as in the case of Ḥasan III. Ḥusām al-Dawla Ardashīr I's response is not known but given that his position was under threat from the Khwārazmshāhs it must have been at least sensible to seek out other allies in western Iran.

But in 592/1196, the Abbasid forces in Rayy were forced to retreat after receiving threats from the Khwāwarzmshāh Tikish, and there is no further reference in the sources to contact between the Abbasid caliph and the Bāwandids. However, the approach to the Bāwandids can be seen as a forerunner to Abbasid overtures to the Nizārī Imam. The apparent acceptance of an Abbasid envoy in Ṭabaristān may have encouraged the dispatch of further delegations to the courts of those threatened by the Khwārazmshāhs. It is clear that during these years a new political alliance was created in northern Iran with Twelver Shiʿis, Nizārīs and Sunnis cooperating closely against the Khwārazmshāhs.[29]

Ḥasan III and the policy in the Caspian provinces

As regards the results of this pro-Abbasid policy of Ḥasan III, there are two events recorded in the Caspian provinces which appear to be important. First, the *Tārīkh-i Uljaytū* relates that Ḥasan III married four daughters of local Gīlānī families, including the daughter of Kay Kā'ūs b. Shāhanshāh, the hereditary ruler of the town of Kūtum, who claimed to have a mythical pre-Islamic lineage.[30] This source, a work written in the late Ilkhanid period, does not name the three other local Gīlānī dynasties, but the daughter of the lord of Kūtum was probably specified because she was the mother of Ḥasan's successor, ʿAlā' al-Dīn Muḥammad III. As mentioned, Ḥasan III's mother was also a Sunni which indicates that marriages between Nizārī Imams and local Sunni families were not unknown even during the apparent isolation of the *qiyāma* times.[31]

It was after the murder of Ḥasan II in 561/1166, that difficulties connected with the succession of the Nizārī Imams arose. Although the concept of *naṣṣ* functioned, i.e. it was never put into abeyance, and all Imams were designated by their predecessor in accordance with the principle of the *naṣṣ*, on some occasions the actions of an Imam were disputed or questioned by other members of the family.

The plot against Ḥasan II, and the eradication of his plotters in 561/1166, the alleged poisoning of Muḥammad II in 607/1210, the supposed plot against Ḥasan III in 618/1221, the question of the involvement of all or some of his wives in some way in it resulting in their execution by the vizier of Ḥasan III, the murder of Muḥammad III, are all instances where the women of the family seem to have played some part in the events. The growing role of wives and concubines suggests the dynasty of the Nizārī Imams had developed the characteristics of a local clan; and though the material in the sources is limited, these recorded conflicts suggest that, alongside the act of *naṣṣ*, the role of influential women and powerful courtiers should not be underestimated. But while the effect of a prestigious marriage with a local Gīlānī or Māzandarānī princess as well as the influence of courtiers or clan figures should not undermine the importance the act of *naṣṣ*, they probably introduced a certain clan-like tradition in which various elements sought to exert influence over the designation of a successor. The cultural background of the wives of Ḥasan III, for instance, was first and foremost a local Caspian one, where legendary ancestry, claims of pre-Islamic lineage, and different Shiʿi groups, could all play a role.

Another interesting but hitherto neglected aspect of Ḥasan III's reign was his advance into Ṭabaristān. After the extirpation of the Iṣfahbadiyya line of the Bāwandids, in which the Nizārīs had played a leading role along with the Khwārazmshāhs, Ṭabaristān came under direct Khwārazmian control at some point after 601/1205, possibly only after 606/1210.

The Khwārazmshāhs, as local governors, quickly adopted and continued the policies of the Bāwandids in the Caspian provinces. They became the new overlords of the Bādūspānids in Rūyān and confrontation with Nizārīs therefore seemed unavoidable. Given that they had adopted Bāwandid political objectives, the leaders of the Nizārī Ismaili state no longer lent support to their expansion westwards. In this rapidly fluctuating political situation in around 596/1200, where coalitions were built, quickly rebuilt and dissolved, the rapid westward advance of the Khwārazmshāhs and their conquest of Caspian polities meant a new period of unification after decades of disintegration during Saljūq decline. The Nizārīs supported the Khwārazmshāhs against their enemies, not against their own territories or interests. When the Khwārazmshāhs defeated the Bāwandids, the Nizārīs in the Caspian area may have briefly experienced a sense of relief, but this would have been quickly replaced by fear and suspicion as the former allies, the Nizārīs and the Bādūspānid-Khwārazmian forces, were now direct neighbours.

On the other hand, the Nizārīs might have extended their own influence towards Ṭabaristān exploiting the fall of the Iṣfahbadiyya branch. The fall of the once powerful *iṣfahbads* created an interim political vacuum which all the major political players immediately tried to fill. It appears that the Nizārīs pursued their tried-and-tested policy, meaning that they had relations with everyone but usually supported those forces that were being suppressed by their opponents. In the case of mountainous Ṭabaristān, the scarcity of our sources means that we do not hear about any new territorial gains made by the Nizārīs after the decline of the Iṣfahbadiyya branch of the Bāwandids. The Bādūspānids retained a relatively firm hold on Rūyān. In the works of Āmulī and Marʿashī, there are some laments over the ultimate fall of the Iṣfahbadiyya line of the Bāwandids, the overlords and supporters of the Bādūspānids,[32] but the Bādūspānids themselves were strong enough to withstand the Nizārīs. They apparently pledged their allegiance to Khwārazmshāh ʿAlāʾ al-Dīn Muḥammad and were, at least nominally, loyal to him until the appearance of the Mongols and the fall of his empire not long after. Bādūspānid relations with the Nizārīs, however, remained poor. Zarrīnkamar b. Justān and his descendants represented a branch of the Bādūspānids which enjoyed the support of the Bāwandids and had succeeded in extirpating other, more Nizārī-friendly relatives in Rūyān. Zarrīnkamar's descendants were usually hostile to the Nizārīs in the following decades; after 607/1210 they became the strongest local family in Ṭabaristān and could be seen as the most significant local polity.

The oddity and complexity of the situation is clearly reflected by the fact that the same Bādūspānids actively supported the Bāwandid revival after 607/1210, but at the same time the Bādūspānids remained on friendly terms with the Khwārazmshāhs, who had subdued Bāwandids years before. The Khwārazmshāhs remained the staunch enemies of the Nizārīs who, however, gave support to the Bāwandid revival after 607/1210. Thus, when we start analysing Nizārī policy regarding the eastern areas after 607/1210, we find two opponents of the Nizārīs: the Khwārazmshāhs and the Bādūspānids. As far as the rest of Ṭabaristān is concerned, there were still a number of local rulers who opposed the Khwārazmshāhs, including, perhaps not surprisingly, various cadet branches of the Bāwandids. The Nizārīs had penetrated deep into Ṭabaristān, into the major cities as well as more remote areas around Firīm, the ancient place of origin of the Bāwandids. The presence of Nizārī groups can be detected here and their thorough knowledge of political movements in their immediate vicinity is further emphasised by Ibn Isfandiyār and Marʿashī. These sources say that a sister or daughter of Jalāl al-Dīn Ḥasan III became the wife of Kīnkhwār, an obscure Bāwandid prince. From this dynastic marriage, Ḥusām al-Dawla Ardashīr was born, and in 636/1238 he became the founder of the Kinkhwāriyya, the third main branch of the Bāwandids who ruled in some parts of Ṭabaristān until 750/1349. This story is fascinating as it is the only instance in the sources of a marriage between a daughter of an Ismaili Imam and a local ruler.[33]

When we look at this interesting passage in Marʿashī's history, the two different editions display variations to the story, thus making the text more intriguing than one might have expected. In Dorn's edition we find:[34]

> Another Kīnkhwār was born who is the father of Ardashīr and the child of the daughter of Ardashīr b. al-Ḥasan, and Ardashīr b. Kīnkhwār is the maternal nephew of *khudawand* ʿAlāʾ al-Dīn b. Jalāl al-Dīn Ḥasan b. ʿAlāʾ al-Dīn Muḥammad.[35]

The Tasbiḥī edition offers a slightly different version:[36]

> Another Kīnkhwār was born, who is the father of Ardashīr, and the child of the daughter of *khudawand* ʿAlāʾ al-Dīn b. Jalāl al-Dīn Ḥasan b. ʿAlāʾ al-Dīn Muḥammad.[37]

Dorn's edition has a comparatively longer text whereas Tasbīḥī's presents a much-abbreviated version of the same passage. No doubt the editions relied on different manuscript traditions, which may explain the difference. As far as the secondary sources are concerned, Rabino di Borgomale says that the princess was part of the Khwārazmian dynasty.[38] Though he usually offers a detailed and very elaborate analysis, in this case, however, his conclusion appears to be erroneous. Perhaps he thought that the princess was the daughter of Jalāl al-Dīn Mingburnī, the son of ʿAlāʾ al-Dīn Muḥammad. Yet the ruler is called Jalāl al-Dīn Ḥasan, who has a son called ʿAlāʾ al-Dīn Muḥammad. To the best of our knowledge, Jalāl al-Dīn Mingburnī did not bear the name Ḥasan and, furthermore, none of his sons was called ʿAlāʾ al-Dīn Muḥammad.

The passage in Dorn's edition is probably more accurate, but there is no doubt that a Nizārī princess married the Bāwandid prince. Regarding her parentage, it seems to be more plausible chronologically that she was the daughter of Jalāl al-Dīn Ḥasan III rather than of ʿAlāʾ

al-Dīn Muḥammad III. If a son of the princess, Ḥusām al-Dawla Ardashīr II, acceded to the restored throne of the Bāwandids in 636/1238, he would have to have been born around 617/1220 at least.

As has been stated, the heir and successor of Jalāl al-Dīn Ḥasan III was born to the daughter of the prince of Kūtum. This marriage between Jalāl al-Dīn Ḥasan III and the princess of Kūtum took place after Jalāl al-Dīn Ḥasan, as Nizārī Imam, had officially expressed his rapprochement with Sunni Islam. If ʿAlāʾ al-Dīn Muḥammad III was born around 607/1210, he could hardly be the father of a Nizārī princess who married the Bāwandid Kīnkhwār in around 617/1220.[39]

Both Ibn Isfandiyār and Marʿashī tried to suppress or ignore this information. Both of them say that the princess was of Bādūspānid origin, which is improbable since such names as ʿAlāʾ al-Dīn Muḥammad and Jalāl al-Dīn Ḥasan were unknown in the Bādūspānid dynasty in the first half of the 7th/13th century. Both Marʿashī and Ibn Isfandiyār say that the princess was either the daughter or the sister of ʿAlāʾ al-Dīn Muḥammad, whose father was Jalāl al-Dīn Ḥasan, and whose grandfather was ʿAlāʾ al-Dīn (= Nūr al-Dīn) Muḥammad. This lineage completely accords with our knowledge of the Nizārī Imams. In addition, ʿAlāʾ al-Dīn Muḥammad or Muḥammad III (the son and heir of Ḥasan III) was known as *khudāwand*, which was a traditional title for the Nizārī Imams but unknown among the Bādūspānids.

Concerning Bādūspānid-Nizārī contacts under Jalāl al-Dīn Ḥasan III, due to the limitations of the sources there is very little information. Zarrīnkamar b. Justān, the enemy of the Nizārīs and former protégé of the Bāwandid, Ḥusām al-Dawla Ardashīr I, died around 610/1214. His son and successor Bīsutūn ruled from 610/1214 until 621/1224. Although he only ruled for ten years, and although the accounts of Āmulī and Marʿashī are regrettably very limited concerning this period, these sources do indicate that this new *ustāndār* of Rūyān had to wage war against local, but unnamed, princes of Gīlān who were trying to exploit the collapse of the Iṣfahbadiyya branch of the Bāwandids in 607/1210. Neither Āmulī nor Marʿashī name these local Gīlānī princes, so it would be too speculative to say that it was the Nizārīs who attacked Rūyān after 610/1214. However, the Nizārīs, certainly benefitted from the fall of the Bāwandids. Bīsutūn b. Zarrīnkamar spent all of his relatively brief reign fighting local wars. In his sketchy account of events Āmulī praises Bīsutūn for his virtues but, apart from recounting some anecdotal details such as that the *ustāndār* became bald prematurely because he never removed his hat from his head, does not supply us with any pertinent details about his reign.[40]

Regrettably, Āmulī mentions neither the Nizārīs nor the Khwārazmshāhs in this context, yet the fact that the Bādūspānids did survive the collapse of the Iṣfahbadiyya line of the Bāwandids, can be attributed to their allegiance to the Khwārazmshāhs. In fact, it is notable that the Bādūspānids managed to keep their polity intact. Geographical isolation may have been of some importance in their survival too, for it is known that it was owing to their remote location that they also survived the first wave of the Mongol invasion.

The Nizārī Ismaili state in the early Mongol period

Mongol rule was a watershed in the history of the Middle East. As is known, it was the forces of the Mongol Hülegü who eventually brought about the fall of the Nizārī Ismaili state in 654/1256. However, before that catastrophic event, the sources reveal a much more complex relationship between the Mongols and the Nizārīs over some thirty-six years. Despite the fact that this was a relatively brief period, nonetheless Nizārī-Mongol relations during this time influenced the history of the Middle East.

The Mongol conquest of Iranian lands took place over some four decades from the first attacks by Chingiz Khān in 617/1220 up until the military operations of his grandson, Hülegü, in 654–657/1256–1259. The Mongols first brought down the Khwārazmshāh's empire in 617–620/1220–1223, and thereafter Mongol viceroys and military commanders controlled Central Asia and large parts of Khurāsān. The most important military governors of Persian lands were Chormaghan (620–639/1223–1241) and Baiju Noyan (639–654/1241–1256). It is worth noting that in the three decades between 617/1220 and 650/1252, there are no reports of any significant Nizārī-Mongol clashes. Other military targets, internal Mongol disputes and perhaps some kind of Nizārī-Mongol alliance could have played a part in this state of affairs. Most of the Nizārī lands were situated in inaccessible mountainous areas which meant that conquest would be difficult, particularly for a military based on the rapid deployment of mounted horsemen over open expanses of grassland. As a result, the Nizārīs managed to retain their own territories in relatively stable conditions. Once the Mongols had acquired greater siege weaponry, as will be discussed, the situation changed.

Nonetheless, the last years of Jalāl al-Dīn Ḥasan III were marked by the menace of the Mongol conquest. As noted, the Nizārīs were well informed concerning the political events of their age and Jalāl al-Dīn Ḥasan III is recorded as the first Muslim ruler to try to make terms with the Mongols after they had crossed the Oxus in August 616/1219. The period 616–619/1219–1222 saw the first Mongol attacks against Iran and Central Asia. It is not precisely known what the main objective of a Nizārī visit to the Mongol camp was, but it seems reasonable to assume that they realised the menace the Mongols posed to the eastern Iranian world and wished to make diplomatic contact with the Mongols before any potential onslaught. The information comes to us from the vehemently anti-Nizārī chronicler, Juwaynī.[41] But it must be noted that there is no record of any direct confrontation with the Nizārīs during the first Mongol attack on Iran. If this was a result of this early and cautious diplomatic mission, it was indeed a wise move.[42]

The Nizārīs of Quhistān gave shelter to Khwārazmian and Khurāsānī refugees from the Mongol onslaught, which caused anxiety among the Nizārīs of Alamūt. According to Jūzjānī, the *muḥtasham* of Quhistān was immediately reprimanded for this by Jalāl al-Din's successor, ʿAlāʾ al-Dīn Muḥammad III.[43] One refugee was Nāṣir al-Dīn al-Ṭūsī who had fled from Nīshāpūr to Quhistān.[44] Nonetheless, sheltering Khwārazmian refugees can be seen as evidence of regular contact between the local Nizārīs and other Khurāsānīs on the one hand and a constant sense of ambiguity in all their dealings with other powers on the other.

In contrast to this, the *Shengwu qinzheng lu* (*Campaigns of Chingiz Khan*), a Chinese source written in the Yuan (Mongol) era, says that Tolui, the fourth son of Chingiz Khān, plundered Nizārī-populated areas in Khurāsān, too:

> [§51.2] In the winter, the Fourth Crown Prince also sacked Maruchaq, Yeke Maru,[45] and Sirāqs[46] cities, before moving on with his troops. [§51.3] In year *rén/xu* [Year of the Horse, or 619/1222], in the spring, he also sacked Tus, Nicha'ur,[47] and other cities. Since just then the summer-heat was becoming excessive, His Majesty sent envoys summoning Tolui to make

> haste and return. As he was passing through the Mulayid realm,[48] he totally plundered them. Crossing the Choqchoran River, he sacked Heri[49] and other cities.[50]

Almost the same information and the same text can be found in the *Yuanshi*, the official Chinese chronicle of the Yuan period, dealing with Tolui's attack on Khurāsān and Quhistān:

> Year seventeen, that of *ren/xu* [that is, 619/1222]. Spring. The Imperial Prince Tolui conquers Tus, Nicha'ur and other cities. Returning, he passed through the Mulayid kingdom, plundering it heavily. Crossing the Choqchoran River, he conquered Heri and other towns.[51]

The horsemen of Chingiz Khān also penetrated the Caspian region in pursuit of ʿAlāʾ al-Dīn Muḥammad Khwārazmshāh who in his flight from the Mongols found asylum in northern Iran. During his flight, he came to Āmul, the former Bāwandid capital, where unnamed local princes advised him to take refuge on the islands in the Caspian Sea. He died on the island of Ashūrada, according to al-Nasawī of pneumonia.[52] Mongol forces led by the Mongol generals, Jebe and Sübötei, pursued ʿAlāʾ al-Dīn but failed to capture him. Thus, the Mongols entered the Caspian areas for the first time in 618/1221. According to Juwaynī, Jebe's forces caused great destruction in Māzandarān, and pillaged the city of Āmul in their search for ʿAlāʾ al-Dīn Khwāramshāh.[53] Jūzjānī says the Mongols raided the encampment of ʿAlāʾ al-Dīn in Tamīsha, in eastern Māzandarān. Jūzjānī's statement is confirmed by Juwaynī, who says the Mongols invaded Māzandarān for the first time from Gurgān.[54]

Meanwhile, the forces of Sübötei, arriving from the direction of Nīshāpūr, razed the town of Dāmghān almost to the ground. The local aristocracy fled to the neighbouring Nizārī fortress of Girdkūh before the Mongols appeared. According to Juwaynī, only some '*runūd*', or disorganised elements of the Dāmghān population, resisted the invading Mongol forces. The Nizārīs in Girdkūh then captured Dāmghān, and perhaps Qūmis, after the departure of the Mongols.

Sübötei's forces headed westwards, and they swiftly conquered and destroyed Simnān and Rayy, massacring the local population. During this first Mongol campaign, no more is heard about incursions into areas near the Nizārīs or any attacks against them.[55]

Two factors can explain why the Nizārīs kept a low profile. Firstly, they were opponents of the Khwārazmshāhs, but also the Nizārī ambassadors sent to Chingiz Khān would have witnessed the military supremacy of the Mongols. The forces of Jebe and Sübötei did not waste time attacking the Nizārī castle of Girdkūh, because their primary task was to capture the Khwārazmshāh and in the case of the first Mongol attack in the Middle East, we cannot speak of any systematic territorial conquest. It may also have been because they did not have sufficient materiel for an assault on so impregnable a fortress as Girdkūh.

Chapter 7

ʿAlāʾ al-Dīn Muḥammad III and the End of the Nizārī Ismaili State in the Caspian Provinces

The relatively long reign of ʿAlāʾ al-Dīn Muḥammad Muḥammad III can be divided into two main periods. Apparently, in the first period he followed the religious policy of his father. As he was only nine years old upon his accession to power his influence was nominal, and affairs were managed by his vizier, ʿImād al-Dīn Muḥtasham, presumably a former Nizārī governor or from a family of governors of Quhistān. In this very difficult time, when the Mongols had overrun Central Asia and northeastern Iran, there is little information on the minority of the new Nizārī Imam. However, the new leadership at Alamūt gradually distanced itself from Sunni Islam, although without producing apparently any declaration on the matter.

In the period after 618/1221, a twofold situation can be discerned. From a Nizārī perspective, these decades somehow recalled the era of Ḥasan-i Ṣabbāḥ. The political situation seems similar to the years of the founding of the state and to international events before the announcement of the *qiyāma* in 559/1164. Like Ḥasan-i Ṣabbāḥ, who quickly despatched *dāʿīs* to different areas of the Saljūq empire after the deaths of Niẓām al-Mulk and Malikshāh, thus exploiting the chaos and wars of the contending sons of Malikshāh, after 618/1221 the Nizārīs also attempted to fill the political vacuum left by the sudden collapse of the Khwārazmshāh's empire.

Exerting Mongol control over Khurāsān was not without problems. It took time for the new Mongol dispensation to settle in the conquered areas and for the Mongol viceroys to appear in Iran and Central Asia. After the first Mongol attacks, the newly-appointed Mongol viceroys for Central Asia and Khurāsān, such as Chin-Temür and Chormaghan quarrelled with each other on the ruins of the Khwārazmshāh's empire. In the meantime, Jalāl al-Dīn Mingburnī, the last Khwārazmshāh, himself an adventurous character, engaged in tireless efforts to restore some vestige of his father's empire. In this unsettled period, the Nizārī leadership of Alamūt found an opportunity to strengthen its political influence by extending its authority into new areas; some Nizārī circles clearly thought that the dramatic events of the Middle East were an eschatological sign calling on the Nizārī Ismaili state to extend its realms.[1]

In the *Rawḍat al-taslīm* of Nāṣir al-Dīn al-Ṭūsī, written in these decades, we find a striking prophecy of the Nizārī conquest of Asian territories, saying the Nizārī Imam will first conquer the Caspian provinces, after taking Daylamān. Following the conquest of Māzandarān, Gīlān and Mughān, the Imam will continue on his way to Hind, Rūm and Chīn. It is a matter of interpretation what we understand by Hind and Rūm; Hodgson thought it referred to broader areas, roughly equivalent to the climes of Greek origin as they were known in works of medieval Islamic geography and does not see these terms as synonymous with present-day India and Anatolia.[2] Another version of the same prophecy can be found in the *Haft bāb* of Abū Isḥāq Quhistānī.[3] The origin of this prophecy is not known and it is unclear whether it was an earlier legend incorporated into the *Rawḍat al-taslīm* by al-Ṭūsī or whether it is purely a reflection of the Ismaili millenarianism of al-Ṭūsī's age, i.e. the decades after 618/1221. If the latter, the text certainly has further implications as it indicates expectations on the part of contemporaneous Nizārīs who believed in the revival of the Nizārī *da'wa* during these times.

A similar indication of heightened Nizārī political expectation is found in the biography of Jalāl al-Dīn Mingburnī by al-Nasawī, the secretary and occasional diplomat on behalf of Jalāl al-Dīn. He says that upon hearing erroneous reports of the death of his master, Jalāl al-Dīn Mingburnī, a group of Syrian Ismailis boasted to the Saljūq sultan of Rūm, Kay Kubād I, that the Alamūt Nizārīs were on the verge of taking over the province of 'Irāq-i 'Ajam, formerly held by the Khwārazmians.[4]

Yet the situation was not without risks or danger, and in this turbulent state of affairs the Nizārīs sought to maintain good relations with every side. Their presence was noted both in the entourages of the Mongol viceroys and at the court of Jalāl al-Dīn Mingburnī. This kind of diplomacy was a continuation of earlier Ismaili approaches.

The Nizārīs and their Caspian neighbours under Muḥammad III

The imamate of Muḥammad III, which lasted some three decades, may be considered a peak of Nizārī activity and influence in the Caspian provinces. The reason for this intensified activity and success was the fragmented state of the eastern Islamic lands at the time as well as Nizārī victories against local powers in northern Iran.

When one examines local policy in the Caspian provinces in the decades leading up to 618/1221, it is evident that the Nizārī Ismaili state was the only polity which benefited consistently from the political changes in northern Iran between 590/1194 and 629/1231. First, the downfall of the last scions of the Iranian Saljūqs in 590/1194, had opened the way to the Ismailis extending their influence in some parts of western Iran as demonstrated by the bold military actions of Ḥasan III. A more significant political benefit was the fall of the Iṣfahbadiyya branch of the Bāwandids in 601–607/1205–1210, which meant the elimination of their most dangerous local opponent. This had also led to a weakening of the pro-Bāwandid ruling line of the Bādūspānids in Rūyān between Ṭabaristān and Daylamān.

The Nizārīs conquered various areas in Rūyān and Daylamān and perhaps in western Ṭabaristān during these years and their territorial expansion continued further under Muḥammad III. Under Jalāl al-Dīn Ḥasan III, the Nizārīs had begun to support a new branch of the Bāwandids. Ḥasan III married his daughter to the Bāwandid prince Shahriyār in around 617/1220. This fact underlined the growing influence of the Nizārīs in Ṭabaristān, such that even the Bāwandids, who had been their avowed enemies only a few decades before, had accepted their offer of a dynastic alliance.

These successes continued under 'Alā' ad-Dīn Muḥammad III. We know from al-Nasawī that the Nizārīs conquered the city of Dāmghān and perhaps Qūmis (near Girdkūh) following a Mongol attack in 618/1221-22. These new acquisitions were as significant and easier to control being closer to the core lands of the Nizārī Ismaili state than the cities of Abhar and Zanjān that had been held briefly under Ḥasan III.

But the chief goal of the Ismailis now was to move into those areas lost to the Khwārazmshāhs but not yet ruled directly by the Mongols. Al-Nasawī says that for six years there was warfare between the Nizārīs and Jalāl al-Dīn Mingburnī, because he wished to re-establish the Khwārazmian empire in northern Iran. This suggests that the Nizārīs captured the area of Dāmghān soon after the first Mongol invasion, possibly around 619/1222. There was also Ismaili activity in Rayy, where a group of Nizārī *dāʿīs* sought to convert those local people who had survived the Mongol sack of the city, which would have made Rayy loyal to Muḥammad III. However, Rukn al-Dīn, the brother of Jalāl al-Dīn Mingburnī, had the *dāʿīs* arrested and put to death.[5]

Echoes of the Nizārī conquest of Dāmghān, Bisṭām and perhaps Mihrīn can be found in the *Dīwān-i Qāʾimiyyāt*. According to the editor of the recently published text, Jalal Badakhchani, they were written by various Nizārī poets before 638–641/1240–1243.[6] If this is the case, and bearing in mind the caveat that *qaṣīda*s could have undergone changes in subsequent centuries, then this important and hitherto lesser known literary source may be said to contain material relating to the last decades of the Nizārī Ismaili state in the Caspian provinces. *Qaṣīda* 124 may be of particular interest since it appears to celebrate the territorial gains made by the Nizārīs following the end of Khwārazmian rule in northern Iran. The text refers to the Nizārīs entering Dāmghān after the Mongol attack, and says that they conquered castles and citadels (*qalʿahā va qaṣrān*) in western Iran.

Furthermore, the *qaṣīda* mentions an approximate date of (6)20, which is 1223 CE, in relation to Chingiz Khān's assault on Central Asia and Khurāsān. Although this date is erroneous, because the first Mongol attacks against northern Iran and Nizārī-populated areas took place a few years earlier, the chronology is not of great significance.

Īlīāj, the Khwārazmian governor (*ḥākim*) of Khalkhāl is also mentioned in it in relation to these events. A Nizārī raid against Khalkhāl and the death of its governor, which is not referred to elsewhere in contemporaneous sources, is mentioned here.[7] The *Dīwān-i Qāʾimiyyāt* also mentions the conquest of Bisṭām and Mihrīn in *qaṣīda* 73, although Mihrīn is mentioned explicitly only in the prose introduction to the *qaṣīda*. This means that Nizārī forces based in Girdkūh retook some important fortresses that had been lost to Shāh Ghāzī Rustam before 560/1165, and which later could have come into the possession of the Khwārazmshāhs.[8]

There are also references to contacts with the Mongols. The years between 616/1219 and 629/1231, leading up to the death of Jalāl al-Dīn

Mingburnī, formed a period of 'cordial' contacts between the Nizārīs and the Mongols. As stated previously, the Nizārīs had learnt as early as 616/1219 about Mongol military operations, and messengers had been sent to Central Asian Nizārī communities warning of the invasion and Jalāl al-Dīn Ḥasan III was the first Muslim ruler to send envoys to Chingiz Khān's camp on the Oxus river.

The fact that the Ismailis in the Caspian provinces managed to avoid an attack by the armies of Chingiz Khān, is reflected in the *Dīwān-i Qā'imiyyāt.* Here, we see some interesting perceptions relating to the Mongols, who are depicted as part of an eschatological schema culminating in the victory of the Ismailis. It can be argued that the role ascribed in the *Dīwān-i Qā'imiyyāt* to the Mongols and the first Mongol ruler, whose emergence was somehow conceived as being a necessary consequence of the *qiyāma* declaration of 559/1164, is further emphasised by a distinct anti-Khwārazmian attitude, which celebrates the sudden fall of the 'Turk rule' of the Khwārazmshāhs. This is balanced by the expression of sorrow over the destruction of Bukhārā and Samarqand. Several verses therefore suggest this approach as a way of explaining the events of the period and that the Ismailis interpreted the assault of the Mongols against the Khwārazmshāhs as part of the *qiyāma*. It is possible however, that the *Dīwān-i Qā'imiyyāt* reflected only one aspect of Nizārī attitudes to these events, as it is also known that some Nizārīs in the Punjab assisted the Khwārazmshāh Jalāl al-Dīn Mingburnī when he crossed the Indus river in flight from the Mongols; and as we have seen the Nizārī *muḥtasham* of Quhistān, Shihāb al-Dīn, took in Khwārazmian refugees following the Mongol conquest of Central Asia.[9] Bearing these points in mind and given that only the first and second Mongol attacks (616–620/1219–1223; 637–638/1240–1242) are mentioned in the *Dīwān-i Qā'imiyyāt*, Nizārī-Mongol relations now appear to be more complex than is suggested in post-Alamūt sources. This is to some degree corroborated by Juwaynī who claims that an agreement was established with the Mongols following their first invasion.[10] Juwaynī himself states that he did not lend it much credibility but suggests 'it was assumed to be the case by the Heretics (i.e. the Nizārīs themselves)'. It remains unknown what sources Juwaynī might have used here, but the *Dīwān-i Qā'imiyyāt* may be seen as supporting the notion of some kind of Nizārī-Mongol understanding in around 617/1220.[11]

However, the second sub-period, apparently from 629/1231 up until completion of the *Dīwān-i Qā'imiyyāt* in around 641/1243, which is when we have the latest information for the life of its main author, Ḥasan-i Maḥmūd-i Kātib,[12] is more complex. This period covers the second major Mongol military operation, initiated by the Great Khān Ögedei (r. 624–639/1227–1241), when the Mongols invaded parts of Iran and Anatolia in 637–640/1240–1243. The main difference is perhaps the collapse of the Khwārazmshāh's empire. In 617/1220, the main enemy of the Nizārīs was not the emerging Mongol empire, whose dimensions and military potential were doubtless unknown to the Nizārīs, but the Khwārazmshāhs. But now passages relating to the second generations of Chingizids, Chingiz-i thānī (referring to Ögedei) and a certain Chaghtāy instead see the Mongols as the enemy. This reflects the situation around 638/1240, when the Khwārazmian threat to the Nizārīs had been eliminated. By this time, the Nizārīs were experiencing changes in the attitude of the Mongols to them and a souring of relations. As a result, the Nizārīs made some effort to restore themselves in the eyes of the Mongols. Along with envoys of the last Abbasid caliph of Baghdad, al-Musta'ṣim (r. 640–656/1242–1258), and several other Muslim princes, Shihāb al-Dīn and Shams al-Dīn, Nizārī *muḥtashams* in Quhistān, were sent to Karakorum in Mongolia, to participate in the celebrations for the enthronement of the successor to Ögedei, Güyük (r. 644–646/1246–1248). However, the Nizārī emissaries were dismissed peremptorily by the new Great Khan and indeed relations with the Mongols came to an end.[13]

One of the most intriguing parts of the *Dīwān-i Qā'imiyyāt* tells the story of the two Chingizes as related to the second sub-period of the Nizārī Ismaili state and the Mongols. According to the poems of the *Dīwān-i Qā'imiyyāt*, Chingiz Khān showed sincere friendship (*ikhlāṣ-i dūstār*) towards the Nizārīs and at the end of time (*ākhir-i zamān*) the Mongol army (*lashkar-i tatār*) spread throughout the world. According to *qaṣīda* 49 of the *Dīwān-i Qā'imiyyāt* a certain kind of divine blessing (*marḥimat*) contributed to Mongol successes.[14] Yet in *qaṣīda* 78 we learn that Chingiz Khān, who had shown sincere friendship to the Nizārīs as commanded by the Imam, later diverged from the firm advice (*az īn ra'y-i razīn bargasht*) and wanted the Nizārī Imam to show his face at his court (*rukh bi dargāham nahī*).[15] Another legendary element belonging to the second sub-period and incorporated into this story is the account of 'Chingiz-i thānī' or that of Chingiz II (possibly Ögedei r. 624–639/1227–1241),[16] who despatched his brother, Chaghtāy (= Chagatāy), against the Nizārīs. This can be found in *qaṣīdas* 49[17] and 133.[18]

As regards the identification of this 'Chaghtāy', it is unlikely that the passages of the *Dīwān-i Qā'imiyyāt* refer to the second son of Chingiz Khān but instead are about one of the most prominent *noyons* (high-ranking Mongol military leaders), who was also called Chaghtāy. Chaghtāy Qūrchī was a lieutenant of the Mongol viceroy Chormaghan who appeared in 634/1236, in the Caucasus region, where he subjugated numerous important Georgian and Armenian sites such as Lori, Tbilisi, Dumanis and Shamshuldis. Kirakos Gandzakets'i, an Armenian historian of the time, gives a detailed report of the sophisticated methods used by the Mongols in besieging castles and cities.[19] According to Gandzakets'i, Chaghtāy Qūrchī *noyon* was killed by the Ismailis at some time after 638/1240. This episode is also mentioned by the Persian sources.[20]

Timothy May suggests that the killing of Chaghtāy Qūrchī was intended to divert or weaken Mongol military manoeuvres against the Nizārīs, after the fall of the Khwārazmshāhs.[21] By 641/1243, the Khwārazmshāhs had been eliminated and the Rūm Saljūqs reduced to being vassals of the Mongols[22] who had secured areas of Transcaucasia and the Iranian plateau for themselves. It was at this time that their relations with the Nizārīs began to sour. May speculates that the killing of Chaghtāy Qūrchī could have occurred after the death, in 639/1241, of Chormaghan, the highest-ranking Mongol general stationed in Persia, since none of the sources refer to this event occurring during Chormaghan's time and if it had taken place before 639/1241 there would have been some reference linked to Chormaghan in the sources.

However, there are Armenian sources that suggest that Chaghtāy Qūrchī was still alive in 647/1249, when several Georgian and Armenian princes rebelled against the Mongols as a result of the heavy taxes they levied. But it is noteworthy that this revolt was suppressed by Baiju, and not by Chaghtāy Qūrchī, meaning that he could have been killed in around 647-48/1249-50.[23] It is also known that Baiju, the Mongol military governor of Persia after Chormaghan, wrote a letter to Möngke about the Nizārīs in 649/1251 which may be connected with the murder of Chaghtāy Qūrchī.[24] In light of the above-mentioned chronology for Chaghtāy Qūrchī's death in 647-48/1249-50, the argument that the *Dīwān-i Qā'imiyyāt* was finished in the 640s/1240s becomes questionable and, at least in parts, this is likely as much to be a composition that is looking back to an earlier age.[25]

The Mongols' threatening attitude to the Ismailis is attested to elsewhere. As mentioned earlier, Güyük used harsh language against the Nizārī envoys upon his enthronement in 644/1246. One of those who influenced Güyük's opinion was perhaps Shiramun, the son of Chormaghan. According to Rashīd al-Dīn, in 644/1246 Güyük repeated some of these complaints to the Abbasid ambassador.[26] According to Juwaynī, in the same year, Güyük sent military reinforcements to Iran with another Mongol *noyan*, Eljigitei, although it is not said that this new Mongol army was sent directly against the Ismailis in the Caspian mountains.[27]

As for Armenian-Ismaili relations, the Armenian sources suggest these were difficult before 654/1256, one possible reason for the Ismailis' hostile attitude to the Armenians being the role of some Armenians princes who had become the Mongols' vassals. Armenian provinces both in the southern Caucasus and Cilicia were occupied by the Mongols after 620/1223 and provided auxiliary military forces and food supplies for the Mongol armies stationed there. According to the 13th-century Armenian historian Smbat Sparapet, as a result of this the Armenian King Het'um of Cilicia (r. 1213–1270) disguised himself as a cattle-driver when he travelled through Ismaili-populated areas in Cappadocia in 651/1253 on his way to Möngke Khān's court.[28]

As for the origins of the some of the conciliatory attitude in some poems of the *Dīwān-i Qā'imiyyāt*, they may be found in the cautious approach of the Imam 'Alā' al-Dīn Muḥammad towards the Mongol threat. As we have seen, the Nizārīs also acquired new territories following the first Mongol assault on Iran. On the other hand, the influence of this attitude among the Nizārī elite as early as 617–619/1220–1222 helps in understanding subsequent actions that are seen as controversial in secondary sources. Those influential figures such as Nāṣir al-Dīn al-Ṭūsī can now be seen in a different way. His later role in persuading Rukn al-Dīn Khurshāh to come down from the castle of Maymūndiz and hand the Ismaili fortresses over to the Mongols can be perhaps in part explained if a different attitude towards the Mongols was prevalent before 654/1256.[29] It is fairly likely that Ḥasan-i Maḥmūd-i Kātib and Naṣīr al-Dīn al-Ṭūsī knew each other in Quhistān before going to the Caspian region; and the attitude which can be seen in some of the *qaṣīdas* of the *Dīwān-i Qā'imiyyāt* could also suggest that a significant number of those in Alamūt may have hailed the initial appearance of the Mongols as a fortuitous development, although of course this opinion was later revised.[30]

The Khwārazmian response to Ismaili successes after 617/1220

As noted, modest but constant Ismaili territorial expansion can be discerned around Ṭārum and on the southern slopes of the Alburz mountains following the first Mongol assault, which suggests an intention to subdue ultimately the entire area of northern Iran. The Khwārazmshāh's empire, having lost its central government, was unable to topple the Nizārīs and it was only the reappearance of the last Khwārazmshāh, Jalāl al-Dīn Mingburnī, that compelled the Nizārīs to withdraw and to make a treaty. Jalāl al-Dīn Mingburnī had spent three years in India after suffering several defeats at the hands of the Mongols in 618/1221, and then in 621/1224 he finally made his way to southern and western Iran to restore some parts of his father's empire.[31]

Jalāl al-Dīn Mingburnī's attempts to restore his western provinces met with resistance from his brothers as well as from local powers, including the Nizārī Ismaili state. By 622/1225, Jalāl al-Dīn Mingburnī had managed to remove his brother Ghiyāth al-Dīn from central Iran, Iṣfahān and Hamadān, and in 622/1225 he subdued Muẓaffar al-Dīn Uzbak, the last Īldigüzid *atabeg* in Tabrīz. Then, he turned his attention to northern Iran. The Nizārīs were traditionally considered enemies of the Khwārazmshāhs, for they had allied themselves with the Abbasid caliphate and with the Īldigüzids under Ḥasan III against the Khwārazmian empire. After 622/1225 Jalāl al-Dīn tried to eject the Nizārīs from their newly-acquired possessions, but was unsuccessful. The details of this campaign, however, are obscure. A peace treaty was drawn up following the murder of Urkhān, a Khwārazmian leader and close confidante of Jalāl al-Dīn Mingburnī, which Nasawī says was carried out by Nizārī *fidā'īs*.[32] Urkhān had held Khurāsān as an *iqṭā'* from Jalāl al-Dīn Mingburnī and had carried out raids against the

Nizārīs in Quhistān and possibly in northern Iran. Kirakos Gandzakets'i also recounted the murder of Urkhān and ascribes it to the 'Mulheds'.[33]

After the death of Urkhān, Jalāl al-Dīn Mingburnī made concessions to the Nizārīs in northern Iran. However, there is no mention in Nasawī's *Sīra* of Nizārī raids against Khalkhāl as found in the *Dīwān-i Qā'imiyyāt.*[34]

The treaty between the Nizārīs and the Khwārazmshāh was drawn up in 624/1227.[35] The circumstances of the agreement are particularly interesting in elucidating the details of the dealings of the Nizārīs with the Khwārazmshāh. The details of the agreement were prepared by Sharaf al-Mulk, the vizier of Jalāl al-Dīn Mingburnī, and Badr al-Dīn Aḥmad, the envoy of 'Alā' al-Dīn Muḥammad III. Originally, it was agreed that the Nizārīs would remain in possession of Dāmghān, the city they had taken from the Khwārazmshāhs after the Mongol invasion of 617-18/1220-21,[36] conditional upon an annual payment of 30,000 gold dinars.

Nasawī records an episode that he says occurred during the preparatory negotiations. Badr al-Dīn Aḥmad revealed the power of the Ismailis, praising those Nizārīs who had been operating in the Khwārazmian administration. To prove his words to his surprised hosts, Badr al-Dīn Aḥmad summoned five Nizārīs working in the Khwārazmshāh's service. A furious Jalāl al-Dīn Mingburnī ordered Sharaf al-Mulk, his vizier, to put them to death. Sharaf al-Mulk nonetheless felt that this action could greatly jeopardise the success of the peace talks and lead to further needless bloodshed between the Nizārīs and the Khwārazmshāh, when the main issue was confronting the Mongol threat. He pleaded in vain with Jalāl al-Dīn Mingburnī to change his decision, but the latter remained firm and the Nizārīs were burned alive, defiantly shouting the name of 'Alā' al-Dīn Muḥammad. The Nizārīs responded to the brutality of Jalāl al-Dīn Mingburnī in a sophisticated manner by despatching Ṣalāḥ al-Dīn 'Alī, another Nizārī envoy, to the Khwārazmshāh's camp. Ṣalāḥ al-Dīn 'Alī openly threatened Jalāl al-Dīn Mingburnī over the execution of the Ismailis and demanded 10,000 dinars in compensation. An agreement was finally reached whereby the Khwārazmshāh's vizier, Sharaf al-Mulk, who had far more diplomatic sense than his master, decided to reduce the annual tribute payable by the Nizārīs by 10,000 dinars to be paid over five years.[37] These negotiations were recorded by Nasawī, who was an active participant in the Nizārī-Khwārazmian negotiations.

Yet this agreement of 624/1227 did not last long and relations remained relatively poor. Al-Nasawī informs us that the Nizārīs welcomed two high-ranking individuals in Alamūt. One of them was Malik Khāmūsh, son of the last, deposed, Īldigüzid ruler, Muẓaffar al-Dīn Uzbak, who had been defeated by Jalāl al-Dīn Mingburnī in 622/1225.[38] That this Īldigüzid prince found shelter in Alamūt is also mentioned in the *Dīwān-i Qāʾimiyyāt*.[39] As has been shown, the Īldigüzids, after earlier hostilities, became partners and allies of the Nizārīs under the Nizārī Ismaili Imam, Ḥasan III, who had helped Muẓaffar al-Dīn Uzbak to topple his rebellious governor Minglī in 614/1217. The Nizārīs and their western neighbours, including the Īldigüzids, had been opposed to the Khwārazmshāh; and contacts between them apparently continued into the reign of ʿAlāʾ al-Dīn Muḥammad III.

In 625/1228, the Nizārīs in Daylamān had another, perhaps more prestigious, guest. This was Ghiyāth al-Dīn, the younger brother of Jalāl al-Dīn Mingburnī, who had ruled western Iran as a semi-independent Khwārazmian governor; however, upon the arrival in 622/1225 of his older brother, Jalāl al-Dīn, he was forced to surrender power to him. According to al-Nasawī, the Abbasids also supported Ghiyāth al-Dīn financially, so it would seem that the Nizārīs, Abbasids and the Īldigüzids continued their cooperation well into the reign of ʿAlāʾ al-Dīn Muḥammad III. Jalāl al-Dīn Mingburnī was greatly angered by his brother having been offered shelter in Alamūt and he blocked the roads in the region so his brother could be captured. In spite of this blockade, though, the Nizārīs managed to smuggle Ghiyāth al-Dīn out as far as Kirmān; there, however, he was betrayed by his entourage and put to death on the orders of Jalāl al-Dīn Mingburnī. Al-Nasawī, Ibn al-Athīr and Juwaynī all mention the presence of Ghiyāth al-Dīn at Alamūt with al-Nasawī explicitly stating that the Nizārīs gave Ghiyāth al-Dīn active support and despatched three or four hundred Nizārī horsemen with him to Kirmān.[40] Juwaynī, who had an especially hostile attitude towards the Nizārīs, says that Ghiyāth al-Dīn decided to leave Alamūt on his own during the Nizārī-Khwārazmian negotiations.[41] Ibn al-Athīr remarks that although ʿAlāʾ al-Dīn Muḥammad welcomed Ghiyāth al-Dīn in Alamūt, he was nonetheless disinclined to pit Ghiyāth al-Dīn against his brother, an indication once again of the cautious diplomatic approach of the Ismailis.[42]

According to al-Nasawī, after this truce of 624/1227, Nizārī envoys from Alamūt appeared in Rayy at the court of Jalāl al-Dīn Mingburnī, where they offered their services as fighters to the Khwārazmshāh. Jalāl al-Dīn Mingburnī after some hesitation declined this offer, fearing that the Nizārīs would eventually acquire information about his army.[43]

Not long after these events, Jalāl al-Dīn Mingburnī, whose relations with the Nizārīs fluctuated, had yet another dispute with Alamūt when a high-ranking Ismaili was imprisoned by the Khwārazmian *iqṭāʿ*-holder of the town of Sāwa and put to death. After this incident, the Nizārīs tried to counterbalance the growing power of Jalāl al-Dīn Mingburnī and sent emissaries to both the Abbasids and the Mongols. Al-Nasawī claims that it was the above-mentioned Ismaili diplomat, Badr al-Dīn, who was sent to the Mongols, a claim reiterated by Ibn al-Athīr.[44]

> An official of the Ismaili Malāḥida was sent to the Tatars. He made known to them the weakness of Jalāl al-Dīn with his defeat.[45] He urged [the Mongols] to proceed to him, and follow up on [Jalāl al-Dīn's] weaknesses. And [the Ismaili official] truly guaranteed them victory over [Jalāl al-Dīn] if they went to him.[46]

The most striking piece of evidence regarding this can be read in Chinese annals written about the Yuan dynasty.[47] In the *Shengwu qinzheng Lu* we read that the ruler of the 'Malaya' sent his envoy to the Mongol court in 627/1229:

> In this year, the city ruler of Isbarayin city in the West came to surrender.[48] Also the rulers of the western Hindus[49] and the Malaya realms of the West came personally to attend the court.[50]

As Atwood notes it is almost certain that the Chinese text in fact is referring to the Nizārī diplomat, Badr al-Dīn Aḥmad.

We read the same story in the *Yuanshi*, the other Chinese chronicle of the Mongol period in China:

> The ruler of India and the ruler of the Moloyid Kingdom came to have an imperial audience. The chieftain of the city of Isbarana in the West came to surrender.[51]

According to the narratives by Ibn al-Athīr, al-Nasawī and the Chinese sources, it seems that Badr al-Dīn Aḥmad went directly to a local Mongol court and then to Karakorum, the Mongol capital.

In 627/1229, Jalāl al-Dīn Mingburnī was once again greatly angered by the ongoing Nizārī-Mongol negotiations and ordered the suspension of all trading activities between the Oxus and the Mediterranean, suspecting the presence of Mongol spies in the caravans guided by the Nizārīs to the Abbasids or to other kingdoms hostile to him. Not long after this decision, Sharaf al-Mulk, the vizier of Jalāl al-Dīn Mingburnī, executed seventy Nizārī merchants in Ādharbāyjān who were travelling westwards, suspecting that Mongol spies were hiding among the Nizārīs, or thinking that the Nizārīs had been hired by the Mongols for spying activities. After this incident, the Nizārīs of Alamūt threatened Jalāl al-Dīn Mingburnī with retaliation and demanded compensation and the making of some sort of amends, which things were promised but, according to al-Nasawī, never fulfilled.[52]

Perhaps in consequence of this bloody incident as well as the lack of compensation for the loss of lives and goods, the Nizārīs refused to pay the full amount of tribute due for Dāmghān. Angered, Jalāl al-Dīn Mingburnī then sent al-Nasawī to Alamūt. The latter, according to his own narrative, set out for Alamūt with much anxiety and hesitation, fearing that the Nizārīs would then execute him for the harsh content of his master's letter. After much hesitation, however, he was encouraged by other courtiers to go to Alamūt. Once in Alamūt, al-Nasawī insisted that he should personally meet the Imam and lord of Alamūt. He was finally granted an audience by 'Alā' al-Dīn Muḥammad III and his chief confidant 'Imād al-Dīn Muḥtasham; and despite his earlier hesitation al-Nasawī claims he showed much courage in the presence of the *khudāwand* of Alamūt.

Al-Nasawī says that the claims of Jalāl al-Dīn Mingburnī against the Nizārīs appeared to be very serious. First, Jalāl al-Dīn Mingburnī urged the Nizārīs to reinstate the *khuṭba* given in the name of the Khwārazmshāhs, which they had abandoned after the death of his father in 617/1220. Secondly, he reproached the Nizārīs for having despatched emissaries to the Mongol court. Furthermore, Jalāl al-Dīn Mingburnī wanted the remainder of the tribute that the Nizārīs were still withholding.

Al-Nasawī says that 'Alā' al-Dīn Muḥammad III's response to the demands of the last Khwārazmshāh was more nuanced than expected, at least by himself, and it proved to be enough to have a calming effect on the situation. In his reply ʿAlāʾ al-Dīn Muḥammad III insisted that he and his followers had pledged their allegiance to the Khwārazmshāh, and it was Jalāl al-Dīn Mingburnī who had broken his word by attacking Nizārī merchants.

As far as the Mongol contacts were concerned, ʿAlāʾ al-Dīn Muḥammad III replied diplomatically that the Mongols were neighbours of the Nizārīs and it was consequently the duty of the Nizārīs to have official contacts with them just as they did with the Khwārazmshāh.

Regarding Dāmghān and its tribute, the Nizārīs asked Sharaf al-Mulk, the vizier of Jalāl al-Dīn Mingburnī, for a reduction. Al-Nasawī, perhaps due to his negative opinion of Sharaf al-Mulk, rejected this deal, but in the end, it was agreed that the Nizārīs would pay a reduced tribute for Dāmghān. This was paid in the gold dinars of the Ghūrids.

As is clear from the result of these negotiations, in his dealings with the Nizārīs the Khwārazmshāh generally failed to achieve his objectives, and the Nizārīs were usually successful in defending their positions and could not be forced to accept the conditions he tried to impose on them. Though not overly successful, the peaceful and hospitable atmosphere in which the negotiations were conducted was a great relief to al-Nasawī, and he was personally honoured by ʿAlāʾ al-Dīn Muḥammad III at the end of them. The Nizārī Imam presented lavish gifts to al-Nasawī at the end of his visit. As he wrote:

> ʿAlāʾ al-Dīn Muḥammad favoured me above all the other envoys of the Sultan, treating me with great respect and delicacy. He dealt generously with me, and gave me twice the usual amount in gifts and robes of honour. This is an honourable man. Generosity to such a man is never wasted. The value of what was bestowed on me, in cash and in kind, was near 3000 dinars, including two robes of honour, each consisting of a satin cloak, a hood, a fur and a cape, one lined with satin and the other with Chinese crepe; two belts of 200 dinars weight; 70 pieces of cloth; two horses with saddles, bridles and harness and pommels; a thousand dinars in gold; four caparisoned horses; a string of Bactrian camels; and thirty robes of honour for my suite.[53]

Given al-Nasawī's account, these rich gifts, textiles and exotic clothes of different origin demonstrate the far-reaching diplomatic and mercantile connections, stretching into Central Asia, of the Nizārī leadership in this era, something which has been confirmed by recent excavations at Alamūt carried out by Hamīda Chubak.[54]

Al-Nasawī says that at the end of his mission he wished to purchase sheep in a local market in Alamūt valley, with the intention of donating them to a *khānqah* he had founded in Khurāsān where there was a shortage of cattle in the aftermath of the Mongol ravages. When 'Alā' al-Dīn Muḥammad III heard of this, he himself intervened and gave his guest 400 sheep. Al-Nasawī went to Qazwīn and the livestock was sent on after him. Whether or not the sheep reached the *khānqah* is not known but again the diplomatic sophistication of the Nizārīs is contrasted with Jalāl al-Dīn's increasingly erratic and desperate behaviour.[55]

The curious nature of these provisional political alliances, displaying a mixture of personal sympathy and antipathy, is clearly reflected in Ibn al-Athīr's accounts of events. Continuing the story of Nasawī's mission, Ibn al-Athīr says that a Nizārī envoy was sent back to Jalāl al-Dīn Mingburnī with him. However, this Nizārī emissary was familiar with the courtiers of Jalāl al-Dīn Mingburnī. The Nizārīs seem to have had a good understanding of Jalāl al-Dīn's entourage, where they had both friends and enemies.[56]

Sharaf al-Mulk, Jalāl al-Dīn Mingburnī's vizier and a key protagonist in the Nizārī affair, was said to have been greatly disliked by the new envoy of Alamūt, which statement suggests the closeness of personal relations between the Nizārīs and the Khwārazmshāh in around 628/1230. Indeed, the Nizārī envoy was said to be so familiar with the most intimate circles of Jalāl al-Dīn Mingburnī's court that he had been able to stir up the Khwārazmian court against Sharaf al-Mulk in the past. Sharaf al-Mulk accused him of betraying Khwārazmian interests and of persuading the Mongols to attack Jalāl al-Dīn Mingburnī. Due to the extreme scarcity of other sources,[57] we cannot judge whether this statement was an act of personal revenge or connected to the Nizārī visit to the Mongols discussed above. But in such an ambiguous political atmosphere, when political preferences frequently fluctuated, nothing was improbable. The Nizārīs had contacts with the Mongols and maintained their political philosophy of supporting the enemies of their enemies. In the end, Sharaf al-Mulk had the Nizārī envoy executed, thus perpetuating the constant state of aggression between the last Khwārazmshāh and Alamūt.

In sum, relations between the last Khwārazmian ruler and the Nizārīs were no different to the dealings between the Nizārīs and their former opponents, the Saljūqs and Bāwandids. However as a result of, above all, al-Nasawī's record there is some detail of at least one diplomatic exchange and through these episodes that he recounts, despite his antipathy to the Nizārīs generally, there emerges the character of Nizārī diplomacy at his time. Moreover, it is clear from his account that whatever concessions diplomatically the Nizārī Imams may have felt it necessary to make they saw themselves as the true leaders of the Muslim community and conducted themselves as gracious and generous sovereigns. The wealth that they appear to have amassed, the gifts to al-Nasawī and the store of gold dinars with which to pay revenues to Jalāl al-Dīn, indicate the prosperity and extent of the community as a whole, despite the troubled times in Iran and Central Asia caused by the Mongol onslaught. Besides al-Nasawī, Nizārī sources from the early Nizārī period, later used by Juwaynī and Rashīd al-Dīn, had similar accounts of the manner in which the Nizārīs handled their diplomatic missions, especially in the administration of the district of Girdkūh by Ra'īs Muẓaffar and in the division of revenues with Sanjar. Many indications of pragmatism and flexibility can be perceived from the narrative of al-Nasawī, where the sophisticated methods of Nizārī diplomacy are well documented.

The years after 618/1221, the first decade of ʿAlā' al-Dīn Muḥammad III's rule thus saw an unexpected expansion of the Nizārīs in northern Iran, who quickly and shrewdly exerted their power over areas ravaged the Mongols and abandoned by the Khwārazmians in the collapse of their empire. The attempt to create a greater Nizārī Ismaili state clearly recalls the age of Ḥasan-i Ṣabbāḥ. On the other hand, however, the last two decades of ʿAlā' al-Dīn Muḥammad III's imamate were overshadowed by political isolation and Mongol military manoeuvres, which eventually led to the fall of Alamūt in 654/1256.

The expansionist aspirations of the Ismailis are reflected in the *Rawḍat al-taslīm* and other contemporary sources, all suggesting that the enormous political changes created by the Mongols provoked a great reaction among the Nizārīs comparable to the atmosphere of Ḥasan-i Ṣabbāḥ's time. Regarding their contacts with their Caspian neighbours after 617/1220, one can see a similar impetus when they extended the area under their control to include Dāmghān and Bisṭām. The three main local protagonists in this period were the Bāwandids in Ṭabaristān, the Bādūspānids in Rūyān, and the city of Qazwīn. Unfortunately, sources telling of Zaydī clans and Imams previously active in Daylamān and Gīlān are fragmentary for the period after 617/1220, so one cannot really assess their impact on local history, but some Zaydī Imams survived the havoc wrought by the Mongols and represented a significant form of local power as late as the 8th/14th century.[58]

As for as the Bāwandids, although equally pressurised by the major powers of the age, they had been the most formidable enemy of the Nizārīs in the Caspian provinces before 607/1210, fighting a long series of wars against them around Alamūt and in the area of Girdkūh. The fall of the Bāwandid kingdom in Māzandarān in 607/1210 greatly facilitated Nizārī actions there making them more confident in pursuit of their expansionist policy in northern Iran. After the elimination of the Bāwandids, the Nizārīs turned their attention to the Khwārazmians who had replaced the Bāwandids in the areas they had ruled. Consequently, the Nizārīs started supporting those elements who opposed the Khwārazmian presence in northern Iran and among them one can also include surviving branches of the Bāwandids. Various cadet branches of this clan-like dynasty lived on in Māzandarān as local lords. As noted earlier, Jalāl al-Dīn Ḥasan III gave his daughter in marriage to a Bāwandid prince, Kinkhwār. The circumstances of this marriage are obscure, but it may have been a significant event at a local level as it represented the depth of influence the Nizārīs exerted on the former Bāwandid-ruled areas. As mentioned earlier also, Ḥusām al-Dawla Ardashīr, the son of this obscure Bāwandid prince Kinkhwār and a Nizārī princess, became the founder of the third branch of the Bāwandids which restored the Bāwandid kingdom in around 636/1238.

This year was, however, also marked by other developments when Nizārī envoys appeared in France and in England seeking military aid, or perhaps warning of the invasion of Europe that was to come. This remarkable episode was briefly recorded by the English chronicler of the period, Matthew Paris. A further element in it is the discover of a record of gold dinars in the English treasury, apparently the same kind paid to the Khwārazmshāh.[59]

As regards the contemporary English attitude towards the Ismaili ambassadors, there is the delusional comment of the Bishop of Winchester about both the Muslims and the Mongols:

> Let us leave these dogs to devour one another, that they may all be consumed, and perish; and we, when we proceed against the enemies of Christ who remain, will slay them, and cleanse the face of the earth, so that all the world will be subject to the one Catholic [i.e. universal] Church, and there will be one shepherd and one fold.[60]

The restoration of the Bāwandid kingdom with Nizārī help and dynastic links to the family of the Imam of Alamūt was an important local episode, and later events suggest that the Nizārīs were interested in the restoration of the Bāwandids. After the death of the last Khwārazmshāh, Jalāl al-Dīn Mingburnī, in 629/1231 the Nizārīs felt threatened by the growing menace of Mongol forces and sought new allies against them. The number of possible allies for the Nizārīs was now quite limited. No record of overtures to Muslim states in the Near East on this issue has been identified. The restored Bāwandid kingdom after 636/1238 (that of the Kinkhwāriyya branch) controlled a much more limited area than the Iṣfahbadiyya had before 607/1210, yet their support could be important on the local level as they could operate as a buffer zone for the Nizārīs against possible Mongol attacks.

Māzandarān was twice overrun by the Mongols, in 618/1221 and then in 634/1236. Although, as far as one can tell, these attacks did not affect the Nizārīs they may well have alarmed them. The restored Bāwandid kingdom, led by a nephew of the *khudāwand* of Alamūt, might have helped to halt future Mongol attacks. The Nizārīs, as has been seen, regularly and tenaciously supported their neighbours when they themselves were being threatened by a greater power. It seems that the Nizārīs helped to revive the Bāwandids when they felt threatened by the Khwārazmians and, later on, by the Mongols after the second Mongol attack in Māzandarān in 634/1236. The fact that the Nizārīs calculated accurately as regards Bāwandid support is supported by the fact that after 654–655/1256–1257 the Bāwandids only reluctantly joined the Mongols in their campaigns against the Nizārīs.

Ḥusām al-Dawla Ardashīr's circumstances upon his accession are not well understood due to the paucity of our sources. Ibn Isfandiyār, the main source for local Māzandarānī history, perished in the first Mongol invasion of Khwārazm in 617–618/1220–1221. The anonymous continuer of his work felt no need to explain the events of the decades after 617/1220, thus the transitional period between the fall of the Iṣfahbadiyya branch in 607/1210 and the rise of the Kinkhwāriya branch of the Bāwandids is largely undocumented. Except for the first and last years (636/1238 and 647/1249) of Ḥusām al-Dawla Ardashīr II's reign in Māzandarān practically nothing is known; but it must be noted that Māzandarān was firmly under the control of the Mongols after 618/1221; and Mongol armies regularly appeared there, either parading their power, such as that of Arghūn Āqā, the Mongol viceroy of Māzandarān and Khurāsān in 634/1236, or conducting punitive campaigns against local rulers, as we will see in relation to the Bādūspānids.

The great campaign of Chormaghan, the Mongol viceroy of Iran, against Jalāl al-Dīn Mingburnī in 629/1231 affected northern Iran as well. According to Jūzjānī, in that year Chormaghan raided numerous northern Iranian provinces, including Rūyān and Gīlān, which may have had a great impact on the Nizārīs too, though nothing is known about the Nizārī reaction to such attacks, albeit the sending of envoys to Europe, mentioned above, may have been part of it.[61]

Ḥusām al-Dawla Ardashīr II probably died around 647/1249. He was succeeded by his oldest son, Shams al-Mulūk Muḥammad. As for his name, 'Muḥammad', one should note that previously it had only appeared once among names of the Bāwandid kings, and so may have been a gesture to his influential maternal uncle, ʿAlāʾ al-Dīn Muḥammad III, at Alamūt. Shams al-Mulūk Muḥammad ruled for nearly two decades in central Ṭabaristān. The end year of his reign, however, is uncertain, as Madelung notes.[62] According to Marʿashī, Shams al-Mulūk Muḥammad must have died in 663/1264 but, according to Āmulī, he was present at the Mongol siege of Girdkūh in 669/1270.[63]

One must therefore be realistic regarding the importance of the newly restored Bāwandid kingdom. It could have been only a mere shadow of its predecessor. The effect of Mongol depredations is clear from the fact that the capital was moved from Āmul, which was regularly raided by the Mongols, to the safer city of Sārī. The Nizārī role in the restoration appears to be prominent, and considering the growing Mongol menace after the death of the last Khwārazmshāh in 629/1231, their efforts to rebuild the Bāwandid kingdom as a Nizārī vassal state and perhaps as their eastern 'shield' against the Mongols were undoubtedly significant.

The situation of the Bādūspānids and their relations with the Nizārīs were equally complicated during the imamate 'Alā' al-Dīn Muḥammad III. Most Bādūspānid rulers had long-standing confrontations with the Nizārīs and although occasionally there were pro-Nizārī Bādūspānid princes as governors of Rūyān mentioned in the written sources, a Bādūspānid line eventually took over that was strongly opposed to the Nizārīs.

The first years 'Alā' al-Dīn Muḥammad III's imamate coincided with the last years of the Bādūspānid *ustāndār* Bīsutūn b. Zarrīnkamar. Apart from some anecdotal details, Āmulī says that following the death of Bīsutūn b. Zarrīnkamar in 621/1224, and the succession of his son Fakhr al-Dawla Nāmāwar, opposition elements in Rūyān contacted the '*mulḥids*' i.e. the Nizārīs, who themselves sensed that the political situation might offer them an opportunity to extend their influence into the Bādūspānid-ruled areas of Rūyān. In some very brief passages, Āmulī suggests that the local pro-Nizārī party in Rūyān, which had been suppressed under Zarrīnkamar and Bīsutūn, had nevertheless endeavoured to remain active. Āmulī notes that the revived Nizārī and pro-Nizārī activity in Rūyān was further enhanced by the decline of the Bāwandids in Ṭabaristān in 607/1210, since they had supported the ruling anti-Nizārī line of the Bādūspānids in the past.[64] Therefore, Fakhr al-Dawla Nāmāwar was forced to turn to Jalāl al-Dīn Mingburnī for help since the local pro-Nizārī forces along with the local Nizārīs themselves were advancing quickly into Rūyān. According to Āmulī, Fakhr al-Dawla Nāmāwar spent a year in Khurāsān possibly in the entourage of Jalāl al-Dīn Mingburnī, who then despatched him to Rūyān along with a few thousand Khwārazmian horsemen and a few high-ranking officers to help the embattled *ustāndār* against his enemies. Furthermore, he received regular financial support from the Khwārazmshāh.

After this, Āmulī's record of events pertaining to Rūyān lacks specific detail. When mentioning the death of the Khwārazmshāh he speaks about an unnamed Khwārazmian prince who was forced to escape to Rūyān in 629/1231. Āmulī calls him '*padishāhzādah*', which means he was must have been yet another member of the Khwārazmian royal family. Āmulī relates that this exiled Khwārazmian prince, after lavish ceremonies held at his honour in Kujūr in the capital of Rūyān, was asked to give one of his daughters to Fakhr al-Dawla Nāmāwar. Āmulī, though his account is very short, cannot hide the astonishment the Khwārazmian prince felt at this request which he felt was beneath him, however desperate his circumstances. Nonetheless, the harsh conditions of his situation and the Mongol's surprise attack led by Chormaghan in 629/1231 against the remnants of the Khwārazmians forced this unnamed prince to accept Fakhr al-Dawla Nāmāwar's proposal. Āmulī notes, too, that Fakhr al-Dawla Nāmāwar's second son, Iskandar was born from his marriage with the Khwārazmian princess.[65]

Unfortunately, the wars Fakhr al-Dawla Nāmāwar waged on the Nizārīs and local pro-Nizārī aristocrats remain opaque; nonetheless, it is important to note that his principal achievement was that he succeeded in keeping his throne in Rūyān despite the tempestuous political events which characterised the era. The Bādūspānid dynasty first lost the support of the Bāwandids, then of the Khwārazmians, but they nonetheless managed to weather these calamities and survive in northern Iran.

The Bādūspānid dynasty not only survived but pursued its former anti-Nizārī policy at a local level. Fakhr al-Dawla Nāmāwar died in 640/1242 and his sons were strong enough to divide the traditional areas of Rūyān amongst themselves. His eldest son, Ḥusām al-Dawla Ardashīr, ruled in Daylamān, while another son, Iskandar, the one said to be born of the Khwārazmian princess, ruled the core areas of Rūyān from Nāṭil. The sources do not suggest any sort of conflict between the brothers, however not long after this division a third son of Fakhr al-Dawla Nāmāwar, Shahragīm (r. 640–671/1242–1273), took over Rūyān and ruled for nearly three decades.

During this late period the Nizārīs showed great interest in reviving the Bāwandids. Through dynastic contacts they were somehow able to support the third branch of the Bāwandids in their accession to power. If the Nizārīs main aim was to support local polities against the Mongols by creating a coalition of local princes, then their stance towards the Bādūspānids might have been more flexible accounting for why this local dynasty did not succumb to the Nizārīs. A coalition between local rulers in Māzandarān did in fact develop in the years before Hülegü's campaign. Shahragīm is known to have given one of his daughters to the Bāwandid Shams al-Mulūk Muḥammad (who ruled after 647/1249), whose grandmother was a daughter of Jalāl al-Dīn Ḥasan III.[66]

Our sources are also lacking regarding the Nizārīs' regional policy towards their direct neighbours in the years before the great military expedition of Hülegü and the downfall of the Nizārī Ismaili state in Iran. As far as the Mongols are concerned, after 617/1220 the local rulers in Māzandarān had become their vassals and the Mongol viceroys extended their authority to Māzandarān after 629/1231, most importantly over the Bāwandids, despite the Nizārī role in their restoration in 635/1238, and over the Bādūspānids. The Mongol viceroys inherited by right of conquest the claim to power of the Khwārazmshāhs and in this old-new system the local polities had no option other than to follow the orders of their Mongol masters. But it is clear that the Bāwandids and Bādūspānids also maintained relations with the Nizārīs, and indeed it made sense at the time to do so.

Alamūt and Qazwīn in the reign of ʿAlāʾ al-Dīn Muḥammad III

Despite Imam Jalāl al-Dīn Ḥasan III's attempts at reconciliatory contact with the leadership of Qazwīn, relations between Alamūt and Qazwīn continued to be fraught during the imamate of ʿAlāʾ al-Dīn Muḥammad III. The reasons for this were both contemporary and traditional. Traditionally, Qazwīn, a rich merchant city, which was the main southwestern gateway to Gīlān was also located on the east-west commercial route of northern Iran, part of the Silk Road. Additionally, as already noted, there had been renewed attempts to extend the control of the state to areas nearer Qazwīn. There was also a determined attempt to increase Nizārī influence in the city itself. According to Rashīd al-Dīn and Kāshānī,[67] ʿAlāʾ al-Dīn Muḥammad III was able to develop close contacts with a Sufi shaykh there called Jalāl al-Dīn Gīlī. ʿAlāʾ al-Dīn Muḥammad III was said to have sent the shaykh an annual bursary of 500 gold dinars, presumably the same kind of dinars that were paid to the last Khwārazmshāh and that found their way into the treasury of the king of England. According to the *Dabistān*,[68] a much later account, the Sufi shaykh even converted to Ismailism, an assertion it has to be said confirmed neither by Rashīd al-Dīn nor Kāshānī. But the Nizārī Imam was rumoured to have sent a message to the people of Qazwīn, warning them that his soldiery would have attacked Qazwīn had Jamāl al-Dīn Gīlī not become an Ismaili. Rashīd al-Dīn suggested that the rather extravagant personality of the Nizārī Imam was the main factor in this episode.[69] Yet as noted, many of these accusations are based on the anti-Nizārī bias and hostile attitude of our Sunni sources.

However, two factors can be said to account for the policy of 'Alā' al-Dīn Muḥammad III regarding Qazwīn. First, one can see a continuation of Jalāl al-Dīn Ḥasan III's policy towards Sunni centres of power and the 'courting' by 'Alā' al-Dīn Muḥammad III of the religious circles of Qazwīn might be readily accepted as a reflection of the former policy. Alongside this, we cannot forget that Jamāl al-Dīn Gīlī was a Sufi thinker, and this may have created some common basis in religious matters in Alamūt and also in some of the Sufi circles of Qazwīn. As noted, there had been signs of a similar rapprochment concerning spiritual issues between Baghdad and Alamūt during the era of the caliph al-Nāṣir and Jalāl al-Dīn Ḥasan III, in which elements of both Sufism and Shi'i Islam were blended.

However, a spiritual propinquity could often become a political advantage. It is not exactly known when 'Alā' al-Dīn Muḥammad III contacted Jamāl al-Dīn Gīlī, but Nizārī attempts to gain more influence in Qazwīn may have coincided with their efforts after 618/1221 to exert control over various towns that had been ravaged by the Mongols and abandoned by the Khwārazmians, such as Rayy and Dāmghān.

Any attempts to incorporate Qazwīn into the Nizārī realm, however, eventually failed. Jūzjānī says that it was due to the endless wars between the Nizārīs and Qazwīnīs that Shams al-Dīn, the *qāḍī* of Qazwīn, visited Karakorum, the Mongol capital, several times. According to Juzjānī in 649/1251 he railed against the Nizārīs at the court of Möngke Khan, and Jūzjānī claims that the *qāḍī* appeared in Möngke's court wearing a shirt of mail under his robes as a precaution against them.[70] He called the Nizārīs trouble-makers, saying they always exploited political disturbances; and he placed Sunni Islam, Christianity and the *dīn-i mughūlī* on the same level, i.e. as being threatened by the 'relentless' Nizārīs'.[71] Furthermore, he declared that if Mongol power were to vanish, the Nizārīs would quickly capture their lands in the Middle East. It has been argued that this suggests that

Nizārīs had had some success in Qazwīn in this period.[72] According to Mustawfī Qazwīnī, it was Shams al-Dīn who approved the choice of Hülegü for the military expedition against the Middle East;[73] and though this is hardly credible, such matters being decided by individuals in Karakorum far more powerful than this *qāḍī*, the account of Mustawfī Qazwīnī nevertheless indicates that the Sunni elite of Qazwīn saw itself in collaboration with the Mongols.[74] Hodgson argued that this Sunni Muslim hatred exacerbated Mongol resentment against the Nizārīs.[75]

But the Nizārīs also felt the need to send their envoys to Karakorum upon the enthronement of Möngke in 649/1251, though these envoys were swiftly turned back as had been their earlier delegation upon Güyük's accession in 644/1246.[76]

The visit of this Sunni *qāḍī* to Karakorum, the Mongol capital, points to both the ultimate failure of the Nizārīs to extend their influence over Qazwīn and the Nizārī-friendly Sufis in Qazwīn. Despite the dominance of the Mongol empire, ʿAlāʾ al-Dīn pursued a policy based on the heightened ambitions of the Nizārīs and their aspirations and this was vehemently opposed by certain groups, notably those who felt they had something to lose.

As far as the death of ʿAlāʾ al-Dīn Muḥammad III in 654/1255 is concerned, Juwaynī described it as a plot organised by his boon companion Ḥasan Māzandarānī,[77] but there is also the fact that his eldest son and designated successor, Rukn al-Dīn Khurshāh, had had apparently very poor relations with his father. The main reason was perhaps Rukn al-Dīn Khurshāh's discontent with his father's stance regarding the Mongols.

In the case of ʿAlāʾ al-Dīn Muḥammad III, serious political concerns augmented the rivalries between contending factions. According to Juwaynī and Rashīd al-Dīn,[78] the conspirators against ʿAlāʾ al-Dīn Muḥammad III wished to begin immediate negotiations with the Mongols upon Rukn al-Dīn Khurshāh's accession to power; thus one cannot dismiss the influence of certain pro-Mongol elements among the Nizārīs and a bitter argument over policy in the elimination of ʿAlāʾ al-Dīn Muḥammad III, who, after years of pro-Mongol alliances was now hostile towards the Mongols, although unable to find a counterbalance to the growing existential threat they presented.

This souring of Nizārī-Mongol relations may have commenced after 629/1231, with the death of the last Khwārazmshāh, Jalāl al-Dīn

Mingburnī. 'Alā' al-Dīn Muḥammad had endeavoured to come to terms with the Mongols after 629/1231, but without success. Details of the increasingly uncongenial conditions can only be fragmentarily reconstructed. The failed Nizārī efforts to reconcile themselves with the Mongols included those of 'Alā' al-Dīn Muḥammad's emissaries; a situation in which they were not alone since the ambassadors the Abbasid caliph al-Musta'ṣim were similarly treated by Great Khan Güyük at his enthronement in 644/1246.

A possible Nizārī role in the death of Güyük, as mentioned by Kāshānī, was clearly a later fabrication from the Ilkhanid period. The fable of a Nizārī concubine who seduces Güyük and then kills him in his bed is mentioned only by Kāshānī and this story does not fit the historical context.[79] But this kind of Ilkhanid paranoia concerning the deaths of their rulers is clear from the sources. Their fear of the Nizārīs receives further confirmation from the Franciscan missionary William of Rubruk, who travelled to Mongolia in the reign of Möngke. He says that the Mongols believed 400 Nizārī *fidā'īs* had been sent to Karakorum to kill Güyük's successor, Möngke.[80] The growing Mongol menace hanging over the Nizārīs in Quhistān and in the Caspian provinces, however, was more or less clearly seen by 'Alā' al-Dīn Muḥammad as is evident in a letter addressed to the Abbasid caliph Musta'ṣim, an ally against the Mongols.[81]

The end of the Nizārī Ismaili state in the Caspian

After 629/1231, the Nizārīs became more and more isolated by which time the Mongol army in the southern Caucasus and Persia had eliminated any other possible opposition. The Nizārī murder of Chaghtāy Qūrchī after 647/1249 was probably an important consideration in the decision to eliminate the Nizārī Ismaili state. As mentioned, Nizārī envoys were reproached and treated contemptuously at least twice in Karakorum by the Mongols, once in 644/1246, at Güyük's enthronement, and again in 649/1251, when Möngke Khan suceeded to the Mongol throne. Following the incidents at the enthronement in 644/1246, Güyük sent military reinforcements to the Middle East. Then in 649/1251, Baiju, the military commander of the Mongol armies in the Middle East, sent a message to Möngke complaining about the dangerous behaviour of the Nizārīs;[82]

meanwhile, Shams al-Dīn, the *qāḍī* of Qazwīn, incited Möngke and his court in Karakorum against the Nizārīs. Despite this, it should be remembered that the decision to destroy the Nizārīs in Iran was part of the wider military objectives put in motion on the accession of Möngke, which included further advances in Russia and eastern Europe and a renewed assault in China against the empire of the Southern Sung.

As early as 650/1252, Ket-Buqa arrived in Khurāsān and started attacking the Nizārīs fortresses in Rūdbār and Quhistān.[83] One of the first Mongol attacks in 650/1252 attempted to capture Girdkūh, but without success. Ket-Buqa's expedition is mentioned by Chinese sources too. The *Yuanshi* mentions this event several times and refers to the *mulḥids*, i.e. the Nizārīs, as the targets of Ket-Buqa's military campaign:

> 3rd passage (year 650/1252):
>
> i. English translation: Year two, that of *ren/zi* [that is, 650/1252]. Spring. First moon... He sent Ket-Buqa to attack the Molaid Girduke[84] Fortress.[85]
>
> 4th passage: [Same year]:
>
> ii. English translation: [same year as above] Autumn. Seventh moon. The emperor ordered Qubilai to campaign against Dali, and the princes Turghaq and Sali[86] to campaign against Shindu,[87] Ket-Buqa to campaign against Molqid, and Hüle'ü to campaign against the countries of the sultan in the west.[88]

After the unsuccessful attack on Girdkūh, Ket-Buqa turned his attention to Quhistān and penetrated the area, whereupon a sort of stalemate then set in. Whenever the Mongols entered a town they controlled it briefly only until their departure when the local Nizārīs retook it. Apparently, the Nizārīs always made use of this method which they had honed during conflicts with the Saljūqs and Khwārazmshāhs. Overall, the Nizārīs in Quhistān displayed a steadfast resistance against the forces of Ket-Buqa; yet this was just a minor episode before the storm brought by the army of Hülegü.

Hülegü's enormous army had been recruited from all corners of the Mongol empire, and this time the leadership of the Nizārī Ismaili state in Iran clearly realised that the way they had resisted Ket-Buqa's armies was untenable against the new army. Hülegü was instructed by Möngke to conquer all the areas lying between the Oxus and the Nile with special attention being given to Alamūt and the Nizārī Ismaili state. The newly-discovered *Akhbār-i Mughūlān* gives a vivid description of highly sophisticated military equipment, among other items the giant *kamāncha-i chirkh* or lethal machine, a construction capable of firing explosive materials some 2,500 paces, a considerable distance at that time.[89]

It is still unclear if the Mongols had knowledge of explosives during this campaign. Stephen Haw thinks that we cannot know this, while some elements in Mongol terminology may well refer to gunpowder as '*batan*' or '*panbah*'.[90] Nonetheless, the Mongols had advanced into northern China by this stage, and although 'greek fire' had been long known and deployed in the Middle East, it was in China that these specific forms of weaponry had developed. Hülegü's army was a relatively slow-moving military force due to its special arms and procedures and also its manpower; and in order to feed the vast number of soldiers, provisions had already been put in place by Mongol commanders, such as Arghūn Āqā, operating in Iran, as Juwaynī says: 'emirs and some local rulers... began to prepare provisions and get together *tuzghu* or offerings of food; and they set down their offerings at every stage (of the army's advance).'[91]

Quṭb al-Dīn Shīrāzī sheds further light on the Mongol military preparations, giving us details of the way the Mongols organised Hülegü's expedition using local guides and a highly skilled staff to handle the transportation of their military equipment:

> And from all the provinces they brought out provisions and supplies without limit and beyond compare. They set off by donkey, camel and cow and asses and such like. They had brought limitless noodles and cooked porridge (*tatum ash, tatumaj*), and pounded millet (*gāvrus-i kufteh*) from the provinces of Khitai and Uyghurestan to the foot of Alamut and Mimundaz and that castle, and every half farhang they had stacked ample flour and rice and necessities/ingredients (staples) in bags of fine linen so that everywhere was found great hills [of provisions].[92]

Hülegü arrived in Khurāsān in the month of Rabī' I 654/April 1256 and first invaded the city of Tūn, which had a sizeable Ismaili population. According to Juwaynī, Tūn was plundered by the two Mongol vanguards, those of Ket-Buqa and Köke-Ilgei, who captured the city after a week in the middle of Rabī' II 654/May 1256. Daftary says that the Mongols prevented Hülegü from attending the siege for it was feared that he would be a target of the Nizārīs. The Mongols slaughtered the population of Tūn, albeit sparing the lives of women and perhaps of some groups of artisans.[93]

When Hülegü arrived in Khurāsān, he sent written orders and messengers to *mulūk* and *pādishāhān* (kings and rulers) from every Iranian province to enlist men in his army. He promised peace and prosperity to those who did not refuse to obey his command and who were ready to assist him with troops and military supplies in his forthcoming campaign against the *malāḥida*, but threatened his Iranian vassals with retribution if they defied his command. According to the *Akhbār-i Mughūlān*, the *atabeg* of Shiraz, the sultan of Rūm, the *maliks* of Khurāsān, Sīstān, Māzandarān, Kirmān, Rustamdār, Shīrwān, Gurjistān, ʿIrāq, Ādharbayjān, Arrān and Luristān, were all personally invited to join Hülegü's army, while other rulers delegated such tasks to their relatives or despatched military supplies and gifts. Among the enlisted rulers, according to the *Akhbār-i Mughūlān*, were the princes of Rustamdār and Māzandarān, which means that both the Bādūspānids of Rūyān (Rustamdār) and the Bāwandids of Māzandarān were obliged to provide military support to the Mongols against the Nizārīs.[94]

After capturing Tūn, Hülegü proceeded towards Ṭūs, where Nāṣir al-Dīn, the Nizārī *muḥtasham* of Quhistān, surrendered to Hülegü on the advice of a local ally, Malik Shams al-Dīn (643–677/1245–1278), ancestor of the Kartid dynasty of Herat.[95] Naṣīr al-Dīn obeyed Hülegü but was unable to hand over the fortresses of Quhistān as everything depended on the Lord of Alamūt. However, for his obedience he was rewarded by Hülegü with the city of Tūn, though he died shortly after these events in Ṣafar 655/March 1257.[96]

Diplomatic missions and negotiations were intensifed in this period and the sources relate that, after numerous failed attempts to negotiate with Hülegü, in Jumādā I 654/May 1256 Rukn al-Dīn Khurshāh sent a message to Yasa'ur, the Mongol commander of ʿIrāq-i ʿAjam, offering his own surrender.[97] The head of the Nizārī delegation was his brother, Shāhanshāh, and there were other Nizārī dignitaries present also. The Nizārīs and Mongols met in Qazwīn, and Yasa'ur's son led the delegation to Hülegü's camp.[98] Though Yasa'ur clashed with the Nizārīs in Rūdbār in Jumādā I 654/June 1256, not long after the arrival of the Nizārī delegation, he also showed restraint, perhaps influenced by

Rukn al-Dīn Khurshāh's offer of total surrender and in line with the orders of Hülegü, who received Shāhanshāh and the Nizārīs in Qūchān. Hülegü accepted Rukn al-Dīn Khurshāh's offer and sent his own *ilchis* (envoys) to Alamūt with a *yarlīgh* (decree) at the end of Jumādā II 654/July 1256, which guaranteed the personal safety of the Imam if he pledged his absolute loyalty. In his message sent to Alamūt, Hülegü pardoned ʿAlāʾ al-Dīn's 'crimes', i.e. his actions against the Mongols, with reference being made to the death of Chaghtāy Qūrchī, which occurred in around 647/1250. A more serious Mongol demand was that all Nizārī castles were to be destroyed and that personal homage was to be made to Hülegü, this being so that the Mongol forces would stop devastating further Nizārī areas. Rukn al-Dīn Khurshāh consented to this and indeed he gave orders to have the castles destroyed, under the supervision of Mongol representatives, although at Alamūt, Lamasar and Maymūndiz, he only removed some outer battlements and did not dismantle them completely; furthermore, he showed no sign of preparing to come and pay homage. Mongol inspectors present in Rūdbār reported these anomalies to Hülegü. Apparently, the Nizārīs were playing for time, possibly hoping for the arrival of the winter snows to block the passes up into Daylām, and indeed Rukn al-Dīn Khurshāh asked for one year's grace before presenting himself at the court of Hülegü. But Hülegü replied harshly and demanded homage immediately. Hülegü appointed Tükel Bahadur as a Mongol *basqaq*, or chargé d'affaires, in Rūdbār. However, Rukn al-Dīn Khurshāh again asked for a grace period of a year and the exemption of Alamūt and Lamasar from the list of fortresses to be demolished. He sent the Mongol ambassadors back to Hülegü's camp, along with a relative, Sayf al-Dīn b. Bū Manṣūr b. Nūr al-Dīn Muḥammad (Muḥammad II), and his vizier, Shams al-Dīn Gīlakī, to negotiate with Hülegü on these matters, and they reached the camp on 17 Shaʿbān 654/16 September 1256.[99] Soon, Nizārī envoys appeared from Girdkūh and Quhistān, paying homage to Hülegü. But none of these attempts to appease the Mongols persuaded Hülegü to defer or delay his plans for the core areas of the Nizārī state in northern Iran.

Hülegü ordered more vigorous military action against Nizārī-controlled Daylam and he himself set up camp in Basṭām, slowly moving towards the Nizārī-ruled mountainous areas. The right flank of his army, led by two high-ranking Mongol commanders, Buqa

Temür and Köke Ilgei, quickly moved forward through Māzandarān, while the left flank, under the command of Ket-Buqa and the Chaghtāy prince Tegüder, approached northern Iran via Simnān and Khwār. The Mongol forces stationed in ʿIrāq-i ʿAjam, led by two other Chaghtāy princes of the blood, Tutar and Balaghai, were also ordered to take control of areas in Rūdbār. This was a classic Mongol strategy of approaching a military objective through three routes. Hülegü quickly left Bastām and went to Rayy, then on to Damāwand.

Having reached the valley of Damāwand Hülegü sent another messenger with a threatening message to Rukn al-Dīn Khurshāh, demanding his immediate surrender and that he present himself at Alamūt, adding that were he to be delayed by preparations he should send one of his sons as a 'ransom' to the Mongol camp. Rukn al-Dīn Khurshāh then despatched one of his younger sons in Ramaḍān 654/ October 1256; but Hülegü, though he showed kindness towards the Nizārī envoys, apparently had doubts about the status of the young prince and sent him back to Alamūt, demanding a more senior family member (perhaps Shīrānshāh, a brother of Rukn al-Din Khurshāh) to be sent so as to spare the life of Shāhanshāh, the brother of Rukn al-Dīn Khurshāh who had been the head of the Nizārī delegation to Hülegü.[100] Under growing Mongol pressure, Rukn al-Dīn Khurshāh sent Shīrānshāh with a considerable entourage. Hülegü consented to this and sent back Shīrānshāh with a new message demanding the demolition of Maymūndiz and that personal homage be paid by Rukn al-Dīn Khurshāh to Hülegü, otherwise he would face the Mongol assault.

Yet Rukn al-Dīn Khurshāh waited and did not leave Maymūndiz, where he had been during these months. Instead, the Mongols came closer and Hülegü himself appeared in Rūdbār after razing the area of Ṭāliqān.[101] On 18 Shawwāl 654/8 November 1256 he set up his camp on one of the foothills near Maymūndiz. The fortress itself was so impressive that Hülegü was first said to have hesitated, thinking about withdrawing his forces and waiting until the next spring to act. Ket-Buqa, however, succeeded in persuading Hülegü to persevere and launch an attack against the castle. Hülegü sent a final demand to Rukn al-Dīn Khurshāh for an unconditional surrender, but false news came to him: that Rukn al-Dīn Khurshāh had left Maymūndiz. Nonetheless, the assault against Maymūndiz was launched. The

Mongols cut down the trees around the fortress and the Nizārī hurled stones at the besiegers. After four days of preliminary bombardment, the Mongols deployed the monstrous *Kamān-i gāw*, the giant crossbow that could fire incendiary material at 2,500 paces. This induced Rukn al-Dīn Khurshāh to offer to turn himself over to the Mongols in exchange for his and his relatives' safety.[102] He sent his brother Īrānshāh and one of his sons, whose name according to Rashīd al-Dīn was Tarkiya, to the Mongols.[103] Following ferocious renewed Mongol attacks,[104] in accordance with the advice of Naṣīr al-Dīn al-Ṭūsī who suggested he surrender to the Mongols, Rukn al-Dīn Khurshāh finally came out of Maymūndiz on 29 Shawwāl 654/19 November 1256.[105] This marked the effective end of the Nizārī Ismaili state in northern Iran after 166 years.[106]

Rukn al-Dīn Khurshāh, Naṣīr al-Dīn al-Ṭūsī, Muʾayyad al-Dīn and Aṣīl al-Dīn Zūzānī, along with members of his family all came down from the castle, though scattered groups of Ismailis inside it still fought on for three further days. Rukn al-Dīn Khurshāh was forced to promulgate an order to dismantle the remaining fortresses in Rūdbār. Nearly all the castles opened their gates to the Mongols or were demolished by their guards, except for Alamūt and Lamasar.[107]

At Alamūt, Hülegü brought Rukn al-Dīn Khurshāh to persuade the defenders to surrender. The Mongols, led by Prince Balaghai, despatched their troops to the base of the fortress, calling for the immediate surrender of the commander, Muqaddam al-Dīn. The Mongols declared that if he and his military personnel were ready to submit promptly and pledge their allegiance to Möngke Khān within one day, their lives would be spared. After much hesitation and reluctance, they consented, and were given three days to remove their belongings.[108] As a sign of his obedience to the Imam, Muqaddim al-Dīn and the rest of the military in Alamūt left the fortress and the Mongol army began demolishing the now undefended chief fortress.[109] In the meantime most of the other fortresses in Daylamān had also complied with the orders of Rukn al-Dīn Khurshāh who was even allowed to pay a last visit to Alamūt in Dhu'l-Qaʿda 654/December 1256.[110] Juwaynī was allowed to visit the library of Alamūt and gives a vivid and detailed description of the military takeover of Alamūt; he also described the castle's highly sophisticated system of storage facilities.[111]

Meanwhile, Hülegü advanced towards Lamasar, which however resisted repeated Mongol calls to surrender. The defenders of this castle stood out against the Mongols for more than a year but were finally devastated by an outbreak of the plague (*waba*) at the end of 655/1257.[112] Hülegü then left Rūdbār in Dhu'l-Ḥijja 654/January 1257 and marched towards Hamadān and eventually Baghdad. The young Rukn al-Dīn Khurshāh became a hapless tool in the hands of the Mongols since his status as the Imam helped to speed up the capture of numerous Nizārī fortresses by the Mongols without any fighting. He had to accompany Hülegü, while his family was taken to Qazwīn and he was required to send more letters and envoys to the Nizārīs of Syria, telling them to accept Hülegü as their new ruler before the Mongols arrived there.

However, as the major Nizārī fortresses of the Caspian region surrendered, Rukn al-Dīn Khurshāh's value to the Mongol military machine decreased and on 1 Rabīʿ I 655/26 March 1257 he was despatched to Karakorum with nine companions guarded by a Mongol commander called Bujrai. After a long and exhausting journey replete with notorious episodes such as an unsuccessful appeal to the defenders of Girdkūh to surrender, and fist-fighting with his Mongol guards in Bukhārā, Rukn al-Dīn Khurshāh finally arrived at Karakorum. There, however, Möngke refused to see him, saying that several fortresses in northern Iran were still resisting. Möngke sent Rukn al-Dīn away and, on his orders, the Nizārī Imam was killed by Mongol soldiers in the Khangai mountains in north-western Mongolia. The actual date of his murder is unknown but according to Juwaynī, it coincided with further anti-Nizārī actions. Most of the relatives of Rukn al-Dīn Khurshāh were slaughtered by a Mongol commander, Qaraqai Bitikchi, in Qazwīn shortly after Rukn al-Dīn Khurshāh's departure for Karakorum, and Ötegü-China, another Mongol military leader, was said to have massacred nearly 12,000 Nizārīs in Khurāsān alone.[113] The number and degree of Nizārī deaths were certainly noteworthy, but one should add that survival was also significant as both in Daylam and in Quhistān we hear of a remarkable Nizārī presence after 654/1256, and attempts to reinstate themselves in the castles.[114]

The sources only provide us with detailed information about the situation in the Caspian provinces in the years preceding 654/1256 with regard to the Mongol raids on Rūdbār. Apart from this, one event of note concerns the participation of the Bādūspānid and Bāwandid rulers in Mongol military campaigns against the Nizārīs. For seventeen years Girdkūh, the last Nizārī fortress resisted the Mongols, but capitulated in December 669/1270. Regrettably, accounts of the role and size of local military forces in the campaigns of Hülegü and his successor, Ābāqā, are limited; Ibn Isfandiyār, Āmulī, as well as Marʿashī, recorded only fragmentary information.[115]

But in general, all of the local sources confirm the forced participation of local princes in these Mongol campaigns, though the military importance of such local powers would have been minimal in contrast to the numbers and armaments of the imperial armies of the Mongols. In the siege and fall of Alamūt in 654/1256, the participation of neighbouring principalities would have been in response to Mongol orders, though, interestingly, our local Caspian sources do not mention this. Only in the case of the siege of Girdkūh do we learn a few details about the military service of local princes, each for a period of two to three years.[116] The sources suggest that not only the Bādūspānids and Bāwandids, but perhaps other petty rulers of northern Iran were also summoned by the Mongols to fight the Nizārīs.

On one occasion in around 667/1269 both Fakhr al-Dawla Nāmāwar, the Bādūspānid *ustāndār* of Rūyān, and Shams al-Mulūk Muḥammad, the Bāwandid prince, appeared together at the walls of Girdkūh. The two rulers were avid hunters and since it was springtime they decided leave the Mongol camp at Girdkūh and return to Māzandarān; so they left apparently without permission and the Mongols were enraged at this insubordination.

The local sources relate that the Great Khān of the Mongol empire, Kubilai, gave orders for punitive action to be taken against these two deserters. Soon, a Mongol army led by a certain Ghāzān Bahādur arrived in Māzandarān and plundered the districts of Āmul controlled by the Bāwandids, and Rūdbār, ruled by the Bādūspānids. The local princes first sought to wage guerrilla warfare and hid in the dense forests of Māzandarān.[117] Local aristocrats intervened and tried to win over Ghāzān Bahādur. Finally, and somewhat ironically, Fakhr al-Dawla Nāmāwar appeared in the Mongol camp and took responsibility for their desertion declaring before Ghāzān Bahādur that it had been his decision to return to Māzandarān to rely on the safety it provided. He also suggested that the Bāwandid Shams al-Mulūk Muḥammad, the other deserter, who was his son-in-law as well as his ally, was both too young and too inexperienced to appear at the siege; so he was not to be blamed for any kind of defiance since he had been won over by the decision of his father-in-law. Ghāzān Bahādur finally pardoned both leaders on condition that Fakhr al-Dawla Nāmāwar send auxiliary forces to Girdkūh. In the end, these local rulers managed to avoid further involvement in the siege of Girdkūh, and they kept their thrones, according to the somewhat romantic characterisation of events in the local chronicles.[118]

Subsequently, the two local rulers continued to show signs of insubordination. As Āmulī says, they became as closely allied as father and son. No doubt the 'father' and mastermind behind this insubordination was Fakhr al-Dawla Nāmāwar. The Īl Khān Ābāqā (r. 663–681/1265–1282), Hülegü's successor realised that his northern Iranian vassals were again on the verge of revolt. According to Āmulī, Ābāqā invited Shams al-Mulūk Muḥammad to his camp, where he was put to death. Following this, Ābāqā sent a force to arrest Fakhr al-Dawla Nāmāwar who once again fled to the forests and sent 'harsh messages to the Mongols' according to Āmulī, while in the meantime the Mongols were causing so much damage in Rūyān that 'no one had ever witnessed such a thing'.[119]

Despite his lack of cooperation, the Bādūspānid ruler was once again pardoned by the Mongols and, as Āmulī states, he eventually stayed loyal to the Mongols. The forces of Ābāqā, the second Īl Khān of Persia, concentrated on Māzandarān, which was more accessible and where they slaughtered the remaining Bāwandids. The possible reason for the tenacious survival of Fakhr al-Dawla Nāmāwar was his relatively isolated position in mountainous Rūyān and perhaps in some parts of Rūdbār in former Nizārī areas. It would seem that in contrast to the Nizārīs, his tactics were flexible and not tied to defending great fortresses. Yet as Madelung pointed out, the date given for this last incident (663/1264-65) is too early chronologically, especially if this second Bādūspānid-Bāwandid revolt is supposed to have occurred after the fall of Girdkūh (669/1270), as Āmulī's account suggests.[120]

As far as the local history of the Nizārīs and their neighbouring areas is concerned, one of the earliest episodes of this 160-year-long cooperation was joint Nizārī-Bāwandid resistance against the invading armies of the Saljūq sultan, Muḥammad b. Malikshāh in around

502/1109, when the Bāwandid king Ḥusām al-Dawla Shahriyār rejected the Saljūq order to appear at the walls of Alamūt. Interestingly, the last part of this, often complex, relationship is very similar to the very first being an example of cooperation between local dynasts against offensive major powers. As in 502/1109, when the Bāwandid *iṣfahbad*, Ḥusām al-Dawla Shahriyār, supported the Nizārīs by turning down a Saljūq request for military help against them, so in 668–669/1269–1270 allied Bādūspānid-Bāwandid forces strove to delay Mongol efforts to capture Girdkūh. Mutual interests and local alliances worked remarkably well when pressure from the major regional powers was mounting in the Caspian provinces.

The account of the Nizārī Ismaili state and their Caspian neighbours ends with these anecdotes of cooperation and subversion against a common enemy. Neither the Nizārī Ismailis nor their Caspian neighbours, who were sometimes their allies, sometimes their opponents, disappeared after the downfall of the Nizārī Ismaili state, but found means to survive and eventually flourish, however the history of that perseverance and ultimate survival are beyond the scope of this work.

Chapter 8

The Economy and Social Structure of the Nizārī Ismaili State

One of the most regrettable aspects of Nizārī historiography is the complete loss of economic and administrative documents produced by the Nizārī Ismaili state in northern Iran from the 6th to 7th/12th to 13th centuries.

As a result of this loss of material it is extremely difficult to address questions pertaining to revenue and state structure as well as other subjects. Nevertheless, in some Nizārī-related sources a little light is shed on the economy of the Nizārī state, although it has to be said the reports can be contradictory. This evidence concerns mainly the last decades of the Nizārīs. Ibn al-Athīr speaks about the extreme poverty of the Nizārīs and the serious financial losses sustained by the community in the aftermath of the first disastrous Mongol campaigns.[1] However, the details in al-Nasawī's account of his visit to the Nizārīs that can be used to provisionally reconstruct elements of the economy of their state, would seem to contradict Ibn al-Athīr's statement.

Though the broader Caspian region, the lands ruled by neighbouring polities, was not especially rich in resources before the Mongol conquest, using evidence relating to these provinces from a much broader period of time we are able to reconstruct a theoretical system for the Nizārī economy.

It can be said the Nizārī state had three main sources of income: taxes paid by the local peasantry in Daylamān; tolls on the commerce along the important routes lying south of the Alburz; and, the financial support or *wājibāt* of more remote Nizārī communities,[2] those of Quhistān, and perhaps Syria most importantly, but also of those places such as Cappadocia, Central Asia and in parts of South Asia.

Revenue from Daylamān

The core areas of the Caspian Nizārī state were in Daylamān. The local people were mainly Daylamī peasants who lived in scattered villages in the valleys of the western Alburz. These Daylamīs constituted the vast majority of the local Nizārī converts and supplied the needs of the Nizārī fortresses there. Although we have no taxation lists or *daftars* relating to Nizārī areas for the years between 483/1090 and 654/1256, the *Tārīkh-i Ṭabaristān* of Ibn Isfandiyār and the *Nuzhat-i Qulūb* of Ḥamd Allāh Mustawfī, can help in reconstructing some patterns inherent in the local economy.

The *Tārīkh-i Ṭabaristān* is perhaps the most useful written source for an analysis of the Nizārī economy, since it throws some light on the economic system of neighbouring Ṭabaristān, preserving an interesting inventory of taxes paid in around 145/762 by the *iṣfahbad* Khurshīd, the last Dābūyid ruler of Ṭabaristān, to the Abbasid caliph al-Manṣūr. Given that climatic and geographical conditions were much the same in both Ṭabaristān and in Daylamān, this list provides an indication as to the main goods produced and taxed in the Caspian provinces in the Middle Ages. The list is as follows:

> Manṣūr sent him a royal crown and robe of honour, and the *iṣfahbad*, being pleased thereat, sent the court of Baghdad the land tax (*kharāj*) of Ṭabaristān according to the age (or treaty)[3] of the Kisrās.[4] An amount of 300,000 dirhams, each dirham containing four *dangs* of 'white' silver;[5] 300 bales of green silk stuff consisting of pillows[6] and carpets; the same amount of good coloured flax; the same amount of gold and Rūyānī and Lafūraj woollen garments; ten *kharwār*[7] of saffron, which is of a kind unique throughout the world; ten *kharwārs* of red, good quality, pomegranates, ten *kharwār* of salted fish. All this tribute was loaded onto 40 mules, on each of which was mounted a Turkic page or a maid.[8]

This list provided by Ibn Isfandiyār raises a number of questions. The original document no longer exists. As for his language skills, there are no indications that Ibn Isfandiyār could have understood or deciphered Middle Persian documents. He never mentions this issue, and all of his transcriptions suggest that he preferred Arabised versions of Middle Persian names and titles.

On the basis of his Arabic and Persian, Ibn Isfandiyār tried to collect as much written material as he could from the archives of the Bāwandid bureacracy in Āmul during the late 6th/12th and early 7th/13th centuries; he did the same in Baghdad and, later, in Khwārazm. Yet the documents that were thought to be primary sources relating to the pre-Islamic and early Islamic period remain rather obscure or were simply lost. Ibn Isfandiyār's principal source for the late Sasanian period as well as for the first decades of the Abbasid caliphate was a work by a certain Yazdādī. Of this Arabic book by Yazdādī practically nothing has survived. Given current knowledge of the matter, it can be argued that Ibn Isfandiyār may have culled the so-called Sasanian taxation list from a hitherto unknown Arabic source or from an independent taxation document found somewhere in Baghdad or in other urban centres of medieval Persia, but all of these original sources are now lost.

Regarding the authenticity of this brief inventory of taxes, one needs to note that the measures and names used in it all suggest that it could have come from an early Islamic document that made use of Sasanian technical terms. The occurrence of old monetary units of Iranian origin, such as *drahm* (dirham) and *dāng*, again reveal that Ibn Isfandiyār's information is probably based on an original document dating back to the first centuries of Islam. Another indication of a possible Arabicised Sasanian origin for this document is his use elsewhere of the noun '*lafūraj*', which refers to a local textile, which is in fact an Arabicised form of the Middle Persian '*lafūrag*' (originally from the city of Lafūr).[9]

Concerning the goods listed in the text, the most important item mentioned by Ibn Isfandiyār is silk. We know that the southern coast of the Caspian had been the first and foremost silk-producing area in the Sasanian era from the 6th century CE. This was the time when new taxation measures were officially introduced and the first senior officials of the Sasanian state arrived to count the date palms and meadows in the Iranian countryside. The first successful attempts in northern Iran at developing a silk industry took place in Ṭabaristān.[10] The mention of silk in Ibn Isfandiyār's list may also be an indication that it reflects either a late Sasanian or an early Islamic document drawn up in Ṭabaristān.

Other goods covered include well-known local products. We do not know precisely what sort of clothing the Lafūraj and Rūyānī garments were, but their names derived from two well-known ancient towns of Ṭabaristān, Lafūr and Rūyān, both of which played an active role in the history of Ṭabaristān in the early Islamic era.

Indeed there is ample evidence for widespread silk production in both Māzandarān and Gīlān from the end of the Sasanian period, when the first silk production centres were set up in northern Iran; this went along with widespread cultivation of mulberry trees. Both in Gīlān and Māzandarān silk weaving was already flourishing in the pre-Ilkhanid period. The city of Lāhīj is mentioned by the geographer Yāqūt, in around 612/1216, as the most significant silk-weaving area in Gīlān, though he claimed the quality of the silk was mediocre.[11] According to Marco Polo, in the Mongol era Genoese merchants saw the silk of Gīlān as a viable business, for he refers to ships under their command sailing between ports on the Caspian to transfer woven silk to other trading centres in the Caucasus.[12] In Ṭabaristān the richest silk-weaving manufacturers established their workshops in Āmul, possibly the richest place in the entire province, from where mulberry trees were brought to be planted in more eastern parts of the region, mainly Gurgān. Apart from the silk industry, herding livestock was the main activity of the local population throughout the Middle Ages.[13]

The fact that in northern Iran there was extensive production of various textiles and the cultivation of fruit is further corroborated by the *Nuzhat al-Qulūb* written in the 8th/14th century. Ḥamd Allāh Mustawfī describes the extensive cultivation of citrus fruits, rice, grain and the existence of cotton fields in Daylamān. All these products are more or less similar to the goods mentioned in the list of Ibn Isfandiyār recorded nearly a century before.[14]

As far as the limited economic resources and often harsh economic conditions of northern Iran are concerned, a parallel can be drawn between the Zīyārid Wushmgīr (r. 323–349/935–960) and the Nizārī Imam ʿAlāʾ al-Dīn Muḥammad. An interesting episode is mentioned by later sources: that Wushmgīr was fond of rice planting and on one occasion the emissaries of his brothers, Mardāwīj, found him standing in the middle of a paddy field apparently engaged in planting rice. A not dissimilar scenario is mentioned by Juwaynī for the Nizārī Imam ʿAlāʾ al-Dīn Muḥammad III though in rather contemptuous terms.[15] According to Juwaynī, ʿAlāʾ al-Dīn Muḥammad was fond of goat herding and indeed, he was found dead in his goat herding tent. The parallel is more than striking between the Zīyārid prince and the Nizārī Imam as both are described, albeit in separate ways, as adherents of Caspian rural life. It could be argued, however, that this is a reflection not of personal preference (let alone negative behaviour) but of the realities of life in these provinces. It also may reflect the differences between the southern and northern sides of the Alburz and the agriculture in these different regions.

The fact that goat herding was a good source of income for the *khudāwands* of Alamūt is corroborated by the anecdote recounted by al-Nasawī about his attempt to purchase goats and sheep in the region around Alamūt. In this, al-Nasawī was generously assisted by ʿAlā' al-Dīn Muḥammad III, the penultimate Nizārī Imam of Alamūt, who sent him 400 sheep. Ibn Isfandiyār also supplies evidence for the importance of herding relating that Ḥusām al-Dawla Ardashīr had 280,000 goats and sheep grazing between Astarābād and Daylamān at the end of the 6th/12th century, and these vast flocks were all owned by the *iṣfahbad*, and constantly watched by a thousand shepherds.[16]

Dues levied by the Nizārīs along the great trade routes south of the Alburz

Details in al-Nasawī's account can help in reconstructing elements of the commercial activity of the Nizārīs. The first of these is the occurrence of caravans of Nizārī merchants operating between the Oxus and Syria and Anatolia, which were stopped in Ādharbāyjān by the Khwārazmians in around 628/1230. This episode throws light on another possible source of income for the Nizārīs, namely long-distance commerce. It suggests that the Nizārīs were not only tax collectors at strategic points south of the Alburz but that they were also involved in trade as merchants. Al-Nasawī's account of a Nizārī caravan or caravans is particularly striking after the destruction of ancient trading centres such as Marw, Nīshāpūr, Rayy and Hamadān by the Mongols. It remains questionable whether these caravans of Nizārī merchants were simply supplanting the trading cities eradicated by the Mongols, or whether Nizārī commercial enterprises had existed long before 617–618/1220–1221. It should be remembered that several of the early Imams in the period of *satr* before the establishment of the Fatimid state had posed as merchants, not least ʿAbd Allāh al-Mahdī himself during his momentous journey to North Africa in 291/904. Furthermore, looking at a map of the Ismaili fortresses, it is clear that they fall within three main areas: Daylamān, the area of north of Rayy and the areas around Girdkūh. The well-connected fortresses easily controlled different trade routes.

As for the fiscal system of Alamūt, another interesting point in al-Nasawī's account[17] is a survey of tribute sent by the Quhistānī Nizārīs to Alamūt which confirms that so far from there being a dispersed or fragmentary economy in the Nizārī community linked only to their various localities rather than their spiritual centre, in fact Alamūt was the centre of the economy of their state. Two other earlier examples also support this view. First, the allocation of goods and revenues from Arrajān to Alamūt during the time of Ḥasan-i Ṣabbāḥ and secondly the dues sent from Girdkūh to Alamūt in the first decades of the Nizārī state referred to by Rashīd al-Dīn,[18] both of which serve to reinforce the idea of customary dues being paid to Alamūt well before the Quhistānī donations.

One of the main aims of the Caspian Nizārī state was to extend its boundaries southward. During the 160 years of Nizārī statehood, there were numerous efforts to conquer the towns set along the major trading routes of northern Iran where the goods from China, Central Asia and the Mediterranean had been bought and sold for centuries. Trading routes also meant there was a flourishing agriculture for the settled population that inhabited towns and cities and their environs along them. Thus, the Nizārīs' interest in controlling this area may have been as much economic as political or military. The wealth of these cities, and the taxes and tolls levied along these routes guaranteed a considerable income for those who could control them.

In their mountainous lands in Daylamān the Nizārīs possessed only small villages with a very limited engagement in this long-distance trade, and undoubtedly the majority of the population there were peasants. But in the old urban centres between Abhar and Bisṭām, both the population and their socio-economic institutions were based on long-distance trade and the pursuit of learning, in which nearly all the religious schools of classical Islam, both Sunni and Shiʿi, were represented.

As far as the Nizārīs are concerned there was a continuous interest in incorporating these areas into their northern Iranian state. Their main goals, to control these areas and to levy taxes, occasionally went hand in hand with efforts to convert the local population. But their local rivals, the Bāwandids, also attempted to rule these cities, as did major regional powers, such as the Saljūqs and Khwārazmshāhs, who felt a need to exert their influence over these long-established commercial routes.

The conquest of these areas was partly successful at the beginning of the Nizārī period. The capture of Girdkūh and its neighbouring lands and fortresses by Raʾīs Muẓaffar in 487/1094 was a major step in this direction and benefitted the Nizārī economy. The former Saljūq military leader retained his hold over this area and managed to come to an agreement with Sanjar regarding the division of revenue derived from the *kharāj* or land tax. According to Willey, who bases his claim upon the existence of Nizārī fortresses on both sides of the major route in the area, the Nizārīs soon exerted total control over the roads around Girdkūh.[19] Ruling Girdkūh appears to have been vital to the life of the Nizārī Ismaili state. It successfully resisted successive military campaigns from 493/1100 to 669/1270. Neither the Saljūqs nor the Bāwandids were able to capture it, and Girdkūh remained firmly in the hands of the Nizārīs throughout the period. This meant a strong and constant presence of Nizārīs in south-east of the Caspian region.

Regarding the central and western parts of the southern Alburz, Nizārī attempts to capture Rayy and Qazwīn proved to be less successful. Rayy was the centre of the Saljūq administration until the mid-6th/12th century, and it was later governed by the Bāwandids, the Īldigüzids, the Abbasids and the Khwārazmshāhs. According to the sources, Rayy and Qazwīn were constantly at the forefront of Nizārī concerns. They acquired various posts around both Rayy and Qazwīn but failed to exert complete control over all the trade routes around these cities. The endless campaigns, the steadfastness of the Nizārīs and the obsessions of anti-Nizārī local governors meant constant warfare over control of all the trade routes around them. No doubt, one source of the conflict between the Nizārīs and their opponents was the lack of an agreement over a division of revenues. Here, both the Nizārīs and their adversaries occupied important military positions yet none of them succeeded in capturing the entire area. The Nizārīs endeavoured to expand the areas they held around

Mount Damāwand and Ṭāliqān, which had been constantly and firmly in their possession from the start of their era in the Caspian while their enemies made tireless efforts to push them back and block Nizārī expansionism.

The fact that the Nizārīs made painstaking efforts to capture all the major cities of the region is evident in two successful territorial gains that came at the end of the Caspian era. As discussed earlier, in the early 7th/13th century Jalāl al-Dīn Ḥasan III was rewarded for his military services to the Īldigüzids and Abbasids with the possession of Abhar and Zanjān.

According to both the *Dīwān-i Qā'imiyyāt* and al-Nasawī, the Nizārīs very quickly and astutely exploited the decline of the Khwārazmians after 618/1221 by taking Bisṭām and Dāmghān. In addition, we are informed by al-Nasawī that Nizārī *dā'īs* appeared in Rayy (or in what remained of it after the Mongol raid), attempting to convert the survivors of the Mongol attack to Nizārī Ismailism. The Nizārī *dā'īs* were quickly put to death by the returning Khwārazmian administration, but this episode also suggests intensified Nizārī activity around Rayy in the political vacuum left by the weakened Khwārazmians.

The acquisition of the cities of Abhar and Zanjān was also of huge importance both in terms of the economy and military strength given that the Nizārī Ismaili state already possessed sizeable areas around Dāmghān, Bisṭām and Simnān. From this point of view, the Nizārī request for Abhar and Zanjān seems a natural step to expand their zone of taxation at the foot of the Alburz mountains westwards.

Financial support from more remote Nizārī communities

To what extent the Nizārī communities of Quhistān, or Syria, contributed to the central budget of the Nizārī Ismaili state of the Caspian is not known; and this raises the question of the internal Nizārī administration, autonomous tendencies and self-government in these communities, as well as the degree and nature of centralisation in the Nizārī Ismaili state. If Quhistān and the area of Girdkūh were able regularly to send monies, in particular the religious dues, to Alamūt, were the Syrian Nizārīs also linked to Alamūt through economic ties as well as confessional ones? In the medieval world these two elements were seen as contiguous at the least.

The Nizārīs of Girdkūh had a great deal of contact with those of Alamūt and the Nizārīs of Daylamān generally. As far as the more distant areas are concerned, the scarcity of our sources makes it extremely difficult to assess the issue of socio-economic conditions or relations between Quhistān and the Syrian Nizārīs, not to mention parts of Anatolia, with the central Caspian areas.

Though we lack substantive knowledge of the socio-economic system, the last decades are slightly better known than the early Nizārī period. As has been seen, Nizārī caravans travelled between Anatolia and Alamūt after 618/1221, and were stopped temporarily by Khwārazmians under Jalāl al-Dīn Mingburnī. In 627/1229, Jalāl al-Dīn Mingburnī was greatly angered by hearing about contacts between the Nizārīs and the Mongols and he ordered the suspension of all trading activities between the Oxus and the Mediterranean, fearing that among the caravans there could be Mongol spies guided by the Nizārīs to the Abbasids or to another kingdom hostile to him.[20] This episode is an indication that merchant caravans were a vital means of communication between individuals and communities, as well as a potential object of suspicion for those in authority. What is striking however, is the continuation of trade across these considerable areas of the Middle East and particularly in this period around 627/1229 given the grim reality of the Mongols' plundering and the destruction of the great trading cities of Marw, Nīshāpūr, Rayy and Hamadān.

Al-Nasawī's other account, of the lavish gifts donated by ʿAlāʾ al-Dīn Muḥammad III, including precious robes of honour, Bactrian camels, belts, pommels and other prestigious presents of Far-Eastern origin, reveal a rare glimpse into the possible artefacts in transcontinental trade, in which Nizārīs would appear to have been involved. Of the exact nature of the trade, of its main protagonists, and of Nizārī guilds and trading companies, we have no information. In this respect, the excavations conducted by Hamīda Chubak in Alamūt, during which fine Chinese porcelain and other Central Asian and Iranian ceramics have been found, indicate the wide geographical range of Nizārī contacts. At present, however, the number of publications and surveys undertaken on Nizārī-built fortresses in the Caspian provinces is insufficient to substantively address the question of the commercial contacts the Nizārīs had in this period on the basis of archaeological finds.

Social structure of the Nizārī Ismaili state in the Caspian region

As far as the social structure of the Nizārīs in the Caspian provinces is concerned, it seems to have followed the local patterns seen in other states in the area. In Daylamān and Ṭabaristān, the local Nizārīs were largely the rural peasantry, locals who had been converted by different groups of *dāʿīs* both before and after the foundation of the Nizārī Ismaili state in 487/1094. A significant rural community could have followed Zaydī Shiʿism before their conversion to Ismailism or Nizārī Ismailism. Another aspect of the local Nizārī Ismaili society in the Caspian provinces concerns the Nizārī elite, who seem to have been of local origin, including the founder of the state, Ḥasan-i Ṣabbāḥ, who himself had a good knowledge of the local geography of northern Iran. Apparently, Ḥasan-i Ṣabbāḥ founded the state in his place of origin and Alamūt was one of several options for the centre of the *daʿwa*, in the event perhaps the best. From Kiyā Buzurg-Umīd onwards, all the lords of Alamūt had local Daylamī connections. Though there is no evidence for the existence of specific clans, the Caspian clan system may have continued to be an effective element in the Nizārī Ismaili state.

However, a hereditary and clan-like nature for the Nizārī elite and its consequences are can be clearly seen around the time of the declaration of the *qiyāma* in 559/1164 and, later, in the nearly every succession crisis until 654/1256. The names of the governors and commanders of fortresses are largely omitted from our sources; and in the case of Girdkūh, the hereditary nature of the governors can be seen based on fragmentary information only. As regards contact between major fortresses, the case of Lamasar and Alamūt is of particular importance. A newly discovered source, the *Akhbār-i Mughūlān,* refers to the fortress of Lamasar as the place of residence of the family of the last Imam of Alamūt, Rukn al-Dīn Khurshāh. It is not clear whether Lamasar was a permanent place of residence for the families of the Imams or whether the exceptional and existential conditions of the Mongol siege in 654/1256 compelled the Imam to send his family to this more remote and safer place. But Lamasar was the second most important of the Caspian fortresses. Kiyā Buzurg-Umīd had been the governor of Lamasar before he moved to Alamūt in 518/1124 on the death of Ḥasan-i Ṣabbāḥ. Later, Ḥasan II was killed by his brother-in-law in Lamasar and it was the place where other relatives present were executed on the orders of Nūr al-Dīn Muḥammad (Muḥammad II). All this, along with the testimony of the *Akhbār-i Mughūlān*, suggests that Lamasar was perhaps a place where the closest relatives of the Imam regularly resided.

Apart from the rural and agrarian element of the Nizārī social structure which was, as in most pre-modern societies, the dominant factor, there were other groups who played an important part, possibly reflecting some parts of the structure of the *daʿwa*. There were the Nizārīs who acted as envoys and merchants travelling between Syria, Quhistān and more distant areas, presumably in Central Asia, who could have been of different origins and of diverse social character, from the highly urbanised classes and the intellectual elites of Khurāsān and Central Asia. Nizārī or pro-Nizārī circles were present in Marw, the eastern Saljūq capital, in Baghdad and in the bureaucracy of the later Khwārazmian empire also. These Nizārī diasporas were closely connected by an advanced system of communication and could, it seems, have closely followed orders from Alamūt. Quhistān, an important area for early Nizārī history, had its own *muḥtasham* who was a representative of Alamūt, but had some ability to operate independently. During the 160 years of the Nizārī state, our sources do not reveal any sort of inner-Nizārī mutiny or revolt against directives coming from Alamūt in Quhistān or Central Asia. However, according to Jūzjānī, the *muḥtasham* of Quhistān outraged Muḥammad II who was fiercely anti-Khwārazmian when he took in refugees from Khwārazm and Khurāsān after the first Mongol raids in about 617/1220.[21] In this episode can be glimpsed the nature of the relationship between the centre and the periphery in the Nizārī Ismaili state, one in which loyalty to the Imam was a constant but also operated in tandem with the exigencies of local conditions.

Conclusion

At the end of this analysis and overview of the nearly 160-year long local policy of the Nizārī Ismaili state, it is tempting to see the fall and decline of the Nizārīs as a mere consequence of the military and political failures of the Nizārī Imam 'Alā' al-Dīn Muḥammad III.

The secondary literature sees another paradox in the fall of the Nizārīs. Though some earlier academic works are not without an anti-Nizārī bias reflecting the Sunni primary sources for Nizārī history and treating the Nizārīs as evildoers or simply murderers at the fringes of the Islamic world, on dealing with the end of the Nizārī Ismaili state this anti-Nizārī attitude suddenly changes and accuses the Mongols with similar zeal in their annihilation of the Nizārī state.

But this approach fails to take into account the complex politics of the age. The Nizārī policy of sophisticated diplomacy based on finding a counterbalance between their opponents was remarkably successful up until almost the last decade of the state.

However, a few considerations concerning the vicissitudes of Nizārī policy between 483/1090 and 654/1256 summarising the main characteristics of the subject-matter of this study should be made. Given the information in the primary sources, it is possible to outline the main trends and features of the history of the petty kingdoms of northern Iran, and this can be applied to the Nizārī Ismaili state as well.

For the region of Ṭabaristān, Gīlān and Daylamān there are two recurrent phases: the first is a rising or emerging phase, taking advantage of the fall or dissolution of major neighbouring empires. These fortunate circumstances helped local powers reunite territories and these local forces temporarily made the Caspian provinces an important, regional political centre. Such a rising phase can be seen at least five times in the history of the Caspian provinces before the arrival of the Mongols:

1. The fall of the Sasanians and the rule of the Dābūyids (1st–2nd/7th–8th centuries)
2. The decline of the Abbasid caliphate and the heyday of the Qārinwand Māzyār (r. 201–224/817–839) in the first half of the 3rd/9th century until the rise of the Ṭāhirids.
3. The Zaydī state in the second half of the 3rd/9th century until just before 287/900 and their Daylamī successors.
4. The Bāwandid renaissance in the 6th/12th century at the time of Saljūq disintegration, which manifested itself in considerable political power and the conquests of the Iṣfahbadiyya branch under Shāh Ghāzī Rustam (536–561/1141–1165).
5. The Nizārī takeover of northern Iranian areas and Nizārī expansion following the first Mongol assault in 617–18/1220–21.

In the meantime, there were also defensive tendencies that marked the second phase. Between periods of political stability, the Caspian provinces became a buffer zone for various political influences and one can see a general political and dynastic disintegration due to the lack of any unifying centre or a charismatic local family.

This all suggests that the relatively limited resources as well as the fragmented geography of these areas offered only the prospect of limited success when one of the local rulers tried to extend his power beyond the natural borders of the Caspian provinces. Thus, in purely local terms, neither the Bāwandid Shāh Ghāzī Rustam, nor the Nizārī Imam, ʿAlāʾ al-Dīn Muḥammad III, achieved lasting conquests beyond these well-defended areas; and the Nizārīs and other Caspian rulers were unable to control major trading centres such as Dāmghān, Zanjān or Simnān for anything more than a few years. The Būyids were a notable exception in the first half of the 4th/10th century, but then the main branch of the clan quickly transferred their political centre from northern Iran to Iraq after 329/940.

In the Caspian provinces we can distinguish at least three subdivisions where signs of political disintegration can be seen before 654/1256:

1. Qārinwand-Bāwandid rivalry after the Arab conquest in the second half of the 2nd/8th century, which ended with the victory of Māzyār over his Bāwandid enemies.

2. In the case of Ṭabaristān, whose early medieval history is better known than that of other Caspian provinces, the Qārinwand and Bāwandid families fought each other and later experienced various Zaydī, Daylamī, Ṭāhirid and Sāmānid military incursions into their lands. This created a very fragile political system and a chaotic political map in around 390/1000, and there is scant information about political events then. It seems that, at that time, Ṭabaristān was ruled by local clans and tribal chieftains rather than by a well-organised minor monarchy.
3. After the death of Shāh Ghāzī Rustam in 561/1165, from the end of the 6th/12th century there was another general decline, when the Khwārazmian empire and the Nizārīs led various military expeditions against Bāwandid possessions in and around Ṭabaristān. This eventually led to a very short period of Nizārī supremacy (after 618/1221), which was ultimately unsuccessful due to the presence of the Mongol war machine.

The reason for this ebb and flow can be found in the fact that the Caspian provinces were always relatively isolated and peripheral to the centre of power on the Iranian plateau. This isolation helped them to preserve a sense of an archaic social and political system, because these provinces were never entirely conquered and after every incursion and conquest more or less succeeded in restoring or preserving their original socio-economic conditions. Yet the Caspian provinces, despite their peripheral status, were never cut off from the rest of Iran and political events here were more or less influenced by the neighbouring empires, such as the Abbasid caliphate, the Sāmānids and the Saljūqs. The two opposing processes of isolation and connection simultaneously shaped the history of this region of northern Iran.

Different branches of the early Shiʿis settled in the region from the 2nd/8th century. Their success in propagating their faith was often linked with different degrees of acknowledgement from specific local tribal and cultural traditions. This double system, where a strong tribal and traditionalist social system was headed by a religious group, can be seen in the case of the Zaydīs and the Twelver Shiʿis, and the source material indicates that it was also largely the case with Nizārī Ismailis.

Most of the followers of the Nizārīs were people recruited from local tribes in Daylamān and Gīlān. The traditionalist tendencies can be easily attested to in numerous examples of local Nizārī policy. Their policies were also characterised by a flexibility and versatility, carefully following in the footsteps of preceding Caspian dynasties. Similar indications can be observed in some of the rarely mentioned dynastic marriages. The marriages of the Nizārī Imam Jalāl al-Dīn Ḥasan III to local princesses of ancient origin and the marriage of the daughter of Ḥasan III to a Bāwandid prince certainly refer to the enduring power of local influence. As to what this sort of conservative attitude actually meant, is difficult to assess. Certain pre-Islamic elements undoubtedly persisted in it, but the more distant the Sasanian past became, the more their role diminished. The structure of Nizārī Ismaili beliefs however must have put the local community at a tangent to and at times in tension with this local conservatism. Even in the case of the *qiyāma*, we can discern conflicting ideological and doctrinal elements. Ḥasan II and his supporters in Alamūt adhered to a form of faith which had been established in the wider society of the Islamic world and had been at the centre of an empire, while their opponents, those around Ḥasan b. Nāmāwar in Lamasar, had a different ideological background, where the Būyid-Sasanian legacy seems to have played some role.

As far as the nearly 160 years of the Nizārī Ismaili state are concerned, it displayed many similarities with other Caspian kingdoms despite its wider connections. The Nizārī Ismaili state itself and its Caspian milieu created an interesting context through which we may try to understand its policies. Created during a political vacuum following the disintegration of the Saljūq empire, the Nizārī Ismaili state as an organic institution behaved like any other local kingdom in northern Iran between the fall of the Sasanians up until the age of the Safavid Shāh ʿAbbās in the 10th/16th century, when local kingdoms everywhere in Iran were suppressed. As has been seen,[1] it was not only the Nizārīs but also the Bāwandids who were the winners in the situation after 483/1090, and both of them created ambitious new states exploiting the disintegration of the Saljūqs. Later, the Bādūspānids joined these two local forces in their quest for local Caspian supremacy. The conflicts of these three local powers, the Nizārīs, the Bāwandids and the Bādūspānids, more or less dominated northern Iran between 483/1090 and 654/1256. Other minor protagonists appeared on the scene, such as the Zaydī principalities of Gīlān and Daylamān, but they failed to exert any sort of local influence during the Nizārī period and remained auxiliaries of other powers.

As far as the local policy for this period is concerned, we can detect three attempts to build up Nizārī supremacy in Iran between the first years of Ḥasan-i Ṣabbāḥ and the end of the state under Rukn al-Dīn Khurshāh. It is also clear that these three attempts to supersede the localised nature of a Caspian kingdom and to create a greater Nizārī Ismaili state by capturing larger areas in Iran and Central Asia were not exclusively the result of Nizārī action but also due to major historical events which supplied the Nizārīs with opportunities that they sought to take advantage of. The first of the three main endeavours to create a greater Nizārī state was that of Ḥasan-i Ṣabbāḥ reached as far as the southern Zagros, the area of Arrajān, and also sought to include areas in the provinces of Kirmān and Iṣfahān. Nizārī settlements also appeared in eastern Iran, in Quhistān, and we must take into account the founding of the Syrian Nizārī areas at the beginning of the 6th/12th century, apparently undertaken with the blessing and at the instigation of Ḥasan-i Ṣabbāḥ. However, as known, these events mainly coincided with the very quick disintegration and division of the Saljūq empire. The high expectations of Ḥasan-i Ṣabbāḥ's period could not be fulfilled. Signs of a Saljūq recovery led by Muḥammad can be seen in the later years of Ḥasan-i Ṣabbāḥ's rule after 502/1108, when the Saljūqs fought back and eliminated many Ismaili strongholds outside the Caspian territories. The fortresses in Arrajān, the fortress of Shāhdiz near Iṣfahān, and those of Kirmān were all lost after 498/1105 and the Nizārīs suffered severe territorial losses even in their heartlands in Quhistān and in the Caspian provinces.

The period under Kiyā Buzurg-Umīd and his son and successor Muḥammad I until 557/1162 was chiefly marked by a defensive policy, when local Ismaili leaders were hardly in a position to renew the expansive policy of Ḥasan-i Ṣabbāḥ. Instead, when assessing these decades it can be seen that Kiyā Buzurg-Umīd and his son were forced to lay an emphasis on the local Caspian identity of the Nizārī Ismaili state rather than continue to build a larger entity, as in the time of Ḥasan-i Ṣabbāḥ.

The second attempt of the Nizārīs to break out of the Caspian and to create a greater Ismaili state was also generated by significant historical events. By 559/1164, contemporaries had witnessed the destruction of the Eastern Saljūq empire of Sultan Sanjar and the pillaging of the once glorious Khurāsān, Sanjar's realm, which was devastated by ravaging Ghūzz tribes. The captivity and death of Sanjar led to the fall of the last stronghold of the Sunni Saljūqs on Iranian soil. This caused a major political vacuum, which would be filled a few decades later by the Khwārazmian empire. In this context, the declaration of the *qiyāma* by Ḥasan II may have been seen as a bold step and perhaps an attempt to extend his political influence by reinforcing his position among the Ismailis of the Caspian area and Quhistān, since Sanjar's death marked the real end of a serious threat for the state of Alamūt.

The decline of both the Fatimid and Saljūq states prompted the Nizārīs to fill the spiritual and political vacuum that they left. However, there might have been other motives, such as the annulment of rivalries and hostilities both inside and outside the Ismaili community of northern Iran. It is well known that the reign of Ḥasan *ʿalā dhikrihi'l-salām* between 557/1162 and 562/1166 was not without either personal or internal Nizārī problems, and there were a significant number of local Ismailis who were opposed to him perhaps from a provincial conservative attitude. This opposition group succeeded in killing Ḥasan II in 562/1166 less than two years after the *qiyāma* declaration. By declaring the *qiyāma* and reiterating its ceremony in more remote Ismaili communities in the following months, Ḥasan II may have intended to strengthen his own position against his opponents in the Ismaili community. The ferocious attacks of the Bāwandid kingdom between 536/1142 and 561/1165 could also have had some auxiliary role in the circumstances which led to the declaration.

Despite the declaration of *qiyāma* and the major changes that had taken place in the Middle East, the hopes of the Nizārīs were left unfulfilled once again, since it was the Khwārazmian empire and not the Nizārīs that was able to exploit the political situation and so conquer large areas of the Middle East. In addition, the Nizārīs once again were involved in endless petty warfare with their Caspian neighbours during the time of Nūr al-Dīn Muḥammad II, with little hope of gaining the upper hand. This failed policy consequently led to a second Nizārī defensive sub-period between 562/1166 and 617/1220.

The fall of the Khwārazmian empire after the Mongol attacks between 617/1220 and 629/1231 again aroused hopes of building a greater Nizārī Ismaili state. This was the third event through which the Nizārīs endeavoured to exploit the major changes of the Middle East and Central Asia by reviving their expansionist policy from the past days of Ḥasan-i Ṣabbāḥ. The prophecy in the *Rawḍat al-taslīm* about the world-conquering Nizārī Imam probably underpins these millenarian hopes for the creation of a greater Nizārī empire. The activities of Jalāl al-Dīn Ḥasan III and his official embrace of Sunni Islam by way of *taqiyya* clearly reflect this aspiration. The expansionist attitude can be detected in the case of ʿAlāʾ al-Dīn Muḥammad III, who took bold steps to make these Nizārī hopes real, even in the shadow of the Mongol advance. However, this began to alarm both their Sunni opponents and the Mongols, particularly after the fall of Jalāl al-Dīn Khwārazmshāh in 629/1231. The result was that the Mongols effectively destroyed the Nizārī Ismaili state in their campaigns between 654/1256 and 669/1270 and the third defensive sub-period ended with the Mongol capture of Girdkūh, the last significant Nizārī fortress resisting the Mongols.

It could be argued that the failure of the Nizārīs in resisting the Mongols lay in the fact that there was no state equal to acting as a neutralising counterweight to the Mongol menace. The only possible entity that could have fulfilled this function, the Khwāramian empire, had proved too insubstantial to mount more than a sporadic resistance. Local kingdoms such as the Bādūspānids and the newly restored Bāwandid princes clearly did not have the potential to halt the Mongol armies. The Abbasid caliphate was too far away and indeed under threat itself, and the Nizārī attempt to warn the European powers against the Mongol menace had similarly proved unavailing.

Along with their theological disquisitions, it is also likely that this fluctuating system of expansionist and defensive periods could have to some degree shaped Nizārī thought. Nāṣir al-Dīn al-Ṭūsī's concept in the *Rawḍat al-taslīm* about the *satr*[2] and the *qiyāma* as alternating sub-periods in the life of mankind may well reflect something of the influence of historical events and sub-periods on the doctrines of the Nizārīs. However, an investigation into whether or not al-Ṭūsī's innovation was influenced by these near contemporary historical facts and by considerations about the history of the Nizārī Ismaili state, is perhaps the subject for another study.

Appendix I: Maps of the Caspian Provinces

This appendix presents a summary of the main territorial changes of the Caspian provinces. Hitherto, there have been no attempts to shed light on the territorial changes of the Nizārī Ismaili state in the Caspian provinces.

The Nizārīs ruled three main areas of the Caspian provinces. Following the capture of Alamūt and the establishment of the Nizārī Ismaili state in northern Iran in 487/1094, supporters of Ḥasan-i Ṣabbāḥ mainly took control of fortresses. Most of these fortresses were situated in Daylamān, which served as a stronghold for the Nizārīs. The number and density of their fortresses was highest in this region, though one should stress the fact that the precise number of Nizārī fortresses in northern Iran and other areas is still unknown due to a lack of archaeological fieldwork and related case studies. As has been mentioned several times in this monograph, the want of archaeological studies relating to Nizārī locations constitutes one of the weakest points in current research on the medieval Nizārī Ismaili state.[1]

The second, relatively isolated, region partly occupied by the Nizārī Ismailis can be found around Mount Damāwand, north of the city of Rayy.

The third Nizārī-controlled region in the Caspian provinces was around Girdkūh, in the south-eastern periphery of Ṭabaristān. These areas appeared to have been governed directly from Alamūt.

Between 487/1094 and 654/1256 there are three main periods:

1. the successful territorial expansion of the early Nizārī period, which ended in the first years of Muḥammad b. Buzurg-Umīd (483–534/1090–1140);
2. the years of the Bāwandid wars and a Nizārī territorial setback (534–ca. 607/1140–1210); and

3. a new expansionist period, one with notable conquests and the reacquisition of lost territories (607–655/1210–1257).

The first period saw a successful expansionist policy, and the Nizārīs were able to extend their lands by subduing local rulers in Daylamān and Gīlān. Regarding details of these conquests, we are better informed of the steps taken in Daylamān than in the Damāwand area or around Girdkūh. Sometimes key fortresses were acquired through a peaceful takeover, such as in the case of Alamūt; yet there were also clashes and military expeditions resulting in new conquests. In the case of Girdkūh,

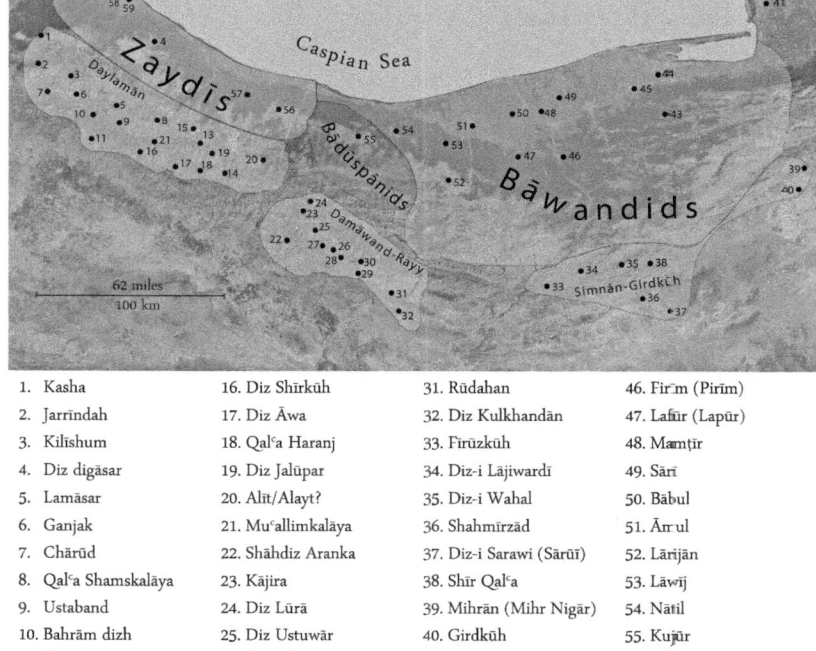

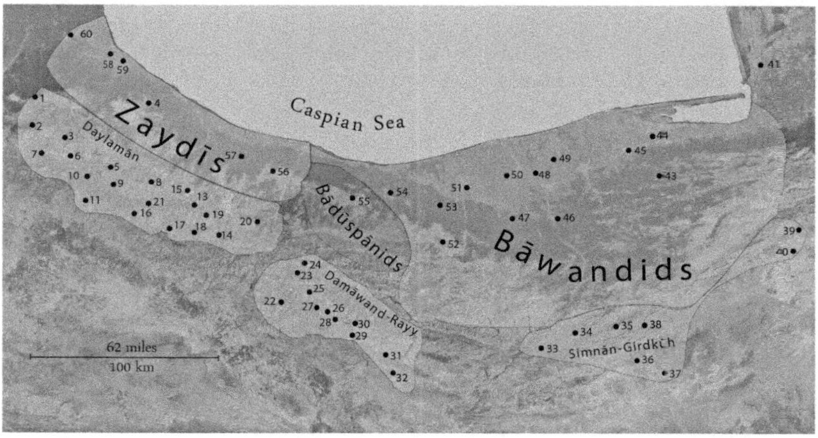

1. Kasha
2. Jarrīndah
3. Kilīshum
4. Diz digāsar
5. Lamāsar
6. Ganjak
7. Chārūd
8. Qalʿa Shamskalāya
9. Ustaband
10. Bahrām dizh
11. Dizwartawān
12. Chanāshak [not seen on map]
13. Alamūt
14. Diz Arzhang
15. Andijrūd
16. Diz Shīrkūh
17. Diz Āwa
18. Qalʿa Haranj
19. Diz Jalūpar
20. Alīt/Alayt?
21. Muʿallimkalāya
22. Shāhdiz Aranka
23. Kājira
24. Diz Lūrā
25. Diz Ustuwār
26. Fašm/Bašm
27. Maygūn
28. Diz Imāma
29. Diz Sarband
30. Ufja/Afja
31. Rūdahan
32. Diz Kulkhandān
33. Fīrūzkūh
34. Diz-i Lājiwardī
35. Diz-i Wahal
36. Shahmīrzād
37. Diz-i Sarawi (Sārūī)
38. Shīr Qalʿa
39. Mihrān (Mihr Nigār)
40. Girdkūh
41. Dihistān
42. Astarābād [not seen on map]
43. Kabūdjāma
44. Bahmanshahr
45. Nikā
46. Firīm (Pirīm)
47. Lafūr (Lapūr)
48. Mamṭīr
49. Sārī
50. Bābul
51. Āmul
52. Lārijān
53. Lāwīj
54. Nātil
55. Kujūr
56. Kalār
57. Gurjiyān
58. Rūdsar
59. Hawsam
60. Fūman

I. Territorial changes in the Caspian Provinces between 483 and 534/1090 and 1140

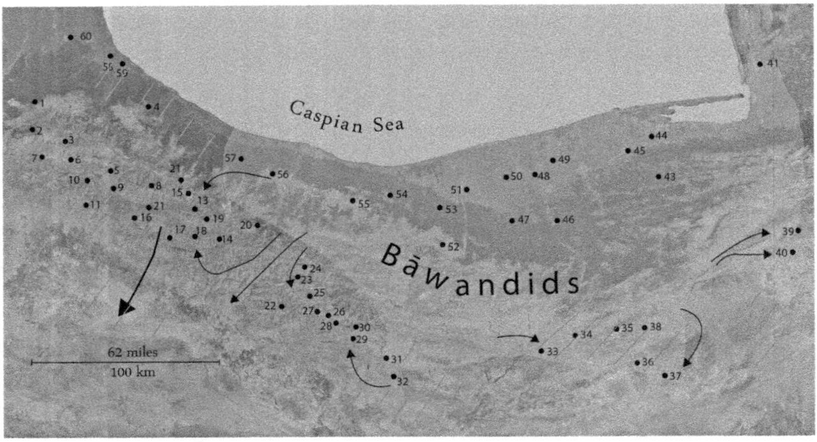

1. Kasha
2. Jarrīndah
3. Kilīshum
4. Diz digāsar
5. Lamāsar
6. Ganjak
7. Chārūd
8. Qalʿa Shamskalāya
9. Ustaband
10. Bahrām dizh
11. Dizwartawān
12. Chanāshak [not seen on map]
13. Alamūt
14. Diz Arzhang
15. Andijrūd
16. Diz Shīrkūh
17. Diz Āwa
18. Qalʿa Haranj
19. Diz Jalūpar
20. Alīt/Alayt?
21. Muʿallimkalāya
22. Shāhdiz Aranka
23. Kājira
24. Diz Lūrā
25. Diz Ustuwār
26. Fašm/Bašm
27. Maygūn
28. Diz Imāma
29. Diz Sarband
30. Ufja/Afja
31. Rūdahan
32. Diz Kulkhandān
33. Fīrūzkūh
34. Diz-i Lājiwardī
35. Diz-i Wahal
36. Shahmīrzād
37. Diz-i Sarawi (Sārūī)
38. Shīr Qalʿa
39. Mihrān (Mihr Nigār)
40. Girdkūh
41. Dihistān
42. Astarābād [not seen on map]
43. Kabūdjāma
44. Bahmanshahr
45. Nikā
46. Firīm (Pirīm)
47. Lafūr (Lapūr)
48. Mamṭīr
49. Sārī
50. Bābul
51. Āmul
52. Lārijān
53. Lāwīj
54. Nātil
55. Kujūr
56. Kalār
57. Gurjiyān
58. Rūdsar
59. Hawsam
60. Fūman

II. Setbacks and losses 534–601/1140–1205

the Saljūq governor of the fortress, Raʾīs Muẓaffar openly declared his pro-Ismaili commitment in 493/1100 and sided with Ḥasan-i Ṣabbāḥ. The Nizārīs suffered some setbacks after 503/1110 when the armies of the Saljūq sultan Muḥammad Tapar invaded Daylamān, but they nevertheless held firm. During the time of Kiyā Buzurg-Umīd and early in that of his son, Muḥammad b. Buzurg-Umīd, there were new conquests, especially in the area of Gurjiyān.

The years of the Bāwandid ruler Shāh Ghāzī Rustam brought a radical change in Nizārī policy in the Caspian provinces as he sought to extend the boundaries of his kingdom. Bāwandid forces routinely attacked all three Nizārī sub-areas after 543/1150 and achieved significant successes. Although information is scarce, there seem to have been Nizārī territorial losses in the Damāwand area, and they had to give up some major fortresses around Girdkūh as well. However, Girdkūh itself was defended successfully. Bāwandid allies raided into deep into Daylamān, reaching both the Alamūt valley and Lamasar, but ultimately failed to eradicate the Nizārīs there. This period is marked generally by territorial setbacks for the Nizārīs. However, the Bāwandid raids ended in 560/1165 when Shāh Ghāzī Rustam died and the Nizārīs restored their positions and went into Rūyān, where they supported pro-Nizārī local Bādūspānid princes. Bāwandid raids

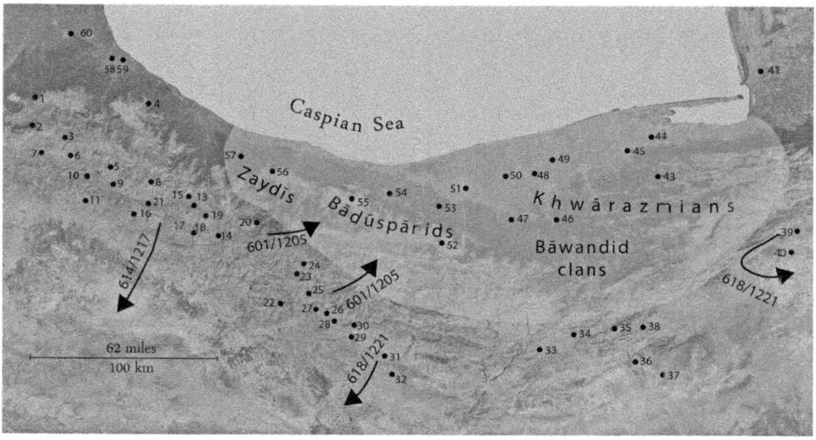

1. Kasha
2. Jarrīndah
3. Kilīshum
4. Diz digāsar
5. Lamāsar
6. Ganjak
7. Chārūd
8. Qal^ca Shamskalāya
9. Ustaband
10. Bahrām dizh
11. Dizwartawān
12. Chanāshak [not seen on map]
13. Alamūt
14. Diz Arzhang
15. Andijrūd
16. Diz Shīrkūh
17. Diz Āwa
18. Qalᶜa Haranj
19. Diz Jalūpar
20. Alīt/Alayt?
21. Muᶜallimkalāya
22. Shāhdiz Aranka
23. Kājira
24. Diz Lūrā
25. Diz Ustuwār
26. Fašm/Bašm
27. Maygūn
28. Diz Imāma
29. Diz Sarband
30. Ufja/Afja
31. Rūdahan
32. Diz Kulkhandān
33. Fīrūzkūh
34. Diz-i Lājiwardī
35. Diz-i Wahal
36. Shahmīrzād
37. Diz-i Sarawi (Sārūī)
38. Shīr Qalᶜa
39. Mihrān (Mihr Nigār)
40. Girdkūh
41. Dihistān
42. Astarābād [not seen on map]
43. Kabūdjāma
44. Bahmanshahr
45. Nikā
46. Firīm (Pirīm)
47. La[illegible]ūr (Lapūr)
48. Mamṭīr
49. Sārī
50. Bābul
51. Āmul
52. Lārijān
53. Lāwīj
54. Nātil
55. Kujūr
56. Kalār
57. Gurjiyān
58. Rūdsar
59. Hawsam
60. Fūman

III. Nizārī renaissance and territorial gains after 607/1210

against the Nizārīs were renewed some twenty years later, in around 581/1185, under Ḥusām al-Dawla Ardashīr, who tried to re-establish the political boundaries of Shāh Ghāzī Rustam. He managed to retake a few fortresses in Rūyān that had been occupied by the Nizārīs.

In return for their military assistance in ʿIrāq, the Nizārīs were given Abhar and Zanjān, in 614/1217, and clearly aspired to acquire areas beyond the southern parts of Daylamān. Following the first Mongol invasion of 617–618/1220–1221, Nizārī groups occupied considerable areas around Dāmghān and Bisṭām. Nizārī influence increased in Ṭabaristān too, where they managed to reinstate the Bāwandids in around 636/1238. This bold policy may have provoked the Mongols, however, and a possible reason for the Mongol expedition against the Nizārīs is this sometimes audacious policy in the last decades of Imam ʿAlāʾ al-Dīn Muḥammad's reign.

Appendix II: The *Dīwān-i Qā'imiyyāt*, Extracts in Translation

qaṣīda 124, 3742–3759, p. 330

3742 He is the Lord who brought new fortune to the world and rejuvenated it with his grace the moment he sat on the throne.

3743 Because this blessed call and sword will unmistakably bring under its rule from China to Qayrawān

3744 The end of all the cycles of the world became manifest and the opening of the supreme cycle was heralded with a sign.

3746 Estates, properties and endless fortunes will be overturned by the decree of the one with knowledge of the unseen.

. . .

3755 The day of the marketplace of guidance was revealed to the people of Truth from behind the veil of the unseen and the caravan was given safe passage on the way.

3757 In the year (6)20, when heaven looked upon us, the most sinful, whose ears had turned deaf through ungratefulness for this blessing,

3758 He was enraged and a flame of His wrath smote this land unwaveringly with the flame of the calamity of Chingiz Khān.

3759 In the year (6)21, the righteous people turned their hearts in worship towards the command of the Lord of the age.

3760 The Lord gracefully showed mercy and happily set wrath aside and expressed kindness to the friends of faith.

3761 That trouble and storm disappeared after the divine intervention
From the area of His Majesty (Alamūt) and the borders (or land) of Qūhistān

3762 Due to the Master's perfect favour towards the righteous people
Heaven dispersed jewels of victory upon them from God

3763 The castles of the Qaṣrān region and the 'borderland' and 'Irāq
were conquered and that region is itself a precious land.
3764 And when a misfortune happened to the governor of Khalkhāl
through his discord the governor rode a horse of sin
3765 Brave *fidā'ī* men, thoughtful servants
made the earth purple, indigo with the blood of the governor
3767 And the accursed Īlīāj made outrageous comments about the virtuous people which cannot be repeated here[1]
3768 And his black soul was burning in his body with envy
that we have managed to conquer the realm of Dāmghān
3769 With all his envy, he was struck by the dagger of great men
and despite his great army and might, he died.

qaṣīda 73, 2180–2186, p. 204

2180 The affairs of the world came under the blessed rule and command of the Lord of Dhu'l-fiqār.
2181 These conquests which were made possible through his name
are constantly the fabric of the garment of the soul and reason.
2182 The world — through His world-conquering flag's sign
became renewed — as are the garden and fields by the gentle breeze
2183 He (the Imam) reconstructed Bisṭām and its fortress
making it sturdy, by divine support, like Iskandar's wall.
2184 He (the Imam) expanded his kingdom and when you leave this kingdom
you may count realms like this up to the gates of Khwārazm
2185 Go and see all the provinces of Khurāsān
there, the decree of the deputy who is appointed as commander.
2186 It is hoped that by the sword and flag of the Lord of faith, conquests will be made from Qayrawān to Qandahār.

qaṣīda 49, 1486–1489, p. 151

1486 The deadline of the Lord of faith came to an end and the pledge of Mustanṣir and Nizār became manifest.
1487 The *fitna* of the end of times by Divine command which had appeared with the Tatar army
1489 Spread all throughout the world and raised dust to heaven from all sides.

The first khān was Chingiz, and he first treated us with sincerity and friendship.

qaṣīda 78, 2281–2292, pp. 211–212

2281 It is time that with blessings, heaven lifts the veil of the darkness of this world from your eyes.

2282 Spiritual miracles which none of you have seen before
since the eyes of your soul were covered with the fog of oppression

2283 But this time with the light of resurrection through physical power, you will see in utter darkness as if you carry a candle with you.

2284 You all looked at the deeds of Chingiz Khān when he appeared with all of his countless graces and friendship

2285 The hand and the eye of the Resurrector grabbed his throat until he died and left this transient world.

2286 The Imam gave an order to Chingiz Khān, saying, 'Speak as a friend with them (the Nizārīs)
and do not cease supporting them in all things.'

2287 Chingiz Khān did so and behaved obediently in his lands
and therefore, he was triumphant over all people.

2288 Then he turned from that firm advice and wrote a command
for his majesty, diverting from the path of human intelligence,

2289 Chingiz Khān wished that 'you (the Imam) should turn your face
to my court now to perfect your cause'

2290 When brave *fidā'ī*s were informed about this plan
they departed, risking their lives sincerely and voluntarily.

2291 The deputy, the commander and the army chief who were said to be up in arms for vengeance like Isfandīyār

2292 He tasted the dagger and his dark soul followed him adding fumes to the flames of hell.

qaṣīda 49, 1508–1509, p. 152

1508 The second Chingiz secured the rank from his brother, Chaghtāy, and he became triumphant

1509 And on the throne of the kingdom the fear of Dhu'l-fiqār put great anxiety in his heart.

qaṣīda 133, 4003–4012, pp. 351–352.

4003 Take heed from the killing of Chaghtāy, because that embodiment of tyranny and the personification of curse

4004 One day boasted to the world,
'I will attack and conquer a thousand well-fortified fortresses

4005 I do not fear any stab wound and I do not
show an iota of dignity to the *mujāhid*s of the world'

4006 Ḥusām al-Dīn Ḥasan b. ʿAlī Jawānmardī
who became the sign of generosity in that world and in this world

4007 He volunteered in his zeal to deal with him with utmost determination, mighty will and upright reason.

4011 Four other commanders also rushed to the scene.

4012 The killing and the turmoil had become so much in that field
as if a cloud had made there a blossoming meadow from rubies.

verses 1704, 1708–09, 1716–1721, p. 169.

1704 O friend, do not worry the about the sorrows of this world
since intelligent men do not worry about things which do not endure for long

1708 Either the lands of Islam will be consumed by Yaʾjūj[2]
or the throne of Khwārazm will be taken away from the sultan

1709 Either the people of Bukhārā and Samarqand will be massacred
or the splendour around Khurāsān will not remain

1716 [Our Lord] has said that in this cycle of *qiyāmat*
secrets will be revealed, and will not remain hidden

1717 And with the glory of this blessed cycle, enemies in the world will have no respite.

1718 The enemy of faith will not have the respite in this world to breathe and be disobedient.

1719 When things develop further, everybody will see
that this Turkic state will not remain long

1720 Not even a small piece all over the world with all its beauties
from their useless (Turkic) state will remain long.

1721 And for these (Turkic) masters of the sword, when they are done with what they do, both their homes will be pillaged and their khān will not last.

Appendix III: Dynastic Tables

The Dābūyids

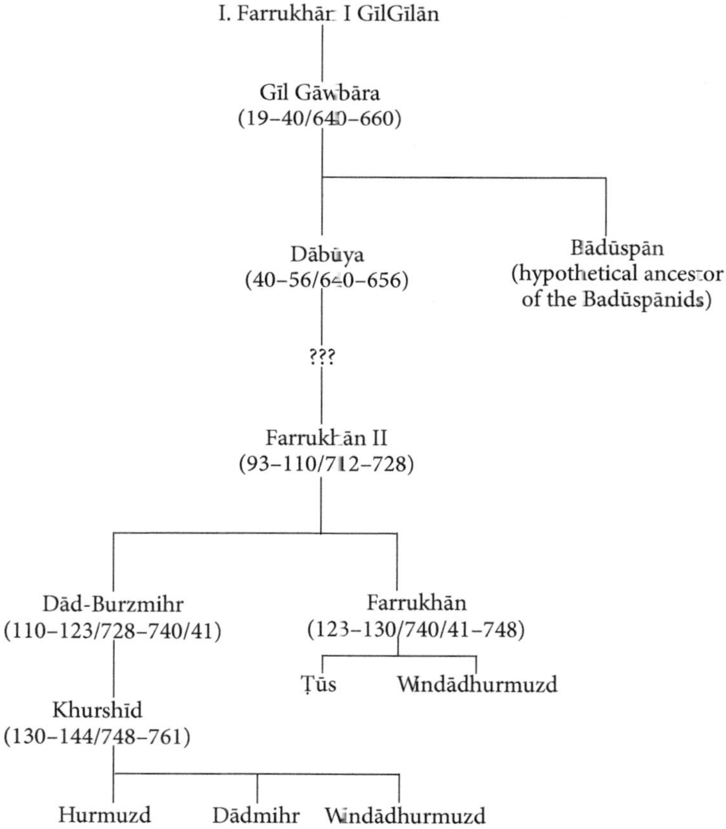

The Early Bādūspānids

Nāṣir al-Dawla Sharaf al-Dīn Naṣr. Shāhriwashn (Shāhrnūsh, 502–524/1109–1130)

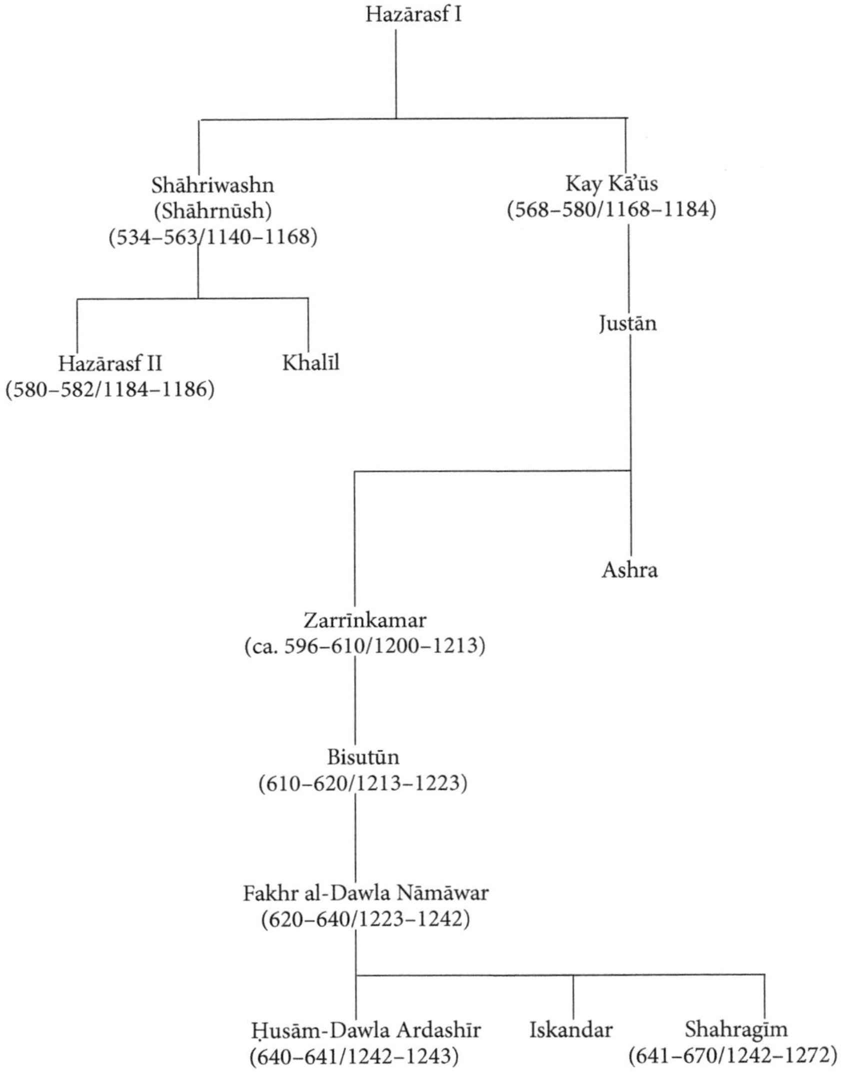

Line of Tāj al-Mulūk Mardāwīj

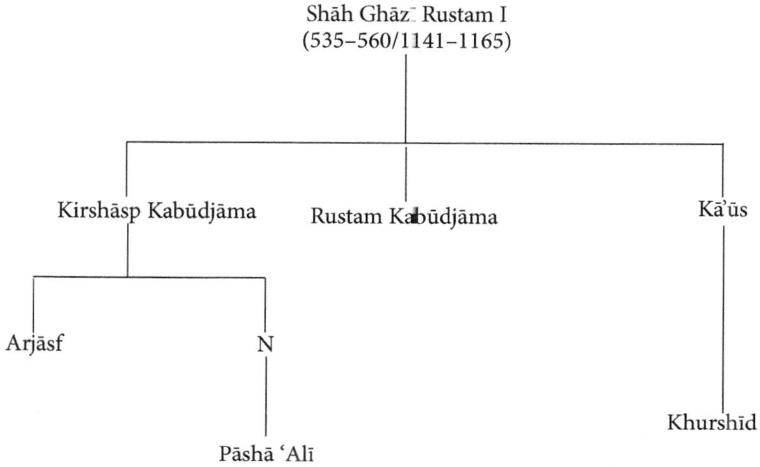

Line of Yazdgird b. Ḥusām al-Dawla Shahriyār

Notes

Chapter 1. Introduction: Sources and Studies

1 F. Daftary, 'Persian Historiography of the Early Nizārī Ismāʿīlīs', *Iran*, 30 (1992), p. 91.

2 The catalogue numbers for these two Mss are Persian Ms 162 and Ms 177. Neither of them has been published. The only major secondary source to assess their origin and issues is by Delia Cortese (D. Cortese, 'Lost and found: the *Sarguzasht-i Sayyid-nâ*. Facts and fiction of Ḥasan-i Ṣabbâḥ's travels to Egypt vis-à-vis the political and intellectual life of 5th/11th century Fâṭimid Cairo', in *Science in Context: The Dustūr al-munjjimīn and its World. An Interdisciplinary Workshop on the Traditions of Science and Learning in the Ismaili Domain*, 22-23 July 2011, Bonn. https://eprints.mdx.ac.uk/9016/1/DCBonn_Paper.pdf, accessed 12 November 2014), p. 3, n. 5.

3 For instance, there is a reference to a *Sargudhasht-i Sayyidnā* manuscript in A. Berthels and M. Baqoev, *Alphabetic Catalogue of Monuments found by 1959–1963 Expedition in Gorno-Badakhshan Autonomous Region* (Moscow, 1976), p. 76, no. 175/1959/95.

4 ʿAlāʾ al-Dīn ʿAṭā-Malik b. Muḥammad Juwaynī, *Tārīkh-i jahān-gushā*, ed. M. Qazwīnī (Leiden–London, 1912–1937), tr. J. A. Boyle as *The History of the World-Conqueror* (Cambridge, 1958). Muntajāb al-Dīn Juwaynī, *ʿAtabat al-kataba*, ed. M. Qazwīnī and ʿA. Iqbāl (Tehran, 2004). Rashīd al-Dīn Faḍl Allāh, *Jāmiʿ al-tawārīkh*, ed. B. Karīmī (Tehran, 1338 Sh./1959), ed. M. Rawshan (Tehran, 1387 Sh./2008); *Jāmiʿ al-tawārīkh qismat-i Ismāʿīliyān va Fāṭimiyān va Nizāriyān va dāʿīyān va rafīqān*, ed. M. T. Dānishpazhūh and M. Mudarrisī Zanjānī (Tehran, 1338 Sh./1959); *Jāmiʿ al-tawārīkh*, partial tr. as *The Successors of Genghis Khan*, tr. J. A. Boyle (New York, 1971). Abu'l-Qāsim Kāshānī, *Zubdat al-tawārīkh: bakhsh-i Fāṭimiyān va Nizāriyān*, ed. Muḥammad Taqī Dānishpazhūh (2nd ed., Tehran, 1366 Sh./1987). Ḥamd Allāh Mustawfī Qazwīnī, *Nuzhat al-qulūb*, ed. M. Dabīr Siyāqī (Qazwīn, 1381 Sh./2003); idem, *Tārīkh-i guzīda*, ed. ʿA Nawāʾī (Tehran, 1339 Sh./1960); idem, *Ẓafarnāma-i Ḥamd Allāh Mustawfī: bih inẓimām-i Shāhnāma-i Abu'l-Qāsim Firdawsī* ed. Naṣr/Allāh Pūrjavādī (Tehran, 1377 Sh./1999).

5 For the different meanings and uses of the term *daʿwa*, see M. Canard, 'Daʿwa', *EI2*, vol. 2, pp. 168–170, F. Daftary, *The Ismāʿīlīs, their History and Doctrines* (2nd ed., Cambridge, 2007), p. 515, 'Dāʿī', *EIR*, vol. 6, pp. 590–593; see also D. Dagiev, *Central Asian Ismailis: An Annotated Bibliography of Russian, Tajik and Other Sources* (London, 2022), pp. 32–35.

6 Cortese, 'Lost and Found', p. 3, n. 5.

7 F. Daftary, *Ismaili Literature, A Bibliography of Sources and Studies* (London, 2004), pp. 46–48.

8 Ḥasan-i Maḥmūd-i Kātib, *Dīwān-i Qāʾimiyyāt*, ed. S. J. Badakhchani (Tehran, 2011).

9 For the theological meanings of the concept of *qiyāma* in Islam, particularly in Shiʿi Islam, see Ḥasan-i Maḥmūd-i Kātib, *Haft bāb*, ed. and tr. S. J. Badakhchani as *Spiritual Resurrection in Shiʿi Islam: An Early Ismaili Treatise on the Doctrine of Qiyāmat* (London, 2017), pp. 10–25.

10 Kātib, *Haft bāb*, pp. 120–134.

11 Persian Ms. N. 32. f. 42r and a fragment from an uncatalogued Persian Ms, ff. 39–40. These two texts along with a brief prayer entitled *Du'ā dar hangām-i shab*, attributed to Kiyā Buzurg-Umīd, are held by the ISCU See D. Cortese, 'Eschatology and power in Mediaeval Persian Ismailism' (PhD, School of Oriental and African Studies, 1993), pp. 141–142, 161 n. 57–58.
12 Daftary, *The Ismā'īlīs*, p. 306.
13 Ibid., p. 306.
14 C. Hillenbrand, 'A Neglected Source on the Life of Hasan-i Sabbah, the Founder of the Nizari "Assassin" Sect', *Iran*, 55 (2017), p. 3.
15 Hillenbrand, 'A Neglected Source', pp. 3–10.
16 Taqī al-Dīn Aḥmad al-Maqrīzī, *Itti'āẓ al-hunafā' bi akhbār al-ā'imma al-Fāṭimiyyīn al-khulafā'*, ed. J. Shayyal and M. H. M. Aḥmad (Cairo, 1387–1393/1967–1973), vol. 1, pp. 22–29, 151–202.
17 Muḥammad b. Aḥmad al-Nasawī, *Sīrat al-sulṭān Jalāl al-Dīn Mīnkubirnī*, ed. and French tr., O. Houdas as *Histoire du Sultan Djelal ed-Din Mankobirti* (Paris, 1891–1895); anonymous Persian translation, *Sīrat-i Jalāl al-Dīn Mīnkubirnī*, ed. M. Mīnuvī (Tehran, 1344 Sh./1965).
18 Ẓahīr al-Dīn Nīshāpūrī, *Saljūq-nāma*, ed. A. H. Morton (Cambridge, 2004).
19 The royal title of *iṣfahbad* has pre-Islamic roots in the Sasanian military administration. However, it only became part of the royal titulature of the Bāwandids in the Islamic period.
20 Bahā' al-Dīn Muḥammad b. Ḥasan b. Isfandiyār, *Tārīkh-i Ṭabaristān*, ed. 'A. Iqbāl (Tehran, 1320 Sh./1941), hereafter referred to as *Tārīkh-i Ṭabaristān I* and *II*; Charles Melville, 'Ebn Esfandīār, Bahā'-al-Dīn Moḥammad', *EIR*, vol. 8, pp. 20–23; idem, 'The Caspian Provinces: A World Apart, Three Local Histories of Māzandarān', *Iranian Studies*, 33 (2000), pp. 45–91.
21 *Tārīkh-i Ṭabaristān I*, p. 82, where the author mentions the year 613 AH as being 'his own time'.
22 Charles Melville, 'The Caspian Provinces', pp. 49–51, 55–59.
23 Ibid., pp. 75–77. Yukako Goto, *Die südkaspischen Provinzen des Iran unter den Safawiden im 16. und 17. Jahrhundert. Eine Analyse der sozialen und wirtschaftlichen Entwicklung* (Berlin, 2011), pp. 25–26.
24 Awliyā' Allāh Āmulī, *Tārīkh-i Ruyān*, ed. M. Sutūda (Tehran, 1347 Sh./1968).
25 Mar'ashī's great-great-grandfather was Fakhr al-Dawla, the last Bāwandid *iṣfahbad* of Ṭabaristān, who died in 750/1349. See Mīr Ẓahīr al-Dīn Mar'ashī, *Tārīkh-i Ṭabaristān va Rūyān va Māzandarān*, ed. M. H. Tasbīḥī (Tehran, 1345 Sh./1966), p. 253; Goto, *Die südkaspischen Provinzen*, p. 28. n. 33.
26 Goto, *Die südkaspischen Provinzen*, pp. 28–31.
27 Mar'ashī's first major work was *Tārīkh-i Gīlān va Daylamistān*, ed. M. Sutūda (Tehran, 1347 Sh./1968; repr. 1364 Sh./1985).
28 Ẓahīr al-Dīn Mar'ashī, *Tārīkh-i Ṭabaristān va Rūyān va Māzandarān*, ed. M. H. Tasbīḥī (Tehran, 1345 Sh./1966). On Mar'ashī, see Melville, 'The Caspian Provinces'.
29 Mar'ashī, *Tārīkh-i Ṭabaristān*, p. 99; Melville, 'The Caspian Provinces', pp. 64, 70–72, Table 3. Mar'ashī made use of the, now lost, chronicle of al-Najībī Rūyānī, who also lived in the 9th/15th century. See Melville, 'The Caspian Provinces', p. 70; Goto, *Die südkaspischen Provinzen*, p. 31.
30 Ḥumayd b. Aḥmad al-Muḥallī, *al-Ḥadā'iq al-wardiyya fī manāqib ā'imat al-Zaydiyya*, ed. M. Maḥṭūṭī (Sana'a, 1423/2002). M. K. Rahmatī, *Zaydiyya dar Īrān* (Tehran, 1392/2013), pp. 56, 97.
31 For the history of Zaydī studies see S. Schmidtke, 'The History of Zaydī Studies: An Introduction', *Arabica*, 59 (2012), pp. 3–4, 185–199; and W. Madelung (ed.), *Arabic Texts concerning the History of the Zaydī Imāms of Ṭabaristān, Daylamān and Gīlān* (Beirut, 1987).

32 ʿAbd al-Jalīl b. Abi'l-Ḥusayn Qazwīnī Rāzī, *Kitāb-i Naqḍ maʿrūf bih Baʿḍ mathālib al-nawāṣib fī naqḍ naʿḍ faḍāʾiḥ al-rawāfiḍ*, ed. J. H. Muḥaddith Urmawī (Tehran, 1358 Sh./1979).

33 Muḥammad b. ʿAbd al-Malik Muʿizzī, *Dīwān-i Amīr al-Shuʿarāʾ Nīshābūrī mutakhalliṣ bih Muʿizzī*, ed.ʿAbbās Iqbāl (Tehran, 1319 Sh./1940).

34 Kirakos Gandzaketsʿi, *Patmuthun Hayots (History of the Armenians)*, ed. Melikʿ-Ohanjanyan (Erevan, 1961).

35 The term '*mulayid*' represents the classical Arab-Persian term *mulḥid* in Chinese and Mongol sources.

36 Christopher Atwood, *The Campaigns of Chinggis Khan: Text, Translation, and Commentary* (Dallas, TX, forthcoming).

37 H. Chubak, 'Kāwushhā-yi bāstānshināsī dar dīzh-i Ḥasan Ṣabbāḥ-i Alamūt' (Archaeological Excavations in the Fortress of Ḥasan-i Ṣabbāḥ in Alamūt), *Guzārishhā-yi bāstānshināsī (7), majmūʿa-i maqālahā-i nuhumīn girdihimaʾī-yi sālāna-i bāstānshināsī-yi Īrān* (Tehran, 1386 Sh./2007), vol. 1, pp. 88–128.

38 G. C. Miles, 'Coins of the Assassins of Alamūt', *Orientalia Lovaniensia Periodica*, 3 (1972), pp. 155–162. P. Casanova, 'Monnaie des Assassins de Perse', *Revue Numismatique*, 3ème série, 11 (1893), pp. 343–352.

39 H. Hamdan and A. Vardanyan, 'Ismaili Coins from the Alamut Period', in Peter Willey, *The Eagle's Nest: Ismaili Castles in Iran and Syria* (London, 2005), pp. 288–307.

40 M. G. S. Hodgson, *The Order of Assassins: The Struggle of the Early Nizârî Ismâʿîlîs Against the Islamic World* (The Hague, 1955), pp. 41–98. Here the term 'Assassins' refers to the Nizārī Ismailis as it does in other titles about them. For a critique of this Western term and its origins see the works of F. Daftary listed below in note 43.

41 C. Melville, 'Persian Local Histories: Views from the Wings', *Iranian Studies*, 33 (2000), pp. 7–14 and 'The Caspian Provinces: A World Apart, Three local histories of Mazandaran', *Iranian Studies*, 33 (2000), pp. 45–91.

42 Goto, *Die südkaspischen Provinzen*.

43 F. Daftary, *The Ismāʿīlīs: their History and Doctrines* (2nd ed., Cambridge, 2007), pp. 324–371, 669–681; *The Assassin Legends: Myths of the Ismaʿilis* (London, 1994); 'Persian Historiography of the Early Nizārī Ismāʿīlīs', *Iran*, 30 (1992), pp. 91–97.

44 W. Madelung, *Religious Trends in Early Islamic Iran* (Albany, NY, 1988), pp. 9–12, 101–103.

45 C. Hillenbrand, 'The Power Struggle between the Saljūqs and the Ismaʿilis of Alamūt, 487-518/1094-1124: The Saljūq Perspective', in F. Daftary, ed., *Mediaeval Ismaʿili History and Thought* (Cambridge, 1996), pp. 205–220.

46 H. L. Rabino, 'Les dynasties locales du Gilan et du Daylam', *Journal Asiatique*, 237 (1949), p. 327; Goto, *Die südkaspischen Provinzen*, p. 12; E. O. Negahban, 'Deylaman', *EIR*, vol. 7, p. 337; W. Madelung, 'Alids of Ṭabarestān, Daylamān, and Gīlān', *EIR*, vol. 1, pp. 881–886, and his 'Gīlān, IV. In the Early Islamic Period', *EIR*, vol. 10, pp. 634–635.

47 R. Strothmann, 'Ḥasan al-Uṭrūsh', *EI2*, vol. 3, pp. 254–255.

48 Hawsam is the modern Rūdsar in present-day eastern Gīlān province of Iran.

49 Madelung, *Religious Trends*, pp. 9–12, 101–103.

50 Goto, *Die südkaspischen Provinzen*, pp. 68–70.

51 Ibid., pp. 70–72.

52 Nāṣir-i Khusraw, *Safarnāma*, ed. M. Dabīr Siyāqī (Tehrān 1375/1996), pp. 7–8.

53 A. Kasrawī, *Shahriyārān-i gumnām* (Tehran, 1377 Sh./1998), pp. 34–120; C. E. Bosworth, 'The Political and Dynastic History of the Iranian World', in *The Cambridge History of Iran*, vol. 5, *The Saljūq and Mongol Periods*, ed. J. A. Boyle (Cambridge, 1968), pp. 30–32; W. Madelung, 'The Justānids and the Sallārids of Ṭārum in the 4th/10th Century', in *The Cambridge History of Iran*, vol. 4, *The Period from the Arab Invasion to the Saljūqs*, ed. R. N. Frye (Cambridge, 1975), pp. 223–226. V. Minorsky, 'Musāfirids', *EI2*, vol. 7,

pp. 655–657; C. E. Bosworth, *The New Islamic Dynasties: A Chronological and Genealogical Manual* (Edinburgh, 1996), pp. 148–149, n. 71; V. Minorsky, and C. E. Bosworth, 'Ṭārum', *EI2*, vol. 10, pp. 311–312; C. E. Bosworth, 'Mosaferids' *EIR Online Edition*, http://www.iranicaonline.org/articles/mosaferids2013, http://www.iranica online.org/articles/mosaferids.

54 W. Madelung, 'Deylamites. ii. In the Islamic Period', *EI2*, vol. 7, p. 346.

55 S. M. Stern, 'The Early Ismaili Missionaries in North-West Persia and in Khurāsān and Transoxania', *BSOAS*, 23 (1960), pp. 56–90.

56 Daftary, *The Ismāʿīlīs*, pp. 147–156.

57 ʿAbd al-Ḥayy Gardīzī, *Zayn al-akhbār*, ed. A. Ḥabībī (Tehran, 1347/1968), pp. 148–149; *Tārīkh-i Sīstān*, ed. M. T. Bahār (Tehran, 1314/1935), pp. 290–294, 300–302; P. Crone and L. Treadwell, 'A New Text on Ismailism at the Samanid Court', in Chase F. Robinson, ed., *Texts, Documents and Artefacts: Islamic Studies in Honour of D. S. Richards* (Leiden, 2003), pp. 37–67; Daftary, *The Ismāʿīlīs*, p. 113.

58 Stern, 'The Early Ismaili Missionaries', pp. 56–90.

59 His full name was al-Ḥasan b. ʿAlī al-Uṭrūsh al-Nāṣir li'l-Ḥaqq.

60 The name Rustamdār may well be a corruption of *ustandār* or a similar popular corruption of the title of the local Bādūspānids. See Minorsky, Vasmer and Bosworth, 'Māzandarān', *EI2*, p. 937.

61 *Ḥudūd al-ʿālam*, p. 391. Barthold, *An Historical Geography*, pp. 231–232. Goto, *Die südkaspischen Provinzen*, pp. 14–15. Interestingly, Marʿashī distinguishes between Rūyān and Rustamdār, saying that Rūyān was located on the Caspian shore whereas Rustamdār was between Ṭabaristān and Daylam. See Marʿashī, *Tārīkh-i Ṭabaristān*, pp. 14, 52–53.

62 It is likely that Rūyān was incorporated into Ṭabaristān only after the Islamic conquest of 149/766, under the latter's first Islamic governor, ʿUmar b. al-ʿAlā', whose coins begin in the year 153/770. See Barthold, *An Historical Geography*, pp. 231–232. This raises the question of an 'autonomous' status of Rūyān between Ṭabaristān and Gīlān. Its direct proximity to Gīlān and Daylamān may help explain its political ambiguities in the Nizārī period, when the local Bādūspānids had 'pro-western' and 'pro-eastern' branches, allying with both the Nizārīs in the 'West' (Daylamān) and their enemies, the Bāwandids, in the 'East' (Ṭabaristān). See Goto, *Die südkaspischen Provinzen*, p. 12.

63 Goto, *Die südkaspischen Provinzen*, p. 15; Marʿashī, *Tārīkh-i Ṭabaristān va Rūyān va Māzandarān*, p. 285.

64 Minorsky, Vasmer and Bosworth, 'Māzandarān'.

65 Sārī was closer to the Caspian in the early Islamic period than nowadays, as according to Ibn al-Faqīh there were only three *farsakhs* between the sea and Sārī. Barthold, *An Historical Geography*, p. 231.

66 Iṣṭakhrī, *Kitāb al-Masālik*, p. 212.

67 al-Hamadhānī, *Compendium libri Kitāb al-buldān*, ed. M. J. de Goeje, p. 310. Barthold, *An Historical Geography*, p. 238. Ẓahīr al-Dīn Marʿashī, *Tārīkh-i Ṭabaristān va Rūyān va Māzandarān*, in *Sehir ed-din's Geschichte von Tabaristān, Rūyān und Māzandarān*, ed. B. Dorn (St. Petersburg, 1850), p. 21.

68 About the area of Hazārjarīb see Y. Goto, 'Der Aufstieg zweier Sayyid-Familien am Kaspischen Meer: "Volkislamische" Strömung in Iran des 8./14. und 9./15. Jahrhunderts', *Wiener Zeitschrift für die Kunde des Morgenländes*, 89 (1999), pp. 45–84.

69 Barthold, *An Historical Geography*, p. 233; Minorsky, Vasmer and Bosworth 'Māzandarān', p. 938; B. Spuler, *Iran in früh-islamischer Zeit* (Wiesbaden, 1952), p. 310.

70 *Tārīkh-i Ṭabaristān I*, p. 175.

71 Ibid.

72 Muḥammad Kāẓim Rahmatī, *Zaydiyya dar Īrān* (Tehran, 1392 Sh./2013), pp. 65–77; Madelung, 'Alids of Ṭabarestān, Daylamān, and Gīlān', *EIR*, vol. 1, pp. 881–882.

73 Mar'ashī, *Tārīkh-i Ṭabaristān va Rūyān va Māzandarān*, p. 162; Goto, *Die südkaspischen Provinzen*, p. 73.
74 For the role of traditionalism in northern Iran see M. Sárközy, 'Indigenous versus International? The Role of "Pre-islamic" Identity and Shīʿī Islam in the Clashes of the Bāwandid Kingdom with the Nizārī Ismāʿīlīs in Northern Iran', in M. Rodziewicz and M. Michalak, ed., *In Quest of Identity. Studies on the Persianate World* (Warsaw, 2015), pp. 129–146.
75 Mar'ashī, *Tārīkh-i Ṭabaristān va Rūyān va Māzandarān*, ed. Tasbīhī, p. 127.
76 Ustandār Kay Kāwūs b. Hazārasf followed the Zaydī school of Aḥmad b. al-Ḥusam al-Mu'ayyad bi'llāh, see W. Madelung, 'Bādūspānids', http://www.iranicaonline.org/articles/baduspanidspp. 385–391; Goto, *Die südkaspischen Provinzen*, pp. 74–75.
77 Madelung, 'Bādūspānids', pp. 386–387.

Chapter 2. The Political Relations of the Nizārī Ismaili State in the Caspian Provinces under Ḥasan-i Ṣabbāḥ

1 C. Hillenbrand, '1092 – A Murderous Year', in *Proceedings of the 14th Congress of the Union Européene des Arabisants et Islamisants* (Budapest, 1995), pp. 281–296.
2 Daftary, *The Ismāʿīlīs*, p. 112.
3 Hodgson, *The Order of Assassins*, p. 78; Madelung, 'Alids of Ṭabarestān, Daylamān, and Gīlān', pp. 882–883.
4 W. Madelung, 'Al-Mahdī al-Ḥaqq, al-Halifa ar-Rashīd und die Bekehrung der Daylamiten zur Shi'a', in H. Biesterfeldt and V. Klemm, ed., *Differenz und Dynamik / Difference and Dynamism in Islam: Festschrift für Heinz Halm zum 70. Geburtstag / Festschrift* (Würzburg, 2002), pp. 122–131.
5 Madelung, *Arabic Texts*, pp. 153–154, 323.
6 Hodgson, *The Order*, p. 78; Madelung, ed., *Arabic Texts*, pp. 153–154, 323.
7 Madelung, 'Alids of Ṭabarestān, Daylamān, and Gīlān', *EI2*, pp. 882–883.
8 For the Ismaili acquisition of Zaydī-ruled areas of Daylamān, see, Juwaynī, *Tārīkh-i jahān-gusha*, ed. Qazwīnī (London, 1912–1937), vol. 3, pp. 193–195, 199, 208–209; and Rashīd al-Dīn, *Jāmiʿ al-tawārīkh: tārīkh-i Ismāʿīliyān*, ed. Rawshan (Tehran, 1387 Sh./2008), pp 105–113.
9 Madelung, *Arabic Texts*, pp. 145, 167, 325, 326. http://www.iranicaonline.org/articles/alids-of-tabarestan-daylaman-and-gilan
10 Not to be confused with the Ismaili Kiyā Buzurg-Umīd, the second lord of Alamūt.
11 *Tārīkh-i Ṭabaristān II*, pp. 66, 69, 87–88, 96, 143.
12 Madelung, *Arabic Texts*, pp. 333–334.
13 Rashīd al-Dīn, *Jāmiʿ al-tawārīkh*, ed. M. Rawshan, p. 124.
14 Anūshtigīn Shīrgīr was the Saljūq governor of Sāwa in central Iran.
15 Al-Fatḥ b. 'Alī al-Bundārī, *Zubdat al-nuṣra*, ed. M. T. Houtsma (Leiden, 1889), pp. 123, 144–147.
16 It is claimed that Ḥasan Jurjānī may have been killed by the Ismailis although Zaydī sources attribute his death to local people in Tanhījān, who arrested him at the instigation of the Gilite and Daylamī Zaydī religious authorities. See, Madelung, ed., *Arabic Texts*, pp. 156–157, 160. On the other hand, Rashīd al-Dīn refers to a certain Ḥasan Girdkānī (or Gurdkānī) who, he says, was killed by the Nizārīs in Tamījān (instead of Tanhījān) in Jumādā I 527/April 1133, Rashīd al-Dīn, ed. Rawshan, p. 143. The placenames 'Gurdkānī' and 'Tamījān' suggest some deterioration in the manuscripts available to Rawshan, the editor of the *Jāmiʿ al-tawārīkh*. But here there is an indication that the death of Ḥasan Jurjānī can be attributed to the Ismailis though why is not clear, which is then repeated by Kāshānī in his *Zubdat al-tawārīkh: bakhsh-i Fāṭimiyān*

va Nizāriyān, ed. Muḥammad Taqī Dānishpazhūh (2nd ed., Tehran, 1366 Sh./1987), p. 182.

17 Marʿashī, *Tārīkh-i Ṭabaristān*, p. 99; Goto, *Die südkaspischen Provinzen*, p. 76.

18 *Tārīkh-i Ṭabaristān II*, pp. 37–38; W. Madelung, 'Āl-e Bāvand', *EIR*, vol. 1, pp. 749–752.

19 Madelung, 'Alids of Ṭabarestān, Daylamān, and Gīlān', pp. 882–883.

20 Bernard Hourcade, 'Alamūt', *EIR*, vol. 1, pp. 797–801.

21 Rashīd al-Dīn, *Jāmiʿ al-tawārīkh*, ed. M. Rawshan, pp. 113–114.

22 According to Juwaynī, Lamasar was conquered by the Ismailis on the night of 24 Dhu'l-Qaʿda 495/10 September 1102), see Juwaynī, *Tārīkh-i Jahāngushā*, ed. Qazwīnī, vol. 3, pp. 208–209.

23 Madelung, ed., *Arabic Texts*, pp. 145, 167; see also his, 'Alids of Ṭabarestān, Daylamān, and Gīlān', pp. 882–883 and 'Hoqayni', *EIR*, vol. 12, pp. 456–457.

24 Madelung, 'Hoqayni', p. 457.

25 Abū Manṣūr Nizār al-Muṣṭafā li-Dīn Allāh, eldest son of the Fatimid Imam-caliph al-Mustanṣir, to whom the *naṣṣ* (designation) had been originally given, see Daftary, *The Ismāʿīlīs*, pp. 241–243.

26 ʿIzz al-Dīn Abu'l-Ḥasan ʿAlī b. al-Athīr, *al-Kāmil fi'l-ta'rīkh*, ed. C. J. Thornberg (Beirut, 1982), vol. 10, p. 112; Daftary *The Ismāʿīlīs* p. 330.

27 See, Rashīd al-Dīn, pp. 121–122; Kāshānī, *Zubdat al-tawārīkh*, pp. 156–157; Ḥāfiẓ Abrū, *Majmaʿ al-tawārīkh al-sulṭāniyya: qismat-i khulafā-i ʿAlawiyya-yi Maghrib va Miṣr va Nizāriyān va rafīqān*, ed. M. Mudarrisī Zanjānī (Tehran, 1364 Sh./1985), p. 211; Ibn al-Athīr, *al-Kāmil fi'l-ta'rīkh*, vol. 10, pp. 112, 151–152, has the fullest details. See also Abū Yalā Ḥamza b. Asad. b. al-Qalānisī, *Dhayl ta'rīkh Dimashq*, ed. H. F. Amedroz (Leiden, 1908), pp. 151–156; Ẓahīr al-Dīn Nīshāpūrī, *Saljūq-nāma*, ed. A. H. Morton (Cambridge, 2004), pp. 48–50; Muḥammad b. ʿAlī al-Rāwandī, *Rāḥat al-ṣudūr*, ed. M. Iqbāl (London, 1921), pp. 158–161; al-Bundārī, *Zubdat al-nuṣra*, ed. M. T. Houtsma (Leiden, 1889), pp. 90–91; Hodgson, *The Order*, pp. 95–96.

28 Juwaynī, *Tārīkh-i Jahāngushā*, ed. Qazwīnī. vol. 3, pp. 109–110; Daftary, *The Ismāʿīlīs*, pp. 335–336.

29 According to the *Qiṣṣa-i Malik-i Sīstān*, an unpublished Nizārī Ismaili treatise, Sultan Muḥammad I died of a tumor. I am indebted to Dr Shafique Virani for this information.

30 Juwaynī, *Tārīkh-i Jahāngushā*, vol. 3, pp. 191–192; Rashīd al-Dīn, ed. M. Rawshan, pp. 102–103. Sh. N. Virani, *The Prince and His Two Captives: A Tale from Alamut*. London: I.B. Tauris in association with the Institute of Ismaili Studies, forthcoming.

31 Qazwīnī Rāzī, *Kitāb-i Naqḍ*, pp. 108–109.

32 F. Daftary, 'Gerdkūh', *EIR*, vol. 10, p. 499. http://www.iranicaonline.org/articles/gerdkuh

33 Hodgson, *The Order*, pp. 49–50, regarded this account as fictitious. Nonetheless a copy of the bill of sale made some time before the 11th/17th century exists, see Daftary, *The Ismāʿīlīs*, pp. 315–316; Daftary and Hirji, *The Ismailis, An Illustrated History* (London, 2008), p. 125.

34 See Juwaynī, *Tārīkh-i Jahāngushā*, vol. 3, pp. 207–208, tr. John A. Boyle, vol. 2, pp. 678–679; Rashīd al-Dīn, *Jāmiʿ al-tawārikh*, ed. M. Rawshan, pp. 116–120; Kāshānī, *Zubdat al-tawārīkh*, pp. 151–155; Ḥāfiẓ Abrū, *Majmaʿ al-tawārīkh*, pp. 208–210; Mustawfī Qazwīnī, *Nuzhat al-qulūb*, vol. 1, p. 161, and vol. 2, p. 158; Ṣadr al-Dīn ʿAlī b. Nāṣir al-Ḥusaynī, *Akhbār al-dawla al-Saljūqiyya*, ed. M. Iqbāl (Lahore, 1933), p. 87; Hodgson, *Order*, pp. 86–87; Willey, *Eagle's Nest*, pp. 147–154; and F. Daftary, 'Gerdkuh', *EIR*, vol. 10, p. 499.

35 *Tārīkh-i Ṭabaristān II*, p. 34; Marʿashī, *Tārīkh-i Ṭabaristān*, p. 23.

36 *Tārīkh-i Ṭabaristān II*, p. 33.

37 Ibid., pp. 33–34; Madelung, 'Alids of Ṭabarestān, Daylamān, and Gīlān', pp. 882–883.

38 *Tārīkh-i Ṭabaristān II*, pp. 34–36; Marʿashī, *Tārīkh-i Ṭabaristān*, pp. 99–103.

39 Ibid.

40 Goto, *Die südkaspischen Provinzen*, p. 73.

41 Rashīd al-Dīn, ed. Rawshan, p. 124.
42 Ibid.
43 *Tārīkh-i Ṭabaristān II*, p. 54.
44 Carole Hillenbrand, 'The Power Struggle between the Saljuqs and the Isma'ilis of Alamūt, 487-518/1094-1124: the Saljūq Perspective', p. 206.
45 Hillenbrand, 'The Power Struggle', pp. 207–208.
46 Ibn al-Athīr, *al-Kāmil*, vol. 10, pp. 213–220.
47 Abu'l-Faraj b. al-Jawzī, *al-Muntaẓam fī ta'rīkh al-mulūk wa'l-umam*, ed. F. Krenkow (Hyderabad, 1357–1362/1938–1943), vol. 17, pp 62–65.
48 Hillenbrand, 'The Power Struggle', pp. 207–208.
49 Ibn al-Athīr, *al-Kāmil*, vol. 10, p. 221. Hillenbrand, 'The Power Struggle', p. 208.
50 Ibid., p. 218.
51 The date of the Saljūq siege of Arrajān is not exactly known, but it probably took place before 511/1118.
52 Hillenbrand, 'The Power Struggle', pp. 213–214.
53 Ṣadr al-Dīn 'Alī b. Nāṣir al-Ḥusaynī, *Akhbār al-dawla al-Saljūqiyya*, ed. M. Iqbāl (Lahore, 1933), p. 81; Ibn al-Athīr, *al-Kāmil*, vol. 10, p. 335; Juwaynī, *Tārīkh-i Jahāngushā*, vol. 3, pp. 211–212, tr. Boyle, vol. 2, p. 680; Hillenbrand, 'The Power Struggle', p. 210.
54 Ibn al-Athīr, *al-Kāmil*, vol. 10, p. 335.
55 Juwaynī, *Tārīkh-i Jahāngushā*, vol. 3, pp. 211–212; tr. Boyle, vol. 2, p. 680.
56 al-Ḥusaynī, *Akhbār al-dawla*, p. 81.
57 Hillenbrand, 'The Power Struggle', pp. 214–215.
58 Juwaynī, *Tārīkh-i Jahāngushā*, vol. 3, pp. 202–203; tr. Boyle, vol. 2, pp. 675–676. Hillenbrand, 'The Power Struggle', p. 211.
59 Ibn al-Athīr, *al-Kāmil*, vol. 10, p. 370; Hillenbrand, 'The Power Struggle', pp. 214–215.
60 Ibn al-Athīr, *al-Kāmil*, vol. 10, p. 370.
61 Hillenbrand, 'The Power Struggle', pp. 214–215; Kleiss, pp. 315–319.
62 Hillenbrand, 'The Power Struggle', pp. 213–214.
63 D. Morgan, *The Mongols* (Oxford, 1990), pp. 17–18.
64 Hillenbrand, 'The Power Struggle', p. 213; Ibn al-Athīr, *al-Kāmil*, vol. 10, p. 213.
65 Bāṭiniyya was one of the derogatory names for Ismailis used mainly by non-Ismailis in this era and is reference to the inner (*bāṭin*) meaning of sacred texts often talked of in Ismaili writings.
66 Ibn al-Athīr, *al-Kāmil*, vol. 10, p. 213; Hillenbrand, 'The Power Struggle', p. 212.
67 Ibn al-Athīr, *al-Kāmil*, vol. 10, p. 313; Hillenbrand, 'The Power Struggle', p. 210.
68 Rashīd al-Dīn, ed. Rawshan, pp. 104, 118, 122, 130; Qazwīnī Rāzī, *Kitāb-i Naqḍ*, pp. 108–109, 399; Muḥammad b. 'Abd al-Malik Mu'izzī, *Dīwān-i Amīr al-Shu'arā' Nīshābūrī*, ed. 'A. Iqbāl (Tehran, 1319 Sh./1939), pp. 103–104, 313–314; Muḥammad Ghaznawī, *Maqamāt-i zhanda pīl*, ed. H. Mu'ayyad Sanandājī (Tehran, 1339 Sh./1960), pp. 59–63. The title ('The Memoirs of the Colossal Elephant') refers to the physique of Shaykh Aḥmad Jāmī who was very tall as well as very strong (*Tārīkh-i Ṭabaristān II*, pp. 50–67).
69 Rashīd al-Dīn, ed. Rawshan, p. 130.
70 Juwaynī, *Tārīkh-i Jahāngushā*, vol. 3, pp. 214–215, tr. Boyle, vol. 2, p. 682.
71 Ibn al-Athīr, *al-Kāmil*, vol. 10, p. 201.
72 Hillenbrand, 'The Power Struggle', p. 209.
73 Daftary, *The Ismā'īlīs*, p. 320.
74 Ghaznawī, *Maqamāt-i zhanda pīl*, pp. 59–63.
75 Ibid., pp. 105–107; see also Daftary, *The Assassin Legends* (London, 1994).
76 See T. Mayer, *Keys to the Arcana, Shahrastani's Esoteric Commentary on the Qur'an* (London, 2009), pp. 14–16, and D. Poor, *Command and Creation, A Shi'i Cosmological Treatise* (London, 2021), pp. 4–7, 28–37.
77 The original text is not yet published and Dr Shafique N. Virani, whose generosity is much appreciated once again, made a copy accessible to me.

78 al-Ḥusaynī, *Akhbār al-dawla*, p. 55; Hillenbrand, 'The Power Struggle', p. 215.
79 Ibn al-Athīr, *al-Kāmil*, vol. 10, p. 393.
80 Juwaynī, *Tārīkh-i Jahāngushā*, vol. 3, pp. 213–214, tr. Boyle, vol. 2, pp. 681–682. Rashīd al-Dīn, ed. Rawshan, p. 123. Kāshānī, *Zubdat al-tawārīkh*, pp. 155, 159. Ḥāfiẓ Abrū, *Majma' al-tawārīkh al-sulṭāniyya: qismat-i khulafā-i 'Alawiyya-yi Maghrib va Miṣr va Nizāriyān va Rafīqān*, ed. M. Mudarrisī Zanjānī (Tehran, 1364 Sh./1985), p. 212.
81 *Tārīkh-i Ṭabaristān II*, p. 64.
82 *Tārīkh-i Ṭabaristān II*, pp. 69–71.
83 Rashīd al-Dīn, ed. Rawshan, p. 138; Kāshānī, *Zubdat al-tawārīkh*, p. 173. As for the dates of construction of Maymūndiz, Daftary points out 'Ḥāfiẓ Abrū does not mention this detail', *The Ismā'īlīs*, p. 625. Both Rashīd al-Dīn, ed. Rawshan, p. 122, and Kāshānī, *Zubdat al-tawārīkh*, p. 158, give earlier dates, 490/1097 and 497/1104 respectively, for the construction of Maymūndiz. According to Juwaynī, Maymūndiz was built much later, during the reign of Imam 'Alā al-Dīn Muḥammad III (r. 618–653/618/1221–1255), *Tārīkh-i Jahāngushā*, vol. 1, pp. 122–123; tr. Boyle, vol. 2, p. 627. The area of Maymūndiz, situated to the north of the present-day village of Shams Kilaya and west of Alamūt, was discovered in 1960 by Peter Willey, see Willey, *Castles of the Assassins*, pp. 158–192, and his *Eagle's Nest*, pp. 114–120. For other discussions about Maymūndiz, see W. Ivanow, *Alamūt and Lamasar* (Tehran, 1960), pp. 75–81; C. E. Bosworth, 'Maymun-Diz', *EI2*, vol. 6, pp. 917–918; and M. Sutūda, *Qilā'-i ismā'īliyya* (Tehran, 1362 Sh./1984), pp. 108–122. It should be noted that Sutuda largely disagrees with Willey.
84 Rashīd al-Dīn, pp. 137, 140.
85 Madelung, 'Āl-e Bāvand'.
86 *Tārīkh-i Ṭabaristān II*, p. 68.
87 Such as in the case of the inscription of the tower of Lajīm, see André Godard, 'Les tours de Ladjim et de Resget (Māzandarān)', *Āthār-é Īrān, Annales du service archéologique de l'Īrān*, vol. 1 (1936), pp. 109–121.
88 *Tārīkh-i Ṭabaristān II*, p. 68; Hodgson, *The Order*, p. 100.

Chapter 3. The Development of Local Powers in the Caspian during Saljūq Decline

1 Rashīd al-Dīn, ed. Rawshan, p. 137; Hodgson, *The Order*, p. 102, n. 11.
2 Madelung, 'Alids of Ṭabarestān, Daylamān, and Gīlān', pp. 882–883.
3 al-Muḥallī, *al-Ḥadā'iq al-wardiyya*.
4 Rashīd al-Dīn, ed. Rawshan, pp. 137–139.
5 The term *zandaqa* referred to a belief in dualism and was applied to various groups that challenged Sunni religio-political authority.
6 Rashīd al-Dīn, ed. Rawshan, p. 139.
7 Ibid.
8 Rashīd al-Dīn, ed. Rawshan, p. 142.
9 This place name is not exactly clear.
10 Rashīd al-Dīn, ed. Rawshan, p. 140.
11 It is only Lewis (*Assassins*, p. 42) who has raised doubts about the identification of Gurjīyān or Gurjistān as Georgia in the Caucasus. But none of the evidence suggests that this is valid.
12 Rashīd al-Dīn, ed. Rawshan, p. 141. For the location of Gurjīyān we have found very limited data at a modest Iranian blog: see http://javaherdeh.blogfa.com/post-379.aspx (accessed 19 August 2019).
13 Rashīd al-Dīn, ed. Rawshan, p. 108.

14 Ibid.
15 Ibid., p. 121.
16 Rashīd al-Dīn, ed. Rawshan, p. 113. Hodgson, *The Order*, p. 78.
17 Rashīd al-Dīn, ed. Rawshan, p. 121.
18 Turshīz is identified as modern Kāshmar in Khurāsān.
19 Rashīd al-Dīn, ed. Rawshan, p. 121.
20 Ibid., p. 138.
21 Rashīd al-Dīn, ed. Rawshan, p. 141.

Chapter 4. Nizārī-Bāwandid Competition for Hegemony, 534–565/1140–1170

1 The full name of the new Bāwandid ruler was Nuṣrat al-Dīn Shāh Ghāzī Rustam.
2 The exact date of Shāh Ghāzī Rustam's succession is not known.
3 H. L. Rabino, 'Les dynasties du Māzandarān de l'an 50 avant l'Hégire á l'an 1006 de l'Hégire (572 á 1597-98), d'aprés les chroniques locales', *Journal Asiatique*, 228 (1936), p. 425; W. Madelung, "Alā' al-Dawla 'Alī', p. 772.
4 Ibn Isfandiyār, *Tārīkh-i Ṭabaristān*, II, pp. 68–69.
5 Mar'ashī, ed. Tasbīḥī, pp. 16–18; Goto, *Die südkaspischen Provinzen*, p. 74.
6 Ibn Isfandiyār, *Tārīkh-i Ṭabaristān*, II, p. 105.
7 She was perhaps the former wife Tāj al-Mulūk Mardāwīj, Shāh Ghāzī Rustam's deposed brother, who had married a Saljūq princess. Ibn Isfandiyār, *Tārīkh-i Ṭabaristān*, II, p. 104.
8 Ibn Isfandiyār, *Tārīkh-i Ṭabaristān*, II, pp. 94–95.
9 Morimoto, K. 'Ketāb al-naqż', *Encyclopaedia Iranica Online Edition*, 2015, http://www.iranicaonline.org/articles/ketab-al-naqz.
10 Ibn Isfandiyār, *Tārīkh-i Ṭabaristān*, II, pp. 68–69.
11 Ibid.
12 Ibn Isfandiyār, *Tārīkh-i Ṭabaristān*, II, p. 68.
13 Ibid.
14 Ibn Isfandiyār, *Tārīkh-i Ṭabaristān*, II, p. 86.
15 Ibid.
16 Rashīd al-Dīn, ed. Rawshan, p. 155; Kāshānī, *Zubdat al-tawārīkh*, p. 192; Ḥāfiẓ Abrū, *Majma' al-tawārīkh*, p. 240; Ibn al-Athīr, *al-Kāmil*, vol. 11, p. 44; Daftary, *The Ismā'īlīs*, p. 357.
17 Rashīd al-Dīn, ed. Rawshan, p. 155; Hodgson, *The Order*, p. 114.
18 Ibid.
19 Rashīd al-Dīn, ed. Rawshan, pp. 152, 157; Kāshānī, *Zubdat al-tawārīkh*, pp. 171–174.
20 Madelung, *Religious Trends*, pp. 10–11.
21 For the Khurramī issue, see: H. Sadighi, *Les mouvements religieux iraniens au IIe et IIIe siècle de l'hégire* (Paris, 1938), pp. 240–287; P. Crone, *The Nativist Prophets of Early Islamic Iran* (Cambridge, 2014), pp. 47–76.
22 Madelung, *Religious Trends*, p. 10; Rashīd al-Dīn, ed. Rawshan, p. 148.
23 Madelung, *Religious Trends*, pp. 10–11; Rashīd al-Dīn, ed. Rawshan, p. 148.
24 Madelung, *Religious Trends*, p. 12, n. 28.
25 Hodgson, *The Order*, pp. 71–72.
26 Hodgson, *The Order*, pp. 143–148, by contrast, regards it as a series of 'minor quarrels'.
27 Rashīd al-Dīn, ed. Rawshan, p. 145.
28 Ibn Isfandiyār, *Tārīkh-i Ṭabaristān*, II, p. 68.
29 Not to be confused with the more renowned second *dā'ī* and lord of Alamūt.
30 Rashīd al-Dīn, ed. Rawshan, pp. 146–147.
31 See the dynastical-genealogical table in Appendix III.

32 *Ḥudūd al-ʿālam*, ed. Sutūda, p. 146; Āmulī, *Tārīkh-i Rūyān*, pp. 23–24; W. Madelung, 'Abu Isḥāq al-Ṣābī on the Alids of Ṭabaristān and Gīlān', *Journal of Near Eastern Studies*, 26 (1967), pp. 17–57; A. H. Morton, 'Dinars from Western Māzandarān of Some Vassals of the Saljūq Sultan Muhammad b. Malik-Shāh', *Iran*, 25 (1987), p. 86; Madelung, 'Bādūspānids', p. 385.
33 Marʿashī, *Ṭabaristān*, ed. M. H. Tasbīḥī, p. 159.
34 Ibn Isfandiyār, *Tārīkh-i Ṭabaristān*, II, p. 96.
35 Ibn Isfandiyār, *Tārīkh-i Ṭabaristān*, II, p. 87.
36 Āmulī, *Tārīkh-i Rūyān*, pp. 127–128.
37 Marʿashī, *Ṭabaristān*, ed. M. H. Tasbīḥī, p. 17.
38 Ibn al-Athīr, *The Chronicle of Ibn al-Athīr for the Crusading Period from al-Kamil fi'l-ta'rikh*, vol. 2 'The Years 541-581/541/1146-1193: The Age of Nūr al-al-Dīn and Saladīn', tr. D. S. Richards (Aldershot, 2007), pp. 91–92: [Events of 552/1157-1158]: This year the Shāh of Māzandarān, Rustum ibn ʿAlī ibn Shahriyār, gathered his troops and marched away, although he told no-one of his destination. He followed narrow passes and made haste towards Alamūt, which belonged to the Ismāʿīlīs. He carried out a raid and burnt villages and the countryside. He killed many, plundered property, seized their womenfolk and enslaved their children, whom he sold in the marketplace, before returning safely and rich in booty. The Ismāʿīlīs were sorely stricken and overwhelmed by a powerlessness, the like of which they had not experienced before. He so ruined their lands that they were not productive for many years.
39 Marʿashī, ed. Tasbīḥī, p. 17.
40 The Persian word '*Kūr*' 'blind' instead of '*Nūr*' 'light, brightness' seems to be a belittling, malevolent anti-Nizārī phrase in the letter.
41 Āmulī, *Tārīkh-i Rūyān*, pp. 127–128.
42 Ibn Isfandiyār, *Tārīkh-i Ṭabaristān*, II, p. 87. Meanwhile, Marʿashī attributes the letter to Kiyā Buzurg Daylamānī, who was waging war against the Nizārīs as ordered by his lord, Shāh Ghāzī Rustam (Marʿashī, ed. M. H. Tasbīḥī, p. 17).
43 Hodgson, *The Order*, pp. 147–148.
44 Ibn Isfandiyār, *Tārīkh-i Ṭabaristān*, II, pp. 103–104.
45 Rashīd al-Dīn, ed. Rawshan, p. 139; Hodgson, *The Order*, p. 103.
46 Rashīd al-Dīn, ed. Rawshan, p. 154.
47 Ibid., p. 155.
48 Ibid., p. 154.
49 Rashīd al-Dīn, ed. Rawshan, p. 155.
50 Rashīd al-Dīn, ed. Rawshan, pp. 153–154.
51 Hodgson, *The Order*, p. 145.
52 Willey, *Eagles Nest*, p. 163.
53 Ibn Isfandiyār, *Tārīkh-i Ṭabaristān*, II, p. 92. Iraq means here ʿIrāq-i ʿAjam, which is in present-day western Iran.
54 Ibn Isfandiyār, II, p. 96, http://www.iranicaonline.org/articles/alids-of-tabarestan-daylaman-and-gilan Marʿashī, 19 states that the auxiliary forces who were summoned after a defeat in Dihistān were Daylamīs and Gilites. See also, Marʿashī, *Ṭabaristān*, ed. M. H. Tasbīḥī, p. 19.
55 Ibn Isfandiyār, *Tārīkh-i Ṭabaristān*, II, p. 95.
56 Willey, *Eagles Nest*, p. 165.
57 For these place names, we have modified Willey's transcription.
58 Daftary, 'Gerdkūh'.
59 Willey, *Eagles Nest*, pp. 147–154.
60 Ibid., pp. 147–154.
61 A Turkic amīr in Khurāsān formerly in the entourage of Sanjar.
62 As for '*kharwār*', this can be translated both as 'ass-load' but, according to some linguistic and historical sources, one *kharwār* weighs 300 kilos. Steingass says that it is

'an ass-load; the measure of a hundred Tabriz *maunds*.' One Tabrīzī *maund* in the 18th century might have been somewhere between 6.66 and 7.38 English pounds i.e. ca. 3–3.3 kilos. If we say each *kharwār* weighs 300 kg then, 10 *kharwārs* equal almost 3,000 kilos. Francis Joseph Steingass, *A Comprehensive Persian-English Dictionary* (rpr. Beirut, 1972), p. 475; R. Greaves, 'Iranian Relations with the European Trading Companies to 1798', in *The Cambridge History of Iran*, vol. 7, *From Nadir Shah to the Islamic Republic*, ed. P. Avery, et al. (Cambridge, 1991), p. 369.

63 Ibn Isfandiyār, *Tārīkh-i Ṭabaristān*, II, pp. 102–103.
64 Ibn al-Athīr, *The Chronicle of Ibn al-Athīr*, tr. D. S. Richards, vol. 2, pp. 117–118.
65 Ibid., pp. 92–94, 139, 154.
66 Ibn Isfandiyār, *Tārīkh-i Ṭabaristān*, II, p. 104.
67 Rashīd al-Dīn, ed. Rawshan, p. 152.
68 Daftary, *The Ismāʿīlīs*, p. 357.
69 Goto, *Die südkaspischen Provinzen*, p. 78.
70 Madelung, 'Bādūspānids', pp. 387–388.
71 Marʿashī, ed. Tasbīḥī, p. 20; Goto, *Die südkaspischen Provinzen*, pp. 74–75.
72 Āmulī, *Tārīkh-i Rūyān*, p. 129.
73 Rashīd al-Dīn, ed. Rawshan, p. 146.
74 Āmulī, *Tārīkh-i Rūyān*, p. 129; Rashīd al-Dīn, ed. Rawshan, p. 146.
75 Āmulī, *Tārīkh-i Rūyān*, pp. 129–131; Madelung, 'Bādūspānids', pp. 385–386.

Chapter 5. Bāwandid-Nizārī Confrontation in the Late 6th/12th Century

1 Morimoto, Kazuo, 'Ketāb al-Naqż', *Encyclopaedia Iranica Online Edition*, 2015, http://www.iranicaonline.org/articles/ketab-al-naqz; Wilferd Madelung, 'Abd-al-Jalīl Rāzī', *EIR*, vol. 1, p. 120.
2 Excerpts from two *qaṣīdas* of Muʿizzī relating to the Bāwandid prince ʿAlāʾ al-Dawla ʿAlī, Muḥammad b. ʿAbd al-Malik Muʿizzī, *Dīwān-i Amīr al-Shuʿarāʾ*, ed. ʿAbbās Iqbāl (Tehran, 1319 Sh./1939), pp. 103–104, 313–314.
3 Daftary, *The Ismāʿīlīs*, pp. 301, 316–317.
4 Kāshānī, *Zubdat al-tawārīkh*, p. 148; *Haft bāb-i Bābā Sayyidna*, ed. W. Ivanow, in his *Two Early Ismaili Treatises* (Bombay, 1933), p. 30; English tr. in Hodgson, *The Order*, p. 314. n. 40.
5 M. Sárközy, 'Indigenous versus International?', pp. 129–146.
6 Uram was a village and a district in Ṭabaristān ruled by the Bāwandids.
7 Qazwīnī Rāzī, *Kitāb-i Naqḍ*, pp. 110–111.
8 Qazwīnī Rāzī, *Kitāb-i Naqḍ*, pp. 200–201.
9 Regarding the identity of this mysterious 'Khwāja', Morimoto writes:

> As its title indicates, the *Naqz* (Refutation) is a refutation against a polemical work impugning the Twelver Shiʿites, entitled *Baʿż fażāʾeḥ al-Rawāfeż* (some of the ignominies of the Shiʿites). Since Qazvinī cites sections of the *Baʿż fażāʾeḥ* and refutes it one by one, the *Naqż* is in fact a composite text that comprises not only Qazvini's own refutation but also what seems to amount to a large portion of the *Baʿż fażāʾeḥ al-Rawāfeż*. The *Baʿż fażāʾeḥ al-Rawāfeż* was written also in Rayy by an anonymous author who was a defector from the Twelver Shiʿite community (*Naqż*, 1980, p. 14; see p. 373 n. 2, for the falsehood of the identification of the author with a certain Shihāb-al-Dīn Tawāriqī Shāfiʿī of the Mashshāṭ family; the author's legal and theological affiliations will be discussed below). Qazvīnī knew the identity of his opponent (*Naqż*, pp. 5, 141 n. 1), but kept him anonymous throughout his refutation, calling him

mockingly by such appellations as 'Khwāja-ye Now-Sonni', 'Khwāja-ye Now-mosalmān', or 'Khwāja-yi Enteiāli' (see, e.g., *Naqż*, pp. 52, 63, 69).

See Morimoto, 'Ketāb al-Naqż'.

10 Qazwīnī Rāzī, *Kitāb-i Naqḍ*, pp. 108–109

11 *Tārīkh-i Ṭabaristān I*, p. 116.

12 Qazwīnī Rāzī, *Kitāb-i Naqḍ*, p. 399.

13 Ibid., p. 131.

14 Ibid., p. 553.

15 Qazwīnī Rāzī, *Kitāb-i Naqḍ*, pp. 110–111.

16 See Sárközy, 'Indigenous versus International?', pp. 137–143.

17 Juwaynī, vol. 3, pp. 225–228; Hodgson, *The Order*, pp. 147–148.

18 D. Cortese, 'Eschatology and power in mediaeval Persian Ismailism' (PhD, School of Oriental and African Studies, University of London, 1993), pp.133–134; B. Lewis, 'Kamāl al-Dīn's Biography of Rashīd al-Dīn Sinān', *Arabica*, 13 (1966), pp. 263–264.

19 Cortese, 'Eschatology and power', pp. 133–134.

20 Hodgson, *The Order*, p. 156; Cortese, 'Eschatology and power', p. 134.

21 See Ḥasan-i Maḥmūd-i Kātib, *Haft bāb*, ed. and tr. S. J. Badakhchani as *Spiritual Resurrection in Shiʿi Islam* (London, 2017), p. 26, n. 78. Referring to Naṣīr al-Dīn Muḥammad al-Ṭūsī's *Rawḍat al-taslīm* (Leiden, 1950), p. 157, Badakhchani suggests that the proclamation of the *qiyāma* was pre-ordained for the year 500 AH.

22 As far as the medieval (Qur'anic, Ismaili, non-Ismaili) interpretations of the *qiyāma* are concerned, Badakhchani's introductory chapter to his edition and translation of Ḥasan-i Maḥmūd-i Kātib's *Haft bāb* has a good summary of different views of the *qiyāma*; Badakhchani, *Spiritual Resurrection*, pp. 10–25. Henry Corbin wrote extensively on the meaning of the *qiyāma* which he considered a real but invisible phenomenon thus giving a strongly esoteric interpretation in which the advent of a pure spiritual Islam and an initiation into the hidden meaning of the divine revelation can both be detected; see, H. Corbin, *History of Islamic Philosophy* (London, 1993), pp. 131–144. However, Buckley saw the declaration of *qiyāma* as a sign of the 'Abnormal-Sacred' (based on anthropological concepts perhaps following the ideas of Mircea Eliade), considering it a phenomenon shifting from the 'Normal-Profane' order (J. Buckley, 'The Nizārī Isma'ili Abolishment of the Shari'a during the 'Great Resurrection' of 559/1164 A.D./559 A.H.', *Studia Islamica*, 60 (1984), pp. 162–164). More recently Christian Jambet addressed the question of the philosophy of the *qiyāma* in his monograph *La grande résurrection d'Alamût: les forms de la liberté dans le Shîʿisme Ismaélien* (Lagrasse, 1990), and in his foreword to Badakhchani, *Spiritual Resurrection in Shiʿi Islam*, pp. xv–xx, 32–36. See also Cortese, 'Eschatology and power', pp. 149–151.

23 Juwaynī, *Tārīkh-i Jahāngushā*, ed. Qazwīnī, vol. 3, pp. 225–230, 237–239; tr. Boyle, vol. 2, pp. 688–691, 695–697; Rashīd al-Dīn ed. Rawshan, pp. 164–166, 168–169, and Kāshānī, *Zubdat al-tawārīkh*, pp. 201–202, 204. All three chroniclers give the same account, probably based on the same Nizārī sources; see Ḥāfiẓ-i Abrū, *Majmaʿ al-tawārīkh*, pp. 252–253. Nizārī teachings relating to the *qiyāma*, as further developed during the time of Ḥasan's successors, are discussed in a few later Nizārī texts, notably in Ḥasan-i Maḥmūd-i Kātib's *Haft bāb* cited above and in Naṣīr al-Dīn al-Ṭūsī's *Rawḍat al-taslīm*, ed. and tr. W. Ivanow (Leiden, 1950), especially the following excerpts: text, pp. 62–63, 83–84, 101–102, 128–149, translation, pp. 68–70, 94–96, 115–116, 149–175; ed. and tr. S. J. Badakhchani as *Paradise of Submission: A Medieval Treatise on Ismaili Thought* (London, 2005), text, pp. 81–83, 109–110, 134–136, 169–198, translation, pp. 70–72, 92, 109–111, 136–159. References to the doctrine of the *qiyāma*, with an important passage on the proclamation, are found in the *Haft bāb* of Abū Isḥāq Qūhistānī, text, pp. 19, 24, 38–39, 40–42 (describing the event), 43–44, 46–47, 53, 58, 65, translation, pp. 19, 23, 38, 40–42, 43–44, 46–47, 53–54, 58, 65, a Nizārī Ismaili

treatise written at the beginning of the 10th/16th century, and in Khayrkhwāh-i Haratī, *Kalām-i pīr*, ed. and tr. W. Ivanow (Bombay, 1935), text, pp. 46, 51, 62–64, 65–66, 68, 90–92, 95–96, 100, 112–113, translation, pp. 38–39, 44, 57–59, 60–61, 64, 84–87, 91, 96, 109, and appendix, pp. 115–116, containing Abū Isḥāq Qūhistānī's original passage on the *qiyāma* declaration. The *Kalām-i pīr*, as argued by Ivanow, is a plagiarised and partly extended version of Abū Isḥāq Qūhistānī's treatise, composed a few decades later and attributed by Khayrkhwāh-i Harātī to Naṣīr-i Khusraw, though the actual author was Khayrkhwāh-i Harātī himself, see: Khayrkhwāh-i Harātī, *Kalām-i pīr, a Treatise on Ismaili Doctrine*, ed. and tr. W. Ivanow (Bombay, 1935); W. Ivanow, *A Guide to Ismaili Literature* (London 1933), pp. 141–143, 162–163; Daftary, *Ismaili Literature*, p. 124.

24 Daftary, *The Ismāʿīlīs*, p. 362.

25 Daftary, *The Ismāʿīlīs*, pp. 360–361.

26 F. Daftary, 'Ḥasan II', *EIR*, vol. 12, pp. 24–25, available online at http://www.iranicaonline.org/articles/hasan-ii

27 Hodgson, *The Order*, pp. 148–151.

28 Besides the translations by Ivanow and Badakhchani, another was made by Hodgson, however it is based on Ivanow's (Hodgson, *The Order*, pp. 149–151). A French translation was also published by Henry Corbin in his 'Huitième centenaire d'Alamût', *Mercure de France* (February, 1956), pp. 284–304. See also Badakhchani, *Spiritual Resurrection*, p. 26, n. 77.

29 Badakhchani, *Spiritual Resurrection*, pp. 26–28. With minor alterations the text can be found also in the *Kalām-i pīr* of Khayrkhwāh-i Harātī, pp. 65–66; F. Daftary, *Ismaili Literature*, pp. 124, 162. Badakhchani has endeavoured to reconstruct the original paragraph of the *qiyāma* announcement read by Ḥasan II in the presence of his followers in Alamūt based on the *Haft bāb* of Abū Isḥāq Quhistānī and other surviving materials attributed to Ḥasan II. His reconstruction is as follows: 'Arise, the *qiyāmat* has arrived! Verily, the epoch of expectations has ended. Now is the Resurrection which is the final amongst all Resurrections. Today is a time when things are demonstrated by proof and reason, and not verses, ideologies, hints and the exhibition of bodily performance. Today bodily actions, discourses, indications and signs have reached the end of their appointed time. Now whoever by his own insight can contemplate the essence will be a witness to the entirety of all the revelations and divine signs, but whoever observes through names and indications is misled, confounded and prevented from the true realisation.' Badakhchani, *Spiritual Resurrection*, p. 27, n. 80.

30 Hodgson's translation in *The Order*, pp. 149–150; Rashīd al-Dīn, ed. Rawshan, p. 123.

31 This passage in Rashīd al-Dīn's version would seem to be a reference to the Shiʿi concept of occultation (*ghayba*) rather than concealment (*satr*).

32 Hodgson's translation in *The Order*, pp. 149–150. Rashīd al-Dīn, ed. Rawshan, pp. 123–124. The reference to wine is clearly a polemical slurr.

33 Juwaynī, vol. 3, p. 228, tr. Boyle, vol. 2, p. 690; Rashīd al-Dīn, ed. Rawshan, p. 165; Kāshānī, *Zubdat al-tawārīkh*, p. 202; Ḥāfiẓ-i Abrū, *Majmaʿ al-tawārīkh*, p. 253; Daftary, *The Ismāʿīlīs*, p. 361.

34 See Badakhchani, *Spiritual Resurrection*, p. 28, n. 81.

35 On the other hand, in the *Haft bāb* of Ḥasan-i Maḥmūd-i Kātib there is a brief reference (paragraph 52) to a son of Nizār, called Ḥasan and his grandson, called Ḥusayn, who could have been the grandfather and father of Ḥasan II of Alamūt, therefore supporting the idea that Ḥasan II was the great-grandson of Nizār b. Mustanṣir. It is known that Nizār had sons and grandsons, some of whom were active in uprisings against the rule of al-Āmir and his successors in Egypt. As a result similar views concerning the direct descent of Ḥasan II from Nizār appear in a several Arabic and Persian sources as well, for instance: Ibn al-Qalānisī, *Dhayl ta'rīkh Dimashq*, ed. Henry F. Amedroz (Leiden, 1908), p. 302; Ibn Ẓāfir, *Akhbār al-dual al-munqaṭiʿa*, ed. André Ferré (Cairo, 1972), pp. 79, 111; Jamāl al-Dīn ibn ʿInaba, *ʿUmdat al-ṭālib fī ansāb Āl Abī Ṭālib* (Najaf, 1961),

p. 237; and the *Dustūr al-munajjimīn* in Muḥammad Aṣl Karīmī Zanjānī, *Tārīkh wa ta'wīl bi riwāyat-i Dustūr al-munajjimīn* (Bonn, 2013), p. 59, quoting *Yāddāshthā-yi Qazwīnī*, ed. Īraj Afshār (Tehran, 1345/1966), see also Badakhchani, *Spiritual Resurrection*, p. 8, n. 24. Other contemporary sources, however, remain silent about the names of the father and grandfather of Hasan II, with the exception of Juwaynī. The names of Ḥasan II's paternal ancestors mentioned by Juwaynī are entirely different from those of the *Haft bāb* of Ḥasan-i Maḥmūd-i Kātib and Juwaynī believes that Ḥasan II was the great-great-grandson of Nizār and not the latter's great-grandson, calling his father, paternal grandfather and great-grandfather al-Qāhir, al-Muhtadā and al-Hādī. Therefore, this al-Hādī should have been the son of Nizār who was saved and brought to Alamūt from Egypt after 488/1095. See Juwaynī, vol. 3, p. 246. See also, F. Daftary, *The Ismaili Imams, A Biographical History* (London, 2020), pp. 118–123.

36 Hodgson, *The Order*, Appendix I, pp. 299–304.
37 Ibid., pp. 151–152.
38 Manuscript n. 32, fragment 42r, held in the Ismaili Special Collections Unit of The Institute of Ismaili Studies, quoted by Cortese, 'Eschatology and power', pp. 141–142.
39 This Raʿīs Muẓaffar is not to be confused with the first governor of Girdkūh.
40 Daftary, *The Ismāʿīlīs*, p. 359.
41 Hodgson, *The Order*, p. 148.
42 Ibid.
43 See Cortese, 'Eschatology and power', pp. 157–158. See also H. Corbin, 'The Realism and Symbolism of Colours in Shiite Islam', in his *Temple and Contemplation* (London, 1986), pp. 1–54, and Badakhchani, *Spiritual Resurrection*, p. 26. n. 79. Of course, all these interpretations could have been present alongside each other.
44 Daftary, *The Ismāʿīlīs*, p. 361.
45 *Qā'im al-qiyāma* or 'the one who establishes the Resurrection'.
46 D. Tor, 'The Importance of Khurāsān and Transoxiana in the Classical Islamic World', in A.C.S. Peacock and D. G. Tor, ed., *Medieval Central Asia and the Persianate World: Iranian Tradition and Islamic Civilisation* (London, 2015), pp. 1–12.
47 Juwaynī, vol. 3, p. 239.
48 Rashīd al-Dīn, ed. Rawshan, p. 146.
49 Daftary, *The Ismāʿīlīs*, p. 361.
50 Mustawfī, *Tārīkh-i guzīda*, p. 523.
51 Ibn al-Athīr, tr. Richards, vol. 2, p. 137. Hodgson, *The Order*, p. 158.
52 Hodgson, *The Order*, pp. 180–185; Daftary *The Ismāʿīlīs*, pp. 363–367.
53 Paragraph No. 12. The original and still unpublished text was kindly made available by Dr Shafique Virani.
54 *Tārīkh-i Ṭabaristān II*, pp. 117–119.
55 Goto, *Die südkaspischen Provinzen*, pp. 78–79.
56 Marʿashī, ed. Tasbīḥī, pp. 28–29.
57 *Tārīkh-i Ṭabaristān II*, pp. 141–145. See the family tree of the Bādūspānids in Appendix III of this volume.
58 *Tārīkh-i Ṭabaristān II*, pp. 143–145. Marʿashī, *Ṭabaristān*, ed. Tasbīḥī, p. 27.
59 Ibid.
60 *Tārīkh-i Ṭabaristān II*, pp. 141–145.
61 Goto, *Die südkaspischen Provinzen*, pp. 74–75.
62 *Tārīkh-i Ṭabaristān II*, p. 144; Marʿashī *Ṭabaristān*, ed. Tasbīḥī, pp. 28–29.
63 *Tārīkh-i Ṭabaristān II*, pp. 144–145.
64 Ibid., pp. 169–170; Rabino, 'Les dynasties du Māzandarān', p. 414.
65 *Tārīkh-i Ṭabaristān II*, pp. 66, 69, 87–88, 96, 143. See the dynastic table in Appendix III.
66 Marʿashī, *Ṭabaristān*, ed. Tasbīḥī, pp. 27–29.
67 *Tārīkh-i Ṭabaristān II*, pp. 144–145; Āmulī, *Tārīkh-i Rūyān*, pp. 147–149.
68 *Tārīkh-i Ṭabaristān II*, pp. 143–145.

69 *Tārīkh-i Ṭabaristān II*, after p. 145 becomes very fragmented and has only brief comments on various historical events. Āmulī and Marʿashī, *Ṭabaristān*, follow mainly Ibn Isfandiyār and consequently have brief reports about this period and there are no other reliable accounts for the local history of northern Iran.
70 Āmulī, *Tārīkh-i Rūyān*, pp. 150–151.
71 *Tārīkh-i Ṭabaristān II*, pp. 144–145. Āmulī, *Tārīkh-i Rūyān*, pp. 147–149.
72 Madelung, 'Bādūspānids', pp. 387–388.
73 Marʿashī, *Tārīkh-i Ṭabaristān*, ed. Tasbīḥī, pp. 29–30.
74 Āmulī, *Tārīkh-i Rūyān*, pp. 150–151. Marʿashī, *Tārīkh-i Ṭabaristān*, pp. 29–30. Material relating to the rule of Bīsutūn b. Nāmāwar remains extremely sparse.
75 Āmulī, *Tārīkh-i Rūyān*, pp. 150–151; Marʿashī, *Ṭabaristān*, ed. Tasbīḥī, pp. 29–30.
76 Āmulī, pp. 152–153; see also Marʿashī, *Ṭabaristān*, ed. Tasbīḥī, pp. 30–31.
77 Rabino, 'Les dynasties du Māzandarān', pp. 430–432.
78 Ibid.; Daftary, *The Ismāʿīlīs*, p. 366; Madelung, 'Āl-e Bāvand', pp. 750–751.
79 Marʿashī, *Ṭabaristān*, ed. Tasbīḥī, pp. 114–117; Rabino, 'Les dynasties du Māzandarān', pp. 430–431; Madelung, 'Āl-e Bāvand', pp. 750–751.
80 *Tārīkh-i Ṭabaristān II*, p. 92.
81 *Tārīkh-i Ṭabaristān II*, pp. 136–140, Marʿashī, *Ṭabaristān*, ed. Tasbīḥī, pp. 114–117, Rabino, 'Les dynasties du Māzandarān', pp. 430–431, Madelung, 'Āl-e Bāvand', pp. 750–751, Daftary, *The Ismāʿīlīs*, p. 374.
82 Minhāj al-Dīn ʿUthmān b. Sirāj al-Dīn Juzjānī, *Ṭabaqāt-i Nāṣirī*, ed. ʿAbd al-Ḥayy Ḥabībī (2nd ed., Kabul, 1342–1343 Sh./1963–1964), p. 403. Muḥammad b. Aḥmad Nasawī, *Sīrat-i Jalāl al-Dīn Mīnkubirnī*, anonymous Persian translation, ed. Muḥammad Mīnuwī (Tehran, 1394 Sh./2015), p. 231.
83 Goto, *Die südkaspischen Provinzen*, pp. 74–79.
84 *Tārīkh-i Ṭabaristān II*, pp. 163, 174; Āmulī, *Tārīkh-i Rūyān*, pp. 150–151; Marʿashī, *Ṭabaristān*, ed. Tasbīḥī, pp. 30, 118.
85 For more on this, see the next chapter.
86 *Tārīkh-i Ṭabaristān II*, p. 174; Marʿashī *Ṭabaristān*, ed. Tasbīḥī, p. 118.
87 C.E. Bosworth, *The Islamic Dynasties* (2nd ed., Edinburgh, 1996), pp. 164–165.
88 W. Ivanow, 'An Ismaili Poem in Praise of Fidawis', *Journal of the Bombay Branch of the Royal Asiatic Society*, New Series, 14 (1938), pp. 63–72.
89 Not to be confused with the *Haft bāb* of Abū Isḥāq Qūhistānī which was composed much later. The *Haft bāb* of Ḥasan-i Maḥmūd-i Kātib was formerly called *Haft bāb-i bābā sayyidnā* when it was first edited and published by Ivanow. However, in the light of recent research and manuscript tradition, Badakhchani revised the title in his edition and translation of the *Haft bāb*. See Jalal Badakhchani, ed. and tr., *Spiritual Resurrection*, pp. 1–3.
90 This name appears in the colophon of one of the manuscripts of the *Dīwān-i Qāʾimiyyāt* dated 1105/1694, preserved in the Ismaili Special Collections Unit of The Institute of Ismaili Studies (MS no. 600). See also Badakhchani, *Spiritual Resurrection*, p. 2, n. 7.
91 Naṣīr al-Dīn al-Ṭūsī, *Sayr wa sulūk*, ed. and tr. S. J. Badakhchani as *Contemplation and Action: The Spiritual Autobiography of a Muslim Scholar* (London, 1998), p. 31.
92 Rashīd al-Dīn, ed. Rawshan, p. 151, where it also says that he wrote this part of the chronicle subsequently re-utilised by Rashīd al-Dīn, during his time working for the *muḥtasham* Shihāb al-Dīn. See also Badakhchani, *Spiritual Resurrection*, p. 2, n. 9.
93 Badakhchani, *Spiritual Resurrection*, p. 2, n. 10, where it says that the name Ḥasan-i Ṣalāḥ-i Bīrjandī appears in al-Ṭūsī's *Majmūʿa-yi Rasāʾil* (Tehran, 1335 Sh./1956), p. 123, and Aḥmad Amīn Rāzī's *Tadhkira-yi haft iqlīm*, ed. Jawād-i Fāḍil (Tehran, 1340/1961), where *qaṣīda* 85 is attributed to Ḥasan-i Ṣalāḥ-i Bīrjandī.
94 Naṣīr al-Dīn al-Ṭūsī, *Rawḍat al-taslīm*, ed. Ivanow, p. 170; Badakhchani, *Spiritual Resurrection*, pp. 2–3.

95 According to Badakhchani, Ḥasan-i Maḥmūd-i Kātib moved to Alamūt in around 634/1237, which can be an indication of the date for the compilation of the *Dīwān-i Qā'imiyyāt* (Badakhchani, *Spiritual Resurrection*, p. 3).
96 *Dīwān-i Qā'imiyyāt*, English preface, pp. 9–20.
97 *Dīwān-i Qā'imiyyāt*, Persian preface, pp. xix–xxiii.
98 C. E. Bosworth, 'Azerbaijan', *EIR*, vol. 3, pp. 226–228. http://www.iranicaonline.org/articles/atabakan-e-adarbayjan
99 *Tārīkh-i Ṭabaristān II*, p. 154.
100 D. Tor, 'A Tale of Two Murders: Power Relations between Caliph and the Sultan in the Saljūq Era', *ZDMG*, 159 (2009), pp. 279–297.
101 *Tārīkh-i Ṭabaristān II*, pp. 136–140, Mar'ashī, *Ṭabaristān*, ed. Tasbīḥī, pp. 114–115. Rabino, 'Les dynasties du Māzandarān', pp. 430–431; Madelung, 'Āl-e Bāvand', pp. 750–751.
102 *Tārīkh-i Ṭabaristān II*, pp. 136–140,
103 *Tārīkh-i Ṭabaristān II*, pp. 152, 154; Ivanow, 'An Ismaili Poem in Praise of Fidawis', pp. 64–67; Rabino, 'Les dynasties du Māzandarān, pp. 430–431; Madelung, 'Āl-e Bāvand', pp. 750–751.

Chapter 6. The Last Decades of the Nizārī Ismaili State

1 Zakarīyā' b. Muḥammad al-Qazwīnī, *Āthār al-bilād wa-akhbār al-'ibād* (Beirut, 1960), pp. 292–293; Hodgson, *The Order*, pp. 212–213.
2 Hodgson, *The Order*, p. 212; al-Rāwandī, *Rāḥat al-ṣudūr*, p. 390.
3 For Mīyājīq's campaigns see, al-Rāwandī, *Rāḥat al-ṣudūr*, pp. 380–399.
4 al-Rāwandī, *Rāḥat al-ṣudūr*, p. 390.
5 Jūzjānī, *Ṭabaqāt-i Nāṣirī*, Part 2, pp. 182–183, tr. Raverty, Part 2, pp. 1197–1198.
6 The term *naw-musalmān* refers to Jalāl al-Dīn Ḥasan III's newly acquired 'Sunni identity' as reflected in Sunni sources. See Juwaynī, vol. 3, pp. 243–249; Rashīd al-Dīn, ed. Rawshan, pp. 171–175; Kāshānī, *Zubdat al-tawārīkh*, pp. 214–217; Hodgson, *The Order*, pp. 217–225; Daftary, *The Ismā'īlīs*, pp. 375–376.
7 See Daftary, *The Ismā'īlīs*, p. 635, nn. 177 and 178.
8 Hodgson, *The Order*, pp. 217–220; Daftary, *The Ismā'īlīs*, p. 175.
9 Hodgson, *The Order*, p. 223.
10 Juwaynī, vol. 3, pp. 243–245.
11 Nasawī, ed. Mīnuwī, p. 230.
12 Ibid., pp. 163–166.
13 Juwaynī, vol. 3, p. 243.
14 Daftary, *The Ismā'īlīs*, p. 377.
15 For Shi'i symphathies and other religious tendencies under al-Nāṣir, see A. Hartmann, *An-Nasir li-Din Allah (1180-1225): Politik, Religion und Kultur in der späten 'Abbasidenzeit* (Berlin-New York, 1975), pp. 109–172.
16 Hartman, *An-Nasir li-Din Allah*, pp. 118–121.
17 Hartmann, *An-Nasir li-Din Allah*, pp. 111–122; al-Shahrastānī, *Kitāb al-muṣara'a*, ed. and tr. W. Madelung and T. Mayer as *Struggling with the Philosopher: a Refutation of Avicenna's Metaphysics* (London, 2001), p. 13.
18 Hodgson, *The Order*, p. 223, n. 32.
19 Tor, 'A Tale of Two Murders', pp. 279–297.
20 Daftary, *The Ismā'īlīs*, pp. 375–376.
21 Juwaynī, vol. 2, pp. 245–246; tr. Boyle, vol. 2, pp. 701–702; Rashīd al-Dīn, ed. Rawshan, pp. 176–177; Kāshānī, *Zubdat al-tawārīkh*, pp. 216–217; Ibn al-Athīr, ed. Tornberg, vol. 12, pp. 114, 116, 118; Daftary, *The Ismā'īlīs*, p. 377.

22 Hodgson, *The Order*, p. 223; Rashīd al-Dīn, ed. Rawshan, p. 176.
23 See below for more on this subject.
24 Hodgson, *The Order*, p. 221.
25 Daftary, *The Ismāʿīlīs*, p. 377.
26 Hodgson, *The Order*, p. 218.
27 Kāshānī, *Tārīkh-i Uljaytū*, pp. 57–58, quoted in Rabino, 'Deux inscriptions du Gîlận du temps des Mongols', *Journal Asiatique*, 238 (1950), pp. 328–329. See also his 'Rulers of Gīlān', *JRAS* (1920), pp. 288–289, 293–295, and 'Les dynasties locales du Gilān et du Daylam', *Journal Asiatique*, 237 (1949), pp. 314–315.
28 See Hartmann, *an-Nasir*, for details of the Abbasid understanding of this event.
29 C.E. Bosworth, 'The Political and Dynastic History of the Iranian World (A.D. 1000-1217)', in *Cambridge History of Iran, vol. 5, The Saljuq and Mongol Periods*, ed. J.A. Boyle (Cambridge, 1968), pp. 201–202,
30 Kāshānī, *Tārikh-i Uljaytū*, pp. 57–58, in Rabino, 'Deux inscriptions du Gîlận', pp. 328–329. See also Rabino, 'Rulers of Gīlān', *Journal of the Royal Asiatic Society* (1920), pp. 288–289; Rabino, 'Les dynasties locales du Gilān', pp. 314–315.
31 Kāshānī, *Tārikh-i Uljaytū*, pp. 57–58.
32 *Tārīkh-i Ṭabaristān II*, pp. 163, 174; Āmulī, *Tārīkh-i Rūyān*, pp. 150–151; Marʿashī, *Tārīkh-i Ṭabaristān*, pp. 30, 118.
33 Goto, *Die südkaspischen Provinzen*, p. 79.
34 و کینه خوار دیگر در وجود آمد که پدر اردشیر است و دخترزاده ملک اردشیر بن الحسن میباشد و اردشیر بن کینه خوار خواهرزاده خداوند علا الدین محمد بن جلال ال دین حسن بن علا الدین محمد است
Marʿashī, *Tārīkh-i Ṭabaristān*, ed. B. Dorn, p. 83.
35 The present author's translation.
36 کینه‌خوار دیگر در وجود آمدکه‌پدر اردشیر است‌و دخترزاده‌خداوند علاالدین‌محمدبن‌جلال‌ال‌دین‌حسن‌بن‌علاالدین‌محمداست‌و
Marʿashī, *Tārīkh-i Ṭabaristān*, p. 32.
37 The present author's translation.
38 Rabino, 'Les dynasties du Māzandarān', p. 432.
39 Hodgson, *The Order*, p. 221. n. 25.
40 Āmulī, *Tārīkh-i Rūyān*, pp. 101–102.
41 'It was alleged that the Heretics and the truth is not clear, but this much is evident, that when the armies of the World-Conqueror Chingiz-Khan entered the countries of Islam, the first ruler on this side of the Oxus to send ambassadors, and present his duty, and accept allegiance, was Jalāl al-Dīn [Ḥasan III]'. Juwaynī, vol. 3, p. 248, tr. Boyle, vol. 2, part 3, p. 703.
42 Hodgson, *The Order*, p. 223; J.A. Boyle, 'The Dynastic and Political History of the Il-Khāns', in *The Cambridge History of Iran*, vol. 5, pp. 304–306.
43 Juzjānī, ed. A. Ḥabībī, vol. 2, pp. 699–700; Daftary, *The Ismāʿīlīs*, p. 376.
44 C. E. Bosworth. 'The Ismaʿilis of Quhistān and the Maliks of Nīmrūz or Sīstān', in F. Daftary, ed., *Mediaeval Ismaʿili History and Thought* (London, 1996), pp. 211–229; H. Dabashī, 'The Philosopher/Vizier Khwāja Naṣīr al-Dīn Ṭūsī and the Ismailis', in F. Daftary, ed., *Mediaeval Ismaʿili History and Thought* (Cambridge, 1996), pp. 321–345.
45 Yeke Maru, that is to say, Marw. The Mongol attack against the city took place on 1–2 Muḥarram 618/25–26 February 1221; see Juwaynī, vol. 1, pp. 125–126; tr. Boyle, vol. 1, part 1, pp. 160–161.
46 Sarakhs near the present-day border of Iran and Turkmenistan.
47 Nicha'ur (Neyshābūr or Nishapur) was an important city in Khurāsān. The decisive Mongol assault took place on 12–15 Ṣafar 618/7–10 April 1221; Juwaynī, ed. Qazwīnī, vol 1, pp. 138–140, tr. Boyle, vol. 1, part 1, pp. 176–177.
48 The term *mulayid* is the usual Mongol name applied to the Nizārīs in this Chinese source; it is almost certainly a borrowing of the Arabic-Persian term *mulḥid*. Here possibly a reference to Quhistān?

49 The river here called the Choqchoran is the modern Harī Rūd, and Heri must be the city of Herat, the most important city in present-day north-western Afghanistan. This first Mongol siege of Herat ended with a negotiated surrender and thus meant the sparing of most of the city's population (material quoted courtesy of Professor C. P. Atwood).
50 §51.3 in Atwood, *The Campaigns of Chinggis Khan: Text, Translation, and Commentary* (forthcoming), (courtesy of Professor C. P. Atwood).
51 *Yuanshi*, ed. S. Lian (Beijing, 1976), p. 1.22.
52 al-Nasawī, ed. Minuwī, pp. 68–69.
53 Juwaynī, vol. 1, p. 115, tr. Boyle, vol. 1, part 1, p. 146.
54 Jūzjānī, ed. Ḥabībī, vol. 2, pp. 108–109.
55 B. Spuler, *Die Mongolen in Iran, Politik, Verwaltung und Kultur der Ilchanzeit, 617/1220-1350* (Leiden, 1985), pp. 23–25.

Chapter 7. ʿAlāʾ al-Dīn Muḥammad III and the End of the Nizārī Ismaili State in the Caspian Provinces

1 See W. Ivanow, 'A Forgotten Branch of the Ismailis', *JRAS* (1938), pp. 64, 67.
2 Interestingly Hodgson does not find an equivalent to Chin. See Hodgson, *The Order*, p. 251.
3 See Badakhchani, *Spiritual Resurrection*, p. 68; al-Ṭūsī, *Rawḍat al-taslīm*, ed. and tr. W. Ivanow (Leiden, 1950), p. 117; Hodgson, *The Order*, p. 250.
4 Hodgson, *The Order*, p. 251; al-Nasawī, ed. Minuwī, pp. 68–69, p. 121.
5 al-Nasawī, ed. Minuwī, pp. 68–69. p. 95; Daftary, *The Ismāʿīlīs*, p. 384.
6 *Dīwān-i Qāʾimiyyāt*, p. 9.
7 See Appendix II of this work for a translation of lines 3742–3759 of *qaṣīda* 124.
8 See Appendix II of this work for a translation of lines 2150–2156 of *qaṣīda* 73.
9 Jūzjānī, ed. Ḥabībī, vol. 2, pp. 182–185, 186–188; See also C. E. Bosworth, *The History of the Saffarids of Sīstān and the Maliks of Nimrūz (247/861 to 949/1542-3)* (Costa Mesa, CA/New York, 1994), pp. 399, 408–409; Daftary, *The Ismāʿīlīs*, p. 383.
10 J. A. Boyle, 'The Ismāʿīlīs and the Mongol Invasion', in S. H. Nasr, ed., *Ismāʿīlī Contributions to Islamic Culture* (Tehran, 1977), pp. 4–5; Juwaynī, vol. 3, p. 248, tr. Boyle, vol. 2, p. 703.
11 T. A. May, 'A Mongol-Ismâʿîlî Alliance? Thoughts on the Mongols and Assassins', *JRAS*, 14 (2004), pp. 231–239.
12 The *Dīwān-i Qāʾimiyyāt* was first presented in 630/1233 by Ḥasan-i Maḥmūd-i Kātib to ʿAlāʾ al-Dīn Muḥammad III; but, as Badakhchani notes, it can be easily argued that it was continued or revised in the remaining years of Ḥasan-i Maḥmūd-i Kātib, after 630/1233, as he was prolific as an author. See *Dīwān-i Qāʾimiyyāt*, English preface, pp. 9–12.
13 Juwaynī, vol. 1, pp. 205, 213; tr. Boyle, vol. 1, pp. 250, 258; Rashīd al-Dīn, ed. E. Blochet (Leiden–London, 1911), vol. 2, pp. 243, 248, also, ed. B. Karīmī (Tehran, 1338 Sh./1959), vol. 1, pp. 568, 570; English trans. by J. A. Boyle in *The Successors of Genghis Khan* (New York, 1971), pp. 181, 184.
14 See Appendix II for a translation of lines 1486–1489.
15 See Appendix II for a translation of lines 2289–2290.
16 Here, interestingly, the name 'Jinghiz' evolves into a royal title of the Mongols such as personal names of Khusraw or Caesar in Iranian and Roman titulatures.
17 See Appendix II for a translation of lines 1508–1509.
18 Not translated here.
19 Kirakos Gandzaketsʿi, *Patmutʿyun Hayocʿ* (*History of the Armenians*), ed. K. A. Melikʿ-Ohanǰanyan (Yerevan, 1961), pp. 264, 275; B. Dashdondog, *Mongols and Armenians*

(617/1220-1335) (Leiden, 2011), pp. 253–254; Juwaynī, vol. 1, p. 277; Rashīd al-Dīn, ed. Karīmī, vol. 2, p. 56; P. Jackson, *The Mongols and the Islamic World, from Conquest to Conversion* (New Haven and London, 2017), pp. 125–126.

20 Kirakos Gandzakets'i, *Patmutyun Hayoc'*, pp. 122–125; Rashīd al-Dīn, ed. Karīmī, vol. 2, p. 56; Juwaynī, vol. 1, pp. 277, 724.

21 May, 'A Mongol-Isma'ili Alliance? Thoughts on the Mongols and Assassins', pp. 231–239.

22 The Rūm Saljūqs were defeated at Köshe Dagh between Erzinjān and Erzurum on 7 Muḥarram 641/26 June 1243 by the Mongols led by Baiju, and his Caucasian allies.

23 Ganjakeçi, *Patmuthun Hayot*, pp. 319–320; Grigor Arkents'i, *History of the Tatars/ History of the Nation of the Archers* (Jerusalem, 1974), p. 36; Dashdondog, *Mongols and Armenians*, pp. 55–57.

24 Dashdondog, *Mongols and Armenians*, p. 123; Rashīd al-Dīn, ed. Karīmī p. 654.

25 *Dīwān-i Qā'imiyyāt*, English preface, pp. 8–9.

26 Rashīd al-Dīn, ed. Karīmī, pp. 570, 654; Dashdondog, *Mongols and Armenians*, p. 122, n. 6.

27 Juwaynī, vol. 3. pp. 212–213; Bar Hebraeus, *The Chronology of Gregory: Abu'l-Faraj 622/1225-1286* (Amsterdam, 1976), p. 411; May, 'A Mongol-Ismâ'îlî Alliance?', p. 238.

28 Dashdondog, *Mongols and Armenians*, p. 125.

29 Dabashī, 'The Philosopher/Vizier Khwāja Naṣīr al-Dīn Ṭūsī', pp. 234–238.

30 For the close contacts of Ḥasan-i Maḥmūd-i Kātib and Nāsir al-Dīn Tūsī, see, *Dīwān-i Qā'imiyyāt*, English preface, pp. 9–12.

31 Mahdī Farhānī-Munfarid, 'Dīplomāsī-i gustarish va guftigū, pazhūsishhi dar takāpūhā-i sīāsī-i Ismailiān-i Alamūt, 618-653/ 618/1221-1255 (The Diplomacy of Expansion and Negotiation. Research on the Political Attempts of the Ismailis of Alamūt)', *Farhang*, 56 (1384/2005), pp. 84, 88.

32 Daftary, *The Ismā'īlīs*, p. 386; al-Nasawī, ed. Minuwī, pp. 161–162, 175–176.

33 Ganjakeçi, *Patmuthun Hayots*, pp. 226–228; Dashdondog, *Mongols and Armenians*, pp. 124–125.

34 *Dīwān-i Qā'imiyyāt*, pp. 327, 330.

35 al-Nasawī, ed. Minuwī, pp. 163–166.

36 May says that the Nizārīs possessed Dāmghān until 629/1231. May, 'A Mongol-Ismâ'îlî Alliance?', p. 235.

37 Daftary, *The Ismā'īlīs*, pp. 384–386.

38 Hodgson, *The Order*, p. 252.

39 As far as Malik Khāmush is concerned, see *Dīwān-i Qā'imiyyāt*, *qaṣīda* no. 72, foreword and lines 161–162, p. 203.

40 al-Nasawī, ed. Minuwī, pp. 175–176.

41 Juwaynī, vol. 2, pp. 204–205.

42 Ibn al-Athīr, vol. 3, tr. Richards, p. 288.

43 al-Nasawī, ed. Minuwī, pp. 161–162, 175–176; Farhānī-Munfarid, 'Dīplomāsī-i gustarish va guftigū', p. 94.

44 Ibn al-Athīr, vol. 3, tr. Richards, p. 303.

45 This is a clear reference to the defeat of Jalal al-Dīn Mingburnī by the Mamlūks and Rūm-Saljūqs.

46 May's translation: Ibn al-Athīr, ed. Tornberg, vol. 12, p. 495, see May, 'A Mongol-Ismâ'îlî Alliance?', p. 239.

47 The author's thanks go to Professor Christopher Atwood for allowing access to these sources and their English translations.

48 Atwood notes: 'I read here Isbarayin (amended from the text's Isbarana); the historical event is certainly connected to Isfarāyin, a medium-sized city northwest of Nisha'ur/ Nīshāpūr. As described in Juwaynī, tr. Boyle, pp. 486–487, the surrender of Isfarāyin — one

of the largest intact cities left in Khurāsān — and the personal attendance of its *malik* or governor, Bahā' al-Dīn, at Öködei's court became a crucial turning point in convincing Öködei Qa'an that Khurāsān was in fact pacified and could be moved from punitive massacre and purely military rule to more stable civilian rule.' *sub anno* 1229 in Atwood, *The Campaigns of Chinggis Khan* (forthcoming).

49 Atwood notes: 'There is no outside corroboration of the surrender of any Indian ruler, but it is likely to have been the Rana (king) of the Salt Range (*Kūh-i Jūd*), one of the few remaining Hindu rulers in the province of Punjab.' Atwood, *The Campaigns of Chinggis Khan* (forthcoming), *sub anno* 1229.

50 Ibid.

51 *Yuanshi*, ed. S. Lian (Beijing, 1976), p. 230.

52 al-Nasawī, ed. Minuwī, pp. 163–166; Ibn al-Athīr, ed. Tornberg, vol. 12, p. 182; Daftary, *The Ismāʿīlīs*, pp. 386–387.

53 al-Nasawī, ed. Minuwī, pp. 231–232; see also Ibn al-Athīr, ed. Tornberg, vol. 12, pp. 192–193, A.H. Morton, 'Ghurid gold en route to England?', *Iran*, 16 (1978), pp. 167–170.

54 H. Chubak, 'Kāwishhā-yi bāstānshināsī dar dīzh-i Ḥasan Sabbāḥ-i Alamūt' ('Archaeological Excavations in the Fortress of Ḥasan Sabbāḥ in Alamūt'), *Guzārishhā-yi bāstānshināsī* (7), *majmūʿa-i maqālaha-i nahumīn girdhimāyi-yi sālāna-i bāstānshināsī-yi Īrān, jild-i awwal* (Tehran, 1386 Sh./2007), pp. 88–128.

55 al-Nasawī, ed. Minuwī, pp. 229–233.

56 Ibn al-Athīr, ed. Tornberg, vol. 12, pp. 192–193; see also al-Nasawī, ed. Minuwī, pp. 229–233.

57 Daftary, *The Ismāʿīlīs*, p. 387.

58 Daftary, *The Ismāʿīlīs*, pp. 415–416. Rabino, 'Rulers of Gīlān', pp. 293–294 and 'Les dynasties locales', pp. 315–318.

59 Matthew Paris, *English History*, tr. J. A. Giles (London, 1852), vol. 1, pp. 131–132. See also, See also, Morton, pp. 167–170.

60 Matthew Paris, *English History*, tr. John A. Giles (London, 1852), vol. 1, pp. 131–132; Daftary, *The Ismāʿīlīs*, p. 525, n. 23.

61 Jūzjānī, ed. Ḥabībī, vol. 2, p. 158.

62 Madelung, 'Āl-e Bāvand', *EIr*.

63 Āmulī, *Tārīkh-i Rūyān*, pp. 152–153. Marʿashī, ed. Shāyān, p. 243.

64 Āmulī, *Tārīkh-i Rūyān*, pp. 152–153.

65 Ibid.

66 Madelung, *Religious Trends in early Islamic Iran*, p. 387.

67 Rashīd al-Dīn, ed. Rawshan, p. 181; Kāshānī, ed. Muḥammad Taqī Dānishpazhūh, p. 222.

68 *Dabistān*, part 1, p. 265.

69 Rashīd al-Dīn, ed. Rawshan, pp. 181–182.

70 Jūzjānī, ed. Habībī, p. 698; May, 'A Mongol-Ismâʿîlî Alliance?', p. 234. Dashdondog, *Mongols and Armenians 1220-1335*, p. 124

71 Jūzjānī, ed. Habībī, p. 698.

72 Nadia Eboo Jamal, *Surviving the Mongols: Nizārī Quhistani and the Continuity of Ismaili Tradition in Iran* (London, 2003), p. 46.

73 Ḥamd Allāh Mustawfī Qazwīnī, *Ẓafarnāma-i Ḥamd Allāh Mustawfī: bih inẓimām-i Shāhnāma-i Abu'l-Qāsim Firdawsī*, ed. N. Pūrjavādī (Tehran, 1377 Sh./1999), vol. 1, pp. 1118–1120.

74 Dashdondog, *Mongols and Armenians 1220-1335*, p. 124.

75 Hodgson appears to accept reluctantly the notion that a secret alliance had existed between the Nizārīs and the Mongols (Hodgson, *The Order*, p. 259) though this may occasionally refer to Mongol-Nizārī cooperation, such as in the Nizārīs' seizing of Dāmghān (ibid., p. 254).

76 May, 'A Mongol-Ismâʿîlî Alliance?', p. 234.

77 Juwaynī, vol. 3, pp. 256–260.

78 Rashīd al-Dīn, ed. Rawshan, p. 181.

79 Kāshānī, *Zubdat al-tawārīkh*, p. 223; Farhānī-Munfarid, 'Dīplomāsī-i gustarish va guftigū', p. 102.

80 *The Mission of Friar William of Rubruck: His Journey to the Court of the Great Khan Möngke*, tr. P. Jackson and ed. David O. Morgan (London, 1990), p. 222.

81 Farhānī-Munfarid, 'Dīplomāsī-i gustarish va guftigū', p. 100. Kāshānī, *Zubdat al-tawārīkh*, pp. 222–223.

82 Rashīd al-Dīn, ed. Karīmī, p. 684.

83 Hodgson, *The Order*, pp. 263–271; Daftary, *The Ismā'īlīs*, p. 392; J. A. Boyle, 'The Ismā'īlīs and the Mongol Invasion', pp. 5–22; Jackson, *The Mongols and the Islamic World*, pp. 125–128.

84 Molaid=*mulāḥida* Girduke Fortress is a clear reference to Girdkūh.

85 *Yuanshi*, p. 345.

86 Sali was more of a Tatar military leader than a prince. According to Atwood's valuable commentary, *Turghaq* 'day guard' is not a separate name but a title indicating Sali's service in the guards. See C. P. Atwood, *The Campaigns of Chinggis Khan: Text, Translation, and Commentary* (forthcoming).

87 Sindh.

88 *Yuanshi*, p. 346.

89 G. Lane, 'Mongol News: The Akhbāri Moghulān dar Anbāneh Quṭb by Quṭb al-Dīn Mahmūd ibn Mas'ūd Shīrāzī', *JRAS*, 22 (2012), p. 546. Stephen Haw, 'The Mongol Empire – the first 'gunpowder empire?', *JRAS*, 23 (2013), pp. 457–458.

90 Lane, 'Mongol News', p. 547; Stephen Haw, 'The Mongol Empire – the first 'gunpowder empire?', *JRAS*, 23 (2013), pp. 441–469.

91 Juwaynī, vol. 3, p. 94; tr. Boyle, vol. 2, part 3, p. 609.

92 Maḥmūd b. Mas'ūd, Quṭb al-Dīn Shīrāzī, *Akhbār-i Mughūlān dar anbāna-i Quṭb* (Tehran, 2011). Lane's translation, Lane, 'Mongol News', p. 547.

93 Juwaynī, vol. 3, pp. 102–103; tr. Boyle, vol. 2, pp. 615–616; Rashīd al-Dīn, ed. Karīmī, vol. 2, p. 691; Daftary, *The Ismā'īlīs*, p. 393.

94 Shīrāzī, *Akhbār-i Mughūlān*, pp. 22–23.

95 The Kartids (643–791/1245–1389) were an important post-Ilkhanid dynasty in Herat especially after 736/1335 and the death of the last significant Īl Khān, Abū Sa'īd.

96 Daftary, *The Ismā'īlīs*, p. 393; Dabashī, 'The Philosopher/Vizier', p. 232.

97 May, 'A Mongol-Ismâ'îlî Alliance?', p. 236. Yasa'ur and his Mongol army controlled Hamadān as well as the area of 'Irāq-i 'Ajam in the close vicinity of the Nizārī heartlands.

98 Hodgson, *The Order*, p. 266.

99 Juwaynī, vol. 3, p. 263; tr. Boyle, vol. 2, p. 714; Rashīd al-Dīn, ed. Rawshan, p. 187; Kāshānī, *Zubdat al-tawārīkh*, pp. 225–226; Daftary, *The Ismā'īlīs*, p. 394.

100 Shafique Virani, 'The Eagle Returns. Evidence of Continued Ismā'īlī Activity in Alamūt and in the South Caspian region following the Mongol conquests', *Journal of the American Oriental Society*, 123 (2003), pp. 355–356; Rashīd al-Dīn, ed. Karīmī, vol. 2, p. 685.

101 Hodgson, *The Order*, p. 266.

102 Willey, *The Eagle's Nest*, p. 79.

103 Virani, 'The Eagle Returns', p. 356.

104 For details of the siege of Alamūt and other Nizārī fortresses, see J. Masson Smith, 'Hülegü Moves West: Living and Heartbreak on the Road to Baghdad', in L. Komaroff, ed., *Beyond the Legacy of Genghis Khan* (Leiden, 2013), pp. 94–110.

105 Juwaynī, vol. 3, pp. 133, 267, who personally witnessed Rukn al-Dīn Khurshāh's surrender. Rashīd al-Dīn places this event a day later, on 1 Dhu'l-Qa'da/20 November, see Rashīd al-Dīn, *Jāmi' al-tawārīkh*, ed. Alizade, p. 35; ed. Karīmī, vol. 2, p. 695. However, as Daftary notes, Rashīd al-Dīn corroborates Juwaynī's

date relating to events connected with Rukn al-Dīn Khurshāh's reign in his Ismaili history, *Jāmi' al-tawārīkh: qismat-i Ismā'īliyān*, p. 190; Daftary, *The Ismā'īlīs*, p. 641, n. 230.

106 Willey, *The Eagle's Nest*, p. 79.

107 Hodgson, *The Order*, p. 267.

108 Willey, *The Eagle's Nest*, p. 79.

109 Rashīd al-Dīn, ed. Karīmī, vol. 2, p. 685 vol. 2, p. 697. Willey, *The Eagle's Nest*, p. 79.

110 Willey, *The Eagle's Nest*, p. 80.

111 Juwaynī, vol. 3, pp. 186, 269–273; tr. Boyle, vol. 2, pp. 666, 719–721; Daftary, *The Ismā'īlīs*, p. 396.

112 Juwaynī vol. 3, p. 273; tr. Boyle, vol. 2, p. 721; Rashīd al-Dīn, ed. Rawshan, p. 192, and Kāshānī, *Zubdat al-tawārīkh*, pp. 230–231.

113 Mar'ashī, ed. Tasbīḥī, p. 118; Juwaynī, vol. 3, p. 275; tr. Boyle, vol. 2, p. 723; see also Rashīd al-Dīn, ed. Rawshan, p. 193; Kāshānī, p. 232; Goto, *Die südkaspischen Provinzen des Iran*, pp. 79–80.

114 See for example the very elaborate work on the post 654/1256 Nizārī presence in northern Iran: Shafique Virani, 'The Eagle Returns'.

115 Āmulī, *Tārīkh-i Rūyān*, pp. 154–159; Mar'ashī, *Tārīkh-i Ṭabaristān*, pp. 31–32.

116 Āmulī, *Tārīkh-i Rūyān*, pp. 161–164; Mar'ashī, *Tārīkh-i Ṭabaristān*, pp. 34–36.

117 Goto, *Die südkaspischen Provinzen*, pp. 79–80.

118 Āmulī, *Tārīkh-i Rūyān*, pp. 161–164; Mar'ashī, *Tārīkh-i Ṭabaristān*, pp. 34-36; Madelung, 'Bādūspānids', *EIr*.http://www.iranicaonline.org/articles/baduspanids

119 Āmulī, *Tārīkh-i Rūyān*, p. 166.

120 Madelung, 'Āl-e Bāvand', *EIr*.

Chapter 8. The Economy and Social Structure of the Nizārī Ismaili State

1 Farhānī-Munfarid, 'Dīplomāsī-i gustarish va guftigū', p. 89.

2 Though we lack the written evidence and the administrative and taxation records, one can posit that Nizārī communities continued the old Ismaili practice of paying a certain amount of their sums which they call *wājibāt* or *māl-i wājibāt* (levied amount) to the Imam. This practice was detected in the post-Alamūt period in the Nizārī communities of India.

3 '*Ahd* can mean both 'age' and 'treaty' in Classical Persian.

4 The name refers to the Sasanian rulers in general, more specifically to Khusraw I (531–579) and Khusraw II (591–628) of which Arabicised name was the Kisrā.

5 The Sasanian weight *dang* was a fraction (one-sixth) of a *drahm*, see, A. Bivar, 'Weights and Measures', *Encyclopaedia Iranica Online Edition, 2010,* http://www.iranicaonline.org/articles/weights-measures-i; Philippe Gignoux and Michael Bates, 'Dirham', *EIr*, vol. 7 pp. 424–428.

6 The Persian word *bālish* can be translated as a pillow, though there are traces that the notion '*bālish*' was also used as a weight. The *Burhān-i qāṭi'* says: '*bālish* is gold to a certain amount, the golden *bālish* is equal to 20,000 dinars and the silver *bālish* is equal to 200 dinars', Muḥammad Ḥusayn b. Khalaf Tabrīzī Burhān, *Burhān-i qāṭi'* (Tehran 1361 Sh./1982), p. 225 (translation by the present author, from Persian). The reason why we prefer pillow rather than golden weight as a translation of the word *bālish* is that after *bālish* there appears the word *basāṭ*, which might be a pair of *bālish* like 'pillow and bedding'. The word *basāṭ* lacks any similar meaning as a possible weight measure, as in the case of *bālish*.

7 *Tārīkh-i Ṭabaristān I*, p. 175, see also n. 322. Rose Greaves, 'Iranian Relations with the European Trading Companies to 1798', in *The Cambridge History of Iran*, vol. 7, *From Nadir Shah to the Islamic Republic*, ed. G. Hambly, C. Melville, P. Avery (Cambridge, 1991), p. 369.
8 Author's translation.
9 For the measures and weights used in pre-Islamic Iran, see Bivar, 'Weights and Measures'; Gignoux and Bates, 'Dirham'.
10 For the history of silk industry in Persia see: W. Eilers et al., 'Abrisham', *Encyclopaedia Iranica. Online Edition.* http://iranica.com/articles/abrisam-silkindex, (accessed on 29 August 2019).
11 Yāqūt al-Ḥamawī, *Muʿjam al-buldān*, vol. 4, p. 344.
12 H. Yule, *The Book of Ser Marco Polo, the Venetian concerning the Kingdoms and Marvels of the East* (London, 1903), pp. 53, 56. [*The Travels of Marco Polo: The Complete Yule-Cordier Edition* (New York, 1992), vol. 1, p. 52.]
13 For the geography of the region see H. L. Rabino di Borgomale, *Māzandarān and Astarābād* (London, 1928), R. R. Vasmer and C. E. Bosworth, 'Māzandarān', *EI2*, vol. 6, pp. 935–942.
14 Ḥamd Allāh Musṭawfī Qazwīnī, *Nuzhat al-qulūb*, ed. M. Dabīr Siyāqī (Qazwīn, 1381/2003), p. 162.
15 Juwaynī, vol. 2, p. 243.
16 *Tārīkh-i Ṭabaristān II*, p. 124.
17 al-Nasawī, *Sīrat-i Jalāl al-Dīn Mīnkubīrnī*, French trans. O. Houdas as *Histoire du Sultan Djelal ed-Din Mankobirti* (Paris, 1891–1895), vol. 1, pp. 157–158, and vol. 2, pp. 262–264.
18 Rashīd al-Dīn, ed. Rawshan, p. 137; Hodgson, *The Order*, p. 102. n. 11.
19 Willey, *The Eagle's Nest*, p. 164.
20 al-Nasawī, ed. and tr., O. Houdas, vol. 1, pp. 157–158, and vol. 2, pp. 262–264.
21 Jūzjānī, ed. Habībī, pp. 699–700; Daftary, *The Ismāʿīlīs*, p. 376.

Conclusion

1 See Chapter 2.
2 *Satr* means concealment, when (during the *dawr al-satr/era of concealment*) the Imam remains in concealment according to different Ismaili teachings. According to Fatimid writings the term *dawr al-satr* refers exclusively to the era of roughly 150 years when the Ismaili Imams were in concealment from public knowledge until 286/899 when ʿAbd Allāh al-Mahdī proclaimed the end of the *dawr al-satr*, starting the period of disclosure (*dawr al-kashf*).

In later theological writings *dawr al-satr* means the time when truth is unknown to mankind, that is, from Adam until Muḥammad b. Ismāʿīl. In the latest development of the concept called *satr*, Nasīr al-Dīn al-Ṭūsī (d. 672/1274) explained that *satr* as a cyclical phenomenon which happens when the Imam's real spiritual authority is not manifested, despite his physical presence among his followers. See, H. Corbin, *Cyclical Time and Ismaili Gnosis* (New York, 1983), pp. 30–58, 76–84.

Appendix I

1 Kleiss, referring to this problem, tries to identify some hitherto unknown Nizārī fortresses in northern Iran, such as that of Ghutinar, near Qazwīn, which was located

not far from Alamūt, Maymūndiz and Lamasar. He firmly contends that it was a Nizārī fortress but admits that 'there is no clinching evidence for this'. See W. Kleiss, 'Assassin Castles in Iran', in R. Hillenbrand, ed. *The Art of the Saljūqs in Iran and Anatolia* (Costa Mesa, CA, 1994), p. 316.

Appendix II

1 Īliyāj was the Khwārazmian governor of Khalkhāl in western Gīlān.
2 Ya'jūj is a mythical, eschatological evil force along with Ma'jūj, the two will destroy the earth before the end of the world according to Islamic eschatology. They correspond to Gog and Magog.

Select Bibliography

Primary Sources

Abū Ishāq Quhistānī. *Haft Bāb*, ed. and tr. W. Ivanow. Bombay, 1959.

Āmulī, Awliyā' Allāh. *Tārīkh-i Rūyān*, ed. M. Sutūda. Tehran. 1347 Sh./1969.

al-Baghdādī, Bahā' al-Dīn Muḥammad b. Mu'ayyad. *al-Tawaṣṣul ilā al-tarassul*, ed. A. Bahmanyār. Tehran, 1314 Sh./1936.

al-Baladhurī, Aḥmad b. Yaḥyā. *Kitāb Futūḥ al-buldān (Liber expugnationis regionum)*, ed. M. J. de Goeje. Leiden, 1866.

Bal'amī, Abū 'Alī Muḥammad. *Tārīkhnāma-i Ṭabarī, Gardānida-i mansūb be Bal'amī*, ed. M. Rawshan. Tehran, 1380 Sh./2001.

Bayhaqī, Abu'l-Faḍl Muḥammad b. Ḥusayn. *Tārīkh-i Bayhaqī*, ed. K. Khaṭīb-Rahbar. Tehran, 1378 Sh./2000.

Dabistān-i madhāhib, attributed to Kaykhusraw Isfandiyār, ed. R. Riḍāzāda Malik. Tehran, 1362 Sh./1983. tr. D. Shea and A. Troyer as *The Dabistān, or School of Manners*. London, 1901.

Dawlatshāh, Amīr b. 'Alā' al-Dawla Bakhtī-shāh al-Ghāzī al-Samarqandī. *Tadhkirat al-shu'arā'*, ed. M. Ramaḍāni. Tehran, 1366 Sh./1987.

Dorn, B. *Auszüge aus Muhammedanische Schriftstellern Betreffend die Geschichte und Geographie der südlichen Küstenländer des Kaspischen Meeres, nebst einer kurzen Geschichte der Chane von Scheki, Arabische, Persische und Türkische Texte*. St. Petersburg, 1858.

Firdawsī, Abu'l-Qāsim Manṣūr. *Shāhnāma*, ed. and tr. J. Mohl as *Le livre des rois par Abou'lkasim Firdousi*. Paris, 1876; Tehran, 1374 Sh./1995.

Fūmanī, 'Abd al-Fattāḥ. *Tārīkh-i Gīlān*, ed. M. Sutūda. Tehran, 1349 Sh./1970; ed. B. Dorn as *'Abdu'l-Fattah Fumany's Geschichte von Gīlān*. St. Petersburg, 1858.

Gardīzī, Abū Sa'īd 'Abd al-Ḥayy b. al-Ḍaḥḥāk b. Maḥmūd. *Zayn al-Akhbār*, ed. A. Ḥabībī. Tehran, 1327 Sh./1948.

Ghaznawī, Muḥammad, Khwāja Sadīd al-Dīn Muḥammad. *Maqāmāt-i Zhanda-Pīl*, ed. Hishmat Allāh Mu'ayyad Sanandajī. Tehran, 1339 Sh./1961.

Ḥāfiẓ Abrū, 'Abd Allāh b. Luṭf Allāh al-Bihdādīnī. *Majma' al-tawārīkh al-sulṭāniyya: qismat-i khulafā-i 'Alawiyya-yi Maghrib va Miṣr va Nizāriyān va rafīqān*, ed. M. Mudarrisī Zanjānī. Tehran, 1364 Sh./1985.

Haft bāb-i Bābā Sayyidnā, ed. W. Ivanow, in his *Two Early Ismaili Treatises*. Bombay, 1933, pp. 4–42.

Ḥamd Allāh Mustawfī Qazwīnī. *Nuzhat al-qulūb*, ed. M. Dabīr Siyāqī. Qazwīn, 1381 Sh./2002.

—. *Tārīkh-i guzīda*, ed. 'A. Nawā'ī. Tehran, 1339 Sh./1960.

—. *Ẓafarnāma-i Ḥamd Allāh Mustawfī: bih inẓimām-i Shāhnāma-i Abu'l-Qāsim Firdawsī*, ed. Naṣr Allāh Pūrjavādī. Tehran, 1377 Sh./1999.

Ḥudūd al-'ālam, ed. M. Sutūdah. Tehran, 1340 Sh./1962; tr. by V. Minorsky as *Ḥudūd al-'ālam. The regions of the world: a Persian geography, 372 A.H. - 982 A.D.* London, 1937.

Ḥasan-i Maḥmūd-i Kātib. *Dīwān-i qā'imiyyāt*, ed. Jalal Badakhchani. Tehran, 2011.

al-Ḥusaynī, Ṣadr al-Dīn ʿAlī b. Nāṣir. *Akhbār al-dawla al-Saljūqiyya*, ed. M. Iqbāl. Lahore, 1933.

Ibn al-Athīr, ʿIzz al-Dīn Abu'l-Ḥasan b. ʿAlī b. Muḥammad. *al-Kāmil fi'l-ta'rīkh*, vols I–XIII, ed. C. J. Tornberg. Beirut, 1982; Partial trans. as *The Chronicle of Ibn al-Athīr for the Crusading Period from al-Kamil fi'l-ta'rikh*, The Years 491-541/1097-1146: The Coming of the Franks and the Muslim Response Part. 1, tr. D. S. Richards. Aldershot, 2006; *The Chronicle of Ibn al-Athīr for the Crusading Period from al-Kamil fi'l-ta'rikh*, The Years 541-581/1146-1193: The Age of Nūr al-Dīn and Saladin, Part. 2, tr. D. S. Richards. Aldershot, 2007; *The Chronicle of Ibn al-Athīr for the Crusading Period from al-Kamil fi'l-ta'rikh*, The Years 589-629/1193-1231: The Ayyubids after Saladin and the Mongol Menace, Part. 3, tr. D. S. Richards. Aldershot, 2008.

Ibn al-Faqīh al-Hamadhānī, Abū Bakr Shihāb al-Dīn Aḥmad. *Compendium libri Kitāb al-buldān*, ed. M. J. de Goeje. Leiden, 1885.

Ibn al-Jawzī, Abu'l-Faraj. *al-Muntaẓam fī ta'rīkh al-mulūk wa'l-umam*, vols I-VII. Hyderabad, 1938–1941; ed. F. Krenkow. Hyderabad, 1357–1362/1938–1943.

Ibn Ḥawqal, Muḥammad Abu'l-Qāsim. *al-Masālik wa'l-mamālik*, ed. J. H. Kramers. Leiden-Leipzig, 1938–1939.

Ibn Ḥawqal, Muḥammad Abu'l-Qāsim. *Kitāb Ṣūrat al-arḍ*, ed. J. H. Kramers. Leiden, 1938–1939.

Ibn Isfandiyār, Bahā' al-Dīn Muḥammad b. al-Ḥasan. *Tārīkh-i Ṭabaristān I-II*, ed. ʿA. Iqbāl. Tehran, 1320/1941.

Ibn al-Qalānisī, Abū Yalā Ḥamza b. Asad. *Dhayl ta'rīkh Dimashq*, ed. Henry F. Amedroz. Leiden, 1908.

Ibn Rusta Iṣfahānī, Aḥmad. *Kitāb al-A'lāk an-Nafīsa*, ed. M. J. de Goeje. Bibliotheca Geographorum Arabicorum [BGA]. Leiden, 1892.

Iṣṭakhrī, Ibrāhīm b. Muḥammad. *Kitāb Masālik al-mamālik*, ed. M. J. de Goeje. Leiden, 1927.

Juwaynī, ʿAlā' al-Dīn ʿAṭā-Malik b. Muḥammad. *Tārīkh-i jahān-gushā*, ed. M. Qazwīnī. Leiden–London, 1912–1937. English tr. by J. A. Boyle, *The History of the World-Conqueror*. Cambridge, MA, 1958.

Juwaynī, Muntajab al-Din. *ʿAtabat al-kataba*, ed. M. Qazwīnī and ʿA. Iqbāl. Tehran, 2004.

Jūzjānī, Minhāj al-Dīn ʿUthmān b. Sirāj. *Ṭabaqāt-i Nāṣirī*, ed. ʿAbd al-Ḥayy Ḥabībī. 2nd ed., Kabul, 1342–1343 Sh./1963–1964; tr. H. G. Raverty as *Ṭabaqāt-i Nāṣirī, A General History of the Muḥammadan Dynasties of Asia*. London, 1881–1899.

Kay Kā'ūs, Unṣur al-Ma'ālā b. Iskandar b. Qābūs b. Wushmgīr b. Ziyār. *Qābūsnāma*, ed. G. Yūsufī. Tehran, 1378 Sh./2000.

Kalām-i pīr, ed. and tr. W. Ivanow. Bombay, 1935.

Kāshānī, Jamāl al-Dīn Abu'l-Qāsim ʿAbd Allāh b. ʿAlī. *Zubdat al-tawārīkh: bakhsh-i Fāṭimiyān va Nizāriyān*, ed. Muḥammad Taqī Dānishpazhūh. 2nd ed., Tehran, 1366 Sh./1987.

Khwāndamīr, Ghiyāth al-Dīn b. Humām al-Dīn. *Ḥabīb al-siyar*, ed. M. Dabīr Sīyāqī. Tehran, 1380 Sh./2001.

Kirakos Gandzaketsʿi. *Patmuthun Hayots* (*History of the Armenians*) ed. Melikʿ– Ohanjanyan. Erevan, 1961.

Lāhijī, ʿAlī b. Shams al-Dīn. *Tārīkh-i Khānī*, ed. M Sutūdah. Tehran, 1353 Sh./1374.

al-Muḥallī, Ḥamīd al-Shahīd b. Aḥmad b. Muḥammad. *al-Ḥadā'iq al-wardiyya fī manāqib a'immat al-Zaydiyya*, 2 vols, ed. al-Murtaḍā b. Zayd al-Maḥṭūrī. 2nd ed., Yemen, 2002.

Manūchihrī Dāmghānī. *Dīwān*, ed. M. Dabīr Sīyāqī. Tehran, 1348 Sh./ 1967.

al-Maqrīzī, Taqī al-Dīn Aḥmad. *Ittiʿāẓ al-ḥunafā' bi akhbār al-ā'imma al-Fāṭimiyyīn al-khulafā'*, ed. M. H. M. Aḥmad. Cairo, 1417/1996.

Marʿashī, Mīr Sayyid Ẓahīr al-Dīn b. Sayyid Naṣīr al-Dīn. *Tārīkh-i Ṭabaristān va Rūyān va Māzandarān*, ed. B. Dorn as *Sehir ed-din's Geschichte von Tabaristān, Rūyān und*

Māzandarān. St. Petersburg, 1850; ed. ʿA. Shāyān. Tehran, 1333 Sh./1954; ed. M. H. Tasbīḥī. Tehran, 1345 Sh./1966.
—. *Tārīkh-i Gīlān va Daylamīstān*, ed. M. Sutūdah. Tehran, 1364 Sh./1985.
Mīrkhwānd, Muḥammad b. Khāwandshāh b. Maḥmūd. *Tārīkh-i rawḍat al-ṣafāʾ fī sīrat al-anbiyā wa'l mulūk wa'l-khulafā*, ed. J. Kiyānfarr. Tehran, 1380 Sh./2001.
Muʿizzī, Muḥammad b. ʿAbd al-Malik. *Dīwān-i Amīr al-Shuʿarāʾ Nīshābūrī mutakhalliṣ bih Muʿizzī: mutazammin-i qaṣāyid va ghazalīyāt va muqaṭṭaʾāt va mushtamil bar ḥawādith-i tārīkhī-i panjāh va panj sāl az ayyām-i salṭanat-i Salājuqa*, ed. ʿA. Iqbāl. Tehran, 1319/1939.
al-Mukhtārāt min al-rasāʾil: majmūʿa-i munshiyāt va faramīn va aḥkām diwānī va sharʿī va ʿarfī-yi az qurūn-i panjum va shishum va haftum-i hijrī az rawī-yi naskhah-i kitābkhanah-i Vasirī-yi Yazd, ed. I. Afshār. Tehran, 1355 Sh./1976.
al-Nasawī, Muḥammad b. Aḥmad. *Sīrat al-sulṭān Jalāl al-Dīn Mīnkubīrtī*, Arabic ed. and French tr., O. Houdas as *Histoire du Sultan Djelal ed-Din Mankobirti*. Paris, 1891–1895; Anonymous Persian translation, *Sīrat-i Jalāl al-Dīn Mīnkubīrnī*, ed. Muḥammad Mīnuvī. Tehran, 1344 Sh./1965.
Nīshāpūrī, Ẓahīr al-Dīn. *Saljūq-nāma*, ed. A. H. Morton. Cambridge, 2004.
Niẓāmī ʿArūḍī Samarqandī. *Chahār maqāla*, ed. M. Qazwīnī and M. Muʿīn. Tehran, 1375 Sh./1996.
Paris, Matthew. *Chronica majora*, vol. 1, tr. J. A. Giles. London, 1852–1854; rp. New York, 1968.
Qazwīnī Rāzī, ʿAbd al-Jalīl b. Abī al-Ḥusayn. *Kitāb-i Naqḍ maʿrūf bih Baʿḍ masālib al-Nawāṣib fī naqḍ baʿḍ faḍāʾiḥ al-rawāfiḍ*, ed. J. H. Muḥaddith Urmawī. Tehran, 1979.
Qazwīnī, Zakariyāʾ b. Muḥammad. *Āthār al-bilād wa akhbār al-ibād*, in *Zakarija Ben Mohammad Ben Mahmud el-Cazwini's Kosmographie. Zweiter Teil. Die Denkmäler der Länder*, part II, ed. F. Wüstenfeld. Göttingen, 1848; rpr. Beirut, 1380/1960.
Qiṣṣa-i Malik-i Sīstān, an unpublished manuscript in the Ismaili Special Collections Unit of the Institute of Ismaili Studies
Rashīd al-Dīn Ṭabīb, Faḍl Allāh b. ʿImād al-Dawla. *Jamīʿ al-tawārīkh*, ed. B. Karīmī. Tehran, 1338 Sh./1959; *Jāmiʿ al-tawārīkh: tārīkh-i Ismāʿīliyān*, ed. M. Rawshan. Tehran, 1387 Sh./2008; *Jāmiʿ al-tawārīkh: qismat-i Ismāʿīliyān va Fāṭimiyān va Nizāriyān va dāʿīyān va rafīqān*, ed. M. T. Dānishpazhūh and M. Mudarrisī Zanjānī. Tehran, 1338 Sh./1959; *Jamīʿ al-tawārīkh: tārīkh-i Ghāzānī*, vol. 2, ed. E. Blochet. Leiden–London, 1911; partial tr. by J. A. Boyle as *The Successors of Genghis Khan*. New York, 1971.
al-Rāwandī, Muḥammad b. Alī. *Rāhat al-sudur*, ed. M. Iqbāl. London, 1921.
al-Shahrastānī, Muḥammad b. ʿAbd al-Karīm. *Kitāb al-Muṣāraʿa*, ed. and tr. W. Madelung and T. Mayer as *Struggling with the Philosopher: A Refutation of Avicenna's Metaphysics*. London, 2001.
—. *Mafātiḥ al-asrār*, tr. by Toby Mayer as *Keys to the Arcana, Shahrastānī's Esoteric Commentary on the Qurʾan*. London, 2008.
—. *Majlis-i maktūb*, ed. and tr. by Daryoush Mohammad Poor as *Command and Creation: A Shiʿi Cosmological Treatise*. London, 2021.
Shīrāzī, Maḥmūd b. Masʿūd, Quṭb al-Dīn. *Akhbār-i Mughūlān dar anbāna-i Quṭb*, ed. I. Afshār. Qum, 2009; English tr. by George Lane as *The Mongols in Iran, Quṭb al-Dīn al-Shirāzī's Akhbār-i Moghūlān*. London and New York, 2018.
al-Ṭabarī, Abū Jaʿfar Muḥammad b. Jarīr. *Taʾrīkh al-rusul wa'l-mulūk*, vols 1–15, ed. M. J. de Goeje et al. Leiden, 1879–1901. German tr. as *Geschichte der Perser und Araber zur Zeit der Sasaniden*. Aus der arabischen Chronik des Tabari übersetzt und mit ausführlichen Erläuterungen und Ergänzungen versehn von Th. Nöldeke. Leiden, 1973; English tr. by various scholars as *The History of al-Ṭabarī*. Albany, NY, 1985–1999.
Tārīkh-i Sīstān, ed. J. Mudarris Ṣādiqī. Tehran, 1373 Sh./1994.
al-Ṭūsī, Naṣīr al-Dīn Abū Jaʿfar Muḥammad b. Muḥammad. *Rawḍat al-taslīm*, ed. and tr. W. Ivanow. Leiden, 1950; ed. and tr. S. J. Badakchani as *Paradise of Submission: A Medieval Treatise on Ismaili Thought*. London, 2005.

—. *Sayr wa sulūk*, ed. and tr. S. J. Badakchani as *Contemplation and Action: The Spiritual Autobiography of a Muslim Scholar*. London, 1998.
Waṭwāt, Rashīd al-Dīn. *Nāmah'hā-yi Waṭwāt*, ed. Q. Tūysirkānī. Tehran, 1338 Sh./1960.
Ya'qūbī, Abu'l-'Abbās Aḥmad. *Ta'rīkh*, 2 vols, ed. M. T. Houtsma. Leiden, 1883.
Yāqūt al-Ḥamawī, Shihāb al-Dīn Abū 'Abd Allāh. *Mu'jam al-buldān*, ed. F. Wüstenfeld. Leipzig, 1866–1873.
Yuan shi, ed. S. Lian. Beijing, 1976.

Studies

Amedroz, Henry Frederick. 'On a Dirham of Khusrau Shāh of 361 A. H.', *JRAS* (1905), pp. 471–484.
Atwood, Christopher. *The Campaigns of Chinggis Khan: Text, Translation, and Commentary*. Dallas, TX, forthcoming.
Aubin, Jean. 'Réseau pastoral et réseau caravanier: Les grand'routes du Khurassan à l'époque mongole', *Le Monde Iranien et l'Islam*, 1 (1971), pp. 105–130.
'Azīzī, Muḥsin. *La domination arabe et l'épanouissement du sentiment national en Iran: Étude politique et sociale sur l'Iran musulman de 651 à 900 av. J. C. Paris*. n.p., 1938.
Barthold, Vasilii Vladimirovich. *An Historical Geography of Iran*, tr. Svat Soucek, ed. C. E. Bosworth. Princeton, 1984.
Bates, Michael. 'History, Geography and Numismatics in the First Century of Islamic Coinage', *Revue suisse de Numismatique*, 65 (1986), pp. 212–267.
Birashk, Ahmad. *Comparative Calendar of the Iranian, Muslim, Lunar and Christian Eras for Three Thousand Years 1260 B. H. - 2000 A.H./639 B. C. - 2621 A. D.* Costa Mesa, CA, 1993.
Bivar, Adrian David Hugh. 'Weights and Measures', *Encyclopaedia Iranica Online Edition*, 2010, http://www.iranicaonline.org/articles/weights-measures-i
Blair, Sheila. *The Monumental Inscriptions from Early Islamic Iran and Transoxiana*. Leiden, 1992.
Bosworth, Clifford Edmund. *The Ghaznavids: Their Empire in Afghanistan and Eastern Iran 994–1042*. Edinburgh, 1963.
—. 'Military Organisation under the Būyids of Persia in Iraq', *Oriens*, 18–19 (1965–1966), pp. 143–167.
—. 'On the Chronology of the Ziyārids in Gurgān and Tabaristān', *Der Islam*, 40 (1964), pp. 37–49.
—. 'The Political and Dynastic History of the Iranian World A. D. 1000–1217,' in *The Cambridge History of Iran*, vol. 5, *The Saljūq and Mongol Periods*, ed. J. A. Boyle. Cambridge, 1968, pp. 1–202.
—. 'Dailamīs in Central Iran: the Kākūyids of Jibāl and Yazd', *Iran*, 8 (1970), pp. 73–95.
—. *The Later Ghaznavids, Splendour and Decay*. New York, 1977.
—. 'The Heritage of Rulership in Early Islamic Iran and the Search for Dynastic Connections with the Past', *Iranian Studies*, 11 (1978), pp. 7–34.
— 'Āl-e Afrāsīāb', *EIR*, vol. 1, pp. 742–744.
—. 'Azerbaijan iv. Islamic History to 1941', *EIR*, vol. 3, pp. 224–231.
—. *The New Islamic Dynasties*. Edinburgh, 1996.
—. 'The Persian Contribution to Islamic Historiography in the pre-Mongol Period', in R. Hovannisian and G. Sabagh, ed. *The Persian Presence in the Islamic World*. Cambridge, 1998, pp. 218–236.
—. 'Sistan and its Local Histories', *Iranian Studies*, 33 (2000), pp. 31–43.
—. 'Khwarazmshāhs i. Descendants of the line of Anushtigin', *EIR Online Edition*, 2009, http://www.iranicaonline.org/articles/khwarazmShāhs-i.
—. 'Ziyārids', *EI2*, vol. 11, pp. 539–540.

—. 'Ziyārids (Āl-e Ziār)', *EIR Online Edition,* http://www.iranicaonline.org/articles/Ziyārids
—. 'Kākuyids [Kakwayhids]', *EIR*, vol. 15, pp. 359–362.
—. 'Mosaferids', *EIR Online Edition*, 2013 http://www.iranicaonline.org/articles/mosaferids, http://www.iranicaonline.org/articles/mosaferids.
Bowen, Harold. 'The Last Buwaihids', *JRAS* (1929), pp. 225–245.
Boyce, Mary. *The Letter of Tansar*. Rome, 1968.
Boyle, John, A. 'The Ismailis and the Mongol invasion', in S. H. Nasr, ed. *Ismaili Contributions to Islamic Culture*. Tehran, 1977, pp. 5–22.
—. 'Dynastic and Political History of the Il-Khans', in *The Cambridge History of Iran*, vol. 5, *The Saljūq and Mongol Periods*, ed. J. A. Boyle. Cambridge, 1968, pp. 303–421.
Brockelmann, Carl. *Geschichte der arabischen Literatur*, Zweite Auflage. Leiden, New York, Köln, 1996.
Browne, Edward G. *An Abridged translation of the History of Tabaristān Compiled about A. H. 613* (A. D. 1216), by Muḥammad b. al-Ḥasan b. Ibn Isfandiyār. Leiden–London, 1905.
Buell, Paul and Anderson, Eugene. *A Soup for the Qan: Chinese Dietary Medicine of the Mongol Era as seen in Hu Sihui's Yinshan Zhengyao*. Leiden, 2010.
Burhān, Muḥammad Ḥusayn b. Khalaf Tabrīzī. *Burhān-i qāṭiʿ*. Tehran, 1361 Sh./1982.
Busse, Heribert. *Chalif und Grosskönig. Die Būyiden in Iraq*. Beirut, 1969.
—. 'The Revival of Persian Kingship under the Būyids', in D. S. Richards, ed. *Islamic Civilization*. Oxford, 1973, pp. 950–1150.
—. 'Iran under the Buyids', in *The Cambridge History of Iran*, vol. 4, *From the Arab Invasion to the Saljuqs*, ed. R. N. Frye. Cambridge, 1975, pp. 250–304.
Cahen, Claude. 'Buwayhids (Būyids)', *EI2*, vol. 1, pp. 1350–1357.
Calmard, Jean 'Marʿashī', *EI2*, vol. 6, pp. 510–516.
Casanova, Paul 'Les Ispehbeds de Firīm', in T. W. Arnold, R. A. Nicholson, ed. *A Volume of Oriental Studies, presented to Edward G. Browne*. Cambridge, 1922, pp. 34–68.
Choksy, Jamsheed Karshasp. *Conflict and Cooperation, Zoroastrian Subalterns and Muslim Elites in Medieval Iranian Society*. New York, 1997.
Christensen, Arthur. *L'Iran sous les Sassanides*. Copenhagen, 1944.
Chubak, Ḥamīde. 'Kāwishhā-yi bāstānshināsī dar dīzh-i Ḥasan Ṣabbāḥ-i Alamūt, Archaeological Excavations in the Fortress of Ḥasan Ṣabbāḥ in Alamūt', *Guzārishhā-yi bāstānshināsī, 7, majmūʿa-i maqālaha-i nuhumīn girdhimāyi-yi sālāna-i bāstānshināsī-yi Īrān, jild-i awwal*. Tehran, 1386 Sh./2007, pp. 88–128.
Cortese, Delia. 'Eschatology and power in mediaeval Persian Ismailism', PhD SOAS, University of London, 1993.
Crone, Patricia. *The Nativist Prophets of Early Islamic Iran*. Cambridge, 2012.
Curiel, Raoul. 'Sur quelques monnaies de gouverneurs ʿabbāsides du Tabaristān, dans Pad nām ī yazdān', *Études d'epigraphie, de numismatique et d'histoire de l'Iran ancien. Travaux de l'Institut d'Études Iraniennes*, 9 (1979), pp. 151–158.
Curiel, Raoul and Gyselen, Rika. 'Une Collection de Monnaies de Cuivre Arabo-Sasanides', *Studia Iranica*, Cahier 2. Paris, 1984.
Curzon, George Nathaniel. *Persia and the Persian Question*. London, 1966.
Dabashī, Hamid. 'The Philosopher/Vizier Khwāja Naṣīr al-Dīn Ṭūsī and the Ismailis', in F. Daftary, ed. *Mediaeval Ismaʿili History and Thought*. Cambridge, 1996, pp. 321–345.
Daftary, Farhad. *The Ismāʿīlīs, Their History and Doctrines*. 2nd ed., Cambridge, 2007.
—. *The Assassin Legends: Myths of the Ismailis*. London, 1994.
—, ed. *Mediaeval Ismaʿili History and Thought*. Cambridge, 1996.
—. *A Short History of the Ismailis: Traditions of a Muslim Community*. Edinburgh, 1998.
—. *Ismailis in Medieval Muslim Societies*. London, 2005.
—. *Ismaili Literature: A Bibliography of Sources and Studies*. London, 2004.
—. 'Ḥasan-i Ṣabbāh and the Origins of the Nizari Ismaili Movement', in F. Daftary, ed. *Mediaeval Ismaʿili History and Thought*, pp. 181–204.

—. 'Persian Historiography of the Early Nizārī Ismā'īlīs', *Iran*, 30 (1992), pp. 91–97.
—. 'Intellectual Life among the Ismailis: An Overview', in F. Daftary, ed. *Intellectual Traditions in Islam*. London, 2000, pp. 87–111.
—. 'Nāṣir al-Dīn Ṭūsī and the Ismailis of the Alamūt Period', in N. Pourjavady and Z. Vesel, ed. *Nāṣir al-Dīn Ṭūsī, philosophe et savant de XIIIe siècle*. Tehran, 2000, pp. 59–67.
—. 'The Isma'ilis and the Crusaders: History and Myth', in Z. Hunyadi and J. Laszlovszky, ed. *The Crusades and the Military Orders: Expanding the Frontiers of Medieval Latin Christianity*. Budapest, 2001, pp. 21–41.
—. 'Fedā'ī', *EIR*, vol. 9, pp. 468–470.
—. 'Ḥasan Ṣabbāḥ', *EIR*, vol. 12, pp. 34–37.
—. 'Gerdkūh', *EIR*, vol. 10, p. 499.
— and Z. Hirji. *The Ismailis, An Illustrated History*. London, 2008.
Daniel, Elton. L. 'Historiography, iii. Early Islamic Period', *EIR*, vol. 12, pp. 337–349.
Dashdondog, Bayarsaikhan. *Mongols and Armenians* 1220–1335. Leiden, 2011.
Dawson, Christopher, ed. *The Mongol Mission: Narratives and Letters of the Franciscan Missionaries in Mongolia and China in the Thirteenth and Fourteenth Centuries, translated by a nun of Stanbrook Abbey*. London, 1955.
Dorn, Bernhard. 'Die Pehlewy-Münzen des Asiatischen Museums der Kaiserlichen Akademie der Wissenschaften III Die Münzen der Ispehbede, Chalifen und deren Statthalter', *Mélanges Asiatiques*, 2 (1856), pp. 249–263.
—. 'Über die letzten dem Asitischen Museum zugekommenen Pehlewy-Münzen', *Mélanges Asiatiques*, 2 (1856), pp. 608–611.
Eboo Jamal, Nadia. *Surviving the Mongols: Nizārī Qūhistānī and the Continuity of Ismaili Tradition in Iran*. London, 2003.
Ehlers, Eckart. *Iran. Grundzüge einer geographischen Landeskunde*. Darmstadt, 1980.
Ethé, Carl Hermann. 'Die älteste Urkunde über Firdausi', *ZDMG*, 48 (1894), pp. 89–94.
Farhānī-Munfarid, Mahdī. 'Dīplomāsī-i gustarish va guftigū, pažūsishhi dar takāpūhā-i siyāsī-i Ismailiyān-i Alamūt, 618-653/1221-1255', *Farhang*, 56 (1384 Sh./2005), pp. 84–112.
Fauth, Wilhelm. 'Der königlicher Gärtner und Jäger im Paradeisos, Beobachtungen zur Rolle des Herrschers in der vorderasiatischen Hortikultur', *Persica*, 8 (1979), pp. 1–53.
Fraehn, Christian Martin. *Recensio Numorum Muhammedanorum*. St. Petersburg, 1826.
Gaube, Heinz. *Arabosasanidische Numismatik*. Braunschweig, 1973.
Gignoux, Philippe. 'La chasse dans l'Iran sasanide', *Orientalia Romana/Serie Orientale Roma* LII/ *Essays and Lectures*, 5, *Iranian Studies* (1983), pp. 101–118.
—. 'Le Spahbed des Sassanides à l'Islam', *Jerusalem Studies in Arabic and Islam*, 13 (1990), pp. 1–14.
—. 'Sur quelques noms propres des sources numismatiques iraniennes', *Proceedings of the First European Conference of Iranian Studies, Part I: Old and Middle Iranian Studies*. Rome, 1990, pp. 135–144.
— and Bates, Michael. 'Dirham', *EIR*, vol. 7, pp. 424–428.
Godard, André. 'Les tours de Ladjim et de Resget (Māzandarān)', *Āthār-é Īrān*, *Annales du service archéologique de l'Īrān*, 1 (1936), pp. 109–121.
Göbl, Robert. *Sasanian Numismatics*. Braunschweig, 1968.
Goto, Yukako. 'Der Aufstieg zweier Sayyid-Familien am Kaspischen Meer: "Volkislamische" Strömung in Iran des 8./14. und 9./15. Jahrhunderts', *Wiener Zeitschrift für die Kunde des Morgenländes*, 89 (1999), pp. 45–84.
—. *Die südkaspischen Provinzen des Iran unter den Safawiden im 16. und 17. Jahrhundert. Eine Analyse der sozialen und wirtschaftlichen Entwicklung*. Berlin, 2011.
Gyselen, Rika and Ludvik Kalus. *Deux trésors monétaires des premier temps de l'Islam*. Paris, 1983.
Hanaway, William. 'Paradise on Earth: The Terrestrial garden in Persian Literature', in E. B. Macdougall, and R. Ettinghausen, ed. *The Islamic Garden*. Washington, DC, 1976, pp. 43–67.

Harmatta, János. 'The Middle Persian – Chinese Bilingual Inscription from Hsian and the Chinese – Sasanian Relations', *La Persia nel Medioevo, Atti del convegno internazionale Roma, 31 marzo – 5 aprile 1970*. Rome, 1971, pp. 363–377.

Harper, Prudence Oliver. *The Royal Hunter. Art of Sassanian Empire*. n.p., 1978.

Haw, Stephen. 'The Mongol Empire – the first "gunpowder empire"?', *JRAS*, 23, 3 (2013), pp. 441–469.

Herzfeld, Ernst. 'Postsasanidische Inschriften', *Archäologische Mitteilungen aus Iran und Turan*, 4 (1932), pp. 140–156.

—. 'Arabische Inschriften aus Iran und Syrien', *Archäologische Mitteilungen aus Iran und Turan*, 8 (1936), pp. 78–90.

Hillenbrand, Carole. '1092 – A Murderous Year', *Proceedings of the 14th Congress of the Union Européene des Arabisants et Islamisants*. Budapest, 1995, pp. 281–296.

—. 'The Power Struggle between the Saljūqs and the Ismāʿīlīs of Alamūt, 487-518/1094-1124: the Saljūq Perspective', in F. Daftary, ed. *Mediaeval Ismaʿili History and Thought*. Cambridge, 1996, pp. 205–220.

Hodgson, Marshall G. S. *The Order of Assassins, The Struggle of the Early Nizārī Ismāʿīlīs against the Islamic World*. The Hague, 1955.

—. 'Alamūt', *EI2*, vol. 1, pp. 352–354.

—. 'The Ismāʿīlī State', in *The Cambridge History of Iran*, vol. 5, *The Saljuq and Mongol Periods*, ed. J. A. Boyle. Cambridge, 1968, pp. 422–482.

Hourcade, Bernard. 'Alamūt', *EIR*, vol. 1, pp. 797–801.

Ivanow, Wladimir. 'An Ismaili Poem in Praise of Fidawis', *Journal of the Bombay Branch of the Royal Asiatic Society*, 14 (1938), pp. 63–72.

—. *A Guide to Ismaili Literature*. London, 1933.

—. *Ismaili Literature: A Bibliographical Survey*. Tehran, 1963.

Jackson, Peter. *The Mongols and the Islamic World: From Conquest to Conversion*. New Haven, 2017.

Jaktājī, Pūr Aḥmad and Muḥammad Taqī, ed. *Gīlānnāma, majmūʿa-i maqālāt-i Gīlānshināsī*, vol 4. Rasht, 1374 Sh./1995.

Jawādī, Sayyid Ḥasan Ḥāj. 'Gīlān az panjhazār sāl-i pīsh tā imrūz', in Ibrāhīm. Iṣlāḥ-ʿArabānī, ed. *Kitāb-i Gīlān*, vol. 2. Tehran. 1374 Sh./1996, pp. 11–120.

Justi, Ferdinand. *Iranisches Namenbuch*. Hildesheim, 1963.

Kabir, Muhammad. 'The Būwayhids of Jibāl and Rayy A.H. 322-420 (933/934-1029)', *Journal of the Asiatic Society of Pakistan*, 3 (1958), pp. 29–42.

—. 'History of Ziyārids of Tabaristān and Gurgān (927/8-1091 A.D.)', *Journal of the Asiatic Society of Pakistan*, 5 (1960), pp. 1–20.

Kasrawī, Aḥmad. *Shāhryārān-i gumnām, pazhūhishī dar Tārīkh-i Īrān*. Tehran, 1379 Sh./2001.

Kawami, Trudy. 'Antike persiche Gärten', in M. Carrol-Spillecke, ed. *Der Garten von der Antike bis zum Mittelalter*. Mainz am Rhein, 1992, pp. 81–97.

Kennedy, Hugh. 'Central Government and Provincial Élites in the Early Abbāsid Caliphate', *BSOAS*, 44 (1981) pp. 26–38.

—. 'The Barmakid Revolution in Islamic Government', in C. Melville, ed. *Pembroke Papers I, Persian and Islamic Studies in Honour of P. W. Avery*. Cambridge, 1990, pp. 89–98.

Khaleghi-Motlagh, Djalal. 'Ferdowsi', *EIR*, vol. 1, pp. 514–523.

Khalidi, Tarif. *Arabic Historical Thought in the Classical Period*. Cambridge, 1994.

Khan, Muhammad Siddiq. 'The Early History of Zaydī Shiism in Daylamān and Gīlān', *ZDMG*, 125 (1975), pp. 301–314.

Khumāmīzāda, Jaʿfar. 'Jughrāfiā-i Tārīkhī', in I. Iṣlāḥ-ʿArabānī, ed. *Kitāb-i Gīlān*. Tehran, 1374 Sh./1996, pp. 469–500.

Kleiss, W. 'Assassin Castles in Iran', in R. Hillenbrand, ed. *The Art of the Saljūqs in Iran and Anatolia*. Costa Mesa, CA, 1994, pp. 315–319.

Knauth, Wolfgang. *Das altiranische Fürstenideal von Xenophon bis Firdausi. nach den antiken und einheimischen Quellen dargestellt in Verbindung mit Sejfoddin Nadjmabadi.* Wiesbaden, 1975.

Kraemer, Joel. *Humanism in the Renaissance of Islam: The Cultural Revival during the Būyid Age*. Leiden, 1986.

Lambton, Ann K. S. *Landlord and Peasant: a study of land tenure and land administration.* London, 1953.

—. *Continuity and Change in Medieval Persia, Aspects of Administrative, Economic and Social History 11th–14th century.* Albany, NY, 1988.

—. 'The Internal Structure of the Saljuq Empire', in *The Cambridge History of Iran*, vol. 5, *The Saljuq and Mongol Periods*, ed. J. A. Boyle. Cambridge, 1968, pp. 203–282.

—. 'Persian local histories: the tradition behind them and the assumptions of their authors', in B. Scarcia and L. Rostagno, ed. *Yādnāma, in memoria di Alessandro Bausani*, vol. 1. Rome, 1991, pp. 227–238.

Lane, George. *Early Mongol Rule in Thirteenth-Century Iran: A Persian Renaissance.* London and New York, 2003.

—. 'Mongol News: The Akhbār-i Moghulān dar Anbāneh Quṭb by Quṭb al-Dīn Maḥmūd ibn Mas'ūd Shīrāzī', *JRAS*, 22 (2012), pp. 541–559.

Laufer, Berthold. *Sino-Iranica. Chinese Contributions to the History of Civilization in Ancient Iran*. Chicago, 1919.

Lewis, Bernard. 'Kamāl al-Dīn's Biography of Rashīd al-Dīn Sinān', *Arabica*, 13 (1966), pp. 225–267.

Luther, Kenneth Allin, 'Atābakān-e Adharbayjān', *EIr*, vol. 2, pp. 890–894.

MacKenzie, David Neil. *A Concise Pahlavi Dictionary*. London, 1971.

Madelung, Wilferd, ed. *Arabic Texts concerning the history of the Zaydī Imams of Ṭabaristān, Daylamān and Gīlān*. Beirut, 1987.

—. *Religious Trends in early Islamic Iran*. Albany, NY, 1988.

—. 'The Minor Dynasties of Northern Iran', in *The Cambridge History of Iran*, vol. 4, *The Period from the Arab Invasion to the Saljuqs*, ed. Richard N. Frye. Cambridge, 1975, pp. 198–226.

—. 'The Justānids and the Sallārids of Ṭārum in the 4th/10th Century', in *The Cambridge History of Iran*, vol. 4, *The Period from the Arab Invasion to the Saljuqs*, ed. Richard N. Frye. Cambridge, 1975, pp. 223–226.

—. 'Al-Mahdī al-Ḥaqq, al-Halifa ar-Rashīd und die Bekehrung der Dailamiten zur Shi'a', in H. Biesterfeldt and V. Klemm, ed. *Differenz und Dynamik/Difference and Dynamism in Islam: Festschrift für Heinz Halm zum 70. Geburtstag.* Würzburg, 2012, pp. 122–131.

—. 'The Alid Rulers of Tabaristān, Daylamān and Gilān', *Atti del III Congresso di Studi Arabi e Islamici*. Naples, 1967, pp. 123–156.

—. 'The Assumption of the Shāhānshāh by the Būyids and the Reign of the Daylam', *Journal of Near Eastern Studies*, 28 (1969), pp. 84–108, 169–183.

—. 'Abu Isḥāq al-Ṣābī on the Alids of Tabaristān and Gīlān', *Journal of Near Eastern Studies*, 26 (1967), pp. 17–57.

—. 'Alids of Ṭabarestān, Daylamān, and Gīlān', *EIR*, vol. 1, pp. 881–886. http://www.iranicaonline.org/articles/alids-of-tabarestan-daylaman-and-gilan

—. 'Āl-e Bāvand', *EIR*, vol. 1, pp. 749–752.

—. 'Awlīā' Allāh Āmoli', *EIR*, vol. 3, pp. 120–121.

—. 'Bādūspānids', http://www.iranicaonline.org/articles/baduspanids *EIR*, vol. 4, pp. 385–391.

—. 'Ismailiyya', *EI2*, vol. 4, pp. 198–206.

—. 'Dābūyids', *EIR*, vol. 6, pp. 541–544.

—. 'Deylamites ii. In the Islamic Period', *EIR*, vol. 7, pp. 343–347.

—. 'Gīlān, IV. In the Early Islamic Period', *EIR*, vol. 10, pp. 634–635.

—. 'Hoqayni', *EIR*, vol. 12, pp. 456–457.

Malek, Hodge, M. 'The Posthumous Arab-Sasanian Coinage of Khurshid in Ṭabaristān', *Numismatic Circular*, 95 (1989), pp. 39–40.
Malek, Hodge, M. 'The Dābūyid Iṣpahbads of Tabaristān', *American Journal of Numismatics*, 5–6 (1993–1994), pp. 105–160.
Marquart, Joseph. *Ērānshāhr nach der Geographie des Ps. Moses Xorenac'i, mit historisch-kritischem Kommentar und historischen und topographischen Excursen*. Berlin, 1901.
Masson Smith, John. 'Hülegü Moves West: Living and Heartbreak on the Road to Baghdad', in L. Komaroff, ed. *Beyond the Legacy of Genghis Khan*. Leiden, 2013, pp. 94–110.
May, Timothy. 'A Mongol-Isma'ili Alliance? Thoughts on the Mongols and Assassins', *JRAS*, 14 (2004), pp. 231–239.
Meisami, Julie Scott. *Persian Historiography to the End of the Twelfth Century*. Edinburgh, 1999.
Melikian-Chirvani, Assadullah Souren. 'The Iranian *bazm* in early new Persian sources', in R. Gyselen, ed. *Res Orientales* IV, *Banquets d'Orient*. Paris, 1992, pp. 95–120.
—. 'Le Livre des Rois, Miroir du Destin', *Studia Iranica*, 17 (1988), pp. 1–14.
Melville, Charles. '"Sometimes by the sword, sometimes by the dagger": the role of the Isma'ilis in Mamluk Mongol relations in the 8th/14th century', in F. Daftary ed., *Mediaeval Isma'ili History and Thought*. Cambridge, 1996, pp. 247–263.
—. 'Persian Local Histories: Views from the Wings', *Iranian Studies*, 33 (2000), pp. 7–14.
—. 'The Caspian Provinces: A World Apart, Three local histories of Mazandaran', *Iranian Studies*, 33 (2000), pp. 45–91.
—. 'Ebn Esfandīār, Bahā'-al-Dīn Moḥammad', *EIR*, vol. 8, pp. 20–23.
Michailidis, Melanie. 'Pilgrims and Patrons: ziyara under the Sāmānids and Bavandids', in F. Suleman, *People of the Prophet's House, Artistic and Ritual Expressions of Shi'i Islam*. London, 2015, pp. 86–95.
Miles, George. 'The Coinage of the Bāvandids of Tabaristān', in C. E. Bosworth ed., *Iran and Islam, In Memory of the late Vladimir Minorsky*. Edinburgh, 1971, pp. 443–460.
—. 'Coins of the Assassins of Alamut', *Orientalia Lovaniensa Periodica*, 3–5 (1972–74), pp. 155–162.
Minorsky, Vladimir. *La domination des Daylamites*. Paris, 1932.
—. *Studies in Caucasian History*. London, 1953.
—. 'Lāhidjān', *EI2*, vol. 5, pp. 602–604.
—. 'Daylam', *EI2*, vol. 2, pp. 189–194.
—. 'Musāfirids', *EI2*, vol. 7, pp. 655–657.
— and Bosworth, C. E. 'Ṭārum', *EI2*, vol. 10, pp. 311–312.
Minuwī, Mujtaba'. *Māzyār*. Tehran, 1320 Sh./1942.
Mordtmann, Andreas David. 'Erklärung der Münzen mit Pehlevi-Legenden', *ZDMG*, 12 (1858), pp. 54–56.
—. 'Erklärung der Münzen mit Pehlevi-Legenden', *ZDMG*, 19 (1865), pp. 474–496.
Morgan, David. *The Mongols*. Oxford, 1990.
Morimoto, K. 'Ketāb al-Naqż', *EIr*, http://www.iranicaonline.org/articles/ketab-al-naqz
Morton, Alexander Hugh. 'Dinars from Western Māzandarān of Some Vassals of the Saljūq Sultan Muḥammad b. Malik Shāh', *Iran*, 25 (1987), pp. 77–90.
—. 'Ghūrid Gold en route to England?', *Iran*, 16 (1978), pp. 167–170.
Mottahedeh, Roy Parviz. 'Administration in Būyid Qazwīn', in D. S. Richards, ed. *Islamic Civilization, 950-1150*. A Colloquium published under the auspices of the Near Eastern History Group Oxford and The Near East Center, University of Pennsylvania. Oxford, 1970, pp. 47–70.
Mu'īn, Muḥammad. *Farhang-i fārsī*, vols 1–6. Tehran, 1379 Sh./2000.
Mūsawī, Sayyid Muḥammad. 'Bāstānshināsī', in I. Iṣlāḥ-'Arabānī, ed. *Kitāb-i Gīlān*, vol. 1. Tehran, 1374 Sh./1996, pp. 501–546.
—. 'Banāhā-i tārīkhī', in I. Iṣlāḥ-'Arabānī, ed. *Kitāb-i Gīlān*, vol. 1. Tehran, 1374 Sh./1996, pp. 547–556.

Nagel, Tilman. 'Buyids', *EIR*, vol. 4, pp. 578–586.
Negahban, Ezat. 'Deylaman', *EIR*, vol. 7, p. 337.
Nöldeke, Theodor. 'Das iranische Nationalepos', in *Grundriss der iranischen Philologie*, 2 vols, ed. W. Geiger and E. Kuhn. Strassburg, 1896–1904, vol. 2, pp. 130–211.
Pāyanda-Langarūdī, Maḥmūd. *Khūnīnahā-i tārīkhī dār al-marz (Gīlān va Māzandarān)*. Rasht, 1370 Sh./1992.
Pezeshk, Manouchehr. 'Jostanids', *EIR*, vol. 15, pp. 44–46.
Pingree, David and Madelung, Wilferd. 'Political Horoscopes relating to Ninth Century Alids', *Journal of Near Eastern Studies*, 36 (1977), pp. 247–275.
Pourshariati, Parvaneh. 'Local Histories of Khurāsān and the Pattern of Arab Settlement', *Studia Iranica*, 27 (1998), pp. 53–57.
Rabino di Borgomale, Hyacinthe Louis. 'Les provinces caspiennes de la Perse. Le Guilān', *Revue du monde musulman*, 32 (1915–1916), pp. 3–110.
—. 'Rulers of Lāhījān and Fūman in Gīlān, Persia', *JRAS*, 85 (1918), pp. 100–134.
—. 'Rulers of Gīlān', *JRAS*, 52 (1920), pp. 277–296.
—. 'Les dynasties Alaoudies du Māzandarān', *Journal Asiatique*, 210 (1927), pp. 253–277.
—. *Māzandarān and Astarābād*. London, 1928
—. 'Les dynasties du Māzandarān de l'an 50 avant l'Hégire á l'an 1006 de l'Hégire (572 á 1597-98), d'aprés les chroniques locales', *Journal Asiatique*, 228 (1936), pp. 397–474.
—. 'Les préfets du califat au Tabaristān de 18 à 328/ 639 a 939-940', *Journal Asiatique*, 231 (1939), pp. 237–275.
—. 'L'histoire du Māzandarān', *Journal Asiatique*, 234 (1943–1945), pp. 211–246.
—. 'Les dynasties locales du Gilān et du Daylam', *Journal Asiatique*, 237 (1949), pp. 301–350.
—. 'Deux inscriptions du Gilān du temps des Mongols', *Journal Asiatique*, 238 (1950), pp. 325–333.
Rehatsek, Edward. 'The Bâw and Gaobârah Sepahbuds along the Southern Caspian Shores', *Journal of the Bombay Branch of the Royal Asiatic Society*, 12 (1876), pp. 410–445.
Rekaya, Mohamed. 'L'integration de l'empire sassanide dans l'aire culturelle islamique au haut Moyen Age VIIe-IXe s.: a propos de travaux récents', *L'Arabisant*, 26 (1987), pp. 54–68.
—. 'La place des provinces sud-caspiennes dans l'histoire de l'Iran de la conquête arabe à l'avenement des Zaydīs (16-250 H/ 637-864 J.C.): particularisme régional ou rôle «national»?', *Rivista degli Studi Orientali* (1972–1973), pp. 117–152.
—. 'Māzyār: Résistance ou intégration d'une province iranienne au monde musulman au milieu du IXe siècle Ap. J.C.', *Studia Iranica*, 2 (1973), pp. 143–192.
Ross, E. Denison, Sir. 'On Three Muhammadan Dynasties in Northern Persia in the tenth and eleventh centuries', *Asia Major*, 2 (1925), pp. 205–225.
Rubrouck, Guillaume de (William of Rubruck). *The Mission of Friar William of Rubruck. His Journey to the Court of the Great Khan Möngke, 1253-1255*, tr. P. Jackson and ed. David O. Morgan. London, 1990.
Rypka, Jan. *Iranische Literaturgeschichte*. Leipzig, 1959.
Sadighi, G. H. *Les mouvements religieux iraniens au IIe et au IIIe siècle de l'hégire*. Paris, 1938.
Sárközy, Miklós. 'Ebn Esfandyār Tārix-e Tabarestān-ja és a Kaszpi-vidék déli partvidékének történeti problémái a 9. század első felében' ['The *Tārīkh-i Ṭabaristān* of Ibn Isfandyār and Historical Problems in the Southern coast of the Caspian Sea]', in Á. Birtalan and M. Yamaji, ed. *Orientalista Nap 2003*. Budapest, 2003, pp. 121–128.
—. 'Ferdousi és a tabarestāni Bāvandida dinasztia' ['Firdawsī and the Bāwandid Dynasty in Tabaristān']', in F. Csirkés et al., ed. *Függőkert, Orientalisztikai tanulmányok 2*. Budapest, 2005, pp. 135–161.
—. 'Vazallus – szövetséges- lázadó: egy kisdinasztia az Īlkhānida periódusban Észak-Iránból: a Bāduspānidák', ['Vassal–Ally–Insurgent, a Local Dynasty of Northern Iran in

the Īlkhānid Period: the Bāduspānids'] *IV. Nemzetközi Vámbéry Konferencia*. Dunájska Streda, 2007, pp. 96–118.
—. 'The Survival of the Myth of the Sasanians in Early Islamic Tabaristān', in Á. Szabó and P. Vargyas, ed. *Cultus deorum studia religionum ad historiam vol. III. Res Medievalia et recentiora ab Oriens ad Europa, In memoriam István Tóth*. Pécs-Budapest, 2008, pp. 21–36.
—. 'A Sasanian taxation list or Early Islamic booty? A Medieval Persian source and the Sasanian taxation system', *Ancient Near-Eastern and Mediterranean Studies, vol. 2., Studies in the Economic and Social History of the Ancient Near East - in Memory of Péter Vargyas*. Pécs, 2014, pp. 701–714.
—. 'Indigenous versus International? The Role of 'Pre-islamic' Identity and Shiʿi Islam in the Clashes of the Bāwandid Kingdom with the Nizārī Ismāʿīlīs in Northern Iran', in M. Rodziewicz and M. Michalak, ed. *In Quest of Identity. Studies on the Persianate World*. Warsaw, 2015, pp. 129–146.
Spuler, Berthold. *Iran in früh-islamischer Zeit*. Wiesbaden, 1952.
—. 'Die historische Literatur Persiens bis zum 13. Jahrhundert als Spiegel seiner geistigen Entwicklung', *Saeculum*, 8 (1957), pp. 267–284.
—. 'Gīlān', *EI2*, vol. 2, pp. 1111–1112.
Stern, Samuel Miklos. 'The Early Ismāʿīlī Missionaries in North-West Persia and in Khurāsān and Transoxania', *BSOAS*, 23 (1960), pp. 56–90.
Stronach, David. 'The Garden as a Political Statement: Some Case Studies from the Near East in the First Millenium B.C.', *Bulletin of the Asia Institute, in Honor of R.N. Frye*, 4 (1990), pp. 171–180.
Strothmann, Rudolf. 'Ḥasan al-Uṭrush', *EI2*, vol. 3, pp. 254–255.
Sūrtījī, Sāmān. *Qilāʿ-i bāstānī-i Māzandarān*. Tehran, 1381 Sh./2002.
Sutūda, Manūchihr. *Qilāʿ-i Ismāʿīliyya dar rishtakuhhā-yi Alburz*. Tehran, 1345 Sh./1966.
Tor, Deborah. 'A Tale of Two Murders: Power Relations between Caliph and Sultan in the Saljūq Era', *ZDMG*, 159 (2009), pp. 279–297.
—. 'The Importance of Khurāsān and Transoxiana in the Classical Islamic World', in A.C.S. Peacock and D. G. Tor, ed. *Medieval Central Asia and the Persianate World: Iranian Tradition and Islamic Civilisation*. London, 2015, pp. 1–12.
Unvala, Jamshedji Maneckji. *Coins of Ṭabaristān and some Sassanian Coins from Susa*. Paris, 1938.
Vasmer, Richard. 'Die Eroberung Tabaristāns durch die Araber zur Zeit des Chalifen al-Manṣūr', *Islamica*, 3 (1927), pp. 86–150.
Vasmer, Richard and Bosworth, C. E. 'Māzandarān', *EI2*, vol. 6, pp. 935–942.
Virani, Shafique. 'The Eagle Returns. Evidence of Continued Ismāʿīlī Activity in Alamūt and in the South Caspian region following the Mongol conquests', *Journal of the American Oriental Society*, 123 (2003), pp. 351–370.
Virani, Shafique N. *The Prince and His Two Captives: A Tale from Alamut*. London: I.B. Tauris in association with the Institute of Ismaili Studies, forthcoming.
Willey, Peter. *Eagle's Nest: Ismaili Castles in Iran and Syria*. London, 2005.
—. *The Castles of the Assassins*. London, 1963.
Yule, Sir Henry. *The Book of Ser Marco Polo, the Venetian concerning the Kingdoms and Marvels of the East*. 3rd ed., London, 1903.
Zambaur, Eduard von. 'Nouvelles contributions à la numismatique orientale', *Numismatische Zeitschrift*, 17 (1914), pp. 115–190.
—. *Manuel de Généalogie et de Chronologie pour l'histoire de l'Islam*. Hanover, 1927.
Zenker, Julius Theodor. 'Mitteilungen über die Länder am südlichen Ufer des kaspischen Meeres, nach G. Melgunof', *ZDMG*, 21 (1867), pp. 232–270.

Index

Ābāqā, Ilkhanid ruler 163–4
ʿAbbās, Saljūq amīr 61
Abbasid/s 17, 94, 118–9, 121–2, 138, 141–3, 172–4
Caliphate of 15, 18, 21, 94, 108, 114, 118–19, 121, 136, 139, 155, 167–8, 178–9, 183
ʿAbd al-Jalīl Qazwīnī Rāzī, Twelver Shiʿi author 10–11, 57, 80, 82–7, 198 n.32, 201 n.31, 202 n.68, 206 n.7, n.8, 207 n.10, n.12, n.15
ʿAbd al-Malik b. ʿAṭṭāsh, Ismaili *dāʿī* 3, 33
ʿAbd Allah al-Mahdī, Ismaili Imam 15, 170
Abhar 119–20, 133, 171, 173, 188
Abū Hāshim Jurjānī, Zaydī leader 48–50, 70
Abū Ḥātim al-Rāzī, Ismaili *dāʿī* 15
Abū Isḥāq Quhistānī, Ismaili author 90, 92, 94, 132, 207 n.23, 207–8 n.23, 208 n.29, 210 n.89
Abū Jaʿfar Bāwandī 46–7, 57
Abū Kālījār, Buyid ruler 15
Abū Ṭālib Akhīr Yaḥyā, Zaydī Imam 25–7, 49, 88
Abu'l-Faḍl Jaʿfar b. Muḥammad 16
Ādharbayjān 15, 63, 99, 108, 112, 116, 119, 143, 158, 170
Akhbār-i Mughūlān 157–8, 175–6
ʿAlāʾ al-Dawla ʿAlī, Bāwandid ruler 27, 29, 31, 33, 35–6, 43–7, 55, 65–7, 77, 206 n.2
ʿAlāʾ al-Dīn Muḥammad III, Nizārī Imam 122, 126, 128, 131–165, 169–70, 174, 177–8, 183, 213 n.12
ʿAlāʾ al-Dīn Muḥammad Khwārazmshāh 129
ʿAlāʾ al-Dīn Tikish Khwārazmshāh 108, 116, 121
Alamūt, castle 1, 4, 11, 14, 24–8, 32, 35, 39, 51, 68–9, 82
library of 2, 6, 40, 161
lords of 2, 4, 6, 79, 112, 158, 175
destruction of 2, 4, 6, 89, 146, 163
Alīābād 17
Āmul 17, 20, 27, 30, 34, 58, 78, 108, 129, 149, 163, 168–9
Āmulī, Awliyāʾ Allāh, historian 8–9, 66, 68, 77–8, 80, 89, 104–6, 124, 126–7, 149–51, 163–4, 210 n.69
Anatolia 11, 21, 54, 132, 136, 170, 174
Anūshtigīn Shīrgīr, Saljūq military ruler 26–7, 36, 38, 45, 200 n.14
Armenian 11, 137–8
Arrajān 30–1, 38, 48, 171, 181, 202 n.51

Asfār, Daylamī military leader 15
Astarābād 17, 55, 75, 170
atabeg 98–9, 108, 112, 139, 158
Atsız 55, 59
Atwood, Christopher xiv, 142, 214 n.48, 215 n.49, 216 n.86

Bābak Khurramī 62
Bādūspānid 8, 17–18, 20, 23, 29, 58, 64–5, 67–8, 71, 76–9, 81, 87, 96, 98–104, 106, 113, 115, 123–4, 126–7, 133, 147, 149–52, 158, 162–5, 180, 183, 187, 193–4, 199 n.60, n.62
Baghdad 21, 35, 61, 119, 153, 162, 167–8, 176
Balaghai, Mongol military leader 160–1
Bārfurūsh 17
Barkiyāruq b. Malikshāh, Saljūq sultan 22, 30, 33, 37, 41
Bastām, 159–60
Bāwandid/s 8–10, 17–20, 22–37, 39–40, 42–8, 53–117, 121, 123–7, 129, 133, 146–52, 158, 162–5, 168, 172, 178–80, 182–4, 186–8, 197 n.19, n.25, 199 n.62, 204 n.1, 206 n.6
Bisṭām 56, 72, 75, 120, 134, 146, 171, 173, 188, 190
Bīsutūn b. Nāmāwar, Bādūspānid prince 78, 96, 103–6, 194, 210 n.74
Bīsutūn b. Zarrīnkamar, Bādūspānid prince 126, 150, 194
Bu'l-Qāsim Shamshīrzan, pro-Nizārī local chieftain 70
Budayl 63
Bukhārā 16, 135, 162, 192
Būyid/s 14–16, 19, 95–6, 178, 180

Casanova, Paul 12
Central Asia viii, 12, 19, 54, 118, 127–8, 131, 134–5, 145–6, 166, 171, 176, 181, 183
Chaghtāy 136, 160, 191–2
Chaghtāy Qūrchī 137–8, 155, 159
Chālūs 17
China 142, 156–7, 162, 171, 189
Chināshak 69, 75
Chinese 11, 128–9, 142, 143, 156, 174
Chingiz Khān 119, 127–30, 134–7, 189, 191
Chormaghan, Mongol military leader 127, 137
Chormaghan, Mongol viceroy 131, 137, 149, 151
Chubak, Ḥamīda 11, 145, 174
coins xiv, 20, 146–6, 152, 199 n.62
  Ghūrid gold 144
Cortese, Delia xiv, 88, 94, 196 n.2

Daftary, Farhad xiv, 13, 72, 76, 81, 89, 94, 157, 203 n.83, 216 n.105
dāʿī viii, 15, 32, 48, 92, 94, 117, 131, 134, 173, 175
Damāwand 71–2, 87, 160, 173, 184–5, 187
Dāmghān 32, 52, 54, 56, 71–2, 75, 99, 108, 113, 120, 129, 133–4, 140, 143–4, 146, 153, 173, 178, 188, 190, 214 n.36, 215 n.75
daʿwa 3, 14–16, 21–2, 30, 32–3, 37, 42, 47, 49–50, 52, 57, 76, 89, 93, 132, 175–6, 196 n.5
al-daʿwa al-hādīya 119
Daylam 14–16, 26, 43, 64, 95–6, 159, 162, 199 n.61

Daylamān 10, 14–16, 20, 23–32, 45–6, 48–9, 51–2, 54–5, 58, 64–9, 75–6, 88, 97, 100, 102–3, 117, 132–3, 141, 147, 151, 161, 166–7, 169–71, 174–5, 177, 179–80, 184–8, 199 n.62
Dihkhudā b. ʿAbd al-Malik b. ʿAlī, author 62, 63
Dihkhudā b. ʿAbd al-Malik Fashandī 4, 63
Dihkhudā Kaykhusraw 63
Dīwān 11, 44, 111
Dīwān-i Qāʾimiyyāt 4, 111–12, 134–41, 173, 189–92, 210 n.90, 211 n.95

Egypt 4, 7, 21–2, 24, 30, 92–4, 97, 196 n.2, 208 n.35
England 147, 152
envoy 32, 49, 52, 59, 61, 74, 93, 101, 109, 117–19, 122, 128, 135–6, 138, 140, 142, 144–5, 147, 149, 154–5, 159–60, 162, 176
Europe vii, 147, 149, 156

Fakhr al-Dawla Nāmāwar, Bādūspānid prince 150–1, 163–4, 194
Fatimid/s vii, 4, 15–16, 21–2, 30, 92–5, 97, 170, 182, 196 n.2, 218 n.2
fidāʾī/s 46, 58–9, 87, 112, 114, 117, 120, 139, 155, 190–1
Firīm 17, 22, 25, 32, 34, 99, 124
Fīrūzkūh 17, 71–2, 108
Fulāl 108

Ghiyāth al-Dīn, Khwārazmian prince 139, 141–2
Ghūrid 109, 117, 144
Gīlān 9–10, 12–17, 20, 23–9, 31, 34, 46, 49–50, 64–5, 77–8, 96, 113, 115, 120–1, 126, 132, 147, 149, 152, 169, 177, 179–80, 185, 198 n.48, 199 n.62
Girdbāzū 59–60, 84
Girdkūh, castle 25, 32–3, 40, 43, 54–5, 69, 71–5, 82, 111, 129–30, 149, 162–4, 171–2, 175, 183, 185, 187, 216 n.84
Gurgān 10, 27, 31–2, 46, 48, 55–6, 60, 75, 129, 169
Gurjīyān 9, 50, 65–6, 69–70, 76, 186, 203 n.11, n.12
Güyük, Great Khān 136, 138, 155

Hādī Ḥuqaynī, Qāsimī Zaydī ruler 24–5, 29, 66
Haft bāb, of Abū Isḥāq Quhistānī 94, 132, 207 n.23, 208 n.29
Hamadān 119–20, 139, 162, 170, 174, 216 n.97
Ḥamd Allāh Mustawfī Qazwīni, historian and geographer 167, 169
Ḥasan b. Nāmāwar 95–6, 180
Ḥasan b. Zayd, Zaydī ruler 18
Ḥasan II *ʿalā dhikrihiʾl-salām ʿalā dhikrihiʾl-salām*, Nizārī Imam 90, 106
Ḥasan Jurjānī, Zaydī leader 27, 48–9, 200 n.16
Ḥasan-i Maḥmūd-i Kātib, Nizārī author 81, 90, 111–14, 117, 136, 139, 208 n.35, 210 n.89, 211 n.95, 213 n.12
Ḥasan-i Ṣabbaḥ, Ismaʿili *dāʿī* and 1st lord of Alamūt 1–4, 6–7, 15–16, 19–48, 50–2, 63–4, 76, 81, 131, 146, 171, 175, 181, 183–4, 186, 196 n.2

Hawsam (Rūdsar), city 14, 16, 23, 25, 26, 27, 46
Hazārasf b. Shahrnūsh 79, 100–4, 113
Hazārjarīb 17
Herat 158, 213 n.49, 216 n.95
Het'um 138
Hizabr al-Dīn Khūrshīd, Bāwandid nobleman 103–4
Hodgson, Marshall G. S. 12, 28, 51, 64, 132, 154, 201 n.33, 215 n.75
Hülegü, Ilkhanid ruler xiii, 5–6, 11, 39, 127, 151–2, 154, 156–64
Ḥusām al-Dawla Ardashīr I, Bāwandid ruler 8, 100–10, 115, 121, 125–6, 147–8, 151, 170, 188
Ḥusām al-Dawla Ardashīr II, Bāwandid ruler 126, 149
Ḥusām al-Dawla Shahriyār, Bāwandid ruler 19, 24, 27–9, 31, 34–6, 65, 165, 195
Ḥusayn b. Ja'far Nāṣir, Nāṣirī Zaydī Imam
Ḥusayn Shā'ir 16

Ibn al-Athīr, 'Izz al-Dīn, historian 6, 30, 37–42, 68, 74–5, 97, 107, 141–3, 145, 166, 205 n.38
Ibn Isfandiyār, historian 8–9, 27, 33–6, 43, 46–7, 56–9, 66, 68–9, 72–5, 78, 80, 84, 86–7, 89, 96, 99, 101–2, 105, 110, 112, 121, 124, 126, 148, 163, 167–70, 210 n.69
Īldigüzid/s, dynasty in Ādharbayjān 98–9, 108, 112–14, 116, 119, 139, 141, 172
Ilkhanid/s 2, 4–6, 17, 122, 155, 169, 216 n.95
'Imād al-Dīn Muḥtasham, Nizārī Ismaili courtier (13th C) 131, 143
Imamate 15–16, 22, 24–5, 30, 49, 92–3, 95, 97–8, 103, 133, 146, 150, 152
Īrānshāh, Nizārī Ismaili prince 161
'Irāq 46, 72, 114, 119, 158, 188, 190
'Irāq-i 'Ajām 44, 120–1, 132, 158, 160, 205 n.53, 216 n.97
Isfaḥān 30–1, 33–5, 38, 52, 120, 139, 181
al-Iṣfahānī, 'Imād al-Dīn Muḥammad, historian 7
iṣfahbad 8, 18, 24, 27, 39, 43, 45, 57–8, 64–6, 70, 72–4, 82, 84, 97, 99, 108, 165, 167, 170, 197 n.19, n.25
Ithnā 'asharī, *see* Twelver Shi'i
Ivanow, Wladimir 11, 112, 207 n.23, 208 n.28

Ja'far b. 'Alī, Justānid vizier 15
Jalāl al-Dīn Ḥasan III, Nizārī Imam 114, 117–18, 125–6, 128, 133, 135, 147, 152–3, 173, 180, 183, 211 n.6
Jalāl al-Dīn Mingburnī Khwārazmshāh 132, 134–5, 139–45, 148–50, 174, 214 n.45
Jāmi' al-tawarīkh, of Rashīd al-Dīn 6, 90, 200 n.16
Jibāl 56, 70, 98–9, 116
Jibāl Bādūspān 17
Jibāl Qārin 17, 56
Juhayna 55
Justān III, Justānid ruler 14
Justānids 14, 66
Juwaynī, 'Aṭā' Malik, historian 2–6, 28, 33, 38–40, 87–88, 96, 107, 118, 128–9, 135, 138, 141,

146, 154, 157, 161–2, 169, 201 n.22, 203 n.83, 208 n.35, 214 n.48
Juzjānī, Minhāj al-Dīn ʿUthmān b. Sirāj al-Dīn, historian 109, 117, 128–9, 149, 153, 176

Kajā 17
Kalā 17
Karakorum 11, 136, 143, 153, 154, 155, 156, 162
Kāshānī, historian 2, 4–6, 38, 57, 62–3, 69, 81, 152–3, 155, 203 n.83
Kawād I, Sasanian ruler 18
Kāwūs, Sasanian prince 18
Kay Kāʾūs 67–8, 78–9, 96, 99–104, 122
Ket-Buqa, Mongol military leader 156–7, 160
Khalkhāl 134, 140, 190, 219
Khānakjā 23, 26
Kharāj 43, 120, 167, 172
see also land tax
Khurāsān 5, 30–2, 37, 41–2, 44, 49, 51, 56, 61, 64, 73–4, 82, 85, 90, 95, 99, 108, 120, 127–9, 131, 134, 139, 145, 149–50, 156–8, 162, 176, 182, 190, 192, 204 n.18, 212 n.47, 214 n.48
Khwārazm 8, 116–17, 148, 168, 176, 190, 192
Khwārazmians 99, 107, 110, 116, 132, 146–8, 151, 153, 170, 173–4
Khwārazmshāh/s 6–7, 46, 55–6, 59, 81, 95, 107–11, 113–18, 121–4, 127, 129–31, 133–7, 139–45, 147–50, 152, 154, 156, 172, 183
Kīnkhwār, Bāwandid ruler 125–6, 147, 195
Kirakos Ganzaketsʿi, Armenian historian 11, 137, 140
Kirmān 38, 52, 141, 158, 181
Kīslīyān 46, 57
Kiyā ʿAlī, Zaydī leader 67
Kiyā Buzurg al-Dāʿī ilaʾl-Ḥaqq Riḍā b. Hādī, Zaydī ruler of Daylamān 25, 66–8, 72, 78
Kiyā Buzurg-Umīd, lord of Alamūt 4, 29, 31 44–50, 52, 54, 66, 67, 175, 181, 186
Kujūr 17, 20, 151

Lafūr 17, 168–9
Lāhījān 9, 16, 27
Lajīm 46–7, 57, 86, 203 n.87
Lamasar 28, 39, 61, 70, 82, 95–6, 159, 161–2, 175–6, 180, 187, 201 n.22
Lāmsālār, Zaydī ruler 28
Luristān 158

Madelung, Wilferd xiv, 13, 20, 23, 48, 62–3, 105, 149, 164
Mahdī b. Khusraw Fīrūz, Justānid ruler 15
Maḥmud b. Malikshāh, Saljūq sultan 22
Malāt 101
Malikshāh Wakhsūdān 15, 49
Malikshāh, Great Saljūq 22, 24, 29–31, 34, 40–1, 131, 164
al-Manṣūr, Abbasid caliph 167
Manṣūrakūh 32–3, 71–2
Marʿashī, Ẓahīr al-Dīn, historian 8–9, 20, 27, 33–4, 55, 66, 68, 77–8, 80, 96, 104–6, 109–10, 124, 126, 149, 163, 197 n.29, 199 n.61, 205 n.42
Mardāwīj Daylamī, military leader 15
Marw 40–2, 59, 170, 174, 176, 212 n.45

Marzbān b. Muḥammad 15, 19
Masʿūd b. Muḥammad, Saljūq sultan 61, 66
May, Timothy 137
Maymūndiz 6, 39, 45, 63, 138, 159–61, 203 n.83
Māzandarān 9, 12, 16–20, 34, 46, 65, 73, 82–4, 86, 129, 132, 147–9, 151–2, 158, 160, 163–4, 169
merchants 83, 120, 143–4, 169–70, 176
Mihrīn 68, 71–2, 134
Miles, George 12
Möngke, Great Khan 137–8, 153–6, 161–2
Mongol conquests 3–4, 8, 11, 39–40, 111, 119, 127–9, 133–6, 138–40, 146, 155, 161–3, 166, 188, 212 n.47
Mongols 11, 119, 127–32, 135–8, 142–5, 148–9, 152–63, 165–6, 169, 173–6, 178–9, 182–3, 213 n.49, 215 n.75
Mubārakkūh 66
Mughān 132
al-Muḥallī, Ḥumayd b. Aḥmad al-, historian 197 n.30
Muḥammad b. Ismāʿīl, grandson of Imam Jaʿfar al-Ṣādiq 15, 218 n.2
Muḥammad b. Buzurg-Umīd, lord of Alamūt 2, 4, 5, 55, 58–9, 63, 65, 68, 70, 75–6, 87–8, 92, 186
Muḥammad b. Malikshāh 31, 34, 76, 164
Muḥammad b. Musāfir, Musāfirid ruler 14–15
Muḥammad Pahlawān, Ildigüzid ruler 108
Muḥammad Tapar 37, 56, 186
Muḥammad Zayd, Zaydī ruler 18
Muḥammad, the Prophet 63
al-Muʿizz, Fatimid caliph 15
al-Mustanṣir, Fatimid caliph 21–2, 30, 93, 95, 201 n.25
Muʿizzī, Muḥammad b. ʿAbd al-Malik, poet 80
Muʾminābād 93–4
Muqaddam al-Dīn, Nizārī military leader 61
Muẓaffar al-Dīn Uzbak, Īldigüzid ruler 119–20, 139, 141

Najm al-Dawla Qārin Nāmāwar, Bādūspānid ruler 27, 31, 34–5, 43–4
Nasawī, historian 7, 109, 129, 132–3, 139–46, 170, 173
Naṣīr al-Dawla Rustam, Bāwandid ruler 8
al-Nāṣir li-Dīn Allāh, ʿAbbāsid caliph 108, 119
al-Nāṣir li'l-Ḥaqq, Ḥusayn Mahdī 23–4, 199 n.25
Nāṣir Uṭrūsh 16, 24
Nāṣirī Zaydīs 23, 25
Nātil 17, 77, 151
Nīshāpūr 36, 75, 128–9, 170, 174, 212 n.47, 214 n.48
Nīshāpūrī, Ẓahīr al-Dīn, historian 7
Niẓām al-Mulk, Saljūq vizier 22, 29, 52, 131
Nizār b. al-Mustanṣir bi'llāh, Nizārī Imam 22, 30, 93, 95, 190, 201 n.25, 208 n.35
Nizārī state vii, 31, 52, 106, 118, 120, 131, 150, 159, 166–7, 171, 175, 177, 181
Nūr al-Dīn Muḥammad II, Nizārī Imam 97–112, 182
Nuzhat al-qulūb 169

Ögedei, Great Khān 136–7
Oxus river (Amu Darya) 119, 135

Paradise, 89
Paris, Matthew 147

qā'im 91, 94–5, 112
Qaraqai Bitikchi, Mongol military leader 162
Qārin b. Shahriyār, Bāwandid ruler 18
Qārin b. Surkhāb, Bāwandid ruler 19
Qārinwand 17, 178–9
qaṣīda 112, 134, 136
Qāsimī Zaydīs 23, 25, 28
Qaṣrānī, ʿAbd al-Malik, Saljūq amīr 61
Qazwīn 10, 29, 32, 50–4, 56, 66–7, 69–70, 76, 82, 97, 105, 113, 115–16, 120, 145, 147, 152–6, 158, 162, 172
Qazwīnī Rāzī, ʿAbd al-Jalīl theologian 10–11, 57, 80, 82–7
Qiṣṣa-i Malik-i Sīstān 42, 99
qiyāma 87–95, 98, 106, 122, 135, 180, 183, 196 n.9, 207 n.22
  declaration of 4–5, 87–97, 111–12, 131, 135, 175, 182
Qizil Arslān, Ildigüzid ruler 112–14
Quhistān 37–8, 41–3, 52, 93, 95, 109, 111, 117, 128–9, 131, 135–6, 139–40, 155, 156, 158–9, 162, 166, 173–4, 176, 181–2, 189, 212 n.48
Quhistānī, Abū Isḥāq, Nizārī author 92, 94, 132
Qumm 21
Qur'an 61, 88
Quṭb al-Dīn Muḥammad, Khwārazmshāh 46
Qutlugh Ābā 67

Rabino di Borgomale, Hyacinth Louis 12–13, 125
Ra'īs Muẓaffar
  governor of Girdkūh 25, 33, 40, 43, 55, 146, 172, 186
  muḥtashām of Quhistān 93
Rāmsar 50
Rasāmūj, Zaydī ruler 28
Rashīd al-Dīn Faḍl Allāh, historian 2–6, 26, 28, 32–3, 35, 40, 48–52, 57, 59, 61–3, 65–7, 69–71, 76–8, 87, 91–2, 94–6, 107, 120, 138, 146, 152–4, 161, 171
Rāshid al-Dīn Sinan, Nizārī leader in Syria 88
al-Rāwandī, Muḥammad, historian 7, 116–17
Rayy 3, 10–11, 17, 32, 36, 42, 46, 50–4, 56–9, 61–2, 69–71, 76, 82, 86, 99, 105, 108, 113, 120–1, 129, 134, 142, 153, 160, 170, 171, 172–4, 184, 206 n.9
revenue/s 40, 57, 59, 60, 62, 120, 166–70, 172
Rūdbār 3, 6, 9, 16, 22, 29, 31, 34, 44–5, 50, 52, 56, 61, 70, 76, 90, 116–17, 156, 158–64
Rukn al-Dawla Qārin, Bāwandid 109–10
Rukn al-Dīn Khurshāh, Nizārī Imam and last lord of Alamūt 6, 138, 154, 158–62, 175, 181
Rukūna 46, 57
Rūm 132, 137, 158, 214 n.22, 214 n.45
Rustam b. Sharwīn, Bāwandid ruler 19
Rustam b. Surkhāb, Bāwandid ruler 18
Rustamdār 17, 158, 199 n.60

Rūyān 9, 17, 20, 23–4, 27, 29, 46, 58, 64–71, 76, 78–9, 96, 98–107, 109–10, 115, 123–4, 126, 133, 147, 149–51, 158, 163–4, 169, 187–8, 199 n.62

Saʿādatkūh 45, 48, 66
Sābiq Qazwīnī, Saljūq Turkic leader 56, 62, 67, 70, 75, 82
Sakhtsar 101
Ṣalāḥ al-Dīn ʿAlī, Nizārī envoy 140
Salgham Khātūn 44
Saljūq/s 6–7, 10, 13–14, 19–22, 24–8, 30–1, 33–48, 50–6, 58–62, 65–7, 71–2, 74–7, 80–7, 95, 97–9, 103, 107–8, 110, 112–14, 120–1, 123, 131–3, 137, 146, 156, 164–5, 172, 176, 178–82, 186, 202 n.51, 204 n.7, 214 n.22, 214 n.45, 218–19 n.1
Samarqand 135, 192
Sanjar, Saljūq sultan 22, 30–1, 33, 36–8, 40–7, 55–6, 59–62, 64–5, 67, 71, 75, 80, 85–6, 95, 107, 120, 146, 172, 182, 206 n.61
Sarakhs 59, 212 n.46
Sargudhasht-i Sayyidnā 2–4, 6, 32, 35, 40, 81
Sārī 17, 30, 34–5, 58, 82–3, 85–6, 99, 108, 149, 199 n.65
Sasanian/s 13, 17–20, 80, 168–9, 180, 197 n.19, 217 nn.4–5
Sawādkūh 17, 46
sayyid 84
Shafīʿī-Kadkānī, Muḥammad 112
Shāh Ghāzī Rustam, Bāwandid ruler 39, 44, 46–7, 55–60, 64–75, 77–9, 82–7, 97, 99–100, 102, 109–10, 134, 178–9, 186–8, 195, 204 n.1
Shāh Ghāzī Rustam II, Bāwandid ruler 109–10, 115
Shāhanshāh, Nizārī Ismaili prince 122, 158–60
Shāhdiz, castle 30–1, 35, 38, 181
Shāhragīm, Bādīspānid ruler 151, 194
Shāhriyārkūh 22, 32
Shahrnūsh b. Hazārasf 77
Shams al-Dīn, *muḥtasham* of Quhistān 136
Shams al-Dīn, *qāḍī* of Qazwīn 153–4, 156
Shams al-Mulūk Muḥammad, Bāwandid ruler 149, 152, 163–4
Sharaf al-Mulūk Ḥasan, Bāwandid ruler 97, 99–100, 108, 113
sharīʿa 61, 63, 91
Sharwīn b. Rustam, Bāwandid ruler 18
Shaykh Aḥmad-i Jām, Sunni Sufi master 41
Shengwu qinzheng lu 11, 128, 142
Shihāb al-Dīn, Ghūrid sultan 109, 117, 119, *206 n.9*
Shihāb al-Dīn, *muḥtasham* of Quhistān 111, 135–6
Shīrānshāh, Nizārī Ismaili prince 160
Shīrwān 158
silk 167–9
Silk Road 50, 152
Simnān 54, 56–8, 75, 99, 129, 160, 173, 178
Sīstān 158
Sīyāhrūd 77–8, 96, 100
Smbat Sparapet, historian 11, 138
Sübötei, Mongol military leader 129–30
Sulaymān Shāh, Saljūq prince 56

Sunqur Inānj, Saljūq Turkic leader 56, 62, 67, 70–1, 75, 82, 99, 113
Sutūda, Manūchihr 11
Syria vii–viii, 21, 93, 119, 162, 166, 170, 173, 176

Ṭabaristān 7–10, 16–19, 22, 24–5, 29, 31–2, 36, 42–7, 50, 55, 58, 60, 64–6, 72, 82, 86, 96–9, 106–10, 115, 122–5, 133, 147, 149–50, 167–9, 175, 177, 179, 184, 188, 199 n.62, 206 n.6
Ṭabas 37–41, 86
Tāj al-Mulūk Mardāwīj 55–6, 60, 67, 77, 195
Tālār 17
Ṭalīqān 17, 45, 51, 71, 86, 160, 173
Tamīsha 17, 55, 74, 108–9, 129
Tamurtughān, Saljūq military leader 45
Tanhijān 49–50
Tarasf b. Malikshāh Gurjī 65
Tārīkh-i jahān-gusha 2
Tārīkh-i Rūyān 8–9
Tārīkh-i Ṭabaristān 8–9, 84, 167
Tārīkh-i Ṭabaristān va Rūyān va Māzandarān 9
Tasbīḥī, Muḥammad Ḥusain 125
Tikish, Khwārazmshāh 108, 116, 121
Ṭughril III, Saljūq ruler 103, 108, 113
Turshīz 51
al-Ṭūsī, Naṣīr al-Dīn Muḥammad, Shiʿi scholar 5, 111, 128, 132, 138–9, 161
Twelver Shiʿi xiii, 6, 8, 10–11, 13, 19–21, 24, 27–8, 35, 46, 50, 57, 59, 65, 80–5, 87, 118

Urkhān, Khwārazmian leader 139–40
Ustunāwand 32, 71, 108
Uzbak, of Adharbayjān 116, 119–20, 139, 141

Wakhsūdān b. Muḥammad 15
Willey, Peter 12, 71–3, 172
Wushmgīr, Ziyārid ruler 169

Yaranqūsh, Saljūq military leader 45
Yasa'úr, Mongol leader 158, 216 n.97
Yuanshi 11, 129, 142, 156

Zanagū 58
Zangiyān 57
Zanjān 54, 119–20, 133, 173, 178, 188
Zarrīnkamar b. Justān b. Kay Kā'ūs, Bādūspānid 100–6, 124, 126, 194
Zaydī Imam/s 16, 24–6, 48–9, 54, 64–8, 70, 147
Zaydī theology 13–15, 24, 29, 48, 175
Zaydī/s xiii, 9–11, 14–18, 23–9, 32, 49, 52, 58, 64–7, 70–2, 78, 96, 102–3, 110, 118, 147, 178–80, 200 n.16